The Nelson Encyclopedia

The

NELSON
ENCYCLOPEDIA

Colin White

STACKPOLE
BOOKS

In Association with the Royal Naval Museum

Foreword

IT SEEMS to have become almost a tradition that new books about Nelson should start with an apology. The underlying assumption appears to be that we already know almost everything about Nelson that is important and so it is unlikely that any new study will be able to say much that is genuinely new about him beyond a few insights into very specific areas of his life and career.

In this, as in many other ways, this book will break with tradition. It has become increasingly apparent in recent years that the underlying assumption is wrong and so no apology is needed for taking a new look at the Nelson story. Recent research into all aspects of Nelson's life – and, most important, into the wider context of the times in which he lived – has yielded fascinating new insights. Moreover, *The Nelson Letters Project*, sponsored by the Royal Naval and National Maritime Museums, has now identified a large body of hitherto unpublished primary source material. As a result of all this new work, the traditional version of the story is being challenged. This book aims to highlight those areas where reassessment is required in the light of the new material and, where appropriate, to offer a new version of the story based on the latest and most accurate research. To make it easier to identify the new insights, the material has been arranged in encyclopaedic form, rather than as a traditional biography. Quotations from the newly-discovered letters are intentionally verbatim, including idiosyncratic spelling and punctuation.

This process of challenge and reconstruction is still going on. To give just one example, we await the major revision of the *Dictionary of National Biography*, which will offer new insights into the people who served with Nelson and reassessments of their careers in the light of modern scholarship. Inevitably, therefore, some of this book's judgements will, in their turn, be overtaken by new research. But it does, at least, offer a snapshot of the current state of our understanding of Nelson and the Royal Navy in which he served.

It also offers an unashamedly Nelson-centric view of that Navy. The individual essays do not attempt an exhaustive treatment of their subject – rather, they aim to show the part that the person, or ship, or place in question played in Nelson's life and how they are interrelated. As will, it is hoped, become apparent, this approach has, in its turn, yielded some interesting insights. But those seeking definitive studies of, say, John Jervis or HMS *Agamemnon* will need to look elsewhere and so, wherever possible, suggestions for further reading have been included to aid this process.

The book has its origins in the research work carried out by me and my colleagues at the Royal Naval Museum during our preparations for the Museum's award-winning exhibition, *Horatio Nelson: the hero and the man*, opened in January 1999. I am especially grateful to the Museum Director, Campbell McMurray, for encouraging me to develop this material into a book and for his unswerving support for my efforts to get it published. I would also like to thank my colleagues, Matthew Sheldon and Stephen Courtney, for their generous assistance with locating and photographing the images for the book, most of which come from the superb collections of the Museum and a number of which have never been published before. I am also grateful to the Museum's librarians, Allison Wareham and Holly Downer, who have borne my persistent requests for obscure books and articles with such patience, and delivered them with such efficiency.

Some of the new insights offered here are the direct product of *The Nelson Letters Project*, in the course of which I am currently transcribing the unpublished Nelson letters that I have located in public and private collections all over the world. In this task I have been greatly helped by colleagues in a number of institutions and I would like especially to mention Jill Davies and Daphne Knott of the National Maritime Museum, Christopher Wright of the British Library and Andrew Helme of the Nelson Museum in Monmouth. The full, and very exciting, results of this new work will be published in due course but some of the new material has been included in this book as a 'taster' – especially in the section entitled *Nelson – in his own words*.

I owe particular thanks to a number of friends at Chatham Publishing: Robert Gardiner who not only agreed to publish the book in the first place, but also has given me the benefit of his own considerable knowledge of the Nelsonian Navy and saved me from some howlers. Needless to say, however, the remaining mistakes are my responsibility and not his! Julian Mannering who has guided the book through its production stages and borne patiently all my last-minute additions, as new material kept popping up, Linda Jones and Stephen Chumbley, who have carried out the detailed editing that has toned down my authorial idiosyncrasies and Tony Hart who created the handsome design. I would also like to thank Michael O'Callaghan of CDA Design, who has created the splendid new plans of Nelson's four great battles, based on the very latest insights of historical research and marine archaeology.

Finally, I owe warm and heartfelt thanks to all those who have supported me during the long gestation of this book: valued friends in the field of Nelson studies who have generously shared the results of their own work with me, especially Tom Pocock, Ann-Mary Hills, Richard Walker, Brian Lavery, Roger Knight, Joe Callo and Peter Goodwin; my dear mother, Margaret, who has typed out all the letter transcriptions; and my dear Peter, who has borne so patiently with my absence and distraction during the writing process and has also helped me to shape some of the insights that have emerged.

In one of the many new letters that I have recently located and transcribed, dated 6 January 1802, Nelson told Captain Henry Digby, '. . . I can never forget all your kindness towards me and I beg that you will ever Believe me your obliged Friend.' Two hundred years later, almost to the very day, I echo those words to all who have helped with this book, with sincere gratitude and affection.

Colin White
Portsmouth, January 2002

A NOTE ON THE ILLUSTRATIONS

The illustrations are taken from the collections of the Royal Naval Museum, except where stated otherwise in the caption.

The battle plans are completely new and have been prepared especially for this book. They are based on the wealth of new information that has emerged as a result of a series of international conferences held to mark the anniversaries of Nelson's battles. These have revealed that the standard plans are out of date and in need of revision.

The Unconventional Hero

'The most like me.' This profile by Simon de Koster was the portrait that Nelson thought was the best likeness of him. This print of it is accompanied by a list of his titles, as of January 1801, in his own handwriting.

A CAPTAIN BEFORE he was twenty-one, a household name throughout most of Europe at thirty-nine and killed in action just three weeks after his forty-seventh birthday, Nelson lived a colourful and crowded life. Not content with winning some of the most resounding victories in British history at the Nile (1798), Copenhagen (1801) and Trafalgar (1805)–and losing an arm and the sight of an eye in the process–he also had a tempestuous and very public love affair with Emma Hamilton, one of the most beautiful women of his day. Affection-ate, engaging and a devoted friend and father, he was also ruthless and occasionally even cruel. Uninspiring and unheroic in his personal appear-ance, he was nonetheless one of the most charismatic leaders Britain has ever produced, able to inspire devotion, even love, in those who served with him.

It is the combination of opposites that makes him so fascinating and, as a result, there always seems to be something new to be said about him, some new light to be shed on his complex character.

New light on a familiar story

This is especially true at the moment, as the 'Nelson Decade' approaches its climax with the commemoration of the bicentenary of Trafalgar in 2005. Much new research is being produced that is throwing new light on the familiar story. International conferences on his battles have brought together scholars from both sides of former conflicts in a sharing of infor-mation that has changed our perception of the conduct and progress of those battles. For the first time, it has become possible to see them in the round and to understand more clearly the reasons why Nelson and his col-leagues were so successful. New research into the British primary sources has given us a better understanding of what actually happened during the battles and has unearthed some hitherto untapped personal accounts. Even the discoveries of modern marine archaeology have been brought into play. As a result of all this work, the traditional narratives of the bat-tles are now seen as being incomplete, and even inaccurate, in places and new narratives are being constructed.[1]

At the same time, research has been carried out into specific aspects of Nelson's life and career. His health has been analysed in the light of modern medical knowledge and a number of long-standing diagnoses challenged.[2] His conduct during the civil war in Naples in 1799–a source of controversy even in his lifetime–has been subjected to new scrutiny.[3] His relationship with women, and in particular with Emma Hamilton, has

1 Details of the latest research into Nelson's battles will be found at the end of the entry for each battle.

2 See entry on 'Nelson's health', p148.

3 See especially Carlo Knight, 'The British in Naples, 1799', *The Trafalgar Chronicle* 10 (2001).

been examined without the fastidious squeamishness that so hampered his earlier biographers.[4] In each of these areas, new insights have emerged that are helping to create a more rounded and balanced picture of Nelson the man.

That picture has been further enhanced by the discovery of significant new primary source material. A survey of Nelson's letters, commissioned by the National Maritime and Royal Naval Museums, has revealed that there is a large amount of unpublished, and largely untapped, Nelson material in all the major public and private collections – at the last count

'His first farewell.' This circa late nineteenth-century lithograph is typical of the way in which Nelson's story was sentimentalised by the Victorians. Nelson's mother had died before he went to sea, so he was shown saying goodbye to his grandmother instead.

well over 500 individual documents. Additionally, the study has shown that some of the key 'runs' of published letters to well-known personalities, such as the Duke of Clarence or Lord St Vincent, have been edited, and indeed censored. These passages relate not only to personal matters – such as Nelson's relationship with Emma Hamilton – but also to public affairs. Nothing so far found in this unpublished material has challenged the core Nelson story in a fundamental way, but some interesting light and shade can now be added to the familiar narrative.[5]

This process has been further advanced by the insights offered by other branches of historical studies. Cultural and social historians have examined the Nelson story itself, as it has been handed down to us, and have analysed the way in which it was constructed, especially at the time of Nelson's death and again around the end of the nineteenth century, when he became a symbol of Britain's naval resurgence. Some aspects of the story have been shown to be pure hagiography.[6]

Most important, much new work has been done on the Royal Navy in which Nelson served, its ships, people and organisation, so that we now understand better the extent to which he fits into the pattern of his times. Studies of the development of naval tactics in the late eighteenth century have placed his tactical ideas in their historical context and have shown that they represent a summation of those developments, rather than a complete break with the past, as used to be suggested. Research into the careers of naval leaders who came before him, and of his key contemporaries, has shown, on the one hand, that he did not spring suddenly from nowhere and, on the other, that he was not an isolated genius.[7] Nelson is now seen both as the inheritor and perfecter of a long naval tradition, and as the foremost representative of one of the most gifted generations of naval officers that Britain has ever produced.

EARLY YEARS: 1758–1784

Born on 29 September 1758, Horatio Nelson was the fourth surviving child of Rev Edmund Nelson, Rector of Burnham Thorpe in Norfolk, and his wife Catherine, and three more children followed after him. He was thus the middle child in a large family. Stories of his youthful prowess that found their way into the early adulatory biographies, and have been repeated unquestioningly ever since, tell of an adventurous and precocious little boy. They all date from after his death and so their details probably owe much to hindsight. But they have two common underlying themes that ring true: that he constantly sought attention and approval from adults and

4 See especially Flora Fraser, *Beloved Emma*, Weidenfeld and Nicolson (London 1986).

5 Colin White, 'The Nelson Letters Project', *The Mariner's Mirror* 87 (November 2001).

6 See especially Terry Coleman, *Nelson: The Man and the Legend*, Bloomsbury (London 2001).

7 See especially Peter Lefevre and Richard Harding (eds), *Precursors of Nelson*, Chatham (London 2000).

that he was naturally impulsive, especially in his affections. These two strands – both of which are, of course, classic characteristics of a middle child – run right through his life and provide the background pattern to all his actions, public as well as private.

He did not have a conventional childhood. His mother died when he was nine, a psychological blow that left a permanent scar. Years later he wrote to a childhood friend, '. . . the thoughts of former days brings all my Mother into my heart which shews itself in my eyes.'[8] He then spent a significant part of his short schooldays in the progressive Paston School at North Walsham, where the curriculum was much more liberal and arts-based than in the standard grammar schools of the time. The results of this schooling can be seen in his marvellous letters, which flow from his pen in an exhilarating stream of consciousness that vividly captures his impulsive and eager way of speaking. Punctuation is minimal, paragraphing almost non-existent and yet the sense is almost always easy to follow. Finally, in March 1771, aged only twelve, he joined the Royal Navy under the patronage of his maternal uncle, Captain Maurice Suckling, and was away from home for most of his teens.

Even in the Navy his training was unconventional. Suckling did not keep his protégé close by his side as was usual; instead, he seems to have deliberately planned for young Horatio to have as wide a variety of experiences as possible. A short spell in Suckling's ship, the 64-gun HMS *Raisonnable*, in the Thames estuary was followed first by a voyage to the West Indies in the merchantman *Mary Ann* and then by another spell in the Thames, when the boy was sent out constantly in small boats. As he later remembered, this experience made him 'confident of myself among rocks and sands, which has many times since been of very great comfort to me.'[9] Then, still aged only fourteen, he took part in an expedition to the Arctic and finally completed his early training with a two-year stint in the crack frigate HMS *Seahorse* in the East Indies, during which he saw action for the first time. At that point, he fell dangerously ill with malaria in 1775 and had to be invalided home. Even so, his first four years in the Navy had been packed with activity and had given him a wide range of experience, in different types of ship and different environments, which helped to nurture his natural independence and energy.

Having recovered from his illness, and made up his necessary sea-time as an acting lieutenant in the battleship HMS *Worcester*, Nelson passed his lieutenant's examination on 5 April 1777 and so began his most intense period of apprenticeship. Yet even here, the pattern of his career was unusual. After only a year in the frigate HMS *Lowestoffe* on the West Indies

8 Nelson to Rev Dean Allott, 14 May 1805, Private collection.

9 Sir Nicholas Harris Nicolas, *The Dispatches and Letters of Vice Admiral Lord Nelson* (1844), Vol I, p2.

10 N A M Rodger, 'Commissioned Officers' Careers in the Royal Navy, 1690–1815', *Journal of Maritime Research* [National Maritime Museum's online journal] June 2001.

11 For example: William Cornwallis and James Saumarez both commanded battleships, and played key roles in Sir George Rodney's great victory over the French at the Battle of the Saintes (12 April 1782); Thomas Foley and Ben Hallowell served as lieutenants in the same battle; and Thomas Troubridge took part in a series of actions in the Indian Ocean under the command of Sir Edward Hughes.

station, her captain, William Locker, gave him command of a small schooner that acted as the frigate's tender. He then transferred to the station flagship HMS *Bristol* as third lieutenant, under the aegis of the commander-in-chief, Sir Peter Parker, who, following the death of Maurice Suckling in 1778, became his chief patron. After less than a year he was promoted to commander and was given his first independent command, the brig HMS *Badger*, and six months later, in June 1779, he received the key promotion to post captain when he was still just three months short of his twenty-first birthday. Although modern research into the careers of naval officers of the period has shown that promotion this rapid was not as unusual as some of his biographers have suggested in the past, it was nonetheless impressive.[10] It also shows just how important it was to have influential patrons, as well as ability, in the eighteenth century. Moreover, his swift rise meant that he had served as a lieutenant for less than three years and so had spent very little time in the strict hierarchy of a wardroom. His natural independence survived.

Lieutenant Nelson leaving HMS Lowestoffe *in rough seas to board an American prize. One of Nelson's early exploits captured realistically in this pen and wash drawing by William Bromley.*

Nelson now spent eight years almost continuously in command of frigates: first the *Hinchinbrooke*, then the *Albemarle* and finally the *Boreas*. For the early part of this period, Britain was at war with the American colonists and was also fighting the French and Spanish who entered the war on the American side. So there were a number of major fleet actions and most of Nelson's contemporaries – including those with whom he later formed some of his closest professional partnerships – served in the battle squadrons.[11] Nelson, by contrast, took part in only one action of any consequence in 1780, when he was involved in the small-scale amphibious attack on the Spanish Fort San

Juan in Nicaragua, following which he suffered a second, and prolonged, bout of sickness which kept him out of active service for almost a year. When, eventually, he did manage to get himself attached to Lord Hood's fleet in November 1782, the war was already beginning to wind down and the opportunity for active service had passed. So by the time Nelson reached the midpoint in his naval career he had not served for any length of time with a battlefleet—nearly all his service had been on detached duty and much of it had been in unusual circumstances. His instinct for initiative and independent action remained as strong as ever.

MARRIAGE AND UNEMPLOYMENT: 1783–1793

At this point, however, his career faltered and almost ended. A peacetime appointment in command of the frigate HMS *Boreas* in the West Indies between 1784 and 1787 was not a happy one. His natural impulsiveness, and occasionally over-rigid sense of duty, led him to handle a dispute over illicit trading between the colonies and the newly-independent American states insensitively, which created powerful enemies among the rich British traders and senior officers in the area, most notably with the commander-in-chief Rear Admiral Sir Richard Hughes. Hitherto, it has been supposed that this was their first encounter but recently-discovered letters have revealed that Nelson had already clashed with Hughes in 1782, while in command of the *Albemarle*.[12] At the same time, he mishandled a delicate situation involving one of the sons of King George III, Prince William Henry, at that time serving in the Navy in command of the frigate HMS *Pegasus*. When the Prince had a disagreement with his first lieutenant, William Schomberg, Nelson failed to defuse the potentially embarrassing incident and allowed the Prince to flout naval rules, thus earning the displeasure of the Admiralty and, indeed, of the King himself. So, between 1788 and 1793 he was unable to get any employment, despite repeated requests. Later, in 1799, when asked to write an account of his life for public consumption, he tactfully said that his difficulties had been due '. . . to a prejudice at the Admiralty evidently against me, which I can neither guess at, or in the least account for.'[13] But in a recently discovered letter to his brother-in-law Thomas Bolton, dating from 1790, he made it clear that he knew exactly how to account for it, saying that he had been 'as ill treated as any person could be for taking the part of the King's son against as gross a calumny as ever was utter'd.'[14]

In the meantime, he had married Frances Nisbet, a pretty and delightful young widow whom he had met on the island of Nevis. Women had not featured much in his life before then. Indeed, despite his later reputation as a passionate lover, as a result of his relationship with Emma Hamilton, it is clear that he was actually most happy emotionally in the male environment of the Navy. Throughout his life, he had close, and often quite intense, male friendships, for example with Thomas Troubridge whom he first met when they served together as midshipmen in the *Seahorse* in 1773, or later with Thomas Hardy from whom he famously asked for a kiss when he was dying. He often looked up to older men and even talked of them as father figures, notably Lord Hood, Sir John Jervis and Sir William Hamilton. He also had a particular affinity with young men and for much of his life surrounded himself with surrogate sons, notably John Weatherhead, William Hoste and Edward Parker. He was also able to inspire devotion among many of the men who served with him and it is clear that most of his comrades in arms found him fascinating, even loveable. Clearly, then, he was essentially a man's man — which is scarcely surprising, since he was almost continuously in male company from the age of twelve.

He was attracted to women of course but had a tendency all his life to idolise them and to fall in love very quickly. His first serious love, in 1782, was Mary Simpson whom he met in Quebec, but he was sent away on a mission before he could propose to her. The following year he met Elizabeth Andrews during a peacetime visit to France and wooed her, but it would appear that she turned him down. Then, in an interesting foreshadowing of his later *grande passion*, he fell deeply in love with Mary Moutray, the pretty young wife of the elderly commissioner of English Harbour in Antigua in 1784. But she tactfully kept him at arm's length while retaining his friendship. So when in early 1785 he first met Frances Nisbet, who was not only attractive and reasonably well off but also available, he proposed quickly, and this time was successful. They were married on Nevis in March 1787 and returned almost at once to Britain. Their courtship had been warm and affectionate but the marriage was severely tested in its early years. Unable to obtain another appointment in the Navy, Nelson became frustrated and irritable; while Fanny, used to the warm climate and relative luxury of the West Indies, had to adjust to living in genteel poverty in the icy winters of Norfolk. Also, as the years dragged by, it became clear that there were not to be any children. Fanny already had a son by her first marriage, Josiah Nisbet, but Nelson, who loved children, longed for some of his own. A note in his autobiographical 'sketch' of 1799 records that he married Fanny in 1787 but adds sadly, 'by whom I have no children'.[15]

12 Letterbook of the *Albemarle* and *Boreas*, British Library: Add MSS 34961.

13 Nicolas, *op cit*, Vol I, p10.

14 Unpublished letter: Nelson to Thomas Bolton, 15 November 1790, Private collection.

15 Nicolas, *op cit*, Vol I, p10.

THE RISE TO FAME: 1793–1796

Finally, after many disappointments, in early 1793 he was offered command of the 64-gun battleship HMS *Agamemnon*. Having gathered a ship's company, including a largely hand-picked contingent from Norfolk, he sailed in her to join the Mediterranean fleet, under Lord Hood. Even there, his role tended to be unconventional, involving much detached duty. In September 1793, he was sent on a diplomatic mission to Naples to persuade the King to send troops to help the British to defend the French port of Toulon, which had been surrendered by royalist sympathisers. Then in the following year, Hood placed him in command of naval forces ashore during the capture of the island of Corsica and he was present at the siege and capture of two key towns: first Bastia, and then Calvi, where he was hit in the face by gravel thrown up from a parapet by a French cannonball. Although he made light of it at the time, recent research has established that the wound was in fact quite serious.[16] As it was, he lost almost all sight in his right eye and thereafter was only able to distinguish light from dark with it.

In 1795, he had a brief spell with the main fleet, by then commanded by Admiral William Hotham, during which time he took part in two fleet battles, the first of his career. At the Battle of the Gulf of Genoa (13/14 March 1795) he showed his independent approach by taking the *Agamemnon* to attack a disabled French ship, the *Ça Ira*. He dealt the much larger ship and her crew such a heavy blow that she fell an easy prey to the British when the fighting resumed the next day. But he was furious when Hotham ended the action when only two prizes had been taken. As he wrote later to Fanny, 'Sure I am had I commanded the fleet on the 14th, that either the whole French fleet would have graced my triumph or I should have been in a confounded scrape.'[17]

He was then detached again, this time as a commodore in command of a small squadron, to Italy where he assisted the Austrian army in its fight against the victorious French armies under the rising new general Napoleon Bonaparte. In the course of this campaign he not only instituted a tight blockade of French-held ports, but also organised a further two successful amphibious operations: the capture of the islands of Elba and Capraia in 1796. He also found time to court his first mistress, the opera singer Adelaide Correglia, whom he met in Leghorn. But there was an element of business combined with his pleasure, since it has recently been established that she supplied him with intelligence of ship movements, as well as sexual favours. His daily routine was largely mundane, and the bat-

16 When Nelson wrote to the Navy Board in 1798, to ask for a pension for the loss of his eye, he mentioned that he was 'carried to my tent from the Battery', which suggests that the wound was rather more serious and disabling than he admitted in his letters at the time. Unpublished letter: Nelson to Commissioner Hope, 1 October 1798. National Maritime Museum, MON 1/8.

17 George Naish, *Nelson's Letters to his Wife*, Navy Records Society (London 1958), p204.

18 The only full-length examination of Nelson's operations in 1795/6 is in A T Mahan, *The Life of Nelson: The Embodiment of the Seapower of Great Britain*, pp155–258.

19 See p82 for details of the latest research into the Battle of Cape St Vincent.

tles were small-scale, so this period has not been studied in much detail in the past.[18] But it is now recognised as a very important stage in his career. First, it gave him experience of independent command, in which he took important operational decisions himself. Second, his exploits won him the regard of a number of influential people, notably the First Lord of the Admiralty, Lord Spencer, and the new commander-in-chief in the Mediterranean, Sir John Jervis, both of whom were to have considerable influence on his career. He also caught the attention of the viceroy of Corsica, Sir Gilbert Elliot, who became a close friend and loyal supporter in later years. But, despite the approval of such men, he began to feel that he was not sufficiently appreciated back home in Britain and his letters to his wife and family at this time are full of complaints that his actions had not been publicly recognised or rewarded.

Nelson at the Battle of Cape St Vincent, 1797. Richard Westall produced this sanitised and romanticised image for the 'official' biography by Clarke and M'Arthur in 1809. In fact, Nelson's uniform was in tatters and his face blackened with gunsmoke.

THE BATTLE OF CAPE ST VINCENT: FEBRUARY 1797

All that was to change dramatically early in 1797. In December 1796, Jervis was forced to abandon the Mediterranean by the victories of the French armies in Italy and by the entry of Spain into the war. Early the following year, France and her allies planned a major invasion of British-held Ireland backed by their fleets, but the opening moves were thwarted by Jervis's remarkable victory over the Spanish fleet at the Battle of Cape St Vincent (14 February 1797), in which Nelson played a leading role. Past accounts of the battle have tended to portray Nelson as a lone genius who saved the day for the British by his unconventional approach. Modern research into the logbooks of the ships involved, and into other contemporary accounts, including material from Spanish sources, has revealed a much more complex picture.[19] It is now appar-

ent that Jervis himself handled the battle unconventionally right from the outset. First, he formed his ships into a loose line of battle and drove swiftly for a gap in the Spanish line. Then, having split the enemy fleet into two unequal groups, he subdivided his own fleet into divisions in order to attack the larger group. Nelson played a decisive role in this second phase of the battle with an act of inspired initiative. Noticing that his divisional flagship, the *Britannia*, was not complying with Jervis's signals, he took his ship, HMS *Captain*, out of the line and sailed directly to assist the British van, which had by then begun to catch up with the rearmost Spaniards. In the past, this act has been described as an act of disobedience that could have cost him his career but it is now clear that he was acting in accordance with Jervis's intentions.[20]

A fierce mêlée ensued, in which a number of Spanish ships suffered badly from the fast and accurate British broadsides. Two of them, the *San Nicolas* and the *San José*, while trying desperately to get out of range, collided and became entangled. Seeing this, Nelson ordered the *Captain* to be placed alongside the *San Nicolas* and then personally led a boarding party to capture her. The *San José*, which had already been badly mauled by gunfire from other British ships, began firing on Nelson and his party in an attempt to help their comrades. So he led his men up her sides and captured her as well. He thus was personally responsible for capturing two of the four prizes that were taken on that day.

It was a remarkable feat, unprecedented in naval history, and Nelson was deservedly the hero of the hour. But his earlier lack of recognition still rankled and so he made sure he was not overlooked on this occasion by sending a personal account of his exploits to his former captain, William Locker, with a request that he have it published in the papers. This account overemphasised his own role in the battle and even suggested that the *Captain* and the *Culloden*, commanded by his friend Thomas Troubridge, had fought alone 'for near an hour'.[21] He obviously believed this sincerely but it was demonstrably not true and the claim made him unpopular in the victorious fleet, where the general opinion was that everyone had contributed to the great victory. Jervis himself wrote in a private letter to the First Lord of the Admiralty that it would be '. . . improper to distinguish one from the other.'

On the other hand, Jervis obviously valued Nelson highly. Following the Battle of Cape St Vincent, the Spanish fleet took refuge in Cádiz and was blockaded by the British. Jervis formed a special inshore squadron of battleships, which he placed under the command of Nelson, by now promoted to rear admiral. He also recognised his gift for inspiring men. When

HMS *Theseus* joined the fleet in May with a half-mutinous crew, Jervis responded by asking Nelson and his flag captain, Ralph Miller, to transfer to her. It is clear that he placed the blame squarely on the shoulders of the ship's officers. Writing to his friend the Duke of Clarence, Nelson explained that 'Sir John for certain reasons has wished Me to Join this Ship which has hitherto not been commanded to his liking.'[22] A fortnight later a note was dropped on the *Theseus*'s quarterdeck, 'Success attend Admiral Nelson God bless Captain Miller we thank them for the officers they have placed over us. We are happy and comfortable and will shed every drop of blood in our veins to support them, and the name of the *Theseus* shall be immortalised as high as *Captain*'s. Ship's Company.'[23]

The reference to 'the officers they have placed over us' is significant. As was customary, Nelson had taken with him a number of his young 'followers', including his two particular favourites, John Weatherhead and William Hoste, and they had obviously been instrumental in establishing good order, helped by some old Agamemnons who had accompanied their commander. The transformation of the *Theseus* was certainly a tribute to Nelson's leadership skills, as his biographers have often pointed out. But it was also a striking demonstration of how important it was for an eighteenth-century officer to surround himself with high-quality followers – and on the lower deck as much as in the wardroom.

SANTA CRUZ DE TENERIFE: JULY 1797

Shortly after arriving off Cádiz, Nelson learned that his exploits had at last received the official recognition that he longed for: he had been made a Knight of the Bath, with the right to wear the distinctive star of the order on the breast of his uniform coat. Delightedly, he set about designing himself a coat of arms, choosing the figure of a sailor as one of the 'supporters' for the shield. This is yet another fascinating insight into his contradictory personality. On the one hand, he was still seeking public recognition of his deeds; on the other, he was acknowledging the debt he owed to the officers and men who served with him. It was a pattern that was to be repeated throughout his life.

The Spanish fleet remained behind the defences of Cádiz, despite all that Nelson and his comrades could do to dislodge them. So, instead, Jervis sought other ways of bringing pressure to bear and in July 1797, remembering Nelson's previous successes against Elba and Capraia, he sent him with a small squadron to attack the Spanish island of Tenerife. This was Nelson's first major operation as an admiral and he tackled it

20 See Colin White, *1797: Nelson's Year of Destiny*, Royal Naval Museum (Portsmouth 1998), p58.

21 Nicolas, *op cit*, Vol I, p341.

22 Nelson to the Duke of Clarence, 26 May 1797. National Maritime Museum, AGC/27/24. (Only parts of this letter have been published. The passage from which this quotation is taken was edited out by Clarke and M'Arthur.)

23 Naish, *op cit*, p326.

with great thoroughness, consulting with his captains regularly, ordering special equipment and insisting on daily training for the men who would be landed. In the end, all his careful preparations were frustrated by the one factor for which he could not plan – the weather. His landing force was prevented from reaching their objective by contrary winds and currents and by the time they did manage to get ashore the well-organised Spanish defenders had taken up strong defensive positions from which they could not be dislodged. At this point, Nelson could quite legitimately have abandoned the operation, but he received intelligence from the shore that the Spanish had very few professional soldiers and that they were in a state of disarray and confusion. At a council of war with all his captains, Nelson was urged to attack again and he needed little persuasion – as he later admitted, 'my pride suffered'.[24] It was the decision of an inexperienced leader who had not fully weighed the risks against the likely gains.[25]

The new attack was a bloody disaster that lost Nelson almost a quarter of his force in killed and wounded. The first part of the intelligence report was correct: the Spanish defenders were indeed very thin on the ground. But the second part was completely wrong: carefully organised by the island's governor, Antonio Gutiérrez, an experienced professional soldier, the small Spanish defending force was in fact alert and ready. As the British sailors stormed the town mole and citadel, they were mown down by concentrated fire, including Nelson himself whose upper right arm was shattered by a musket ball. A few small parties managed to struggle ashore and barricaded themselves in a monastery. But they were surrounded and cut off from their comrades and eventually agreed to surrender.

Luckily for Nelson, his stepson, Josiah Nisbet, was at his side in the boat and he saved his life. First, he staunched the flow of blood from the dangerous wound and then he managed to get him back to his flagship, where the arm was amputated. At this point, it seemed that the attack was succeeding, and so within moments of the operation, Nelson was using his left hand to apply a wavering signature to an ultimatum addressed to the Spanish governor. But, shortly after, more accurate news came from the shore and so his second and slightly more legible attempt at a signature was at the bottom of a letter to General Gutiérrez, thanking him for the very humane way in which he had treated his British prisoners, offering them food and drink and taking their wounded into the town's hospital. With the letter went a cask of beer and some cheese, to which Gutiérrez responded by sending Nelson some Malmsey wine.[26]

It was a severe setback, the worst Nelson had so far suffered in his career, and showed that his tactics of shock and surprise could be countered by a determined and experienced opponent. Not unnaturally, he was very depressed, both by the large number of casualties and by the blow to his own future prospects. As he wrote in a letter to Jervis, '. . . a left handed admiral will never again be considered as useful therefore the sooner I get to a very humble cottage the better and make room for a better man to serve the state.'[27] To make matters worse, the casualties included Lieutenant John Whitehead, who died of his wounds a few days later. Greatly affected by the loss of one of his protégés, Nelson wrote to the young man's clergyman father, '. . . when I reflect on that fatal night I cannot but bring sorrow and his fall before my eyes. Dear friend he fought as he had always done by my side . . .'[28]

Jervis, who had recently been created Earl St Vincent as a reward for his great victory, was sympathetic and sent Nelson home to Britain to recover. After a depressing voyage in which he again talked of finding 'a hut to put my mutilated carcase in', Nelson arrived to find himself the hero of the hour. The disaster at Tenerife was ignored and the hero of St Vincent acclaimed, first by the crowds at Portsmouth where he landed, and then in Bath where he went to join Fanny Nelson and his father. Newspaper articles sang his praises and letters began to arrive inviting him to accept the freedoms of various cities, including the City of London. The first popular prints of him began to appear. This public adulation, the first he had ever received, restored his flagging spirits and within a month he was talking of returning to sea, writing to St Vincent, '. . . if you continue to hold your opinion of me I shall press to return with all the zeal, although not with all the personal ability, I formerly had.'[29]

First, however, he had to recover from the loss of his arm, but this was still causing him such pain that he had to take opium in order to sleep. None of the doctors in Bath was able to help and so he and Fanny travelled to London where they consulted a number of specialists. The consensus was that the arm was best left to heal by itself and in the end this is exactly what happened. One morning Nelson woke after an unusually sound sleep to find that the pain had suddenly disappeared. Characteristically, one of his first acts was to send a note to the nearest church, St George's in Hanover Square, asking for special prayers of thanks to be said the following Sunday.

Nelson's empty sleeve is such a familiar feature of his appearance that it is easy to forget what a psychological shock the loss of his arm must have been. It involved many changes in his everyday life, the most obvious of which was the switch to left-handed writing. There were alterations to his

24 Nelson to Captain Sir Andrew Snape Hammond, 8 September 1797, Nicolas, *op cit*, Vol II, p443.

25 For an analysis of all the new evidence about the council of war, and Nelson's decision to attack, see White, *op cit*, pp112–114.

26 For details of all the latest research on the Tenerife operation, see p230.

27 Nelson to Sir John Jervis, 16 August 1797, Nicolas, *op cit*, Vol II, p435.

28 Nelson to Rev Weatherhead, 31 October 1797, *ibid*, p451.

29 Nelson to Jervis, 6 October 1797, *ibid*, p448.

clothes: the empty sleeve itself, pinned across his chest; specially short-ened right sleeves for his shirts; breeches, stockings and shoes instead of boots. His pens were cut differently and he even acquired a combined knife and fork to help him to cut up his food more easily.

There was also a mental adjustment to make. To this he brought his religious faith, which had a strong element of predestination in it, and also his distinctive sense of humour. He gave his stump a nautical nickname and his 'fin', as he always called it, became part of his public image. 'I'm Lord Nelson, see here's my fin!' he shouted one dark night in the Baltic when a ship he was visiting challenged his boat. He was also prepared to

Nelson wounded at the Nile. This pen and wash drawing by William Bromley shows the wounded Nelson being brought on deck to witness the destruction of the French flagship L'Orient.

make jokes about his loss. On a visit to Great Yarmouth, the landlady of the Wrestler's Arms asked permission to rename her pub The Nelson Arms. 'That would be absurd,' came the reply, 'seeing I have but one.'

He even used a joke about his arm to cover a royal gaffe. On 25 September 1797, he was presented to the King at St James's Palace following his formal investment with the Order of the Bath, but the notoriously tactless George III had not been well briefed. 'You have lost your right arm!' he exclaimed. 'But not my right hand,' replied Nelson quickly, turning to one of his companions, 'as I have the honour of presenting Captain Berry.' This visit to St James's was but one of a number of public engagements that he undertook at this time and, ironically, by holding him in London, his troublesome wound actually worked in his favour. If he had remained with the fleet off Cádiz, his exploits would soon have been forgotten. His regular attendance at Court, and at official Admiralty functions, kept him in the public eye – and, most important, in the minds of men such as the influential First Lord of the Admiralty, Lord Spencer – while his empty sleeve was a visible reminder of his remarkable achievements. This combination was now to give him a unique career opportunity, which was to transform him from one hero among many to *the* hero.

THE NILE CAMPAIGN: JUNE–SEPTEMBER 1798

While Nelson was recovering, the war against France had entered a new phase. Peace negotiations, which had been going on intermittently throughout 1797, had finally broken down and so Britain was now working to construct a new coalition against France. At the same time, Admiral Adam Duncan's victory over the Dutch at Camperdown on 11 October finally ended the threat of invasion, which had been hanging over Britain for more than a year, and so the Cabinet now felt able to look once again at the situation on the Mediterranean. Britain's withdrawal of its fleet in 1796 had been used by the Austrians to justify their own withdrawal from the war, and ministers knew that if they wished to construct a new coalition they had to make a show of strength in the sea again. At the same time, they were beginning to receive intelligence reports of a major expeditionary force being prepared at Toulon. So the idea began to grow of sending a special detached squadron to operate there independently. It would be a highly responsible command for which special qualities of leadership would be needed, and suddenly everybody seemed to think of Nelson. Later, after he had won his stunning victory at the Battle of the Nile, the Duke of Clarence wrote to his friend to assure him that it had been the King's idea. Sir Gilbert Elliot, now Lord Minto, wrote reporting a conversation in which he had suggested the idea to Lord Spencer. Spencer did indeed write to St Vincent, but by the time this letter arrived off Cádiz in early May 1798, St Vincent had already detached Nelson on his mission with a small squadron.

Left in full control of the Mediterranean following the British withdrawal in late 1796, the French used the opportunity to plan a bold and imaginative stroke that they hoped might win the war for them: an invasion of Egypt, followed by an overland attack on British trade in India. In overall command was the brilliant young General Napoleon Bonaparte, fresh from his recent conquest of Italy. Sailing on 19 May 1798 with 35,000 troops in 400 transports, escorted by thirteen battleships, the French went first to Malta, which was surrendered without a fight, and from there to Egypt, where they arrived on 1 July. The army was landed without opposition and, by the end of the month, Egypt was under French control.

The British knew that the expedition was preparing but they did not know where it was heading. So Nelson's first task was to discover the destination of the force and then to destroy it. Having received a large detachment from the Channel fleet, St Vincent reinforced Nelson, giving him a powerful squadron of fourteen battleships, commanded by some of the most experienced captains of his fleet. Mostly the same age as their new commander, and old comrades, they formed an élite team which worked together superbly—a 'Band of Brothers' as Nelson later termed them (quoting from his favourite Shakespeare play, *Henry V*). After only just over a year as an admiral, and aged only thirty-nine, Nelson now found himself with a level of responsibility that would have taxed an older and more experienced man. He rose to the challenge superbly, tracking the French fleet down in Egypt after a long and frustrating chase and destroying them at anchor in Aboukir Bay on 1 August 1798, in one of the most ferocious and decisive naval battles of the sailing era.

Thanks to the insights of modern French research,[30] we now know rather more about the difficulties under which the French commander-in-chief, Vice Admiral François Brueys, was labouring. Even so, the extent and completeness of the victory was remarkable: out of the thirteen French battleships, eleven were captured or destroyed. Remarkable too was the lack of central control that Nelson exercised over the battle. The essence of the attack had been agreed with his captains some time before: a concentration in force on the van of the enemy line, until it had been overwhelmed by rapid gunfire, and then a piecemeal destruction of the rest. As a result, having made his decision to attack at once, even though

30 See especially Michelle Battesti, *La Bataille d'Aboukir*, Economica (Paris, 1998).

31 For details of latest research on the Battle of the Nile, see p192.

night was already falling, he was able to leave the detailed conduct of the action to his individual captains, allowing them as a commander the same independence that he had exercised as a subordinate. It was to become one of the most distinctive hallmarks of his style of leadership.[31]

As the British fleet sailed headlong into Aboukir Bay, without waiting to form a proper line of battle or to gather stragglers, Captain Foley in the leading ship HMS *Goliath* noticed that the French had left enough room between the head of their line and the shoals for him to round their van and attack on the landward side. His bold initiative was followed by the ships immediately astern of him until Nelson, arriving in his flagship HMS *Vanguard*, began a second attack on the seaward side. So, right at the outset, the French van was overwhelmed, crushed on both sides by superior numbers and firepower. And, since the wind was blowing directly down their line, the rearmost ships were unable to do anything to help their comrades and were forced to wait helplessly as the battle rolled inexorably towards them.

Nelson was wounded at the height of the action, when a piece of shrap-

The Nile celebrations. The news of Nelson's victory at the Nile was celebrated all over Europe. This contemporary engraving shows the festivities in London.

'The hero of the Nile.' In this caricature, published only weeks after the news of the victory of the Nile arrived in Britain, Gilray pokes fun at Nelson's new honours, which he suggests are weighing him down.

nel struck him on the forehead, causing a flap of skin to fall over his good eye. Blinded with blood, he at first thought it was a mortal wound and collapsed into his flag captain Berry's arms saying, 'I am killed. Remember me to my wife.' In fact, although messy and very painful, the gash was not life threatening and within an hour he had begun composing his official despatch (see p265 for a transcription).

The Battle of the Nile is now generally regarded as Nelson's most decisive victory, surpassing even Trafalgar. In immediate tactical terms, it was far more complete than Trafalgar: the French Mediterranean fleet was almost eliminated and a completely new force had to be assembled. Its strategic effects were even more wide ranging. It galvanised the opponents of France, and encouraged them to form the Second Coalition, thus breathing new life into a war that had almost come to a standstill following the remarkable successes of the French armies. And Nelson became an international celebrity almost overnight. When the news finally reached Britain, in October 1798, there was an overwhelming sense of relief, expressed in thanksgiving services, bonfires and bell-ringing and special theatrical performances. Above all, there was a flood of commemorative material that stamped his image on the public mind. For the rest of his life, he was known as 'The Hero of the Nile'.

However, at this time, the hero was again at a low ebb. Modern medical opinion is divided as to whether his head wound actually caused major concussion.[32] What is certain, however, is that for months afterwards he suffered from sharp headaches and nausea. At the same time, he was mentally exhausted after the strain of the long drawn out campaign in which he had borne the heavy responsibility of command alone and, for the first time in his career, without any direct support from a senior officer. If he had gone home once again to rest, he might have recovered fully, as he did following the loss of his arm at Tenerife. But, instead, he went to Naples.

32 For a rehearsal of the various points of view, see Leslie LeQuesne, 'Nelson and his surgeons', *Journal of the Royal Naval Medical Service* 86 (2000).

NAPLES AND EMMA: 1798–1800

Nelson's close involvement with Naples between September 1798 and June 1800 was the most controversial period in his career, even during his lifetime, and it has remained controversial ever since. When he first arrived there he was expecting to stay only long enough to refit the *Vanguard*, which had been badly damaged in the battle, and to have a short rest himself. But he became caught up in Neapolitan affairs and gradually began to neglect the needs of his wider command. Having urged the King of Naples to take advantage of the French disarray to attack Rome in the autumn of 1798, he then felt responsible when the Neapolitan armies were routed, and the royal family forced to flee to

The 'Tria Juncta in Uno': Nelson, Emma and Sir William, all portrayed by the same artist, Charles Grignon, in Palermo in 1799. The portrait of Nelson is one of the few informal studies of him to have survived. The portrait of Emma shows her performing one of her famous 'attitudes'.

their second capital of Palermo in Sicily the following December. And when the French occupied Naples and established a republic there, he felt obliged to help the King to recover his throne in June 1799, so becoming directly involved in a very bloody and vicious civil war. He was personally implicated in some ugly incidents, such as the trial and summary execution of one of the republican leaders, Commodore Francesco Caracciolo, and the surrender for brutal execution of a number of other key Neapolitan revolutionaries.

A more experienced man would have remained detached, offering help from a distance. But such was not Nelson's way: impulsive and eager as always, he threw himself into the thick of the fray, just as he had done at Cape St Vincent and again at Tenerife. This time, however, it was not his body that was wounded but his reputation. Questions were asked in Parliament about his conduct in Naples, and the debate about his complicity in the atrocities, and whether or not he should be held responsible for them, has continued ever since. In the past such debates have tended to seek either to exonerate him wholly or wholly to blame him, which is too simplistic a way to judge such a complex affair. More recently, an alternative view has begun to emerge that he must indeed shoulder some of the responsibility, but that others must share it, including Sir William Hamilton and, indeed, the Neapolitans themselves who actually carried out the killings for which their descendants blame Nelson.[33]

The other product of the strange and strained period was his extraordinary relationship with Emma Hamilton. She nursed him tenderly when he first arrived in Naples, sick and shaken with his head wound. They shared danger together when the royal family was evacuated to Palermo in December 1798 in the middle of a fierce storm, during which Emma behaved with magnificent courage when all around her were prostrated with seasickness and terror. And she was at his side throughout the events of July 1799 when he was wrestling with the complexities of Neapolitan politics. In such an intense atmosphere it was, perhaps, not surprising that two such impetuous and impulsively affectionate people should become close friends, and then lovers.

What is surprising is that they did so little to hide it. Modern commentators have suggested that they probably did not start having sex together until late in 1799 or even early 1800,[34] but long before then their public behaviour had already made them a rich source of gossip and scandal. Both of them suffered, but it is arguable that it was Emma who suffered most. Nelson was certainly criticised for his over-close involvement with Neapolitan affairs and was eventually recalled home to Britain in disgrace in June 1800. But the country needed its successful leaders and so his naval career did not suffer a serious setback. Emma, on the other hand, lost at a stroke all the hard-won respectability that she had gained by her own talents and by her marriage to Sir William Hamilton, and she never again recovered it. Sir William suffered too, acquiring in his declining years a reputation as a cuckold that for long overshadowed the memory of his own achievements, both as a diplomat and as a connoisseur and vulcanologist. It is only recently that this talented man has received the recognition that he deserves. Modern studies also suggest that he probably played an important role in the Nelson/Emma relationship. Far from being supine and weak, as has often been suggested in the past, his acquiescence is now seen as the civilised response of an accomplished diplomat who wished both to save his marriage and to keep his best friend.[35]

Hamilton was recalled home at the same time as Nelson and so the trio set off together through the German states on what quickly became a triumphal progress. Nelson was one of the few leaders who had succeeded in beating the French and, as a result, he was a household name in Europe as well as in Britain. Wherever they went there were special ceremonies, and princes and people alike crowded to see the Hero of the Nile. As a result, they stopped so many times en route that a journey they could have expected to make in a few weeks in fact took three and a half months. It was an extraordinary interlude in Nelson's life and shows how, at least in the early stages, his relationship with Emma affected his professional judgement. Elsewhere, the war was still raging furiously, and British forces were engaged in a number of vital operations. Against such a background, Nelson's leisurely progress through Germany did him much harm with the authorities in Britain, especially since most reports of their activities highlighted his very obvious infatuation with Emma.[36]

That infatuation was now to cause him trouble at home. It appears that Nelson genuinely believed that Fanny would be prepared to be as complacent as Sir William was, so that the liaison with Emma could continue. But Fanny had her own brand of quiet and dignified courage, against which Nelson's ruthless eagerness beat in vain. In the end, he was forced to choose between his wife and his lover, a decision that clearly wracked him with guilt. In a letter to Emma dating from this period, he refers to having passed '. . . a very indifferent night'[37] and his state of mind is vividly captured in an oil sketch of him produced at this time by the artist John Hoppner, in which he looks haggard and haunted (see colour plate *IV*). But Emma had one great advantage over Fanny for, by then, she knew that she was pregnant. The prospect of a child of his own at last obviously

33 See Knight, *op cit*.

34 Fraser, *op cit*, p225.

35 See Colin White, 'Tria Juncta in Uno: Nelson and the Hamiltons', *The Trafalgar Chronicle* 6 (1996).

36 For details of the latest research on the tour through Germany, see p131.

37 Unpublished letter: Nelson to Emma Hamilton, 15 December 1800, Private collection.

decided Nelson and the separation from Fanny that followed was cruelly decisive, and so swift that for a while she could not believe it had happened. But he was relentless and, having made a generous financial provision for her, cut her out of his life and refused to see her, or even to communicate with her, again.

The misery of these domestic wrangles was cut short by a summons to serve at sea once more with the Channel fleet, under his old mentor Lord St Vincent, and he hoisted his flag in his former trophy from the Battle of Cape St Vincent, now HMS *San Josef*, on 17 January 1801. But it is clear from the letters he was writing to Emma at this time that he was in a very unstable state mentally. Worry about Emma's pregnancy was followed by wild exhilaration when she gave birth to a daughter, Horatia, only to be replaced by an obsessive jealousy when he learned that Emma was going to dine with the notoriously amorous Prince of Wales. St Vincent, obviously exasperated by the extraordinary change in the man who had once been his most trusted subordinate, wrote angrily to the Secretary of the Admiralty, '. . . his ship is always in the most dreadful disorder and he can never become an officer fit to be placed where I am.'[38] If Nelson had remained with the Channel fleet, the boredom and routine of blockade duty may well have exacerbated his already unbalanced mood and led him into behaviour that would have justified St Vincent's characteristically irascible hyperbole. In fact, events were about to give him a chance to prove just how wrong St Vincent's judgement was.

COPENHAGEN AND THE BALTIC: JANUARY–JUNE 1801

At that time, the Baltic was a vital source of trade and maritime supplies for Britain, worth over £3 million in the prices of the day. So when in early 1801, under the influence of a pro-French Russia, the Baltic states formed themselves into an 'Armed Neutrality of the North' and placed an embargo on British ships, the British government felt compelled to take action. A special fleet was formed at Great Yarmouth, on the coast of Norfolk, under the overall command of Admiral Sir Hyde Parker, an experienced, if rather unadventurous, commander, with a good prior knowledge of the Baltic. Nelson was appointed his second in early March 1801 and, leaving the *San Josef*, moved to the shallower-draught *St George*.

From the first, there was tension between the two men; the rather reserved Parker obviously regarding his younger and more charismatic subordinate with a certain amount of suspicion and reserve. As always, Nelson favoured aggressive, impetuous action: a sudden descent with the whole fleet on Copenhagen, capital of Denmark, one of the key members of the Armed Neutrality. As he wrote to the Duke of Clarence, in a letter that has recently been rediscovered, '. . . from reports the Danes say <u>War</u> therefore War they must have and enough of it to make them sick.'[39] Parker, bound by his orders to exhaust the diplomatic options first, proceeded with caution and was clearly overwhelmed by the responsibility that had fallen on him; so much so that, according to recent research, he was unable to sleep and so became progressively more strained and depressed.[40]

Negotiations with the Danes broke down and so Parker eventually agreed to move on Copenhagen. By now, Nelson had managed to exert his considerable charm upon the older man and a rapport had grown up between them; so much so that Parker handed over the entire direction of the offensive operations to his subordinate. The Danes had placed a defensive line of hulks and floating batteries in front of Copenhagen, designed to keep an attacking force out of bombardment range of the city. This had first to be subdued, a task made the more difficult by the very complicated shoals that surrounded the approaches to the city and by powerful forts protecting the flanks of the floating line.

Nelson was at his charismatic best, filling everyone with confidence, arranging for careful surveys to be made of the surrounding waters, drawing up detailed plans to deal with the Danish line and then, finally, dining with some of his key subordinates to brief them and infuse them with his fighting spirit. As at the Nile, the essence of his plan was concentration: bringing overwhelming force to bear on one part of the enemy line and then moving on to deal with the rest. He impressed all those who were present, including Lieutenant Colonel William Stewart, one of the founders of the Rifle Brigade, who had been attached to the expedition with some of his troops to assist in the assault on the city. A few days after the battle, Stewart wrote to Sir William Clinton, 'The Conduct of Ld Nelson, to whom alone is due all praise both for the attempt & execution of the Contest, has been most <u>grand</u> – he is the admiration of the whole fleet.'[41]

Nelson deserved this praise, for it is clear from all the accounts that it was his determination that eventually won the day for the British – but only by a narrow margin. The Battle of Copenhagen, fought on 2 April 1801, has tended in the past to be presented as a hard-won, but ultimately overwhelming, victory over a gallant and determined foe. But modern Danish and British research has established that it was in fact an extremely close contest.[42] Nelson himself admitted as much in a letter to his friend

38 Jervis to the Secretary to the Admiralty, January 1801, *The Naval Miscellany*: Vol I, Navy Records Society (London 1912), p330.

39 Unpublished letter: Nelson to the Duke of Clarence, 23 March 1801, British Library, Add Mss 46356, f36.

40 Peter Lefevre, 'Little merit will be given to me: Sir Hyde Parker', *Proceedings of the Copenhagen 200 Conference*, The 1805 Club (Shelton 2002).

41 Unpublished letter: William Stewart to William Clinton, 6 April 1801, National Maritime Museum, AGC/14/27.

42 See *Proceedings of the Copenhagen 200 Conference*.

the Duke of Clarence, which was later suppressed by his early biographers and has only recently been rediscovered: '. . . the loss of service in the stations assigned to them of three sail by their getting on shore prevented our success from being so compleat as I intended but I thank God under those very untoward circumstances for what has been done.'[43]

Having lost a quarter of his attacking force in the opening moments of the battle, Nelson then found that the Danish resistance was stronger, and

The Battle of Copenhagen, 2 April 1801. The view of the battle seen from the south. The Danish line is on the left with Nelson's attacking ships on the right. On the extreme right are the British ships that went aground.

more prolonged, than he had expected. As a result the battle dragged on for longer than planned, causing Parker, watching nervously from a distance, to send his notorious signal of recall. Nelson ignored the signal, telling Colonel Stewart, 'Well Stewart, these fellows hold us a better Jug than I expected, however we are keeping up a noble fire and I'll be answerable that we shall bowl them out in four if we cannot do it in three hours, at least I'll give it them till they are sick of it.'[44] Then, sensing that

43 Unpublished letter: Nelson to the Duke of Clarence, 4 April 1801, British Library, Add Ms 46356, f37.

44 Stewart to Clinton, see note 40.

'John Bull partaking of a luncheon.' In this caricature of 1798, John Bull is being fed tasty dishes of French, Spanish and Dutch ships by his admirals. Note, however, that Nelson is portrayed well in the foreground – he is already seen as the main hero.

the Danish line was at last beginning to give way, he sent a message to the Danish Crown Prince offering a truce. By the time the Crown Prince, watching the battle from the shore, received Nelson's letter, the centre of the Danish line had collapsed and the way was open for a British bombardment of his city. So he agreed to Nelson's suggestion and the battle ended.

Having begun the negotiations, Nelson was encouraged by Parker to continue them and he now displayed a talent for diplomacy that suggested he had learned some lessons from his experiences in Naples. The Danes, subjected to a judicious combination of threat and charm, were on the point of agreeing to an armistice when the news arrived that Tsar Paul of Russia, the main architect of the Armed Neutrality, had been assassinated. With the fear of Russian reprisals removed, Denmark felt able to withdraw from a confrontation with Britain that had never been popular and Nelson was free to start cajoling Parker to move up the Baltic to deal with the other partners in the alliance.

By now, however, news of the battle had reached Britain and the results were surprising. Parker was abruptly recalled and St Vincent, now First Lord of the Admiralty and the man who less than five months before had written that Nelson could 'never become an officer fit to be placed where I am,' appointed Nelson commander-in-chief in the Baltic. It was a tribute not only to his fighting abilities but also to the skill he had displayed in the negotiations.

Nelson held this new command for only two months and this period in his life has not been much studied in the past. But it is now becoming clear that it was an important turning point in his professional career, when he first showed that he was more than merely a fighting admiral. He handled the complex administration of his large fleet skilfully, and displayed a sure hand in dealing with the intricate diplomacy of the Baltic region. His official correspondence brought him for the first time into regular contact with leading politicians, such as the prime minister, Henry Addington, and he clearly impressed them, both with his commitment and with his grasp of international affairs. On the other hand, his health was severely undermined by the Baltic cold and, eventually, he had to request to be allowed to return home. As he told an old colleague, 'the cold air of the North has struck me to the heart and I cannot get rid of my Cough. In short I am in a final stage of consumption.'[45]

THE CHANNEL AND PEACE: JULY 1801–MAY 1803

Nelson reached Britain in early July 1801 to find the country in the grip of an invasion scare. For example, the July edition of *The Naval Chronicle* spoke of 'the immense preparations making all along the French coast for the long-talked-of INVASION.'[46] We now know, from recent French research,[47] that these preparations were very largely a bluff by Napoleon, designed to bring Britain, his last remaining major adversary, to the negotiating table. But in Britain the threat was believed, not least by Lord St Vincent, and so he once more decided to appoint Nelson as a commander-in-chief; this time of a large fleet of small vessels in the Channel. He was tasked specifically with defending the south coast and the Thames estuary and with attacking and destroying the French invasion forces.

It was essentially a public relations exercise, intended to calm public fears by placing the Hero of the Nile in the front line and, for this reason, many of Nelson's biographers have tended to by-pass this period in his career and to downplay the importance of the command. Certainly, when measured against the achievements of his other great campaigns, the three months he spent in the Channel appear almost as an interlude. But the force he commanded was far from insignificant: indeed in terms of numbers it was by far the largest that he ever commanded. The detailed daily orders for the campaign have recently been discovered and they show that, as in the Baltic, he proved himself a skilful fleet administrator.[48] And the appointment again brought him into close and regular contact with the country's leaders, thus further reinforcing his reputation as a good man of business as well as a fighter.

Nelson threw himself into the post with his customary enthusiasm, issuing a stream of invigorating orders to his captains and embarking on a

45 Unpublished letter: Nelson to Admiral Dickson, 23 May 1801, Huntington Library, HM34048.

46 *The Naval Chronicle*, Vol VI, p73.

47 Rémi Monaque, 'Latouche-Tréville: The admiral who defied Nelson', *The Mariner's Mirror* 86 (August 2000).

48 See Colin White, 'Nelson's Channel Order Book', *The Naval Miscellany*: Vol VI, The Navy Records Society (London 2003).

Nelson and his prizes. In this print, published in March 1802, Nelson is shown with all the ships he had been responsible for capturing or destroying since 1793. He chose the portrait in the centre himself, rejecting the engraver's choice and telling him to substitute instead the profile by Simon de Koster.

whistle-stop tour of his new command. St Vincent commented admiringly, 'you are so rapid in your movements that it is difficult to know where to write at your Lordship.'[49] But he quickly realised that the invasion threat was a sham and it was not long before he began to feel the command was not a suitable one for him. He made one major attempt to attack the French forces, at Boulogne on 15 August, but his opponent, Admiral Louis de Latouche Tréville, was an experienced commander who had studied Nelson's methods and made careful preparations to counter them. As a result, the British attack was repulsed with heavy casualties, including Captain Edward Parker, who having become one of Nelson's special protégés in the Mediterranean some three years before, had served at his side ever since. He had clearly become particularly attached to the young man, referring to him as 'my son Parker', and so when he later died from his wounds, Nelson was distraught.

Indeed, his letters at this time show that Nelson was once again under severe emotional strain. His health, which had never recovered fully from the punishing it had received in the freezing Baltic, gave way again. Now that the opportunity for action had passed, he was missing Emma and began to suspect that his old friend Thomas Troubridge, now one of the Lords of the Admiralty, was conspiring with St Vincent to keep him apart from her. As the rumours of approaching peace with France began to circulate in early September, he pleaded to be allowed to relinquish his command. But his requests were gently but firmly turned down, first by St Vincent and then by the prime minister himself, which only increased Nelson's sense of persecution. Eventually, however, at the end of October, the peace negotiations had reached a point where the government at last felt able to release him and he went ashore to join the Hamiltons.

While Nelson had been battling with equinoctial gales in the Channel, Emma had been house hunting for him. Eventually, she found a house with a small estate attached at Merton, then a small village in Surrey, and despite a very bad surveyor's report, he purchased it with the help of a loan from his friend and agent Alexander Davison. For the next eighteen months, he and the Hamiltons lived often there together in a curious, but obviously very amicable, *ménage à trois*. Always an affectionate family man, he surrounded himself with his brothers and sisters and their children, and all his nephews and nieces retained warm memories of a gentle and friendly uncle. George Matcham, son of his favourite sister Catherine, later remembered, 'He was remarkable for a demeanour quiet, sedate and unobtrusive, anxious to give pleasure to everyone about him, distinguishing each in turn by some act of kindness and chiefly to those who seemed

49 D Bonner-Smith (ed), *The Letters of Admiral of the Fleet the Earl of St Vincent*, Navy Records Society (London 1926), p135

to require it most.'[50] It was a happy period of quiet retirement, broken only by visits to London, where he took part in debates in the House of Lords and, in the summer of 1802, by a protracted tour of South Wales and the Midlands with the Hamiltons. Like their earlier tour of Germany, it quickly turned into a triumphant progress, which showed Nelson at first hand just how popular he was with the ordinary people of Britain.[51]

That popularity was now manifesting itself in a flood of Nelson commemorative material. Nelson's rise to fame coincided with the rise of the cheap press and with the start of mass production of popular goods. The papers recorded all his movements and carried stories about him and his battles; while his image appeared in every possible medium, from prints and caricatures to ceramics and glassware. As a result, he became instantly recognisable and wherever he went a crowd was sure to gather. He was, to some extent, the first 'pop hero'. He obviously found this phenomenon fascinating. Recent research has established that during this period of comparative idleness, when he had time to spare for such matters, he became personally involved in the production of prints of his battles and even in the selection of the portraits of him with which some of those prints were augmented (see illustration on p38).[52]

There were now many different portraits to choose from. The demand for images of the hero was so great that, by 1802, Nelson had sat for some twenty-five different artists and sculptors.[53] Some of them had produced a number of different versions of their finished work, and most of the paintings had been reproduced as prints. People noticed that no two portraits were the same and, in early 1802, a Mr Thomas Forsyth wrote to Nelson asking him which he thought was the best likeness. Interestingly, Nelson did not select one of the heroic images, but chose instead a very ordinary little profile of his head by Simon de Koster, which, he said, was 'the most like me'.[54] Apparently, Emma Hamilton agreed with him, for she had a miniature copy made, which she wore in a locket around her neck (see colour plate *XX*). Perhaps for her it was a memento of the happy times she had spent with her lover in those peaceful days of 1802/3.

There was, however, a shadow to all this happiness, centring on the continued separation from Fanny Nelson. When she attempted to bring about a reconciliation, her letter was returned with an endorsement by Alexander Davison, 'Opened by mistake by Lord Nelson but not read.' Thereafter Nelson took elaborate pains to avoid meeting her and even made it clear to his family that he expected them to avoid her too. In 1802 he did not visit his father on his final sickbed because Fanny was known to be with him, nor did he even attend the old man's funeral. The significance of this self-exclusion from his beloved father's last moments was made more pointed in April the following year, when Sir William Hamilton died. As he breathed his last, his wife was supporting the pillows under him and Nelson was holding his hand.

So the 'Tria Juncta in Uno', as they had called themselves in joking reference to the motto of the Order of the Bath, of which both Hamilton and Nelson were members, was finally broken. But Nelson and Emma were destined never to be properly alone together for, at almost the same time, war with France again became likely. Even before hostilities broke out, Nelson was appointed commander-in-chief of the Mediterranean. At forty-four, he was one of the youngest men ever to hold that important post and, once again, he owed his appointment to Lord St Vincent, who was still First Lord of the Admiralty. As in 1798, St Vincent chose Nelson over the heads of senior and more experienced admirals, including Lord Keith who had been the Mediterranean chief at the end of the previous war and had expected to be appointed again. Whatever he may have felt about Nelson's suitability for higher command in 1800, St Vincent had clearly changed his mind, for it was now the third time he had given Nelson a commander-in-chief's post, and this was the most prestigious appointment of them all.

THE MEDITERRANEAN: MAY 1803–AUGUST 1805

The next two years have not been much dealt with in biographies of Nelson and there is a wealth of hitherto untapped material in a number of the key collections that deserves a full scholarly study.[55] Even so, we already know enough to see that this was a remarkable climax to Nelson's career that showed what he might have achieved had he survived Trafalgar. He remained as impetuous as ever, always talking of his longing to get at the French Mediterranean fleet which was safe in the heavily defended port of Toulon. As he put it in a letter to Sir Richard Strachan, 'we are all healthy and await a little impatiently the sailing of the French.'[56] But he also demonstrated his ability to play a long game and to handle the very varied demands of his post efficiently. He again proved an excellent administrator, keeping his ships afloat and in fighting trim without any dockyard refits and his men happy, healthy and well fed. He ran a most efficient intelligence service, gathering information from all the corners of his command. For example, in November 1804 he knew exactly what stores the governor of the Spanish island of Minorca was short of and where the Spanish thought the British would land if, as expected, they invaded

50 George Matcham: Letter to *The Times*, 6 November 1861.

51 See Edward Gill, *Nelson and the Hamiltons on Tour*, Sutton (Gloucester 1987).

52 A note from Nelson to a print-maker has recently been discovered, instructing him about which portrait to use in a print showing the ships Nelson had captured up to 1802. British Library, Eg 1614, ff51/52.

53 See Richard Walker, *The Nelson Portraits*, Royal Naval Museum (Portsmouth 1998).

54 Nelson to Thomas Forsyth, 2 February 1802, Walker, *op cit*, p248.

55 The best account is still Mahan's, *op cit*, Vol II, pp179–266.

56 Unpublished letter: Nelson to Richard Strachan, 27 September 1803, Peter Tamm Collection.

the island.[57] Finally, he continued to display a sure touch as diplomat in his dealings with the rulers of the many different countries that came within his area of interest and never allowed himself to become too attached to the fortunes of any one of them, as he had in Naples in 1799. Indeed, when the siren voices began to call from Naples, inviting him to go ashore there to rest, he resisted, telling Emma in March 1805, 'You will see that both the King and Queen of Naples are angry with me but I cannot help it.'[58]

With Emma, he appears to have achieved a serenity that was lacking from the earlier years of their relationship. His letters to her are calmer, even mundane, with none of the jealous anguish of the ones he had written in early 1801. Now he wrote to her as if they were married, with gossip about mutual friends, instructions about building projects at Merton and plans for Horatia's future. Even so, he still loved her fervently, and longed to see her again, writing in March 1805, '. . . you are ever with me in my Soul, your resemblance is never absent from my mind and my own dearest Emma I hope very soon I shall embrace the substantial part of you instead of the Ideal, that will I am sure give us both <u>real pleasure</u> and <u>exquisite happiness</u>.'[59]

Nonetheless, his longing to see Emma again was now balanced by an even greater longing to beat the French one more time. Having applied for sick leave, he more than once delayed his departure when it looked as if they might be on the point of emerging from Toulon. Emma complained bitterly about this habit, just as Fanny had done before her. Indeed, instead of blockading them closely in harbour, as his old friend William Cornwallis was doing off Brest, he constantly tempted them to come out by keeping the main body of his force well out of sight of land. The risk was, of course, that they might be able to escape without him seeing them and this is exactly what happened twice in 1805. In January the French admiral Pierre de Villeneuve managed to elude Nelson's watching frigates but was forced to return to port after encountering a heavy storm. The following March he got clean away at the start of the grand campaign by which Napoleon hoped to unite his fleets with those of the Spaniards and bring them as a single, large force to the Channel to cover his invasion of Britain. Having eventually established that the French had joined with their Spanish allies at Cádiz and sailed for the West Indies, Nelson chased after them, and succeeded in driving them back to European waters before they could do much damage to the rich British possessions. Then, having taken his ships north to join with the Channel fleet under Cornwallis, he returned home to Britain for a rest, arriving at Portsmouth on 19 August 1805.

His role in the campaign has not always been fully understood and it has even been suggested that his chase to the West Indies was foolhardy and risky. But such criticism is misplaced. Far from dashing impetuously after Villeneuve, Nelson spent almost a week in the mouth of the Straits of Gibraltar gathering information before he set off. By the time he began his voyage he knew that the rest of the British fleets had gone northwards and he knew that British possessions in the West Indies were defended by only a few ships. His decision to pursue Villeneuve was therefore based on a careful assessment of the risks. Even so, he was agitated and nervous throughout the voyage and concerned about what his reception might be when he arrived home. On 18 June he wrote to Sir John Acton in Naples, 'I am very very unwell and vexed. . . . I have done all that mortal man could do, therefore I must try and be content.'[60]

He need not have worried. He had saved the West Indies trade from a major threat, which had delighted the London merchants and the government, and the public imagination had been captured by the story of his impetuous chase of a superior force half across the world and back again. He arrived to find himself the man of the moment. Politicians, from Prime Minister William Pitt down, wanted to consult him and ask his advice; leading figures in all walks of life asked for interviews; and whenever he appeared on the streets of London, he was surrounded by cheering crowds. Before, in Naples, adulation of this sort had turned his head: now he was well aware of the danger in which he stood, telling Captain Richard Keats, who had chased after the French fleet with him, 'I am now set up for a <u>conjurer</u> and God knows they will very soon find out I am far from being one . . . if I make one wrong guess the charm will be broken.'[61]

TRAFALGAR: SEPTEMBER–OCTOBER 1805

He had, of course, hoped for some quiet leave at Merton with Emma and Horatia but this was not to be. The Combined French and Spanish fleets were known to have taken refuge in Cádiz and the Admiralty began assembling a special fleet to deal with them for once and all. The command was offered to him as a matter of course and he accepted it with resignation, but also with a strong sense of personal destiny that informed all he did during his last days in Britain. Before he left Merton for the last time, he went with Emma to the local parish church, where they took private communion and then exchanged rings in a quasi-marriage service. On the journey to Portsmouth from Merton, where he had knelt before leaving at the bedside of his sleeping child, he wrote a prayer in his diary ask-

57 Unpublished letter: Nelson to General Villettes, 28 November 1804, Peter Tamm Collection.

58 Nelson to Emma Hamilton, 13 March 1805, Royal Naval Museum, 1973/233 (parts only of this letter have been published before).

59 Unpublished letter: Nelson to Emma Hamilton, 16 March 1805, National Maritime Museum, TRA/13.

60 Nicolas, *op cit*, Vol VI, p460.

61 *Ibid*, Vol VII, p16.

ing God to '. . . enable me to fulfil the expectations of my Country,' adding '. . . If it is His good providence to cut short my days upon earth I bow with the greatest submission.'[62]

Our perception of these last days is coloured by our knowledge that death was now stalking him closely and some historians have fallen into the trap of interpreting these acts and words, and similar things he said and did at this time, as evidence that he was deliberately seeking death. Such an idea is nonsense and completely out of character but it contains perhaps a small grain of truth. He was, as he had been throughout his life, apparently unafraid of death but in 1805 he seems to have been prepared to offer his life if that was the price that was required for a victory that would finish the war. He wrote to his friend Alexander Davison, 'If I fall on such a glorious occasion, it shall be my pride to take care that my friends shall not blush for me. These things are in the hands of a wise and just Providence and His will be done.'[63]

He arrived off Cádiz on 28 September. Only a handful of the captains in the hastily assembled fleet had served with him before and so he had to build a new band of brothers in just a few days. The next day, his forty-seventh birthday, he held a dinner party in the *Victory* at which he explained to his captains his plans for defeating the enemy, which he then committed to writing in a memorandum. With hindsight, 'The Nelson Touch', as he called it, can be seen as a perfect summation of all the tactical ideas he had developed during his career. As at the Nile and Copenhagen, his aim was to bring overwhelming force to bear on one part of the enemy's line, so that it would be crushed as quickly as possible. In a throwback to the lessons he had learned at Hotham's indecisive actions in 1795, he directed that the order of sailing was to be the order of battle, thus avoiding any waste of time in forming a line. And, in a single phrase, he vividly summed up his leadership ethos: '. . . in case signals can neither be seen or perfectly understood, no captain can do very wrong if he places his ship alongside that of an enemy.'[64] The man who had seized the initiative at Cape St Vincent was now empowering his subordinates to do the same. No wonder that some of the captains gathered round his table shed tears of excitement.

The Combined Franco-Spanish fleet emerged from Cádiz on 19 October 1805, heading south. Having abandoned his plans for an invasion of Britain, Napoleon had now started a new campaign against Austria, and Villeneuve had now been ordered into the Mediterranean in support. Nelson shadowed them until they were well clear of harbour and then, on the morning of 21 October, turned to attack. The battle unfolded very

62 *Ibid*, Vol VII, pp33–35.
63 *Ibid*, Vol VII, p56.
64 *Ibid*, Vol VII, p91.

much as he had planned. One British division, under Vice Admiral Cuthbert Collingwood, enveloped the allied rear, crushing it with superior gunfire, while another under Nelson's direct command smashed through the centre of the allied line, cutting it in two and preventing the van from helping their comrades until it was too late. Having led the way through a hail of shot, the *Victory* became entangled with a smaller French battleship, the *Redoutable*, and it was from her that the bullet was fired which struck Nelson, at about 1.15pm, as he was pacing the quarterdeck with Captain Thomas Hardy. Carried down to the cockpit below the *Victory*'s waterline, where the wounded were treated in comparative safety, he lingered, in great pain, long enough to learn that he had won a decisive victory. Of the thirty-three French and Spanish ships that had begun the battle, eighteen had been either captured or destroyed, four escaped only to be captured a fortnight later at the Battle of Cape Ortegal and the remaining eleven managed to struggle back into Cádiz.

However, rejoicing at this remarkable result was overshadowed by grief

The Battle of Trafalgar, 21 October 1805. In this fine oil painting dating from 1807, Thomas Luny shows the battle at its height. In the central group, the Victory *(left) is still flying Nelson's last signal, 'Engage the enemy more closely!', as she fights it out with the* Redoutable.

The funeral service in St Paul's Cathedral, 9 January 1806. In the final moments of the elaborate ceremony, Nelson's coffin is surrounded by the full splendour of an English heraldic funeral. The size of the Spanish flag is not exaggerated – it still survives in the collections of the National Maritime Museum in Greenwich.

at the loss of Nelson. Midshipman Joseph Woollnough of HMS *Agamemnon* recorded that when his comrades heard the news, 'A stranger might have supposed from the gloom that spread among them that they had been beaten instead of being conquerors'[65] and, when the news reached Britain, there was similar subdued reaction. As Robert Southey, the poet laureate, later recalled in his *Life of Nelson*, published in 1813, 'The victory of Trafalgar was celebrated, indeed, with the usual forms of rejoicing, but they were without joy.'[66] Nelson's body was brought home and given a lavish state funeral in St Paul's Cathedral and his sacrifice was celebrated in a surge of heroic paintings, poetry and popular art.

THE IMMORTAL MEMORY

A number of Nelson's contemporaries recorded their first impressions of him and they are remarkably consistent. The Duke of Clarence recalled that when he first saw him on the quarterdeck of Lord Hood's flagship HMS *Barfleur* in 1782, he thought he 'appeared to be the merest boy of a captain I ever beheld,' whose old-fashioned uniform and pigtail made him look quaint. 'My doubts however were removed when Lord Hood introduced me to him. There was something irresistibly pleasing in his address and conversation; and an enthusiasm, when speaking on professional subjects, which showed he was no common being.'[67] Fifteen years later, Lady Spencer, wife of the First Lord of the Admiralty, met him while he was in Britain recovering from the loss of his arm at Tenerife. Many years afterwards, she remembered, 'A most uncouth creature I thought him. . . . He looked so sickly it was painful to see him, and his general appearance was that of an idiot; so much so that, when he spoke and his wonderful mind broke forth, it was a sort of surprise that riveted my whole attention.'[68] The Duke of Wellington had a brief encounter with him in the waiting room at the Colonial Office in September 1805. At first Nelson spoke only about himself '. . . in a style so vain and silly as to surprise and almost disgust me,' but then, having checked whom his companion was, he changed his manner and talked 'like an officer and a statesman. . . . Now if the Secretary of State had been punctual,' Wellington concluded, 'I should have had the same impression of a light and trivial character that other people have had but luckily I saw enough to be satisfied that he was really a very superior man . . .'[69]

Clearly, then, Nelson did not always behave like a conventional hero, and he certainly did not look like one. He was not as short as popular myth commonly suggests but, even so, he was of only average height for his times and slight in build. Although essentially robust, he at times looked frail, especially when he was recovering from one his many wounds or illnesses. But everyone who met him agreed that it was his spirit that made him heroic. They all remembered his energy, his enthusiasm and his engaging directness.

If it was so difficult to sum Nelson up when he was actually present, then it is scarcely surprising that historians have found it difficult to assess him in retrospect. Any attempt to pin him down with a single telling phrase, or to identify a central, unifying trait in his character, is doomed to failure. The Victorians, seeking to enthrone him as an example of spotless, muscular Christianity, ignored the vulnerable and human attributes that helped to make him such a loved – and thus such a successful – leader. The Royal Navy tried to perpetuate his example by codifying his tactics in a set of rules, thus missing the point that flexibility and personal initiative were the keys to his success, rather than any particular set of tactical precepts. Twentieth-century film-makers celebrated the high romance of his relationship with Emma Hamilton and missed its underlying destructiveness: a Shakespearean tragedy rather than a Mills and Boon bodice-ripper. Modern journalists, looking for easy labels to hang on him, such as 'war criminal', have overemphasised his cruel and ruthless streak and missed the essential complexity of a man who could, on the one hand, approve of hanging mutineers on a Sunday and, on the other, pray with transparent sincerity, 'may humanity after Victory be the predominant feature in the British Fleet.'

Many attempts to sum him up have also missed the fact that Nelson changed during the course of his life, often quite strikingly. The man who attempted to command the Mediterranean from a ship moored in Palermo harbour in 1799, so that he could be close to his mistress and to the Court of one of his allies, developed and matured into an assured and statesmanlike admiral, who in 1803/5 exercised command over the same area from his constantly-moving flagship, never once setting foot on shore for nearly two years. The emaciated, doubt-ridden, white-haired invalid, portrayed by Lemuel Abbott in the months immediately following the amputation of his arm in 1797, had by 1805 changed into the tanned, confident

65 Journal of Midshipman Joseph Woollnough, Private collection.

66 Robert Southey, *The Life of Nelson* (1922 edition edited by Geoffrey Callender), p321.

67 Duke of Clarence speaking to Rev James Stanier Clarke, quoted in J S Clarke and J M'Arthur, *The Life of Admiral Lord Nelson* (2nd ed, 1839), Vol I, p78.

68 Countess Spencer speaking to Lady Shelly, quoted in Richard Edgcombe, *The Diary of Frances Lady Shelley 1787-1817* (London 1912).

69 Duke of Wellington speaking to John Wilson Croker, quoted in J L Jennings (ed), The Croker Papers: *Correspondence and Diaries of J W Croker*, John Murray (London 1884), Vol II, pp233–234.

Nelson as Victorian Hero. Daniel Maclise's monumental wall painting of the death of Nelson in the Royal Gallery of the Palace of Westminster. Nelson is portrayed as a typical example of the stoic, Christian heroes whom the Victorians so admired.

70 Alexander Scott to Emma Hamilton, 8 January 1806, Alfred Morrison, *The Hamilton and Nelson Papers*, privately published (London 1893/4), Vol II.

national hero whom all his friends thought had put on weight when they saw him during his brief leave in Britain. To be successful, any biographical study of Nelson must both fully capture and fairly balance all these contradictory elements.

Every year, around the end of October, Trafalgar Night Dinners are held in ships and shore establishments of the Royal Navy and, increasingly, by other navies and even civilian organisations as well. After the Loyal Toast, a toast is drunk to 'The Immortal Memory' and the tradition is for it to be proposed in a speech that sets Nelson in his modern context, and shows why he still offers useful lessons to his descendants. Those who give such speeches, and the historians who seek to capture and portray his complex and elusive spirit, continue to find, in the words of his Chaplain, Alexander Scott, 'what an affectionate, fascinating little fellow he was.'[70]

The Encyclopaedia

The Immortal Memory. An engraving produced in December 1805 to commemorate Nelson's death. The portrait is based on a miniature of Nelson by Thomas Bowyer – one of the last likenesses taken from the life.

Abbott, Lemuel (1769–1821)

Although not in the front rank of portrait painters, Abbott created the image of Nelson that has become by far the most familiar of all his portraits. He owed his commission, in 1797, to Captain William Locker, Nelson's old friend and former commander. Locker already had a portrait of Nelson in his possession,

Nelson by Lemuel Abbott. This is one of many variations that Abbott produced, based on his original half-length sketch. It shows Nelson sick, white-haired and emaciated, following the loss of his arm.

painted by Francis Rigaud some fifteen years before. But it showed Nelson as a young man in a captain's uniform. Now the country was clamouring for a likeness of the hero of the Battle of Cape St Vincent and Locker turned to Lemuel Abbott, who had already painted a number of distinguished naval officers of the day, including Locker himself.

In October 1797, Nelson and his wife stayed with Locker, who had by then become lieutenant governor of the Royal Hospital, Greenwich, at his official residence. While they were there, Abbott had a couple of sittings with Nelson at which he produced a vivid sketch that poignantly captures the suffering that Nelson was enduring at the time. His face is gaunt, his mouth tightly pursed and his naturally sandy hair has turned white with the shock of his wound and the constant pain he was still enduring, more than three months after the loss of his arm. He is wearing the simple, unadorned 'undress' uniform coat of a rear admiral. Only the star of the Order of the Bath on his left chest, and the King's Gold Medal for the Battle of Cape St Vincent on a ribbon around his neck, remind the viewer that this sickly, emaciated figure is the hero of the hour.

Using this sketch as a model, Abbott then created some forty different finished versions for various clients, including Locker himself, Lady Nelson and Nelson's friend and agent Alexander Davison. Some were exact copies of the sketch; in others Nelson was shown full, or three-quarter, length. Most of these versions were then engraved and it has also been reproduced in almost every biography, so that it is now so common that it has become over-familiar, and even hackneyed. The most famous version of all, the image of Nelson that everyone instantly recognises, dates from 1799 and shows him festooned with all his decorations, including the jewelled miniatures of the King and Queen of Naples and with the Sultan of Turkey's 'chelengk', or diamond plume of triumph, in his hat (see p112).

However, the further Abbott went from his original sketch the more he tended to 'adonise' the face and, as a result, in some of the later versions Nelson has lost his warrior's look and has come to resemble what Richard Walker, the leading expert on Nelson's portraits, has called '. . . a charming sweet-tempered country gentleman, not far removed from the breed of Norfolk parsons in which his stock was rooted.' Moreover, because the portrait depicts Nelson at a time when his health and morale were at a particularly low ebb following his wound, it has helped to perpetuate the myth that he was unusually frail and sickly. There are other images that capture Nelson better, such as Heinrich Füger's brilliant evocation of his ruthlessness and fixed purpose or John Hoppner's haunting portrayal of the gentler, more affectionate side of his nature. But, even in these days of mass production of images, these are still far less familiar to the public at large than Abbott's white-haired invalid.

It would seem that Nelson himself was not particularly impressed with the portrait. There is no record that he ever owned a copy himself and when, in 1802, an engraver wanted to include a version of it in a print celebrating the admiral's victories, Nelson sent him a note to say that the portrait was 'disapproved' and instructed him to use, instead, a profile of his head by Simon de Koster.

Abbott's powerful original sketch and the first finished version, which he painted for Locker, are still in private hands but there are examples of the later versions in all the main public Nelson collections. The famous bejewelled and hatted version is in the National Maritime Museum at Greenwich.

SEE ALSO
Decorations, Greenwich, Locker, Portraits

LATEST RESEARCH
Richard Walker, 'Nelson as painted by Lemuel Abbott', *The Trafalgar Chronicle* 4 (1994), The 1805 Club
Richard Walker, *The Nelson Portraits*, Royal Naval Museum (Portsmouth 1998)

Addington, Henry (Lord Sidmouth) (1757–1844)

While prime minister of Britain from 1801 to 1804, Addington came into close touch with Nelson in the immediate aftermath of the Copenhagen campaign and also while Nelson was in command of the anti-invasion forces in the Channel in the summer of 1801. Although Nelson was related through his mother to the great Whig family of the Walpoles, he tended to be a Tory in politics. But, like many other country gentlemen of his class, he preferred the unassuming and mediocre Addington to the more brilliant William Pitt.

Pitt and Addington were in fact close friends and political allies. Addington was Speaker of the House of Commons for eleven years during Pitt's premiership and only agreed to take over the chief office when Pitt fell out with King George III over the issue of Catholic Emancipation. Under Addington's leadership, peace negotiations were opened with France, which led to the Treaty of Amiens, a settlement that Nelson loyally supported in one of the first speeches he made after taking his seat in the House of Lords.

Addington and Nelson corresponded regularly, even after Pitt had returned to office in 1804. In September 1805, Nelson paid a last visit to his friend, by now elevated to the House of Lords as Lord Sidmouth. Dipping his finger in some wine, he traced out the tactics he planned to use in the battle that he felt sure was imminent on a small table, which Sidmouth duly preserved as a treasured relic.

SEE ALSO
Amiens, Nelson Touch, Pitt

Admiralty

In Nelson's day, the Royal Navy was run by the Board of Admiralty, made up of both naval officers and civilians. They controlled the strategic deployment of the fleets, as well as the promotion and appointment of officers, and supervised the work of other specialist bodies, such as the Navy Board, which looked after the construction, maintenance and supplying of ships. The Admiralty was headed by the First Lord of the Admiralty who was a member of the Cabinet and thus a senior member of the government. The post usually went to a senior politician, although sometimes experienced naval officers, such as Lord St Vincent, were appointed. The Board met daily in the gracious, panelled Board Room in the Admiralty Office, a handsome building on Whitehall designed by Thomas Ripley with, at the

front, a grand classical portico and, to the rear, large windows looking out over St James's Park.

Nelson never served on the Admiralty Board but he visited the Admiralty Office on a number of occasions during his life: most notably in the late summer and early autumn of 1805, during his brief spell of leave in Britain in the feverish days before Trafalgar. His body rested there overnight prior to his great state funeral procession through the streets of London on 9 January 1806.

The Admiralty ceased to exist as a separate organisation when the unified Ministry of Defence was formed in 1964 but the Admiralty building has survived, including the splendid Board Room, which is occasionally used for special meetings.

SEE ALSO
Navy Board

LATEST RESEARCH
Brian Lavery, *Nelson's Navy,* Conway Maritime Press (London 1989)
N A M Rodger, *The Admiralty,* Terence Dalton (Lavenham 1979)

The Admiralty Board Room. The nerve-centre of the Royal Navy where many of the key decisions were made that influenced the course of the war against France, including the decision to appoint Nelson to command a detached squadron in the Mediterranean in 1798.

Agamemnon, HMS

Nelson's favourite ship, HMS *Agamemnon,* was a two-decked 64-gun battleship. Nelson was her captain for over three years from January 1793 to June 1796 but she had a most distinguished career, both before and after his time in her.

More lightly armed than their large 74-gun sisters, having only 24-pounder guns on their main deck as opposed to 32-pounders, the 64-gun Third Rate battleships were regarded as old-fashioned by 1793 and the smallest acceptable unit for the battlefleet. On the other hand, they were faster and more manoeuvrable than their heavier sisters, and so were often used on detached duties, escorting convoys or maintaining close blockades. As Nelson was to show while in command of the *Agamemnon*, in the hands of an imaginative captain they could still be very useful warships indeed. He was delighted with her and remained in her even after having been offered a larger ship. His letters home are full of her praises: 'My ship sails well, very few will outsail her,' '*Agamemnon* sails admirably, we think better than any ship in the fleet.'

She was launched on 10 April 1781 in the private shipyard of Henry Adams at Buckler's Hard on the River Beaulieu in Hampshire. She saw action almost at once in the Battle of Ushant off the northwest coast of France, in 1781 under her first captain, Benjamin Caldwell, and again the following year at Admiral Rodney's great victory over the French at the Battle of the Saintes (12 April 1782) in the West Indies.

In 1793, Horatio Nelson became her captain when war with France broke out once again. Nelson had been unemployed for over four years and had begun to fear that his active career was at an end, because of prejudice against him at the Admiralty. So he was excited by his new command and determined to make a success of it. The core of his ship's company was made up of hand-picked men, many from his native Norfolk, and their high morale and professional skill meant that the *Agamemnon* was both a happy and an efficient ship. Under Nelson's command, she took part in the capture of Corsica in 1794, in two indecisive fleet actions under Admiral William Hotham in 1795 and in a large number of small-scale operations against enemy ships and shore installations. And it was in her that Nelson first proudly flew

The launch of HMS Agamemnon *in 1781. This modern oil painting by Harold Wyllie shows the famous ship at her launch at the private shipbuilding yard of Buckler's Hard, near Beaulieu in Hampshire.*

his distinguishing pendant when he was appointed a commodore in March 1796.

By June 1796 she was worn out after over three years continuously at sea without a dockyard refit. So she was sent home to England for major repairs and Nelson transferred to the larger HMS *Captain*, taking many of his key men with him. But the *Agamemnon* continued to be associated with her former commander, taking part in two of his major victories. At the Battle of Copenhagen (2 April 1801) she was part of the squadron under Nelson that attacked the Danish line of defence, although she was unable to weather the shoals at the start of the action and so played little part in the battle. However, at Trafalgar (21 October 1805), commanded by Nelson's friend and associate Edward Berry who had been her first lieutenant briefly in 1796, she was in the thick of the fighting around the *Victory*.

After taking part in one other major action under Berry's command, the Battle of San Domingo in the West Indies in 1806, the *Agamemnon* eventually was wrecked on 16 June 1809 in the mouth of the River Plate in South America. The wreck has recently been discovered and various artefacts raised from it.

SEE ALSO
Berry, Copenhagen, Gulf of Genoa, Hyères, Italian campaign

LATEST RESEARCH
Anthony Deane, *Nelson's Favourite*, Chatham Publishing (London 1996)
Robert Gardiner, *Warships of the Napoleonic Era*, Chatham Publishing (London 1999)

Agincourt Sound

A fine, sheltered anchorage at the La Maddalena Islands, on the northeast coast of Sardinia in the Mediterranean, Agincourt Sound was first surveyed accurately by Captain George Ryves in the 64-gun battleship HMS *Agincourt*, in December 1802. Later, in 1803–5, when Nelson was blockading the French naval arsenal of Toulon on the south coast of France, it became his forward base.

One of the main problems the British encountered in maintaining their constant patrols off Toulon was the distance of that port from their Mediterranean bases at Gibraltar and Malta, each over a week's sail away. Agincourt Sound was only 250 miles from

Toulon and there the fleet could replenish its water and stocks of fresh food and effect essential repairs; while the sheltered Sound offered a brief respite for the crews from the strain of being constantly at sea. Nelson took his fleet to La Maddalena six times in all during his two-year patrol of Toulon, and it was there, on 20 January 1805, that he received news that the French fleet had sailed from Toulon at the beginning of the series of fleet movements that was to develop into the Trafalgar campaign.

Sardinia was technically neutral and so Nelson was always careful to maintain good relations with the local population, often using the *Victory*'s chaplain, Rev Alexander Scott, who was an excellent linguist, as his agent. In October 1804, Scott presented, on Nelson's behalf, a set of silver candlesticks and a crucifix to the local church, where they are still proudly preserved to this day.

SEE ALSO
Alexander Scott, Toulon

LATEST RESEARCH
John Gwyther, 'Nelson's gift to la Maddalena', *The Trafalgar Chronicle* 10 (2000), The 1805 Club
Stephen Howarth, 'Nelson and the Magdalen', *The Trafalgar Chronicle* 1 (1991), The 1805 Club

Albemarle, HMS

Although rated as a 28-gun Sixth Rate frigate, the *Albemarle* was in fact a French merchantman, *La Ménagère*, captured in 1779 and converted. Built for carrying heavy cargoes she was neither swift nor particularly handy, but the war with the American colonies was approaching its crisis, with both France and Spain fighting against Britain, and the country needed every warship it could muster. Having been forced to remain ashore for almost a year by illhealth following his close brush with death in the Nicaraguan campaign, Nelson felt he was lucky to have her, and indeed it has recently been established that he owed his appointment to the direct influence of the First Lord of the Admiralty, Lord Sandwich.

Nelson took command of the *Albemarle* in July 1781. He sailed first in her to the Baltic, where he spent a month off Elsinore, waiting for a large convoy to assemble, and a recently-discovered report to his senior officer, Sir Richard Hughes, reveals that he found she was 'exceedingly crank' and that 'with her present masts it is very dangerous to go to sea in her'. She was then rammed by a storeship in the Downs and was so badly damaged that she had to be taken into the dockyard at Portsmouth for extensive repairs. So it was not until April 1782 that Nelson finally sailed in her to the war zone and, even then, he was ordered to escort a convoy to Quebec in Canada, rather than being posted to the West Indies, where the main naval war was being fought. So it was a frustrating period for him that only ended in November 1782, when he met up with Lord Hood at New York and persuaded the hero of the hour to apply to have the *Albemarle* attached to his fleet. However, it was too late for any glory, for the war was already beginning to wind down and so the only action in which Nelson and the *Albemarle* were involved was the abortive attack on Turk's Island in March 1783. By then he was thoroughly dissatisfied with his slow and unhandy ship and it was clearly with considerable relief that he eventually paid her off in Portsmouth in July 1783, writing to his friend Captain William Locker, 'next Monday I hope to be rid of her.' Once the war was ended, the Royal Navy had no further use for the odd hybrid and she was sold for breaking up in June 1784.

Despite the accidents and frustrations of Nelson's time in her, it is clear that the *Albemarle* was a happy ship. When the time came to pay her off, the whole crew offered to follow Nelson into any ship to which he might be appointed. One reason for this was the care he took of his men. For example, after leaving the *Albemarle* he spent three weeks in London 'attempting to get the wages due to my good fellows for various Ships they have served in the war.'

SEE ALSO
Carver, Lord Hood, New York, Mary Simpson, Turk's Island

Allen, Tom (1764–1838)

Tom Allen was Nelson's personal servant from 1795 to 1802. A Norfolk man, from Burnham Thorpe, he was one of the local youngsters whom Nelson recruited to go with him in the *Agamemnon* in 1793. Two years later, Nelson's servant of some year's standing, Frank Lepée, was dismissed for persistent drunken-

ness and Allen stepped into his shoes. Illiterate and uncouth, with a stubborn sense of his own rightness, he looked after his master like a nanny, with a mixture of tenderness and sharp reprimands. One of Nelson's midshipmen, George Parsons, remembered hearing Allen telling Nelson at a dinner, 'You will be ill if you take any more wine.' To Parsons' amazement, Nelson replied meekly, 'You are perfectly right Tom and I thank you for the hint,' and allowed himself to be led off to bed.

A stocky man, with a stubborn jut to his chin and a full head of tightly curled black hair, Allen retained his broad Norfolk accent to the end of his life, together with his direct countryman's ways. He refused to be overwhelmed by all the great people with whom Nelson associated once he became famous. On one occasion, he delighted his compatriots by seizing the hand that King Ferdinand of Naples had condescendingly extended to be kissed, and pumping it heartily, with the words, 'How d'ye do Mr King?' Nelson regarded him with a mixture of exasperation and affection but clearly allowed him a considerable degree of latitude.

He followed Nelson from ship to ship between 1793 and 1801 and so was with him at most of his key battles. At the Battle of Cape St Vincent (14 February 1797), he was one of Nelson's boarding party that captured the *San Nicolas* and *San José*; he was at his side in the *Theseus* when his arm was amputated at Tenerife (July 1797); and at the Nile (1 August 1798) and Copenhagen (2 April 1801) he fought as a gunner. When the peace came in 1802, he retired to Norfolk with a new wife and a modest fortune of £95.

Thereafter, his story becomes hazy. When an old man, he always claimed he had been with Nelson in the *Victory* in the Mediterranean and added, moreover, that he missed Trafalgar only because he had been sent on an errand and was not able to rejoin the ship before she sailed for Cádiz. However, recently discovered evidence suggests that there had been a falling-out between the two men and it now seems likely that Allen did not serve with Nelson again after 1802.

In later life Allen and his wife fell on hard times but they were looked after in Norfolk by Nelson's protégé, Captain Sir William Bolton. When Bolton died in 1831, a place was obtained for Allen at the

Greenwich Hospital and eventually, in 1837, he was given the post of pewterer at the hospital by the new governor, Rear Admiral Sir Thomas Hardy. This entitled him both to a salary and to a comfortable apartment, where he lived with his wife and grand-daughter until his death in November 1838.

SEE ALSO
HMS *Agamemnon*, Burnham Thorpe

LATEST RESEARCH
HMS Vanguard at the Nile, The Nelson Society (1998)

Amiens, Peace of (1802/3)

The long conflict between Britain and France was broken by one short interlude of peace between March 1802 and May 1803. None of the key issues over which France and Britain had originally gone to war in 1793 had really been resolved and many people, Nelson included, never expected the peace to last. However, the treaty had been concluded by the political party he supported, the Tories under Prime Minister Henry Addington, and so he loyally backed it publicly in one of his first speeches as a newly installed member of the House of Lords.

Nelson was genuinely exhausted, and in poor health, after a long spell of nine months' almost uninterrupted active service, beginning with the build-up to the Copenhagen campaign and ending with his frustrating, and emotionally draining, command in the Channel. So he spent most of the brief peace in semi-retirement with Sir William and Lady Hamilton, at his newly purchased home at Merton Place in Surrey, on the southwestern outskirts of London. There was one brief break, in July and August 1802, when the trio made a private visit to Sir William's estates in Pembrokeshire, South Wales, which turned into a triumphal progress. But Sir William was ailing and eventually, on 6 April 1803, he died in the arms of his wife and with Nelson holding his hand. By now the fragile peace was already fracturing and a month later Nelson was appointed commander-in-chief of the Mediterranean fleet and hoisted his flag in the *Victory* at Portsmouth.

SEE ALSO
Addington, Channel Command, Merton, Nelson's tour of Wales and the Midlands

Andrews, Elizabeth (1762–1837)

The daughter of Rev Robert and Sarah Andrews from Tiverton in Devon, Elizabeth was living with her family in the small northern French town of Saint-Omer when Nelson visited there in the autumn of 1783. The War of American Independence had just ended and he had crossed the Channel to spend some time in France, hoping to learn the language.

Nelson was introduced to Elizabeth by her younger brother George, who was a midshipman in the Royal Navy. A miniature of her dating from around this time shows that she was very pretty, with a fresh complexion, big soulful brown eyes and tumbling locks of dark brown hair. Soon, Nelson was a regular visitor to her father's house and, when he received news of his sister Anne's sudden death in November, Elizabeth comforted him.

Sympathy combined with beauty was a sure way to Nelson's heart and, by December, he was in love and contemplating marriage, calling Elizabeth 'the most accomplished young woman my eyes ever beheld!' But there was a problem. She was known to have an income of £1000 a year, while Nelson could command only £130 at most. So he wrote to one of his maternal uncles, William Suckling, to ask if he would give him an allowance of £100 a year. Suckling appears to have been willing to help but, by the time his answer arrived, Nelson was back in England. He told his friends that he had come home to settle some money affairs, but the speed and unexpectedness of his return suggest that Elizabeth Andrews had rejected his offer.

However, the rejection appears to have been made kindly for Nelson remained on good terms with her family and took her brother George to sea with him as a midshipman in HMS *Boreas* the following spring. He later served again with Nelson as a lieutenant in the *Agamemnon* and fought ashore with him in Corsica in 1794. Elizabeth married a clergyman, Rev Richard Farrer, and, after his death, Lieutenant Colonel Roger Warne.

SEE ALSO
HMS *Agamemnon*, HMS *Boreas*

LATEST RESEARCH
Tom Pocock, *Nelson's Women*, André Deutsch (London 1999)

Antigua

One of the British-held Leeward Islands in the West Indies, Antigua was Nelson's base in 1784–1785 when he was senior officer of the northern division of the Leeward Island Station. He arrived there in his frigate HMS *Boreas* on 28 July 1784, to lay her up during the hurricane months in the island's main port, English Harbour, a deep, sheltered inlet in which there was a small but well-equipped dockyard, defended by batteries at the entrance and on the hills above.

It was here that Nelson met Mary Moutray, the wife of the Commissioner of the Dockyard, with whom he fell in love, although she was able to keep him at a distance, without losing his friendship. It was not a happy time in Nelson's life. As well as sexual and emotional frustration, he also suffered professional setbacks in his dealings with his admiral, Sir Richard Hughes, and some of the other British officials in the area, all of whom were adopting what Nelson believed to be an over-indulgent attitude to the Navigation Laws that regulated the exercise of trade. His own rather priggish way of dealing with the problem scarcely helped. For example, when the governor of Antigua, General Sir Thomas Shirley, remarked pompously that old generals were not accustomed to taking advice from young gentlemen, he received the resounding, but hardly tactful, reply, 'Sir, I am as old as the Prime Minister of England [William Pitt] and think myself as capable of commanding one of His Majesty's ships as that Minister is of governing the State.'

English Harbour still survives, although inevitably it is now a yachting marina. Most of the surviving buildings of the dockyard date from after Nelson's time (including the one often pointed out to visitors as the house in which he stayed). However, across the harbour from the dockyard stands Clarence House, built in 1787 for Nelson's friend Prince William Henry (later the Duke of Clarence and King William IV), when he commanded the frigate HMS *Pegasus* in the West Indies. Even more evocative, perhaps, is the water-catchment just outside the dockyard where successive generations of British sailors have scratched the names of their ships. There is a small museum on the site of the Moutrays' house that contains a collection of Nelson memorabilia.

SEE ALSO
HMS *Boreas*, Collingwood, Mary Moutray

LATEST RESEARCH
Tom Pocock, *The Young Nelson in the Americas*, Collins (London 1980)

Arctic Expedition (June–September 1773)

In the summer of 1773 Nelson, then just fourteen, took part in an expedition to the Arctic which came close to ending his naval career almost before it had begun. The purpose of the expedition was to find if there was a navigable passage north-about between the Atlantic and Pacific Oceans and it was supported by the influential Royal Society and by King George III himself. Two bomb vessels, HMS *Racehorse* and *Carcass*, were fitted out and strengthened under the command of Captain the Honourable Constantine Phipps and a special team assembled, including

Nelson and the polar bear. This highly romanticised image of the famous incident was produced by Richard Westall for the 'official' biography by Clarke and M'Arthur in 1809. In fact, Nelson was separated from the bear by a chasm in the ice.

naturalists and astronomers. It had been decided that boys would not be included, but Nelson used the influence of his uncle, Captain Maurice Suckling, to gain him a place in the *Carcass* as coxswain to her captain, Skeffington Lutwidge.

The expedition failed in its main object. It was an unusually cold summer in the Arctic that year and, as a result, the ships became locked in the ice when they were still in distant sight of Spitzbergen and, despite strenuous efforts, they were unable to cut their way out again. At one point, it appeared that they might have to abandon the ships and attempt to reach land by dragging the ships' boats over the ice. But, on the very day they were to set out on this desperate journey, the wind changed and the ice began to break up. The ships extricated themselves and returned home.

However, for Nelson it had been an important step in his training and helped to boost his growing self-confidence and seamanship skills. He was given command of one of the ship's smaller boats, a four-oared cutter, manned by twelve seamen and, in this, he helped to save the crew of a boat belonging to the *Racehorse* from an attack by a herd of enraged walruses. He also had a more famous encounter with a polar bear, going out one day with a companion to attempt to obtain a bear skin as a present for his father. They found their bear but Nelson's musket misfired and, despite his friend's entreaties, he was apparently preparing to cross the chasm dividing them from their prey, intending to attack it with the butt end of his gun, when they were spotted from the ship. A gun was fired, frightening the bear away, and a sulky Nelson returned to the *Carcass* to explain himself to an angry Captain Lutwidge. Inevitably, this exploit later became part of the Nelson Legend but, in the various paintings of it, the chasm and the companion are always omitted, showing Nelson eyeball-to-eyeball with the bear – and alone. (see colour plate *V*).

SEE ALSO
Lutwidge

Atkinson, Thomas (1767–1836)

Atkinson was master of HMS *Victory* at the Battle of Trafalgar. The master was a key member of any ship's company, in charge of the practical aspects of the sailing and navigation of the vessel. One of Nelson's circle of favoured 'followers', Atkinson served with the admiral on a number of occasions and Nelson clearly thought very highly of him. He once described him as 'one of the best Masters I have seen in the Royal Navy.'

A Yorkshireman, Atkinson joined the Navy as a volunteer in 1793 and was immediately given the rate of able seaman, which suggests he was already an experienced sailor. He qualified as a master in 1795 and was appointed to the frigate HMS *Emerald*, in which he saw action at the Battle of Cape St Vincent (14 February 1797). In the spring of 1797, he transferred to the battleship HMS *Theseus* and it was there that he first came to Nelson's attention, when she became his flagship shortly afterwards. In the *Theseus*, he took part in the attack on Santa Cruz in Tenerife in July 1797, the Battle of the Nile (1 August 1798) and the siege of Acre in May 1799. During the siege, he was slightly wounded in an explosion on board the *Theseus* that badly damaged the ship and killed her captain, Ralph Miller.

In 1801, Atkinson was transferred to Nelson's new flagship, HMS *San Josef*, and there then began an almost uninterrupted spell of service with Nelson. When Nelson transferred his flag to the *St George* for the Baltic campaign, Atkinson went with him and was one of the group of pilots and masters who helped to buoy the treacherous shoals defending the approaches to Copenhagen, enabling Nelson's squadron to make its attack. This won him the first of his testimonials from Nelson, who was also godfather to one of Atkinson's sons.

In 1803, when war broke out again, Nelson wrote directly to Atkinson asking him to be the *Victory*'s master and they served together until the Battle of Trafalgar (21 October 1805). Thereafter, Atkinson served in various naval dockyards, finishing his career as First Master Attendant at Portsmouth where he died in 1836. His obituary pointed out that '. . . the promotions and rewards he obtained were solely the result of his own persevering exertions.'

SEE ALSO
Copenhagen, HMS *Victory*

LATEST RESEARCH
Doreen Scragg, 'The career of Thomas Atkinson', *The Trafalgar Chronicle* 8 (1998), The 1805 Club

Ball, Sir Alexander (1757–1809)

One of the original 'Band of Brothers', Ball remained in close and affectionate touch with Nelson to the end of his life. The son of an old Gloucestershire family with no naval connections, Ball first went to sea at the age of twelve, apparently because he had been inspired by Daniel Defoe's famous book, *Robinson Crusoe*. He served throughout the War of American Independence, and was promoted to commander for his part in the Battle of the Saintes (12 April 1782).

Promoted to post captain the following year, he travelled to France to learn the language and there met Captain Horatio Nelson, who was on the same mission. Nelson was unimpressed, thinking Ball aloof and 'a great coxcomb', and so when they met up again off Cádiz in the spring of 1798, when Lord St Vincent was assembling the squadron that Nelson was to lead into the Mediterranean, relations between them were cool. Shortly after, however, Ball's superb seamanship in HMS *Alexander* saved Nelson's flagship, the *Vanguard*, from almost certain wreck in a violent storm. With characteristic impulsiveness, Nelson reversed his opinion at once, embraced Ball as a dear friend and, during the ensuing campaign, consulted him more frequently than any of the other captains except for his close friend Troubridge.

During the Battle of the Nile (1 August 1798) Ball, in the *Alexander*, engaged the mighty French flagship *L'Orient* and, after the battle, he was sent by Nelson to Malta which the French had captured on their way to Egypt. Ball first organised a blockade and then, with the help of the Maltese, lay siege to the great citadel of Valetta. The French eventually surrendered the island in September 1800 and, in 1801, Ball became the first British governor, a post he held until his death in 1809. He was genuinely mourned by the Maltese, and a handsome monument, in the shape of a small Greek temple, was erected to his memory on the ramparts overlooking Grand Harbour.

A man of studious appearance, with a high domed forehead and thoughtful eyes, Ball was an intellectual who read widely. Although a fine fighting captain, his greatest achievements were as governor of Malta, where he was renowned for his 'conciliating' manner and the soundness of his judgements. When Nelson took on the Mediterranean command in 1803, he worked closely with Ball, writing to him on one occasion, 'you may rely in every situation in life that I shall cherish your friendship.'

SEE ALSO:
'Band of Brothers', Malta, Nile

'Band of Brothers'

Nelson used this phrase on a number of occasions to describe the remarkably close and friendly relationship that existed between him and the captains who served under his command at the Battle of the Nile on 1 August 1798. It is a quotation from the famous Agincourt speech in his favourite Shakespeare play, *King Henry V*. By extension, it has come to encompass all those officers who were particularly close to Nelson, or who served with him in his battles, and thus has become a metaphor for his distinctively 'collegiate' style of leadership, a style that set him apart from most other admirals of his time. It has also become part of the 'Nelson Legend' and so has tended to obscure the often quite subtle ways in which his professional relationships actually worked.

In fact, the phrase is most apt when applied to the original Nile captains. They represented the élite of the Royal Navy at that time, a group of highly professional and experienced men, all of whom had been rigorously trained under Lord St Vincent. Most were the same age as Nelson, in their late thirties or early forties, and most had known him, and served with him, for a number of years. The trust and instinctive

The 'Band of Brothers'. This engraving, produced to celebrate the British victory at the Battle of the Nile in August 1798, features portraits of all the captains who served with Nelson. Nelson himself is shown suspended halfway up the palm tree.

understanding that existed among them was therefore unique and was not repeated to quite the same degree in any other fleet that Nelson commanded.

Moreover, it is now clear from recent research that not all his captains were equally close to Nelson. Instead, he tended to gather around him an 'inner circle' of particularly trusted officers with whom he consulted regularly, and then conveyed the results of those consultations to the remainder by various means. So, for example, a close inspection of the log-books of the ships in the Nile fleet has revealed that Nelson consulted most often with Troubridge, Saumarez (his second in command) and Ball and then transmitted his ideas to the rest of the captains through written orders. Similarly, on the eve of Copenhagen, he dined with close friends such as Hardy, Foley and Fremantle and then stayed up for most of the night dictating his orders to the remainder of his subordinates.

Nor was the composition of the inner circle static. Of the original Nile 'band', only Hardy served with Nelson in all his battles. Some former close colleagues, such as Berry, became physically separated; or even estranged, such as Troubridge. New men, such as Keats or Blackwood, joined the group. So we can now see that, unsurprisingly, Nelson's pattern of relationships was rather more complex and fluid than the older accounts of his life have suggested.

SEE ALSO
Ball, Berry, Blackwood, Foley, Fremantle, Hallowell Hardy, Samuel Hood, Keats, Louis, Miller, Murray, Battle of the Nile, Saumarez, Shakespeare, Thompson, Troubridge

LATEST RESEARCH
Brian Lavery, *Nelson and the Nile*, Chatham Publishing (London 1998)

Barham, Lord *See: Middleton, Charles*

Bastia, Siege of (4 April–23 May 1794)

A heavily fortified port on the north coast of Corsica, Bastia was besieged by the British in the summer of 1794 and Nelson played a key role in the operation.

Bastia in Corsica. This engraving, based on a drawing by Nicholas Pocock, shows Bastia shortly after it fell to the British forces. Lord Hood's flag is flying from the mainmast of HMS Victory *(left).*

'The Comforts of Bath': This contemporary caricature vividly captures the sort of gout-ridden patients the Bath doctors were used to treating. Scarcely surprising, then, that they were unable to do much to help Nelson with his troublesome war wound.

The British had been asked by Corsican nationalists under General Pasquale de Paoli to assist them in driving out their French overlords. Having established a foothold in Corsica in February, by capturing San Fiorenzo in the south of the island, the British then decided to move on Bastia, which was one of the key French strongholds.

Major General Dundas, commanding the British troops, did not wish to begin operations until reinforcements had arrived from Gibraltar but Lord Hood, the commander-in-chief of the Mediterranean fleet, realised that the momentum of the campaign had to be maintained. So he took the fleet to Bastia and landed guns and seamen from his ships to fight alongside Paoli's Corsicans. This naval contingent was commanded by Captain Nelson of the *Agamemnon*, who set up and manned a series of batteries encircling the town. At the same time, Hood instituted a strict naval blockade to prevent any supplies reaching the garrison and continually harassed the French from the sea with gunboats. After enduring thirty-seven days of incessant bombardment from land and sea and with all help of relief gone, the French surrendered on 23 May. General Paoli formally transferred Corsica's allegiance to Great Britain and Bastia became the centre of government under a British viceroy, Sir Gilbert Elliot.

Nelson's energy and enterprise had been essential to the British success and no one realised this more keenly than his commander-in-chief, Lord Hood. But Hood had to tread very delicately. Not only were relations with the army very strained but there were a number of officers senior to Nelson in the fleet who would have been resentful if the young captain had been given too much overt credit for the operations. So, while in private Hood was very generous with his praise of Nelson, in his official despatches he rather played down his role and, as a result, Nelson did not receive the public recognition he felt he deserved.

SEE ALSO

Calvi, Corsica, Samuel Lord Hood

LATEST RESEARCH

Tom Pocock, *Nelson's Campaign in Corsica*, The 1805 Club (Shelton 1994)

Bath

A spa town in southwest England, Bath was at the height of its popularity at the end of the eighteenth century. Nelson's father, Rev Edmund Nelson, went there almost every year to escape from the cold Norfolk winters and eventually died there in April 1802. Other members of Nelson's family stayed there at various times and his wife, Fanny Nelson, whose health was always delicate, lived there for long periods.

Nelson stayed in Bath on two key occasions. In 1781 he went there after the disastrous campaign in Nicaragua, in Central America, to recover from the near-lethal cocktail of tropical illnesses he had contracted. They had had left him weak and occasionally in great pain and he also periodically lost the use of his left arm and leg. He lodged at No 2 Pierrepont Street, conveniently close to the Pump Rooms and the consulting rooms of his doctor. He told his friend Captain William Locker, 'I am physicked three times a day, drink the waters three times and bathe every other night, besides not drinking wine, which I think the worst of all.' The regime obviously worked, for three months later he reported, 'I never was so well in health since you knew me.'

Sixteen years later, he returned to Bath to recover from the loss of his arm following the abortive attack on Santa Cruz de Tenerife (July 1797). His stump was not healing properly and was causing him a great deal of pain and fever. Fanny Nelson was already installed in lodgings at 17 New King Street and he joined her there. By now he was a household name, because of his exploits at the Battle of Cape St Vincent (February 1797) and the *Bath Journal* recorded, 'The Rear Admiral, who was received at Portsmouth with universal greeting, reached Bath on Sunday evening in good health and spirits, to the great joy of his Lady and Venerable Father, and the gratification of every admirer of British Valour.'

Nelson arrived in a very depressed state, believing that his career was finished. But the cheers of the crowds and a flood of congratulatory letters from friends and naval colleagues raised his spirits and he began to look forward to returning to active service. However, his arm was still causing problems and his doctor, William Falconer, a specialist in rheumatology at the Bath Royal Mineral Hospital, was not expert in the treatment of war wounds. He advised Nelson to consult an eminent London surgeon and so the Nelsons left Bath for London.

Nelson paid one very short visit to the city later in the year and, thereafter, never visited it again. Bath was, after all, one of Fanny Nelson's main places of residence and, after the break up of their marriage in January 1801, Nelson always took elaborate precautions to avoid meeting her. Both of the houses in which Nelson stayed have survived and are marked with commemorative plaques. And many of the buildings that he knew and used have survived, notably the Pump Rooms and the great Abbey.

SEE ALSO
Family, Health, Locker, Frances Nelson, Wounds

LATEST RESEARCH
Tom Pocock, 'In Nelson's Footsteps', in Colin White (ed), *The Nelson Companion*, Sutton and Royal Naval Museum (Stroud & Portsmouth 1995)

Beatty, Sir William (d1842)

Beatty tended to Nelson on his deathbed and later published a detailed account of the event, which has formed the basis of every subsequent description of the scene. He joined the Royal Navy in 1793 and saw service throughout the war with Revolutionary France. Eventually, in December 1804, he was appointed surgeon of the *Victory* and served in her throughout the Trafalgar campaign. In 1806 he was promoted to physician and he ended his medical career as Physician of Greenwich Hospital. He was knighted by King William IV in 1831 and died in London in 1842.

In 1806, Beatty published 'An Authentic Narrative of the Death of Lord Nelson', which was very popular and ran through several editions. As well as describing the events of Nelson's death, Beatty also included fascinating details about his daily life, and his health, before the battle and the findings of the autopsy, which he performed on the body before it was handed over for burial. During the course of this operation he retrieved the fatal bullet, which he had mounted in a special locket. He later presented this to King William IV and it remains in the Royal Collection to this day.

SEE ALSO
Death, Relics, Wounds

Nelson by William Beechey (1800). An engraving based on the most 'heroic' of the portraits of Nelson, commissioned by the City of Norwich. Leaning against the cannon on the left is the sword of the Spanish admiral that Nelson captured at the Battle of Cape St Vincent in 1797 and then presented to the city.

Beechey, Sir William (1753–1839)

A fashionable portrait painter, Sir William Beechey painted a most striking likeness of Nelson in 1800/1. The commission came from the city of Norwich, in Norfolk. Three years earlier, Nelson had presented to the city one of the Spanish swords he had captured at the Battle of Cape St Vincent (14 February 1797) and the city authorities decided they wished to have a portrait of Nelson to accompany the sword.

Beechey's Nelson is every inch the hero. In the massive, life-sized, painting he is shown full-length, tall, sturdy and confident, standing on his quarter-deck and surrounded by trophies of his battles,

including the Spanish sword. The portrait was not popular with contemporary art critics, one reviewer remarking that 'the spare war and weather worn Admiral is swelled into an overgrown figurehead.' But the general public loved the heroic image and many engraved copies of it were sold. Still more significantly, Beechey also received a number of commissions for painted copies, including one from the City of London and another, rather later, from the Duke of Wellington.

During the course of the sittings, Beechey and Nelson became firm friends. Nelson presented Beechey with the battered cocked hat he had worn at the Battle of the Nile and also was godfather to Beechey's son Charles, who was later to become a naval officer himself.

SEE ALSO
Cape St Vincent, Portraits

LATEST RESEARCH
Richard Walker, *The Nelson Portraits*, Royal Naval Museum (Portsmouth 1998)

Bellerophon, HMS

The 74-gun battleship HMS *Bellerophon* had the most distinguished battle record of any ship in Nelson's navy. Known affectionately by the sailors as 'Billy Ruffian', she was built in 1786, to a design of Sir Thomas Slade (who also designed the *Victory*) and first commissioned in 1790. In 1794, she took part in Admiral Lord Howe's great victory over the French at the Glorious First of June, helping in the capture of the 100-gun *Revolutionnaire*. Four years later, she once again took on one of the large French ships at the Battle of the Nile (1 August 1798), when she was badly mauled by the huge 120-gun French flagship *L'Orient*.

She was present at the Battle of Trafalgar (21 October 1805), where her captain, John Cooke, was killed while in action with the Spanish *Monarca*. She was so badly damaged that she was sent home to Britain, escorting the *Victory* with Nelson's body on board. After extensive repairs, she continued in active service throughout the rest of the war, including a key role in the Baltic campaign of 1808/9.

However, her greatest moment of glory came right at the end of the war, in July 1815. Fleeing from the

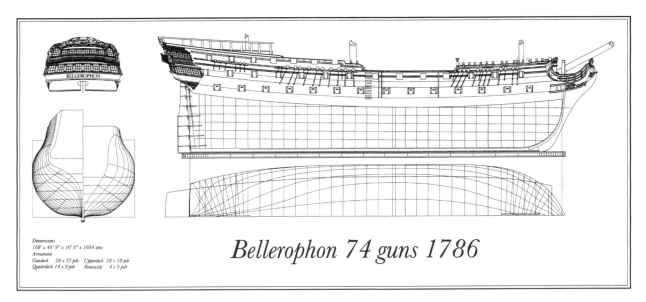

Bellerophon 74 guns 1786

Dimensions
168' x 49' 9" x 16' 9" x 1604 tons
Armament
Gundeck   28 x 32 pdr   Upperdeck 28 x 18 pdr
Quaterdeck 14 x 9 pdr   Forecastle   4 x 9 pdr

victorious allied armies after the Battle of Waterloo, Napoleon headed for the port of Rochefort on the French Atlantic coast, hoping to escape to America. Finding his way blocked by the *Bellerophon*, he decided, instead, to surrender to her captain, Frederick Maitland. He was transported to Britain to learn his fate and during the voyage he took the opportunity to learn more about the Royal Navy, which had done so much to bring about his eventual downfall. 'If it had not been for you English,' he told Maitland ruefully, 'I should have been Emperor of the east; but wherever there is water to float a ship, we are to find you in our way!'

Shortly afterwards, the *Bellerophon* was paid off from active service and, after a number of years as a convict hulk, was finally broken up in 1834. Her figurehead was preserved and is now displayed in the Royal Naval Museum in Portsmouth.

SEE ALSO
L'Orient, Napoleon, Nile, Trafalgar

LATEST RESEARCH
C Pengelly, *The First Bellerophon: The Life of a Famous Ship*, John Baker (London 1966)

Berry, Sir Edward (1768–1831)

Berry was one of Nelson's closest professional friends, and a key member of the 'Band of Brothers'. As well as serving with Nelson at Cape St Vincent,

HMS Bellerophon. *A distinguished veteran of the war against France, it was to her Captain, Frederick Maitland, that Napoleon surrendered after Waterloo in 1815.*

Captain Sir Edward Berry. Nelson's flag captain at the Battle of the Nile and close associate over a number of years.

the Nile and Trafalgar, he took part in six other fleet battles and a large number of smaller actions. A slight, rather delicate man with fair hair and piercing blue eyes, Berry was quick-witted, impulsive and aggressive to the point of recklessness. When he joined the fleet off Cádiz in HMS *Agamemnon* in early October 1805, just prior to Trafalgar, Nelson is supposed to have said, 'Here comes that fool Berry. *Now* we shall have a fight!'

He was born in 1768, the son of a London merchant. His father died young leaving his large family with little means of support and so the boy entered the Navy in 1777 at the very early age of eleven as a midshipman in the *Burford*. Promoted lieutenant in 1794, for bravery in boarding a French man of war while serving in the West Indies, his conduct came to the attention of the commander-in-chief, Admiral Sir John Jervis. So when later, in 1796, Commodore Horatio Nelson was looking for a new first lieutenant for his ship HMS *Agamemnon*, Jervis (by then commanding in the Mediterranean) recommended Berry. The two took an instant liking to each other and formed a close partnership. When Nelson transferred to the *Captain* in 1796, Berry went with him.

Jervis continued to support Berry and obtained his promotion to commander in early 1797. But there was no ship ready for him and so he remained in the *Captain* as a passenger. He was thus with Nelson at the Battle of Cape St Vincent (14 February 1797) and fought alongside him in the boarding party that captured two Spanish ships. Running out along the *Captain*'s bowsprit, he led one division onto the poop of the *San Nicolas* while Nelson led another through her stern windows.

In March 1798, Berry was made a post captain and Nelson (who was at that time in England recovering from the loss of his arm) immediately asked him to be his flag captain in the *Vanguard*. He fought with distinction at the Battle of the Nile (1 August 1798) and it was into his arms that Nelson fell when he was hit on the forehead by a piece of flying shrapnel with the words, 'I am killed. Remember me to my wife.' Given the honour of carrying Nelson's despatches home in HMS *Leander*, Berry was captured by one of the French battleships that had escaped from the Nile, the *Généreux*, and badly wounded in the arm. He was exchanged and finally reached England in December where he was knighted and presented with the freedom of the City of London.

After a long convalescence from the effects of his wound and imprisonment, he was given command of the Third Rate battleship *Foudroyant* and sent out in her to the Mediterranean in June 1799, to replace Nelson's battered flagship *Vanguard*. He commanded the *Foudroyant* during the capture of Malta from the French occupying force and also at the capture of his former captor the *Généreux* and her fellow escapee from the Nile, the *Guillaume Tell*. But his relationship with Nelson was never as close as it had been: partly because of Nelson's distraction with Emma Hamilton; but also because, in the interval, Nelson had found his ideal flag captain in the efficient and seamanlike Thomas Hardy. Nelson was now all too aware of Berry's shortcomings, both as an administrator and as a practical sailor.

Nelson left the Mediterranean in the summer of 1800 and Berry took the *Foudroyant* home to England, where he remained until the summer of 1805, when he was appointed to the *Agamemnon* and joined Nelson in time for Trafalgar. The following year, he also took part in the Battle of San Domingo (6 February 1806) and was made a baronet. He remained in active service until 1813 when he was placed in command of one of the royal yachts but his health was broken and, although he became a rear admiral in 1821, he never hoisted his flag. He died in Bath on 13 February 1831.

SEE ALSO
HMS *Agamemnon*, 'Band of Brothers', Cape St Vincent, HMS *Foudroyant*, Nile

Biographies of Nelson

More than a thousand books have been written about Nelson and new titles are still published almost every year. Much of this material is second rate or worse, but there are a few really top-rank biographies which have stood the test of time (see also the Bibliography on p281).

One of the first, and still one of the most popular, was Robert Southey's *Life of Nelson*. First published in 1813, it has hardly ever been out of print since. However, although it is undoubtedly fine literature, and a useful insight into how Nelson was seen by his contemporaries, Southey's slim book is full of errors, especially in matters relating to the sea and Nelson's battles. So it is best read in the version edited in 1922 by Geoffrey Callender, which corrects the major mistakes.

Most of the biographies published in the nineteenth century were patriotic and laudatory in tone, concentrating overmuch on the central figure of Nelson, who was usually portrayed as a genius towering above his contemporaries. The first seriously to analyse Nelson's leadership qualities, and set them in their historical context, was the great American naval historian Alfred Thayer Mahan. His closely written two-volume work is still regarded as one of the best studies of Nelson as a naval commander, although it is less sure-footed on his private life. In particular, its judgements on Nelson's relationship with Emma Hamilton are seriously flawed by Victorian moralising.

Indeed, until quite recently, biographers tended to separate Nelson's embarrassing private life from his public career and to suggest that the private Nelson was unimportant. The first to challenge this approach, and to concentrate on Nelson the Man, was Carola Oman. In 1947, she produced an intensely personal book, distilled from painstaking reading of hundreds of his letters and, for the first time, the women in Nelson's life were allowed their rightful place. The result is the most intimate and vivid picture available of the man himself and it is still highly regarded.

At this time, more original source material was emerging as private family collections were sold, and as the great public collections became more accessible through detailed catalogues. It became clear that the earlier, published sources were incomplete, and in places, inaccurate. Letters began to appear in various publications: sometimes singly, sometimes in larger collections.

This new material, and the continuing public interest in Nelson, have inspired a spate of biographies since the Second World War – at least two each decade. Two men have dominated Nelson studies in the postwar years: Oliver Warner and Tom Pocock. As the new material emerged, both wrote books and articles covering particular aspects of Nelson's life. Each then distilled their considerable knowledge into short biographies, both of which remain excellent introductions to Nelson's life and career.

It was Warner who once remarked that there was little new to be discovered about Nelson and suggested that future studies would tend to concentrate on very particular aspects of his life. Certainly, most of the postwar biographies, Warner's included, have been little more than reworkings of the familiar material, with the addition of some modern insights. But recently, a new trend in the study of naval history has emerged that may lead eventually to a full-scale re-evaluation of Nelson's life and career.

Since the mid-1980s, naval historians have been concentrating on the context in which Nelson lived and worked, and some interesting results have emerged. Studies of the social history of the eighteenth-century Royal Navy have challenged the old perception that Nelson was a uniquely humane man in an inhumane age. Detailed examination of the development of naval tactics has shown that many of Nelson's tactical ideas were inherited from his predecessors. And the publication in English of research by Spanish and French historians into the difficulties that both navies encountered in the Napoleonic period has helped us to understand better why Nelson and his colleagues were so remarkably successful.

Moreover, scholarly interest in Nelson's life has also been rekindled recently by the discovery of a significant body of new primary source material. A survey of Nelson's letters, commissioned by the National Maritime and Royal Naval Museums, has revealed that there is a large amount of unpublished Nelson material in all the major public and private collections: at the last count well over 500 individual documents. Additionally, the study has shown that some of the key 'runs' of published letters to well-known personalities, such as the Duke of Clarence or Lord St Vincent, have been edited, indeed censored. These passages relate not only to personal matters – such as Nelson's relationship with Emma Hamilton – but also to public affairs. Nothing so far found in this unpublished material challenges the core Nelson story in a fundamental way, but some interesting light and shade can now be added to the familiar narrative.

SEE ALSO
Dispatches and Letters of Vice Admiral Lord Nelson, Letters, Nelson's

LATEST RESEARCH
Michael Nash, 'Building a Nelson Library', in Colin
White (ed), *The Nelson Companion*, Sutton and Royal Naval
Museum (Stroud & Portsmouth 1995)
Colin White, 'The Nelson Letters Project', *The Mariner's
Mirror* 87 (November 2001)

Blackwood, Sir Henry (1770–1832)

Although Blackwood's name is now closely associated with Nelson's, the two men only served together for two brief periods: in 1800, and again for a few weeks in 1805. Born on 28 December 1770, the older accounts of his life state that he joined the Royal Navy in time to serve at the Battle of Dogger Bank in 1781 but recent research suggests that he in fact began his service some years later. What is certain, however, is that he was made a lieutenant in 1790 by Lord Howe and served as first lieutenant in HMS *Invincible* under Captain Packenham at the Glorious First of June (1794). He was promoted to commander for his services and reached the rank of post captain in 1795.

He then began a long career as a frigate captain during which he established a reputation as a dashing and gallant commander: always thoroughly professional but prepared to take risks as well. He showed these qualities to perfection in the Mediterranean in March 1800 when, in the 36-gun frigate HMS *Penelope*, he attacked the 80-gun French battleship *Guillaume Tell*, slowing her down sufficiently for British battleships to come up and capture her. When Nelson heard of this exploit he wrote one of his wonderful warm letters to Blackwood, talking of 'a sympathy which ties men in the bonds of friendship without having a personal knowledge of each other'.

When war broke out in 1803 after the Peace of Amiens, Blackwood was appointed to HMS *Euryalus*. During the next two years, he served mainly off the coast of Ireland but in July 1805, on his own initiative, he shadowed the combined French and Spanish fleet as it made its way south after the Battle of Cape Finisterre. Having tracked them to Cádiz, he returned to Britain with the news, calling on Nelson at Merton on his way to London. When Nelson sailed in the *Victory* for Cádiz a few days later, Blackwood and the *Euryalus* went with him. He soon found himself commanding Nelson's inshore squadron, watching the movements of the allied fleet and reporting them in detail to his admiral, using the flexible telegraphic code for signals recently devised by Sir Home Riggs Popham.

By now, Nelson regarded Blackwood as one of his inner circle – so much so that he invited him on board the *Victory* on the morning of 21 October and asked him to witness, with Hardy, the famous codicil to his will in which he left Emma Hamilton and Horatia as 'a legacy to my country'. Having tried, unsuccessfully, to persuade Nelson to shift his flag to the *Euryalus*, Blackwood left the flagship as the first shots flew overhead, with Nelson's prophetic last words in his ears, 'God bless you Blackwood. I shall never speak to you again.'

During the battle, Blackwood took his frigate into the thick of the fray and received Vice Admiral Collingwood on board after his flagship, the *Royal Sovereign*, had been badly damaged. He then took his ship home to Britain, bearing the captured French admiral, Pierre de Villeneuve. He arrived in time to take part in Nelson's funeral, where he was the train-bearer to the chief mourner, Admiral of the Fleet Sir Peter Parker.

Blackwood was then appointed to command the battleship HMS *Ajax* and served in her in the Dardanelles campaign of 1807, during which the *Ajax* caught fire and was totally destroyed. Blackwood survived, however, and took command of the battleship HMS *Warspite*, serving in her in the North Sea and the Mediterranean. At the end of the war, he was Captain of the Fleet to the Duke of Clarence (later King William IV) at the grand fleet review held at Spithead to celebrate the victory and was rewarded with a baronetcy. Promoted to rear admiral the same year, and vice admiral in 1821, he eventually died on 17 December 1832.

SEE ALSO
'Band of Brothers', Battle of Trafalgar

Bligh, William (1754–1817)

Although best known for his role in the famous mutiny in HMS *Bounty* in 1789, Bligh also had a most distinguished fighting career, including a brief spell of service under Nelson in the Baltic campaign of 1801.

Bligh sailed with the great explorer and navigator Captain James Cook on his second voyage round the world in 1772–1774. He took part in the Battle of Dogger Bank (5 August 1781) and the relief of Gibraltar (1782) and established such a reputation as a navigator that he seemed the ideal choice for the command of the *Bounty* expedition in 1787. Despite the notorious mutiny that ensued, Bligh's reputation was enhanced still further by the remarkable 3618 mile voyage he made in an open boat after he and his followers were set adrift by the mutineers on 28 April 1789. So he continued to receive promotion and employment.

Promoted to post captain in 1790, he served throughout the war with Revolutionary France and, in 1797, commanded the battleship HMS *Director* at the Battle of Camperdown (11 October). In 1801, in command of the battleship HMS *Glatton*, he took part in the Battle of Copenhagen (2 April) where he was Nelson's next astern. He succeeded in setting the Danish flagship *Dannebrog* on fire very early in the action, thus forcing the Danish commander-in-chief, Commodore Olfert Fischer, to shift his pendant to another ship. After the battle, Nelson sent for him and thanked him personally for his support.

Thereafter, however, his career faltered. Appointed governor of the penal colony of New South Wales in Australia, he again found himself embroiled in a mutiny and, although he received the official support of the government, he was never employed in any major post again. Promoted to rear admiral in 1811, he died a vice admiral in 1817.

As is now well known, he was certainly not the tyrant portrayed in successive Hollywood films. But he was an awkward, irritable man with a graceless manner that often offended even those people who were well disposed to him, among them Nelson. Most captains would have been very happy with a public statement of thanks from the Hero of the Nile, but Bligh evidently asked for confirmation in writing. A tetchy note from Nelson, dated 14 April 1801, begins, 'Captain Bligh has desired my testimony to his good conduct which although perfectly unnecessary I cannot refuse. His behaviour on this occasion can reap no additional credit from my testimony.'

SEE ALSO
Copenhagen, Fischer

'I really do not see the signal!' This early twentieth-century illustration by A D McCormick, painted for the 1916 edition of Southey's Life of Nelson, *shows a famous moment at the Battle of Copenhagen (1801) when Nelson is supposed to have claimed that he could not see his superior's signal ordering him to discontinue the action.*

Blind Eye, The

One of the most well-known incidents in Nelson's life, and the origin of a much-used popular phrase, the 'blind eye' incident occurred at the height of the

Battle of Copenhagen, at about 1.00pm on 2 April 1801. At that time, Nelson's squadron was hotly engaged with the Danish line of defence. Three of his ships – a quarter of his available force – had gone aground on the treacherous shoals and the Danes were putting up a much stouter and prolonged fight than expected. Seeing this, Nelson's senior officer, Admiral Sir Hyde Parker, anxiously watching the battle from a distance, ordered signal number 39 to be hoisted, 'Discontinue the engagement'. Nelson realised that if he obeyed the signal and withdrew his force when the Danes were still undefeated, his ships would be subjected to a withering and potentially fatal fire as they left the battleground. He therefore decided to ignore the signal and fight on and, eventually, about an hour later, his persistence was rewarded when the Danish resistance finally began to collapse.

The story of how Nelson received the news of Parker's signal has been told in almost every account of the battle. When the admiral's order to withdraw was seen on board his temporary flagship HMS *Elephant* and reported to him, Nelson appeared to ignore it; then, when his signal lieutenant asked whether he should repeat the signal (that is, pass the order on to the ships of the attacking squadron), Nelson told him curtly, 'No, acknowledge it' (that is, indicate to Parker that he had seen it). He then asked, 'Is No. 16 [the signal for Close Action] still hoisted?' On being told it was, he said, 'Mind you keep it so.' He then resumed his customary pacing of the quarterdeck; but the stump of his right arm was twitching uncontrollably, a sure sign to those who knew him that he was extremely agitated.

Eventually, he stopped alongside Colonel William Stewart, the commanding officer of a corps of riflemen serving in the *Elephant*, and said, 'Do you know what is shown on board the commander in chief? No. 39.' Stewart asked what this meant. 'Why, to leave off action. Leave off action! Now, damn me if I do!' and turning to Captain Thomas Foley, commanding the *Elephant*, who was also at his side, he said, 'You know Foley I have only one eye – I have a right to be blind sometimes!' Then he put a telescope to his blind right eye and said, 'I really do not see the signal! Damn the signal! Keep mine for close action flying.'

The story of this famous theatrical gesture has become hackneyed by constant repetition and, inevitably, there has been a reaction against it. Some authorities have questioned whether it was necessary at all; for example, it has been suggested that Parker never intended the signal to be regarded as a direct order but that it was instead a 'permissive' order, allowing Nelson to withdraw if he thought it right to do so. It has been suggested that Parker and Nelson had agreed beforehand that if the attacking force was seen to be suffering too greatly, the signal would be made so that Nelson could retreat if he thought fit. But recent research has unearthed a hitherto unknown account of the battle by a young signal midshipman called John Finlayson, which confirms that Stewart's recollection of Nelson's incredulous reaction to the news of the signal was accurate. There can be no longer be any doubt about the matter: Nelson neither expected nor welcomed Parker's untimely interference.

Recently, however, the suggestion has even been made that the famous incident with the telescope never happened at all! The theory is that it was invented by Stewart when he wrote an account of the battle for Nelson's early biographers Clarke and M'Arthur in 1809. Certainly, Stewart's 1809 account of the battle is the only one to mention the telescope but it is not clear why he should have deliberately fabricated such a tale. In fact, the story has a strong ring of truth to it: both the gesture itself and Nelson's reported words are wholly characteristic.

Whether it actually happened or not, Nelson's gesture with the telescope has become one of the most famous moments in his life, endlessly depicted in books, paintings and films. In more modern times, it has been lampooned by cartoonists and comedians who have created a new, and very persistent, myth that what he actually said was 'I see no ships'!

SEE ALSO
Copenhagen, Parker, Stewart

RECENT RESEARCH
Terry Coleman, *Nelson: The Man and the Legend*, Bloomsbury (London 2001)
Dudley Pope, *The Great Gamble*, Chatham Publishing (London 2001)
Colin White (ed), 'A Signal Midshipman at Copenhagen', *Trafalgar Chronicle* 11 (2001)

Boreas, HMS

A 28-gun Sixth Rate frigate, HMS *Boreas* was designed by Sir Thomas Slade, Surveyor of the Navy. Slade was responsible for some of the most successful ships of the period, including the *Victory*, but the *Boreas* and her small, lightly armed sisters were old-fashioned even before they came into service and were only built to meet an urgent wartime need for convoy escorts. Constructed in a private yard in Hull, she was launched in 1775 and immediately went into active service in the West Indies under Captain Charles Thompson between 1775 and 1780.

Nelson became her captain in 1784. She was the third small frigate he had commanded but in the much-reduced peacetime Navy he was lucky to get her. He told his brother William that he had gained the appointment by his own merit but he probably owed it more to the political influence of his powerful patron Lord Hood, whom he had recently helped in his successful campaign to be elected member of parliament for Westminster.

In the event, the next three years were to prove the most frustrating of Nelson's naval career. He encountered problems right at the start of the commission, when a Thames pilot ran the *Boreas* aground and, when he finally arrived in the West Indies, he quickly became embroiled in controversy with his senior officer Sir Richard Hughes, and the rich local British merchants, over illicit trading with the newly independent American states. Recently-discovered letters have shown that Nelson had already clashed with Hughes while in command of the *Albemarle* in 1782 and now they fell out again even more seriously.

At the same time, he renewed his friendship with Prince William Henry, who was now a full captain in command of the frigate *Pegasus*, only to be involved in further controversy when the Prince had a public and acrimonious dispute with his first lieutenant Isaac Schomberg. It was an altogether unhappy time, relieved only by his slowly blossoming love affair with Frances Nisbet, whom he wooed for two years before they eventually married on the island of Nevis, on 11 March 1787.

Shortly after the wedding, Nelson returned home to England in the *Boreas* and eventually paid her off at Sheerness on 30 November. But controversy dogged him to the last, when the Admiralty disputed some of the decisions he had made while acting as senior officer in the West Indies. He ended this thoroughly unsatisfactory period ill with a severe cold and with his frigate acting as a receiving ship for pressed men. The ship's punishment record reveals that during the last eighteen months of the commission he flogged almost half of the ship's company for offences such as mutinous language and attempts to desert. Such a high level of punishment was unusual for him and is striking evidence of just how deeply unhappy the whole ship had become.

The *Boreas* continued to be dogged by ill-fortune. Although she survived to serve in the next war, she was eventually wrecked off Guernsey on 28 November 1807.

SEE ALSO
Frances Nelson, Nevis, Schomberg, King William IV

LATEST RESEARCH
Robert Gardiner, *The First Frigates*, Conway (London 1992)

Boulogne, Battle of (15/16 August 1801)

Although comparatively small-scale, involving some 1000 men on either side, the Battle of Boulogne was one of the worst defeats of Nelson's career. Like the attack on Santa Cruz de Tenerife (July 1797), with which it had many similarities, it showed that, when opposed by a determined and experienced commander, with a well-motivated force, Nelson's tactics of shock and surprise could be countered successfully.

In early July, Nelson was appointed to command a special anti-invasion force in the Channel. He soon discovered that the invasion threat was largely a bluff, nonetheless, he sought ways of attacking his opponents in their home ports. The most likely target appeared to be Boulogne, where a defensive line of small vessels had been placed across the harbour mouth by the French commander, Admiral Louis de Latouche Tréville. A major bombardment by bomb vessels on 4 August failed and so Nelson began to consider a frontal assault.

The detailed orders for this ambitious attack have recently been discovered and they contradict the

Boulogne. This engraving of the northern French port, based on a drawing made in early in 1805 when Napoleon's 'Army of England' was encamped there, gives a good impression of how the town looked when Nelson attacked the French flotilla in August 1801.

suggestion made in some modern accounts that the attack on Boulogne on 15 August failed because of careless preparation. On the contrary, it is clear from them that, as always, Nelson planned the operation with meticulous care. His aim was to launch a concentrated attack on the French line by four divisions of ship's boats, with a fifth division of boats fitted with eight-inch howitzers to give covering fire. Two boats in each division were equipped with stout hook-ropes and axes so that they could cut the cables of the enemy vessels and take them in tow.

However, the same attention to detail was shown by his opponent. Knowing that Nelson was in command of the British forces, Latouche had always assumed that he would attack Boulogne and had made his preparations accordingly, strengthening his defensive line and securing his ships firmly to each other. And, in a move that showed he had studied his opponent's methods carefully, he also placed two boats at the head and tail of his line, moored at right angles to their comrades. He knew that, at the Battle of the Nile, Nelson had achieved his crushing victory by rounding the head of the French line of battle and attacking it on both sides, and he was determined to prevent this from happening again.

Latouche had installed his headquarters in a tower on the hills above Boulogne and, from this vantage point, he was able to watch the arrival of Nelson's force and to observe the sudden flurry of activity around the flagship as the attacking force of boats gathered on the evening of 15 August. Guessing that an attack was about to be made, he therefore stationed watch-boats well ahead of his line to give advance warning of the enemy's approach and had his men alert and ready at their posts.

As a result, the British attack went disastrously wrong from the outset. Latouche's advance forces gave the alarm as soon as the first boats were sighted and the attackers were overwhelmed by heavy fire. Moreover, the four British divisions became separated in the dark, and some of them were held up by a strong tide, so that they did not arrive in one wave as planned. As a result, the French were able to deal with the divisions piecemeal and the attack was repulsed with heavy loss: forty-five killed and 128 wounded. Among the latter was Nelson's aide-de-camp and a particular favourite of his, Captain Edward Parker, whose thigh was shattered.

It was a humiliating defeat. In public, Nelson tried to explain his failure by claiming rather fancifully that the French had chained their vessels to the seabed. In private, however, he admitted that his plans had not been properly carried out and he worried that the battle might have been more successful if he had led the attack in person. 'I own I shall never bring myself again to allow any attack to go forward where I am not personally concerned,' he wrote, 'my mind suffers more than if I had a leg shot off.'

SEE ALSO
Channel Command, Latouche Tréville, Edward Parker

LATEST RESEARCH
Rémi Monaque, 'Latouche-Tréville: The admiral who defied Nelson', *The Mariner's Mirror* 86 (August 2000)
Tom Pocock, 'The Summer of 1801: Nelson at Deal and Boulogne', *The Nelson Dispatch* 7 (July 2001), The Nelson Society
Colin White, 'Nelson's Channel Order Book', *The Naval Miscellany* VI (London 2003), The Navy Records Society

Bowen, Richard (1761–1797)

An enterprising and highly professional young officer, Richard Bowen was seen as a rising star in the Royal Navy and it is possible that, had he lived, he could have proved a rival to Nelson. His untimely death, during the abortive attack on Santa Cruz de Tenerife in July 1797, was regarded as a serious blow by all who knew him.

A Devonian, from Ilfracombe, he first went to sea with his father in the merchant service but transferred to the Royal Navy in 1778. Three years later, as a midshipman, he was aide to Captain John Jervis when HMS *Foudroyant* captured the French 74-gun *Pégase* and became one of Jervis's most favoured protégés. At the beginning of the war with revolutionary France, he served as Jervis's signal lieutenant in the West Indies and played a key role in the capture of

Captain Richard Bowen. The only known portrait of Bowen, taken from an article in The Naval Chronicle. *The odd black patch on his cheek is a flaw in the original engraving.*

Port Royal, the capital of the French island of Martinique in 1794. For this, he was promoted to commander, rising to post captain a few months later.

He caught up with Jervis again in the Mediterranean in 1796 and was given a number of 'plums', including the command of a detached squadron of frigates defending Gibraltar. 'He is a child of my own,' Jervis wrote to the governor of Gibraltar, 'and you will find in him the most inexhaustible spirit of enterprise and skillful seamanship which can be comprised in any human character.'

After the Battle of Cape St Vincent in February 1797, Bowen, in his 32-gun frigate HMS *Terpischore*, attacked the badly damaged Spanish four-decker battleship *Santissíma Trinidad* which was limping her way into Cádiz. But she was still too strong for his lightly armed ship and managed to escape. At Tenerife the following July, he commanded a division of the British boats that attacked the main Spanish citadel on the town mole and actually managed to gain a foothold. But he was killed, and his small landing party decimated, by the accurate and deadly Spanish fire. His body was recovered and he was buried at sea with full honours. Nelson was greatly affected by his death and wrote in his official report, 'a more enterprising able and gallant officer does not grace His Majesty's naval service.'

SEE ALSO
Jervis, Tenerife, *Santissíma Trinidad*

Brest

Brest is situated at the tip of the Brittany peninsula in northwest France, where it dominates the approaches to the Channel. Close by is a large area of enclosed water, known as Brest Roads, in which fleets could shelter in safety. The 'Rade' could only be entered through a narrow channel known as the 'Goulet', which meant that the anchorage and port were easily defended. A major dockyard was established there in the late seventeenth century, during the reign of King Louis XIV, with massive fortifications designed by the famous engineer Vauban. By Nelson's time, it had become one of the most important French naval arsenals: so much so, that the British Channel fleet maintained a tight blockade of the port throughout the long war with France. It was a feat of collective endurance of ships and men without parallel in the history of war at sea.

Nelson served in the Channel fleet only briefly when he was second in command to Lord St Vincent in the early months of 1801 and so he was not very familiar with Brest, or with the dangerous waters off Ushant in which so many of his friends and contemporaries served.

SEE ALSO
Cornwallis, Toulon

Bronte, Dukedom of

On 13 August 1799, King Ferdinand of Naples made Nelson the Duke of Bronte, a region in the northwest of Sicily close to the famous volcano Etna. With the title went an estate of 15,000 acres at the centre of which was the ancient Castello de Maniace, originally built in the eleventh century by the famous Byzantine general George Maniace. Later a Benedictine monastery had been established there so, technically, Nelson became an abbot as well as a duke. However, by the time Bronte was handed over to Nelson, the area had been devastated by volcanic eruptions, earthquakes and general neglect. Consequently, although on paper it was supposed to yield an annual revenue of £3000, in fact Nelson received very little financial benefit from it at all.

Nonetheless, Nelson was proud of his new title (which, appropriately, means 'thunder') and immediately used it in his signature. He never visited Bronte but often spoke of retiring there with Emma and Horatia. On his death it passed, along with his English title, to his elder brother William. When William later died without a male heir, the English title of Earl Nelson passed to his sister's son. The Italians, however, were more enlightened and allowed titles to descend in the female line, so William's daughter Charlotte became Duchess of Bronte. She later married Lord Bridport and the Bronte title has remained in the Bridport family ever since.

SEE ALSO
Descendants, Signatures

LATEST RESEARCH
Viscount Bridport, 'The Duchy of Bronte', *The Nelson Dispatch* 7 (January 2000), The Nelson Society

Vice Admiral François Brueys d'Aigallers who commanded the French fleet at the Battle of the Nile (1 August 1798) and lost his life there.

Brueys d'Aigallers, François (1753–1798)

Nelson's opponent at the Battle of the Nile (1 August 1798), Brueys was the son of an aristocratic family from Uzes in the Languedoc region of southwest France. He joined the French Marine Royale at the age of thirteen and fought against the British during the War of American Independence (1778–1783) as a lieutenant in the French West Indies fleet. He continued to serve after the Revolution and, by 1792, had become captain of a 74-gun battleship.

During the period known as 'The Terror', all those with aristocratic connections were regarded as suspect and so Brueys was forced into early retirement. However, he was recalled in 1796, promoted to rear admiral, and commanded a squadron based at Corfu, acting in support of the young General Napoleon Bonaparte's successful campaign in Italy. He man-

aged to capture a superior Venetian squadron, a feat that brought him to Napoleon's attention and so he was a natural choice to command the naval element of Napoleon's daring expedition to Egypt in 1798.

From the outset, Brueys was critical about the organisation of the campaign. The expedition was mounted in a great hurry and a number of the ships were ill-prepared for sea, while all of them were very short of experienced sailors. Additionally, Brueys found himself acting under the direct orders of Napoleon who installed himself with his staff in the fleet flagship *L'Orient* and, characteristically, insisted on interfering with the detailed handling of the fleet, about which he knew little.

At first, however, all went well. The expedition sailed from Toulon without being detected, captured Malta almost without resistance, and then managed to reach Egypt and land the army without being intercepted by Nelson and his fleet. It was then that Brueys's problems began. Knowing that there was no safe anchorage in Egypt, he wanted to withdraw the fleet to Corfu and cover the French army from there. But Napoleon insisted on keeping the fleet close to him and so Brueys was forced to take refuge in the only available anchorage, the open roadstead at Aboukir Bay, just to the east of Alexandria.

Here, he attempted to make his position secure by placing his ships in a defensive line as close to the shoals as possible. But since his fleet included the huge three-decker *L'Orient* and three large 80-gun battleships, he was forced to leave a wide gap between his line and the shallow water, which meant that skilfully handled ships could get inside his line and attack him from the landward side. His task was made even more difficult by Napoleon, who stripped the fleet of supplies, and of its most experienced gunners, to reinforce his army.

When Nelson's fleet was sighted in the early afternoon of 1 August, Brueys expected to have the night to strengthen his line and recall his men who had gone ashore in search of water. Instead, he was caught completely off guard by an immediate and furious attack and never really recovered control of his own forces. *L'Orient* herself was assailed by three British ships and succeeded in driving one of them, the *Bellerophon*, out of the battle, before succumbing to the fire that subsequently destroyed her. Brueys was wounded in the head and arm but refused to leave the deck, attempting instead to stanch the blood with his handkerchief. He was then almost cut in two by a cannonball but again refused to be taken below, saying 'a French admiral ought to die on his quarterdeck.' He died a short while later.

Brueys was much criticised by his contemporaries for his positioning of his fleet in Aboukir Bay and their strictures have been echoed by historians. But recent studies of the battle have established the scale of his problem: the poor quality of some of his ships, his lack of experienced men and supplies and, above all, the very inferior anchorage which he was forced to use by his capricious commander, completely against his better professional judgement. Brueys was a brave and experienced naval officer and it is his misfortune to be remembered for a battle in which he fought with considerable handicaps, against one of the best-trained and best-led fleets in history.

SEE ALSO
L'Orient, Napoleon, Nile

LATEST RESEARCH
Michelle Battesti, *La bataille d'Aboukir*, Economica (Paris 1998)
Brian Lavery, *Nelson and the Nile*, Chatham Publishing (London 1998)
John Morewood, 'Vice Admiral François Paul Brueys d'Aigallers', *The Nelson Dispatch* 6 (July 1998), The Nelson Society

Bucentaure

An 80-gun two-decker battleship launched in 1803, the *Bucentaure* was the flagship of the French Mediterranean fleet throughout the Trafalgar campaign. The fine, large 80-gunners were a French speciality. With their upper battery of 24-pounders they were significantly more powerful than the standard 74-gun battleships favoured by the British, while still retaining a good turn of speed. They were therefore often used as flagships by the French admirals, in preference to the more unwieldy three-deckers.

The *Bucentaure* was a flagship throughout her short career: first of Admiral Louis de Latouche Tréville, from January 1804 until his death the following August, and then of Vice Admiral Pierre de Villeneuve. In 1805, she was the command ship of

the Combined fleet on the extraordinary voyage to the West Indies and back. And it was from her that Villeneuve commanded the allies when they made their sortie from Cádiz on 19 October 1805.

The *Bucentaure* was in the very centre of the fighting at Trafalgar. The *Victory* broke the allied line by passing under her stern, firing a shattering broadside as she did so, and most of the other ships in Nelson's line then followed suit. These successive crippling blows quickly reduced the French flagship to a dismasted hulk, thus preventing Villeneuve from controlling his fleet by signal. When he tried to transfer to a less damaged ship he found that all the ship's boats had been destroyed and so he was forced to surrender, less than two hours after the first shots were fired.

HMS *Conqueror* took the shattered hull of the *Bucentaure* in tow; but during the great storm that followed the battle, she was forced to abandon her prize. The French then compelled the small British prize crew left on board to surrender and, erecting single sail on the stump of her mizzen mast, they tried to get the stricken ship into Cádiz. But she struck a rock close to the harbour entrance and sank.

SEE ALSO
Latouche Tréville, Battle of Trafalgar, Villeneuve

LATEST RESEARCH
Robert Gardiner, *Warships of the Napoleonic Era*, Chatham Publishing (London 1999)

Burnham Thorpe

The village where Nelson was born, and spent his early childhood, lies close to the north Norfolk coast, to the east of King's Lynn. A tiny settlement with a large and ancient church, a pub and some scattered houses, it was then – and to a large extent remains – a remote and peaceful place, cut off from the wider world.

Nelson's father Edmund became rector of the parish in 1755 and he and his wife Catherine brought up their family in the old Parsonage House, which lay in its own farmland about a mile to the south of the centre of the village. Once he had left Burnham to join the Navy, Nelson returned only occasionally. However, he did live there with his wife Fanny for

one extended period from December 1787 when he was unable to obtain a peacetime command. When war eventually broke out again in January 1793, Nelson left the village to take command of the battleship HMS *Agamemnon* after throwing a celebration party for his friends in the local pub, The Plough. He never returned to his birthplace again, although he always retained happy memories of it. He once wrote to a childhood friend, Dean Allot, 'Most probably I shall never see dear, dear Burnham again but I have a satisfaction in thinking that my bones will probably be laid with my father's in the village that gave me birth.'

The Parsonage House was pulled down in Nelson's lifetime and replaced with a grander building in the Georgian style. But the church where he

The parsonage at Burnham Thorpe. Nelson's childhood home was pulled down during his lifetime but this near-contemporary oil painting gives a good impression of what it looked like. The figure in the right foreground is supposed to be Rev Edmund Nelson with young Horatio playing beside him.

was baptised still remains, as does the village pub – now, inevitably, renamed The Lord Nelson.

SEE ALSO
Family

LATEST RESEARCH
Tom Pocock, 'In Nelson's Footprints', in Colin White (ed), *The Nelson Companion*, Sutton and Royal Naval Museum (Stroud & Portsmouth 1995)

Cádiz

Cádiz is a major port and naval base, on the south-west coast of Spain, commanding the entrance to the Straits of Gibraltar. Nelson knew the place well and it features in his story on a number of occasions. He first visited it as a friend and ally, in June 1793. Spain had entered the war against France on the side of Britain and so Nelson called in at Cádiz on his way to join the Mediterranean fleet in HMS *Agamemnon*. He was invited to dinner by the Spanish commander-in-chief, Langara, in his splendid flagship the *Concepcion* and allowed to wander freely around the dockyard. His verdict, in a letter to his wife, was that the Spanish had 'very fine ships but shockingly manned.'

His next visit was far less friendly. Four years later, in April 1797, following their victory at the Battle of Cape St Vincent (14 February 1797), the British fleet arrived off Cádiz. In an attempt to goad the Spanish fleet into emerging to fight another battle, it was decided to starve them out by blockading the port to prevent supplies reaching them by sea. Nelson, recently promoted to rear admiral, was given command of an inshore squadron, placed right in the entrance to the harbour. His ships were so close to the town that, as he wrote to a friend, 'We are looking at the ladies walking the walls and Mall of Cádiz.'

When the blockade failed to work, Nelson resorted to more aggressive measures. Bringing up a special mortar ship *Thunder*, he began to bombard the dockyard and arsenal. The Spanish retaliated by attacking the *Thunder* in armed boats and fierce hand-to-hand fighting ensued in which Nelson narrowly escaped being killed, saved largely through the bravery of one his sailors, John Sykes.

His final visit was in September 1805. The combined French and Spanish fleet under Vice Admiral Pierre de Villeneuve had taken shelter there after their failure to force their way into the Channel in support of Napoleon's invasion plan and Nelson was sent out to take command of the British fleet assembled outside Cádiz to deal with them. This time, he remained out of sight of the port, over the horizon, hoping to tempt the Combined fleet to emerge. But he kept in close touch by stationing a small force of frigates close inshore, linked to his main force by a chain of battleships. So, when Villeneuve finally set sail, on his way into the Mediterranean, his movements were reported to Nelson almost as they were happening and the ensuing Battle of Trafalgar was fought only a few miles away on 21 October.

Cádiz bore the brunt of the human suffering after Trafalgar. The crippled French and Spanish ships struggled back there and the hospitals were filled with the wounded and dying. But, in a gesture typical of the times, the Spanish captain-general, the Marquis de la Solana, sent messages to the British ships offering to care for their wounded as well.

SEE ALSO
Sykes, Battle of Trafalgar

LATEST RESEARCH
Colin White, *1797: Nelson's Year of Destiny*, Sutton and Royal Naval Museum (Stroud & Portsmouth 1998)

Calder, Sir Robert (1745–1818)

An efficient though not an exceptional officer, it was Calder's misfortune that at two key moments in his career he was overshadowed by Nelson. He joined the Royal Navy in 1759 and had an early success when the ship in which he was serving captured a Spanish treasure ship in 1762. Even as a lieutenant, his share of the prize money was £13,000, which made him a rich man early in life. He was promoted captain in 1780, a year after Nelson, who was ten years his junior.

In 1796, he joined the Mediterranean fleet as Sir John Jervis's captain of the fleet and served in that capacity during the Battle of Cape St Vincent (14 February 1797). His hesitant, rule-bound approach was completely out of step with the admiral's aggressive, risk-taking handling of the battle, and with the spirit of most his fellow captains, Nelson in particular. At least twice during the fighting Calder was publicly rebuked by Jervis for his negative attitude. Sent home with the despatches, and knighted for his services, he found even this moment of glory overshadowed by the widespread praise for Nelson's remarkable actions.

Promoted rear admiral in 1799 and vice admiral in 1804, he served mainly with the Channel fleet. On 22 July 1805, he was in command of a detachment that intercepted the Combined fleet under Villeneuve as it attempted to slip into the port of Ferrol, on the north coast of Spain, after its extraordinary voyage to the West Indies and back, chased by Nelson. Although outnumbered, and hampered by thick fog, Calder attacked and managed to capture two Spanish ships. But, concerned that a Spanish force in Ferrol might emerge and come to the aid of their comrades, he failed to follow up his success and allowed Villeneuve to escape.

Thinking he had served his country well in difficult circumstances, Calder continued at sea and eventually joined the force assembled off Cádiz to deal with the now very large Combined fleet. But as news came out from England, he was concerned to discover that he was being criticised for failing to do his utmost and, in an attempt to clear his reputation, demanded a court martial. In response to the public anger, the Admiralty had already decided to try him and so

Nelson in the boat action at Cádiz, June 1797. This pen and wash drawing by William Bromley captures vividly the ferocity and confusion of Nelson's bloody little battle with the Spanish gunboats.

Nelson, who had just taken command of the fleet off Cádiz, was faced with the unhappy duty of sending Calder home, in near disgrace. Broken-hearted,

Calder begged to be allowed to return in his flagship, HMS *Prince of Wales*, and unable to bring himself to add further to his colleague's distress, Nelson agreed, thus depriving his fleet of a powerful three-decker at a time when the Combined fleet was daily expected to sail.

Nelson always refused to join in the chorus of condemnation. In a recently discovered letter, written to Calder on the eve of his departure, he wished him 'a quick passage and a happy termination of your enquiry,' and, as the *Victory* sailed into action at Trafalgar, he turned to his officers and said, 'What would poor Calder give to be with us now?' Calder stood his trial, was found guilty of an error of judgement, and was sentenced to be severely reprimanded. He never served at sea again and died on 31 August 1818.

Porto Agro, near Calvi in Corsica. It was in this small bay that Nelson and his men landed their guns and then hauled them up the steep valley sides to form a ring of batteries around the besieged town.

SEE ALSO
Cape St Vincent, Cape Finisterre, Trafalgar campaign

Calvi, Siege of (19 June–10 August 1794)

A strongly fortified port on the northwest coast of Corsica which was besieged by the British in the summer of 1794. Nelson played a key role in the fighting and was severely wounded in the eye. The British had been asked by Corsican nationalists under General Pasquale de Paoli to assist them in driving out their French overlords. Having established a foothold in Corsica in February, by capturing San Fiorenzo in the south of the island, and having captured the port of Bastia in May, the British then laid siege to Calvi.

At Bastia, the operations had been hampered by disagreements between the senior army and navy officers. At Calvi, the British troops were commanded by Lieutenant General the Honourable Charles

Stuart, who was more prepared to work closely with his naval colleagues. As at Bastia, guns and seamen were landed from the ships to assist in the siege and these were placed under the command of Captain Nelson of the *Agamemnon*. He got the guns and equipment ashore at Porto Agro, a small inlet three and a half miles from the town, manhandled them with his crews across rough and rocky terrain and then set up batteries close to the walls of the town. He remained in the batteries to oversee the fire and, on 12 July, he narrowly escaped death when a French shot struck the parapet close to him and ricocheted over his head. Even so, the sand and gravel thrown up by the blow struck him hard in the face, lacerating his cheek and forehead and gouging a deep cut in his right brow. Worst of all, his right eye was damaged internally so that, from then on, he could not see with it, being able only to distinguish light from dark. Characteristically, he made light of the injury in his letters home but we now know from a recently discovered letter that he was so badly hurt that he had to be carried out of the battery to his tent for treatment.

The siege dragged on and the hot Corsican summer began to take its toll on the British, with malaria, heat exhaustion and dysentery decimating the ranks. But on 19 July, they managed to capture Fort Muzello, one of the keys to the Calvi defences, and this enabled them to bring their guns to bear on the town itself. Shortly after, the French commander asked for a twenty-five day truce, promising to surrender if he was not relieved during that time. No help materialised and so, on 10 August, the town formally surrendered and the Corsican campaign was finally over.

Nelson had expected to be recognised for his exploits and both General Stuart and Admiral Hood did indeed mention him briefly in their official despatches. But, even so, he was very disappointed not to be singled out, telling his elder sister Susannah Bolton, 'They have not done me justice in the affair of Calvi; but never mind one day I'll have a Gazette of my own.'

SEE ALSO
Bastia, Corsica

LATEST RESEARCH
Tom Pocock, *Nelson's Campaign in Corsica*, The 1805 Club (Shelton 1994)

Cape Finisterre, Battle of (22 July 1805)

The battle which ended finally Napoleon's ambitious plans for the invasion of England, Cape Finisterre (also known as 'Calder's Action' to distinguish it from earlier battles fought in the same waters), has been overshadowed by Nelson's much more decisive victory at Trafalgar three months later. Indeed, this engagement, although so wide-ranging in its results, was viewed by the British at the time as almost a defeat and is now virtually forgotten.

In the spring of 1805, the Emperor Napoleon ordered all his fleets to escape to sea and, having joined together in the West Indies, to return to the mouth of the Channel, sweep aside or defeat the British Channel fleet, and then sail north to the Straits of Dover to cover his invasion flotilla as it crossed to England. In the event, only the French Mediterranean fleet under Vice Admiral Pierre de Villeneuve managed to escape, pursued by Nelson and his fleet. The other British squadrons responded by concentrating at the mouth of the Channel: the usual British strategy in the face of such a threat.

Villeneuve did not wait long in the West Indies, sailing for home on 5 June, little more than a fortnight after he had arrived. Misled by inaccurate information, Nelson missed encountering his opponent by a matter of hours and had to content himself with sending a fast brig to England with the news that Villeneuve was heading east. This warning reached the Admiralty in London just before midnight on 8 July and, the following morning, the First Lord, Lord Barham, ordered the commander-in-chief of the Channel fleet, Vice Admiral William Cornwallis, to detach a squadron under Vice Admiral Robert Calder to patrol off Cape Finisterre on the northwest coast of Spain. So when, on 22 July, Villeneuve arrived in the Bay of Biscay, heading for the Spanish port of Ferrol where a squadron of Spanish battleships was waiting to join him, he found Calder blocking his way.

Calder had only fifteen battleships to Villeneuve's nineteen and the day was very misty, with shifting winds. Nonetheless he attacked, forming his fleet into a line of battle and attempting to concentrate on the van of the Franco-Spanish fleet. As gun smoke was added to fog, the conditions became very confusing and neither side could see the other clearly. Even so, the British managed to capture two Spanish ships and inflicted nearly 650 casualties for the loss of only 198. The following day, the two fleets were still in sight but Calder, knowing that there was a Spanish reinforcement not far away in Ferrol, decided not to renew the action. So Villeneuve was able to withdraw first into Vigo Bay and then into Ferrol. A few days later, he re-emerged but, clearly disconcerted by the way in which he had been intercepted so efficiently before, he sailed south to Cádiz, thus abandoning any attempt to force the Channel. When the news reached Boulogne, an irate Napoleon finally abandoned his plans for an invasion and marched, instead, on Austria, which had just signed a treaty with Britain.

Calder had won with an inferior force and had deterred Villeneuve from making any further attempt to reach the Channel. Strategically, therefore, his battle was an important victory and effectively marked the end of the campaign. But the British public had expected something much more dramatic and there was an outcry in the press. Calder demanded a court martial, expecting to clear his name but, instead, he was reprimanded for not having done his utmost to renew the action. He was never employed at sea again.

SEE ALSO
Calder, Napoleon, Trafalgar campaign, Villeneuve

LATEST RESEARCH
Robert Gardiner (ed), *The Campaign of Trafalgar*, Chatham Publishing (London 1997)
Alan Schom, *Trafalgar: Countdown to Battle*, Michael Joseph (London 1990)

Cape Ortegal, Battle of (4 November 1805)

The decisive British victory at Trafalgar on 21 October 1805 was completed by the capture two weeks later of four French battleships that had escaped at the end of the battle, bringing the total captured or destroyed to twenty-three out of a fleet of thirty-three. They were intercepted and brought to action a fortnight later off Cape Ortegal on the northwest coast of Spain, by a squadron under the command of Captain Richard Strachan. The battle is also known as 'Strachan's Action'.

During the closing stages of the Battle of Trafalgar, five ships from the Combined fleet's van, under the command of Rear Admiral Dumanoir de Pelley, made an attempt to help their beleaguered comrades in the centre. However, they were repulsed by the British and lost the Spanish *Neptuno* in the process. The remaining four managed to escape and made a wide sweep, first to the west and then north, hoping to find refuge in one of the French Atlantic ports.

However, a number of British squadrons were patrolling in the Bay of Biscay, looking out for another French force under Rear Admiral Allemand, which had escaped earlier from Rochefort and, on 2 November, some British frigates sighted Dumanoir's ships. They then found Captain Strachan and gave him the news. Strachan's four battleships were spread widely in a search pattern and he needed time to concentrate them, so the frigates *Santa Margarita* and *Phoenix* attacked the rearmost ship of Dumanoir's force, compelling him to slow down and cover her.

Meanwhile, Strachan gathered three of his battleships into line of battle. He then attacked, concentrating on the rear and centre of the French line, and a fierce battle ensued, with much manoeuvring, as the French tried to shake off their pursuers. Eventually, however, all four of their ships were forced to surrender. They were taken into the Royal Navy and one of them, the *Duguay Trouin*, survived until 1949 as the training ship *Implacable*. Strachan was promoted to rear admiral, made a baronet, and given a pension of £1000 a year.

SEE ALSO
Battle of Trafalgar

LATEST RESEARCH
Robert Gardiner (ed), *The Campaign of Trafalgar*, Chatham Publishing (London 1997)

Cape St Vincent, Battle of (14 February 1797)

On St Valentine's Day 1797, a British fleet of fifteen battleships, under Admiral Sir John Jervis, defeated a superior Spanish fleet of twenty-five battleships under Teniente General José de Córdoba y Ramos,

capturing four and badly damaging a number of others. It was Nelson's first full-scale fleet action, and the one where he first won public renown by his remarkable personal feats of courage.

At that time, the war was going badly for Britain. Six months before, Spain had allied herself with France, bringing with her a powerful fleet of some forty battleships. At the same time, the successes of the French army in Italy under their young general Napoleon Bonaparte had closed off all sources of supply. As a result, Britain had been forced to withdraw her fleet from the Mediterranean and now the French and Spanish fleets were known to be combining for a major invasion attempt.

The French had already concentrated their fleets in Brest and, in January 1797, the Spanish began moving their ships out of the Mediterranean in support. Their ships looked impressive enough but they

The Battle of Cape Ortegal, 4 November 1805. A British squadron under the overall command of Captain Sir Richard Strachan, captures four French ships that had escaped from Trafalgar.

were short of experienced seamen and supplies and so their progress was extremely slow. Additionally, the Spanish government had ordered Córdoba to escort a convoy of five merchant ships, bearing a valuable convoy of mercury to the silver mines, to Cádiz and these slowed the fleet down still further.

Stationed at Lisbon, in Portugal, Jervis was kept informed of the Spanish approach by his efficient scouting ships. But he too had his problems. His fleet had been steadily reduced by wreck and other accidents, and it was only when he received a last-minute reinforcement of five ships that he felt able to consider giving battle. Although he knew he was still

CAPE ST VINCENT
14 February 1797

1. The order of the ships in the British line of battle is different to the traditional plans. It is taken from a number of contemporary sources, most especially, a list, 'The British Line of Battle as Formed' in the *Naval Chronicle* (Vol. IV p38) and an exactly similar list in the biography of Theophilus Lee, who served as a midshipman in HMS *Barfleur*. For a full rehearsal of the evidence see: Colin White, 'The Midshipman and the Commodore: Reconstructing the British Line of Battle at Cape St Vincent,' *The Nelson Dispatch* (April 1997).

2. The small plans showing how the British attack developed are taken from Colin White, *1797: Nelson's Year of Destiny* in which the battle is reconstructed using the ship's logs and contemporay accounts.

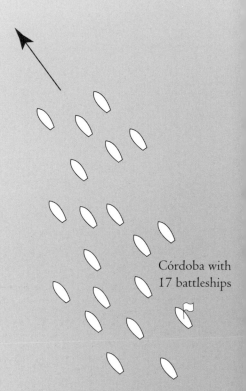

Córdoba with 17 battleships

Culloden

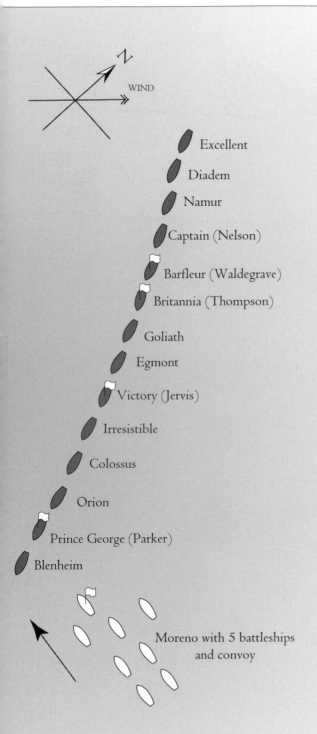

Excellent

Diadem

Namur

Captain (Nelson)

Barfleur (Waldegrave)

Britannia (Thompson)

Goliath

Egmont

Victory (Jervis)

Irresistible

Colossus

Orion

Prince George (Parker)

Blenheim

Moreno with 5 battleships
and convoy

WIND

N

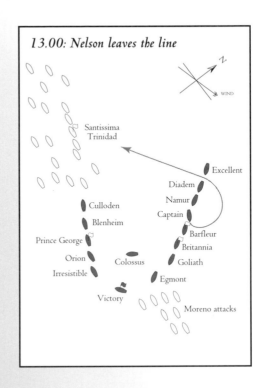

13.00: Nelson leaves the line

Santissima
Trinidad

Excellent

Diadem

Namur

Culloden

Captain

Blenheim

Barfleur

Prince George

Britannia

Orion

Colossus

Goliath

Irresistible

Egmont

Victory

Moreno attacks

WIND

N

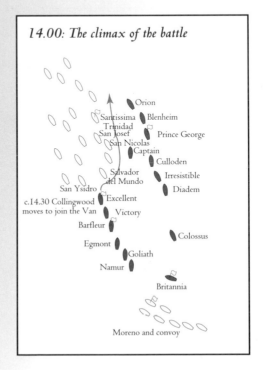

14.00: The climax of the battle

Orion

Santissima
Trinidad

Blenheim

San Josef

Prince George

San Nicolas

Captain

Culloden

Salvador
del Mundo

Irresistible

San Ysidro

Diadem

c.14.30 Collingwood
moves to join the Van

Excellent

Victory

Barfleur

Colossus

Egmont

Goliath

Namur

Britannia

Moreno and convoy

outnumbered, he was confident that the superior training and experience of his officers and men would tip the balance.

The Spanish were sighted at dawn on the morning of 14 February, sailing north in two unequal divisions. The smaller division was the vital convoy, with its escort, but Jervis was unaware of its presence and concentrated his attention, instead, on the gap between the two groups. Hurriedly assembling his line of battle, he drove his ships quickly towards it like an arrow, intent on dividing the Spanish fleet in two. It was a bold and unorthodox move but, as he later wrote in his official despatch, 'I felt myself justified in departing from the regular system.'

The Battle of Cape St Vincent, 14 February 1797. HMS Victory *(centre), flying the flag of Admiral Sir John Jervis from her mainmast, fires a broadside into the stern of the Spanish* Salvador del Mundo.

Seeing the danger, the Spanish ships in the smaller division tried to close the gap and for a while it looked as if there would be a collision between them and the leading British ship, HMS *Culloden*, commanded by Captain Thomas Troubridge. But Troubridge kept his nerve, and just managed to slip through in time, pouring a murderous double-shotted broadside into the nearest Spanish ship, and forcing her to veer her away, her sides visibly shuddering with the impact of the shot.

Having achieved his first aim, Jervis now turned his attention to the larger Spanish division, intending to launch his main attack on them. He therefore ordered his ships to tack in succession and head in their direction. As they did so, the commander of the smaller division, Teniente General Joaquin Moreno, began a series of determined attempts to break through the British line, hoping to rejoin his comrades. Each time, he was met by the disciplined,

well-aimed British broadsides and forced to retreat and so, eventually, he gave up the uneven struggle and turned away. But his attack had slowed down Jervis's manoeuvre to such an extent that it began to seem likely that the larger Spanish division might escape.

Seeing the danger, Jervis signalled to his rear division to tack immediately towards the Spanish, without waiting to follow in the wakes of the leading ships. But for some reason, the signal was not seen in the division flagship, HMS *Britannia*, and with every moment that passed the enemy drew further away. However, it was noticed by Commodore Nelson in HMS *Captain*, positioned three from the end of the British line. From this vantage point, he could also see that the larger Spanish division had begun to turn to head across the British rear, obviously hoping to join up with their comrades. Realising that urgent action was required and acting, as he felt, within the spirit of the order Jervis had just given, he wore his ship out of the battle line and headed straight for the oncoming Spanish ships. He placed himself just ahead of Troubridge's *Culloden*, which was now coming up fast and overtaking the enemy.

Traditional accounts of the battle have tended to portray this as an act of disobedience that could have led to professional ruin. But modern research into the exact sequence of signals and events has shown that Nelson was acting more in line with Jervis's intentions than has been supposed. So his manoeuvre is now seen rather as a demonstration of the remarkable degree of understanding and trust that had grown up between Nelson and his commander-in-chief. It is only fair to add, however, that few other captains would have risked it.

Whatever its exact nature, Nelson's action certainly saved the day for the British. Faced with this onslaught from a small group of well-fought ships, the Spaniards veered back onto their original course. But the delay had given the rest of the British fleet time to catch up and soon a confused, close-quarters action developed in which the superior British gunnery began to tell. Nelson's *Captain* was in the thick of the fighting and was soon a shattered wreck with a large number of her crew killed or wounded, including Nelson himself, who was hit in the stomach by a piece of flying wood. Then he spotted that two of the large Spanish ships, the *San Nicolas* and *San José*, had collided with each other and become entangled. Ordering his captain, Ralph Miller, to place the *Captain* alongside the former, he called for boarders and placed himself at their head.

It was not at all usual for a flag officer, however junior, to lead a boarding party in person. But Nelson always instinctively led from the front, especially when the action he was contemplating appeared risky. As it was, the 80-gun *San Nicolas* had already suffered heavy casualties in the earlier gun battles and so, after only a few minutes of bloody hand-to-hand fighting, she surrendered. The even larger three-decker *San José* was still trapped alongside and her crew now started firing on Nelson's party. It was an awkward moment. If the Spanish had managed to rally, Nelson and his boarders could easily have been overwhelmed.

Instead there now came the most extraordinary act in an extraordinary day. Having secured his rear by placing sentries at the hatchways, and calling for reinforcements to keep the Spaniards below, Nelson led his boarders in another furious rush, this time up the sides of the *San José* looming above them. His magnificent bluff succeeded and moments later he was receiving the surrender of a second Spanish ship (see colour plate *VI*). In the meantime, other British ships had captured a further two Spaniards and it looked as if their great four-decker flagship, the *Santíssima Trinidad*, might be taken too. But at that moment, Jervis noticed that the smaller Spanish division had at last succeeded in catching up and was beginning to threaten his rear. Reluctantly, therefore, he ordered his fleet to break off action and secure the prizes.

It was, by any standards, a remarkable victory. The confident attack in the face of such superior numbers, and the determined way in which that attack had been pressed home at every stage of the battle, demoralised the Spaniards and made them reluctant to take on the British again at sea. It gave the British a much-needed boost in morale at a dark time and confirmed the Royal Navy's reputation for victory, even against great odds. Jervis, deservedly, became Earl St Vincent and there were many other rewards, including a knighthood for Nelson.

It was a pivotal moment in Nelson's career. Before, he had been highly regarded within the Navy itself but little known outside of it. Now he became a household name. His boarding action was dubbed, 'Nelson's Patent Bridge for Boarding First Rates' and, for the first time, he found himself featured in popular prints and ballads. The glory he had sought for so long was his at last.

SEE ALSO
HMS *Captain*, Collingwood, Jervis, Miller, Saumarez, Troubridge, *San José, Santissíma Trinidad*

LATEST RESEARCH
M A J Palmer, 'Sir John's Victory: The Battle of Cape St Vincent Reconsidered', *The Mariner's Mirror* 77 (February 1991)
José Gonzales-Aller, 'The Spanish Navy in the Eighteenth Century', in Stephen Howarth (ed), *Battle of Cape St Vincent 200 Years*, The 1805 Club (Shelton 1998)
Nicholas Tracy, *Nelson's Battles*, Chatham Publishing (London 1996)
Colin White, 'The Battle of Cape St Vincent', in Stephen Howarth (ed), *Battle of Cape St Vincent 200 Years*, The 1805 Club (Shelton 1998)
_____ *1797: Nelson's Year of Destiny*, Sutton and Royal Naval Museum (Stroud & Portsmouth 1998)

Capraia, Capture of (September 1796)

A small island in the Mediterranean, lying just to the northeast of Corsica, Capraia was captured by Nelson in September 1796 in a classic small-scale combined operation. Nelson was then a commodore in command of a detached squadron operating off the northwest coast of Italy. He was sent in HMS *Captain* to the supposedly neutral port of Genoa to organise the transport of a drove of cattle to the Mediterranean fleet – an urgently needed supply of fresh meat. But he found that the French were there before him and had set up their batteries. After a few days of tense stand-off, the *Captain* was fired on and the commodore was brusquely informed that all the ports of the Republic were now closed to British ships. Nelson immediately cast about for the most effective way to make the Genoese aware of the power of the British fleet. The small Genoese-held island of Capraia had long been a thorn in the side of the British, since it acted as a safe haven for French privateers. Nelson now decided to seize the island and so he hurried to Bastia in Corsica to consult with the British viceroy, Sir Gilbert Elliot.

Elliot agreed on the need to act decisively and quickly and so, on 15 September, he gave Nelson orders to attack and capture the island. He also persuaded Lieutenant General de Burgh to give Nelson some 300 troops from the 51st and 69th Regiments to assist with the capture, under the command of Major James Logan. The troops were hurriedly embarked in HMS *Captain* and *Gorgon*, which then sailed from Bastia less than twenty-four hours after Nelson's arrival. With them went the brig *Vanneau* and a cutter, the *Rose*, and they were joined the following day by another frigate, HMS *Minerve*, under Captain George Cockburn, one of Nelson's protégés.

Despite this speedy start, the squadron took two days to reach the island because of 'excessive calm weather', as Nelson put it in his official despatch, but Nelson and Logan made good use of the time to plan their attack in more detail. The captains of the other vessels were summoned on board the *Captain* for a conference at which it emerged that Lieutenant Gourly, commanding the *Vanneau*, knew Capraia well. He told Nelson that there was a landing place on the north side of the island, close to a hill commanding the main town. It was decided that troops and guns would be landed at this point to take the town in the rear, while the rest of the squadron made a show of force in front of the town itself.

The plan worked smoothly. On 17 September, 200 troops were safely landed from the *Rose* and *Vanneau* at the appointed place and a party of seamen from the *Captain*, under the command of her second lieutenant, James Spicer, landed some cannon, which they manhandled easily up the hill and erected a battery on top of it, thus threatening the town with plunging fire. Four privateer vessels in the port attempted to escape but were prevented by Gourly in the *Vanneau*, who took his little ship right into the harbour mouth and remained there until Cockburn came up in the *Minerve* to support him. The *Minerve* had also brought Nelson and Logan to the scene and at first light on the morning of the 18th, they sent in their summons to the island authorities. Carefully drawn up by Viceroy Elliot, these offered very liberal terms: all local officials would retain their offices, local laws and religion would be preserved and all local private property would be protected. The padri del commune tried to gain time by asking permission to seek orders from Genoa but received in reply only a brusque, more threatening, letter from the British commanders, giving them just one more hour to agree to terms. With a strong force of warships off their port and a small but professional body of troops in their rear, backed by a battery of guns aimed at their houses, the padri duly surrendered.

It had been a textbook combined operation: 'I do not believe the two services ever more cordially united than on the present occasion,' Nelson later reported to Elliot. Capraia fell into the hands of the British without any bloodshed on either side, barely a week after the *Captain* had been fired upon in Genoa Roads. Retribution had been swift and ruthlessly efficient.

SEE ALSO
Cockburn, Elliot, Italian campaign

Captain, HMS

A 74-gun Third Rate battleship, HMS *Captain* was Nelson's pendant ship for almost a year, between June 1796 and May 1797. Launched in a private yard in Limehouse, London, in 1787, she had already seen much service in the Mediterranean in the early part of the war against France, including the capture of Toulon and Admiral Hotham's two indecisive actions in 1795.

In 1796, Nelson's first battleship command, HMS *Agamemnon*, was in urgent need of a full refit and was

HMS Captain *(centre). As her crew climb along her bowsprit ready to board, Nelson's pendant ship ranges alongside the Spanish* San Nicolas *at the Battle of Cape St Vincent (14 February 1797).*

ordered home to Britain. By this time, Sir John Jervis had taken command of the Mediterranean fleet and, sensing that dramatic events were about to unfold, Nelson did not wish to leave. So he arranged an exchange with Captain John Smith of HMS *Captain*, who took the *Agamemnon* home instead.

Nelson flew his commodore's pendant in the *Captain* at the Battle of Cape St Vincent (14 February 1797). It was in her that he made his famous move out of the battle line to attack the Spanish fleet and from her deck that he launched his remarkable boarding attack on two much larger Spanish ships. The *Captain* was so badly damaged in the fighting that she had to be towed to Lisbon for repairs and Nelson transferred his pendant to HMS *Irresistible*. A month later, the *Captain* returned but he remained in her for only a few weeks before transferring again, this time permanently, to HMS *Theseus*.

The *Captain* remained in active service, taking part in the capture of the West Indies island of Martinique in 1809 but, in 1813, she was accidentally burned at Plymouth.

SEE ALSO
Berry, Cape St Vincent, Capraia, Elba, Miller

Carnegie, William, Earl of Northesk (1758–1831)

The Earl of Northesk, then a rear admiral, was the third in command of the British fleet at the Battle of Trafalgar (21 October 1805), flying his flag in HMS *Britannia*. His father, the sixth earl, had also served in the Navy and so the young William went to sea in 1771, the same year as Nelson. He served as a lieutenant at Rodney's victory over the Spanish off Cape St Vincent in January 1780 and was promoted to post captain in 1782.

In 1797, he was in command of the battleship HMS *Monmouth*, one of those involved in the Mutiny at the Nore, the great naval anchorage at the mouth of the River Thames. He was asked by the delegates to take their proposals to the King, which he agreed to do; and, when the proposals were rejected, he remained in London and resigned his command.

In 1803, he was appointed to command the First Rate battleship *Britannia* and when he was promoted

to rear admiral in 1804 he remained in her. At Trafalgar, the *Britannia* lay sixth in Nelson's line and was hotly engaged with a number of allied ships, including the *Santíssima Trinidad*. Northesk was made a Knight of the Bath but did not serve at sea again. He died on 28 May 1831 and was buried in St Paul's Cathedral alongside Nelson and Collingwood.

SEE ALSO
Santíssima Trinidad, Battle of Trafalgar

Caracciolo, Francesco (1752–1799)

Commodore Prince Francesco Caracciolo of the Neapolitan Navy was found guilty of treason during the restoration of the monarchy in Naples in June 1799 and hanged from the yardarm of his flagship. Nelson's close involvement in his trial and death has been a source of controversy ever since.

A nobleman, Caracciolo was born in 1752 and saw service in the Royal Navy under Rodney during the war against America. Having distinguished himself in actions against the Algerine pirates, he rose to high rank in the Neapolitan Navy, which at that time consisted of a small but powerful squadron of five battleships with numerous small craft. As one of Britain's key allies in the Mediterranean, Naples sent troops and ships to assist in the capture and defence of Toulon in 1793 and, in 1795, Caracciolo flew his pendant in the Neapolitan 74-gun battleship *Tancredi* at the Battle of the Gulf of Genoa (13/14 March), where Nelson distinguished himself by helping in the capture of the large French battleship *Ça Ira*. Later, in December 1798, by then commander-in-chief of the Neapolitan Navy, Caracciolo helped Nelson to evacuate the royal family to Palermo when Naples fell to the advancing French armies.

Having fled to Palermo himself, he later returned to Naples to prevent his estates being confiscated by the new Parthenopean Republic. While there, he was persuaded by the Republic's leaders, many of whom were close friends and former colleagues, to take command of the Neapolitan Navy. He fought on the republican side when the British returned to Naples in June 1799 to recapture it for the King and so was regarded as a traitor by the royalists. When the republican resistance collapsed, he attempted to escape, disguised as a peasant, but was recognised and dragged back to Naples, where he was sent on board Nelson's flagship *Foudroyant* on 29 June. He was seen there by Midshipman George Parsons who noted he was '. . . haggard with misery and want; his clothing in wretched condition but his countenance denoting stern resolution to endure that misery like a man.'

He was to need all the resolution he could muster because he found Nelson in an implacable mood. A court consisting entirely of royalist officers of the Neapolitan Navy was hurriedly convened in the *Foudroyant*'s wardroom and when the inevitable guilty sentence was handed down, Nelson insisted that the execution should be conducted at once. Caracciolo's pleas for time to prepare himself, and to be executed by firing squad as befitted his noble rank, were curtly refused and he was taken across to his former flagship *Minerva* and hanged at the yardarm the same evening.

It was an ugly incident that showed the darker side of the ruthlessness that won Nelson some of his most notable successes. The sentence was not in itself wrong: in the circumstances then obtaining in Naples, Caracciolo had clearly committed treason. But the speed and apparent callousness with which the trial was conducted, and the sentence carried out, caused considerable unease at the time and still casts a shadow over Nelson's reputation today.

SEE ALSO
Gulf of Genoa, Naples, Neapolitan campaign

Carver, Nathaniel (1740–1815)

Carver was a prosperous merchant from Plymouth, Massachusetts, who was captured by Nelson in 1782 and who helped him escape from a superior French squadron. In the summer of 1782 Nelson, commanding the frigate HMS *Albemarle*, was patrolling in Massachusetts Bay (then known as 'Boston Bay'). On 14 July, he captured a Plymouth fishing schooner, the *Harmony*, and not having anyone in his ship who knew the bay and its dangerous shoals, he ordered her master, Nathaniel Carver, to come on board the *Albemarle* and act as her pilot. Despite being a prominent Massachusetts citizen, and a signatory of the 'Plymouth Petition' of 1773 against British tyranny, Carver agreed to help.

A month later, the *Albemarle* encountered a French

squadron of four battleships and the frigate *Iris*. With Carver's assistance, Nelson ran his ship among the treacherous shoals of the St George's Bank. The battleships abandoned the chase, upon which Nelson backed his main topsail and challenged the French frigate to fight but she refused and rejoined her consorts. Characteristically, Nelson decided to reward Carver for his services. He returned his schooner to him with the words, 'You have rendered us, sir, a very essential service and it is not the custom of English seamen to be ungrateful. In the name therefore, and with the approbation of the officers of this ship, I return your schooner and this certificate of your good conduct. Farewell and may God bless you!' The certificate, intended to protect Carver in case he was captured by another British ship on his way home, noted that 'on account of his good services, I have given him up his vessel again.'

So Carver went free and returned with his ship to Plymouth. But he was in a difficult position because he had, technically, been assisting the enemy. He therefore invented a remarkable story of how, having lost his ship to Nelson, he had then placed some sheep and vegetables in a small boat and sailed out to the *Albemarle*, offering these gifts in exchange for his precious schooner. Nelson, so Carver's story went, had been so overwhelmed by his kindness that he had handed back the schooner along with the certificate.

Carver's story was clearly believed for, in December 1805, when the news of Nelson's death reached America, a letter was sent from Boston to *The Naval Chronicle*, repeating the tale and reporting that the certificate 'is framed and glazed and hangs in a gentleman's parlour in Boston.'

SEE ALSO
New York

Channel Command (July–September 1801)

During the summer of 1801, Nelson was placed in command of a special anti-invasion force in the Channel. It was by far the largest fleet he ever commanded and during this time he suffered his only defeat at the hands of the French. Yet it is one of the least-known aspects of his career.

Returning home from the Baltic in early July 1801, exhausted after a long and demanding campaign following the Battle of Copenhagen, Nelson found Britain in the grips of an invasion scare. Rumours were flying around about French troops massed in Boulogne and the neighbouring ports, ready to cross the Channel. We now know that these threats were largely a bluff by Napoleon, designed to bring Britain, his last remaining major opponent, to the negotiating table. But, at the time, the British took the threat very seriously. Even the First Lord of the Admiralty, the veteran Admiral Lord St Vincent, was convinced by the intelligence reports. He decided to deal with the threat by creating a new, unified and mobile force of small vessels, with the sole purpose of 'frustrating the enemy's designs'. And in what was clearly meant as a public relations exercise – to show the French that he meant business, and to calm fears at home – St Vincent gave command of this new force to the Victor of the Nile and Copenhagen. Nelson was ordered first to make arrangements for defending the mouth of the Thames and then to find a way of destroying the enemy's flotilla.

Nelson arrived in Deal on 29 July and hoisted his flag in HMS *Medusa*, a fine new 32-gun frigate. Three days later he appeared off Boulogne where he found that the French admiral, Latouche Tréville, had moored a line of small ships outside the harbour to defend the approaches. On 4 August, Nelson ordered his bomb vessels to shell these ships and a major bombardment ensued, without much effect. But Nelson had now seen for himself that the feared invasion was not going to come from Boulogne and so he set off on a tour of his command, trying to discover where the invasion army was based. A reconnaissance of Ostend and Blankenberg revealed that there were only sixty or seventy boats in the ports, scarcely enough to transport 3000 men. 'Where, my dear Lord,' Nelson asked St Vincent, 'is our Invasion to come from?' Even so, characteristically, he was looking for a target at which to launch a major offensive blow: 'to crush the enemy at home', as he put it. So, eventually, almost by a process of elimination, the idea grew of a full-scale attack on the French flotilla defending Boulogne. That attack, launched during the night of 15/16 August, was repulsed with heavy loss.

A few weeks after the battle, the British government opened peace negotiations with France: Napoleon's bluff had succeeded. As soon as Nelson heard of this, in early September, he began asking to be relieved of his command. His health was beginning to give way again and he was depressed by the long drawn out sufferings of Captain Edward Parker, who had been dangerously wounded in the thigh at Boulogne and whom he regarded almost as a son. Eventually, after bravely enduring the agonies of amputation, Parker died on 27 September and at his funeral in the burial ground of St George's Church, Deal, a distressed Nelson was seen leaning against a tree weeping. But Lord St Vincent, while offering sincere sympathy for his personal troubles, firmly refused to release him. He was kept at his post until 22 October when, finally, he was allowed to go on leave and hastened to join the Hamiltons in his new home at Merton Place in Surrey, which Emma Hamilton had purchased for him while he was still fretting at sea.

SEE ALSO
Boulogne, Latouche Tréville, Edward Parker

LATEST RESEARCH
Rémi Monaque, 'Latouche-Tréville: The admiral who defied Nelson', *The Mariner's Mirror* 86 (August 2000)
Tom Pocock, 'The Summer of 1801: Nelson at Deal and Boulogne', *The Nelson Dispatch* 7 (July 2001), The Nelson Society
Colin White, 'Nelson's Channel Order Book', *The Naval Miscellany* VI (London 2003), The Navy Records Society

Chatham

Situated on the south side of the mouth of the River Thames, where it commanded the approaches to the Port of London, Chatham was one of the three key Royal Dockyards in Nelson's day. The dockyard itself lay along the banks of the River Medway and close by was the sheltered anchorage of the Nore, where large ships could lie at anchor.

Nelson visited Chatham many times. He joined his first ship there, HMS *Raisonnable*, in early 1771 and commissioned his first battleship command there, HMS *Agamemnon*, in 1793. His famous flagship HMS *Victory* was built there, and returned often for refits, including the great repair she underwent after the Battle of Trafalgar in late 1805.

Abandoned by the Royal Navy in the 1980s, the eighteenth-century Royal Dockyard has been preserved as a heritage area. Many of the buildings Nelson knew have survived, including the grand entrance gateway through which he would have passed so often, the elegant Commissioner's House where he attended formal functions and the great storehouses where he obtained supplies for his ships.

SEE ALSO
HMS *Raisonnable*, HMS *Victory*

LATEST RESEARCH
Roger Morriss, *The Royal Dockyards during the Revolutionary and Napoleonic Wars*, Leicester University Press (Leicester 1983)
Jonathan Coad, *The Royal Dockyards, 1690–1850*, Scholar Press (Aldershot 1989)

Clarence, Duke of *See: William IV*

Coat of Arms, Nelson's

In 1797, Nelson was made a Knight of Bath as a reward for his exploits at the Battle of Cape St Vincent (14 February 1797). His family already had a coat of arms but Nelson's knighthood entitled him to a full set of supporters on either side of the shield and, with his customary interest in the promotion of his own image, he set about designing some that would reflect his recent deeds. On one side of the shield, he wanted a sailor holding a commodore's pendant and, on the other, a British lion tearing a Spanish flag. Above the shield was a crest featuring the stern of the *San José*, one of the two Spanish ships he had captured.

Chatham Royal Dockyard, c1790. This shows the famous dockyard very much as it appeared when Nelson joined his first ship, HMS Raisonnable, *there in 1771.*

Nelson's coat of arms. This is the final version of Nelson's arms, produced after the Battle of Copenhagen, when he was made a viscount. The sailor 'supporter' was Nelson's own idea – it was more usual to have 'heraldic' figures on either side of the shield. (Courtesy The Nelson Society)

At the time, the College of Arms in London – which then, as now, controlled all matters to do with heraldry in Britain – was headed by Sir Isaac Heard, Garter King at Arms. Heard had served in the Royal Navy as a young man and had designed for himself a coat of arms that reflected his own naval service. So he was generally sympathetic to Nelson's wishes, although he was concerned about the use of the Spanish flag, which at that time included the arms of the Spanish royal family. He suggested that such a gesture '. . . might hereafter be considered as indelicate from a truly gallant hero to a subdued enemy which may . . . become a friendly power.' So Nelson's supporters duly appeared, but with the Spanish flag arranged so that the royal coat of arms was not visible. Nelson's use of a sailor as a supporter was a heraldic innovation and set a precedent, which has been followed by a number of naval knights and peers since.

The following year, Nelson was created a baron as a reward for this victory at the Battle of the Nile and so became entitled to 'augment' his arms. On this occasion, Heard himself suggested an addition to the shield itself of a seascape representing the battle, fea-

turing a palm tree, a disabled ship and a ruined battery. Such pictorial heraldry was much frowned on by heraldic purists, but Nelson naturally was delighted and agreed to the change, together with an addition to his crest that showed the famous 'chelengk' or plume of triumph, awarded to him by the Sultan of Turkey. At the same time, the motto was changed from the original and rather uninspiring 'Faith and Works', which had been suggested by Nelson's clerical brother William, to the more imaginative 'Palmam qui meruit ferat' (Let him who has deserved it bear the palm), with its punning reference to the Nile. The supporting sailor and lion each acquired a palm branch and the lion was given a French flag to tear as well as the Spanish one.

These were the last changes made to the arms in Nelson's lifetime, although they were of course extensively changed after Trafalgar when they passed to his brother William. Nelson remained keenly interested in them and a recently discovered letter reveals that, as late as April 1805, he was still corresponding with Heard about their details: '. . . there is one omission in the drawing, the Spanish flag is omitted upon the second flag staff . . . <u>do not</u> forget the Spanish flag.'

SEE ALSO
Decorations and medals

LATEST RESEARCH
Ron Fiske, 'Nelson's Arms and Hatchments', *The Nelson Dispatch* 6 (1999), The Nelson Society
David White, 'The Arms of Nelson', *The Trafalgar Chronicle* 8 (1998), The 1805 Club

Cockburn, Sir George (1772–1853)

George Cockburn served with Nelson in the Mediterranean during 1795–1797 and commanded the frigate HMS *Minerve* when Nelson flew his pendant in her during the evacuation of Elba in January 1797. Even though he joined the Navy during peace, the assistance of some influential patrons – including Admiral Lord Hood and Lord Chatham, the First Lord of the Admiralty – ensured that he received very rapid promotion, becoming a post captain in 1794, when he was just twenty-two.

Appointed to command the frigate HMS *Meleager*, he was sent to the Mediterranean where he was present at Hotham's two actions in March and July 1795. The following year, the *Meleager* was part of Commodore Nelson's detached squadron operating off the northwest coast of Italy and it was during this time that the two men came to appreciate each other's qualities. Nelson once wrote to him, '. . . we think so alike on points of service that if your mind tells you it is right, there can hardly be a doubt but I must approve.' Cockburn returned this admiration fully, writing, '. . . next to my own father, I know of none whose company I so much wish to be in or who I have such real reason to respect.'

Cockburn's services with Nelson were rewarded with the command of a larger frigate, the 42-gun *Minerve*, and in December 1796 Nelson selected her as his temporary pendant ship when he was sent by Admiral Sir John Jervis to organise the evacuation of the British forces from Elba, following the withdrawal of the British fleet from the Mediterranean. Nelson was on board for less than two months but it proved an eventful cruise. On the way to Elba, the *Minerve* fell in with the Spanish frigate *Santa Sabina*, which she captured in a fierce night action. On the way back to join Jervis in February 1797, the frigate sailed right through the middle of the main Spanish fleet, which was then making its way through the Straits of Gibraltar en route to join with the French Brest fleet in an invasion of Ireland. Nelson and Cockburn shadowed the Spaniards until they were sure of their course and then sailed north to bring the news to Jervis, thus enabling the admiral to place his fleet in the most advantageous position to give battle. Cockburn and the *Minerve* played no part in the ensuing action off Cape St Vincent but, following the battle, Jervis detached them to hunt for the badly damaged Spanish flagship *Santissíma Trinidad*.

Thereafter, apart from a brief spell in the Mediterranean in 1799, Cockburn did not serve with Nelson again. Promoted rear admiral in 1812, he was sent to the American station where he commanded the British squadron operating in the Chesapeake. He is famous for his riverborne attack on Washington in 1814 when the newly constructed White House was burned. In 1815, he commanded the squadron that conveyed Napoleon to captivity on St Helena and was the first governor of the island until relieved by Sir Hudson Lowe in 1816. He was one of the last sur-

vivors of Nelson's captains and, by the time he eventually died in 1853, he had risen to admiral of the fleet.

SEE ALSO
Hardy, Italian campaign

LATEST RESEARCH
Roger Morriss, *Cockburn and the British Navy in Transition*, Exeter University Press (Exeter 1997)
A J Pack, *The Man who burned the White House*, Mason (Emsworth 1987)

Codrington, Sir Edward (1770–1851)

One of Nelson's captains at Trafalgar, Codrington remained in active service long enough to command the British fleet in the last major battle fought wholly under sail, Navarino, in 1827. Having joined the Navy in 1783, he became a lieutenant in 1793 and was signal officer of Admiral Lord Howe's flagship, HMS *Queen Charlotte*, at the Glorious First of June in 1794. A personal protégé of Howe, he was given the honour of taking home the admiral's victory despatch and, as was customary, was rewarded with promotion to the rank of commander. The following year he was made a captain.

In 1805, he commanded the 74-gun battleship HMS *Orion* at Trafalgar (21 October 1805) and played a key role in the closing stages of the battle, helping to save the badly damaged *Victory* from a Franco/Spanish counterattack and assisting in the capture of the very gallantly fought French ship *Intrépide*. He continued in active service throughout the rest of the war, serving in the disastrous amphibious attack on the Dutch island of Walcheren in 1809 and off the coast of Spain in support of Wellington's land campaign in 1811/12. Promoted to rear admiral in 1814, he was captain of the fleet to the commander-in-chief of the North American station, Sir Alexander Cochrane, during the closing stages of the war with America, and took part in operations in the Chesapeake River and in the attack on New Orleans.

In 1827, by then a vice admiral, he became commander-in-chief in the Mediterranean, with his flag flying in HMS *Asia*. At that time, the Greeks were in open revolt against their Turkish overlords. Britain, although not formally at war with Turkey, was generally sympathetic to the Greek cause, which placed Codrington in a very difficult position. The growing tension eventually led to a full-scale battle in the Bay of Navarino in southern Greece, on 20 October 1827, where the Turkish fleet was annihilated by a combined British, French and Russian fleet under Codrington's command, thus paving the way for Greek independence which came two years later.

Although the victory was popular with the people of Britain, Codrington was recalled 'for explanations' by a government embarrassed by such overt intervention: the new prime minister, the Duke of Wellington, attempted to dismiss it as 'an untoward incident'. However, Codrington was cleared of blame and continued to serve in the Navy. He commanded the Channel squadron in 1831/2 and then ended a long and distinguished career as commander-in-chief at Plymouth during 1839–1842.

SEE ALSO
Battle of Trafalgar

Coffin, Nelson's

Nelson's body lies in the crypt of St Paul's Cathedral inside an elaborate marble sarcophagus. It is protected by no fewer than three coffins: an elaborate external, or 'state', casket, decorated with gilded emblems celebrating his victories and achievements; a lead shell; and, inside them all, a very plain, roughly made wooden coffin. It is the wooden coffin that is the most historically interesting.

After the Battle of the Nile, a piece of the mainmast of the French flagship *L'Orient* was found floating in Aboukir Bay. It was rescued by sailors from the British battleship *Swiftsure* and their captain, Ben Hallowell, ordered his carpenter to make a coffin from it. Some nine months later, on 23 May 1799, he presented it to Nelson with the wish 'that when you are tired of this life, you may be buried in one of your trophies.'

The coffin arrived at a time when Nelson was suffering from depression – caused, at least in part, by his growing passion for Emma Hamilton and consequent guilty conscience – and Hallowell's macabre gift appears to have suited this black mood. He first had it displayed publicly on the quarterdeck of his flagship and, spotting some of his officers eyeing it in astonishment, he said, 'You may *look* at it, gentlemen, as long as you please; but depend upon it, none

of you shall *have* it.' It was then moved to his cabin, where it stood upright behind his chair where he sat at dinner, and subsequently accompanied him, as part of his luggage, during his long overland journey home to England with the Hamiltons in 1800.

In London, the coffin was lodged with Nelson's agents, Messrs Marsh, Page and Creed. During his brief spell of leave in the autumn of 1805, just before the Battle of Trafalgar, Nelson visited them and asked them to have the coffin's history engraved upon the lid, as he felt he might have need of it on his return. His wishes were honoured and the coffin was duly ferried out to the *Victory* to receive his body when it arrived back in England in December 1805.

SEE ALSO
HMS *Foudroyant*, Funeral, Hallowell, *L'Orient*, Nile

Collingwood, Cuthbert Lord (1750–1810)

Nelson's relationship with Collingwood was very different to that which he shared with most of the 'Band of Brothers'. They served together on a number of occasions throughout their lives, and were close, and even affectionate, personal friends. But 'Col', as Nelson always called him, was by nature an aloof and reserved man, except with his family and a few close friends. So their friendship remained essentially a one-to-one affair and Collingwood was never really part of the intimate inner circle that surrounded Nelson.

A Northumbrian, Collingwood was born in Newcastle on 26 September 1750 and educated at the local grammar school. He first went to sea in 1761 in the frigate HMS *Shannon* with a cousin, Captain Braithwaite, with whom he continued to serve for the next eleven years. At the outbreak of the war with America in 1775, he served ashore with a party of seamen at the Battle of Bunker Hill, was promoted to lieutenant, and later saw service in the West Indies where he was appointed as first lieutenant of the frigate *Lowestoffe* under Captain William Locker in 1778. The vacancy had occurred because Horatio Nelson had just been made first lieutenant of the flagship HMS *Bristol* and, for the next few years, Collingwood's career shadowed Nelson's. When

Nelson was promoted post captain and took command of the frigate HMS *Hinchinbrooke* in 1779, Collingwood was made commander and given Nelson's former sloop, the *Badger*. The following year, when Nelson was given the larger frigate HMS *Janus*, Collingwood followed him into the *Hinchinbrooke*.

During the peace, they met up again in the West Indies when Collingwood commanded the frigate *Mediator* and Nelson the *Boreas*. They collaborated in the campaign against illicit trading that later caused Nelson so much trouble, and they also fell in love with the same woman, Mary Moutray, the wife of the Commissioner of English Harbour in Antigua. Instead of causing friction between them, this shared unrequited love appears to have cemented their friendship and, at some point, they each drew the other's portrait. Nelson's likeness of Collingwood is a reasonably accomplished silhouette; Collingwood's response is a rather wooden profile, showing Nelson wearing a most unflattering wig.

In 1786, Collingwood returned home and spent a happy time in Northumberland with his family; in marked contrast to Nelson's frustrated and unhappy years 'on the beach' during the same period. In 1793, he was appointed to command the battleship HMS *Prince* and then the *Barfleur*, flying the flag of Rear Admiral George Bowyer, in which he played a key role in the Battle of the Glorious First of June in 1794. Then, in 1795, he was appointed to command HMS *Excellent* and was sent in her to the Mediterranean, where he met up with Nelson again, then in command of the *Agamemnon*. The two old friends subsequently served together at the Battle of Cape St Vincent (14 February 1797) where Collingwood played as important a role as Nelson, securing the surrender of two Spanish ships; almost capturing the great four-decker flagship *Santissíma Trinidad*, and at one point even coming to the rescue of Nelson's *Captain*, which had been battered by the broadsides of at least four large Spanish ships. The day after the battle, Nelson wrote to him, '…"A friend in need is a friend indeed" was never more truly verified than by your most noble and gallant conduct yesterday in sparing the *Captain* from further loss.' To which Collingwood replied, 'It added very much to the satisfaction which I felt in thumping the Spaniards that I released you a little.'

Vice Admiral Cuthbert Lord Collingwood. Collingwood is shown in c1802. He is wearing his full dress uniform, with the medals for the Battles of the Glorious First of June and St Vincent in his lapel.

For the next two years, Collingwood and the *Excellent* remained with Lord St Vincent's fleet off Cadiz. Having returned to Britain in early 1799, Collingwood was promoted to rear admiral in February and appointed to the Channel fleet, flying his flag in HMS *Triumph*, and then moving to his old ship the *Barfleur* in early 1800. He and Nelson met again when Nelson was appointed to the Channel fleet in January 1800 and there is a rather poignant story of how they dined together in Plymouth with Collingwood's beloved wife and daughter, who had travelled the length of England to be with him. Collingwood described the scene to their old friend Mary Moutray, 'How surprised you would have been to have popped into the Fountain Inn and see Lord Nelson, my wife and myself sitting by the fire cosing and little Sarah teaching Phyllis, her dog, to dance.' Such a scene of domestic bliss must have been peculiarly painful for Nelson at a time when his own marriage was on the point of breaking up.

The two friends did not meet again for over five years. Collingwood remained with the Channel fleet until the Peace of Amiens in 1802, returning to the station after a short break in 1803. There he continued until the great naval campaign in the summer of 1805, during which he was detached with a small squadron to Cádiz, where the Combined fleet under Villeneuve took refuge in August. So it at first fell to him to watch them until he was joined, and superseded, by Nelson on 28 September. It could have been an awkward moment but the two friends worked well together, as always, and Nelson treated Collingwood with special consideration, consulting him about all his decisions and giving him on the day of battle complete control of his division of the fleet. Collingwood responded magnificently, leading his line with panache and gallantry.

Nelson's death came as a shocking blow and Collingwood was greatly shaken by it, referring in all his letters to the 'most poignant grief' that he felt at the loss. But he also shouldered the unexpected burden of command with courage and considerable skill; so much so, that he was confirmed as Nelson's successor as commander-in-chief of the Mediterranean, thus following in his friend's footsteps for the last time. He remained at his post for over four more years without relief, growing more and more ill with the strain of command, and eventually died on 7 March 1810, while on his way to take some long overdue sick leave. His body was brought back to Britain where it first lay in state in the Painted Hall at Greenwich and was then buried in the crypt of St Paul's alongside Nelson.

Collingwood was a distinguished ship's captain who played an important part in three of the most important naval battles of his period. But his career as an admiral was less noteworthy and so in the past historians have tended to compare him unfavourably with the more glamorous Nelson. Nowadays, he tends to be valued rather more highly, both for his leadership qualities, and for his personal integrity and essential decency; qualities that Nelson himself recognised and respected. As he told him in a letter written just before Trafalgar, 'No man has more confidence in another than I have in you, and no one will

Staffordshire figure of Nelson. This is an early piece of 'Nelsonia', produced in 1798, immediately after the news of the Battle of the Nile reached Britain.

render your services more justice than your very old friend.'

SEE ALSO
'Band of Brothers', Cape St Vincent, Mary Moutray, Battle of Trafalgar

LATEST RESEARCH
Piers Mackesy, *The War in the Mediterranean, 1803–1810*, Longmans (London 1957)

Commemorative material

Nelson is one of the most commemorated people in British history. Large amounts of commemorative items were produced in his lifetime and he has remained popular with the producers of popular art ever since. The first great flood of material came in 1798 following his stunning victory at the Nile and the second came after Trafalgar. After a decline in the middle of the nineteenth century, there was a fresh surge in the build-up to the centenary of his death in 1905 and even to this day new pieces are regularly produced. As the Trafalgar Bicentenary approaches, yet another revival of interest is inevitable.

The media in which Nelson has been commemorated are many and varied. Most numerous are ceramics but he has also appeared on glassware, fans, enamels, metalware, textiles, waxes – in short, in any form available (see colour plates *XVII* and *XVIII*).

'Nelsonia', as it is called, is very popular with collectors, and items that once sold for a few pence now fetch high prices in the sale-rooms. Collections of such items can be seen in all of the museums with Nelson exhibitions but, by common consent, one of the very finest is the Lily Lambert McCarthy Collection at the Royal Naval Museum in Portsmouth. Built up with diligent care over a period of forty years by an American lady with a special affection for, and knowledge of, Nelson, it contains excellent examples of almost every type of commemorative item.

SEE ALSO
Museums, Relics

LATEST RESEARCH
John May, 'Nelson Commemorated', in Colin White (ed), *The Nelson Companion*, Sutton and Royal Naval Museum (Stroud & Portsmouth 1995)
Lily McCarthy, *Remembering Nelson*, The Royal Naval Museum (Portsmouth 1995)

Comyn, Rev Stephen (1766–1839)

Nelson's chaplain from 1798 to 1801, Stephen Comyn served with the admiral at the Battle of the Nile (1 August 1798) and the Battle of Copenhagen (2 April 1801). He first went to sea at the age of thirty-two in March 1798, as the chaplain of HMS *Vanguard*. A religious man himself, Nelson always took special care to ensure that his ships had good chaplains and he also made special arrangements with the Society for the Promotion of Christian Knowledge (SPCK) for the supply of bibles and prayer books to his ships' companies.

During the Battle of the Nile, Comyn helped to attend to Nelson when he was wounded at the height of the battle and received messages from him for Lady Nelson. Afterwards he conducted a public service of thanksgiving on the quarterdeck of the *Vanguard*, an act that much impressed the captured French officers who happened to be on board. Later, in June 1799, he transferred with Nelson to his new flagship the *Foudroyant* and continued to serve with him until Nelson left the ship in the summer of 1800.

The young clergyman had obviously impressed Nelson for, when he went to sea again in January 1801, Comyn was summoned to join him, first in HMS *San Josef* and then in HMS *St George*. He served with Nelson throughout the Baltic campaign. By now, however, he was ready to return to a career ashore and so he persuaded Nelson to use his influence to obtain a parish for him. Nelson duly obliged and, in June 1802, Comyn was made rector of St Mary's, Bridgham, in Norfolk. He served there for thirty-seven years, dying eventually on 17 March 1839.

SEE ALSO
HMS *Foudroyant*, Religious faith, HMS *Vanguard*

LATEST RESEARCH
The Nelson Society, HMS *Vanguard at the Nile*, The Nelson Society (1998)

Copenhagen, Battle of (2 April 1801)

The second of Nelson's three great victories, Copenhagen was his hardest fought major battle, in which he came close to defeat and eventually won by a characteristic combination of determined ruthlessness and humanity.

In 1800, the Baltic was a vital source of trade and maritime supplies for Britain, worth over £3 million in the prices of the day. So when, under the influence of a pro-French Russia, the Baltic states formed themselves into an 'Armed Neutrality of the North' and placed an embargo on British ships, the British government felt compelled to take action. A special

COPENHAGEN
2 April 1801

1. Most plans currently available are based entirely on British records but a lot of new information about the exact composition of the Danish line of defence is now available, based on Danish sources. The Danish line shown here is therefore based on this new material.

2. The plan showing the development of the battle is taken from material put together by 'The Inshore Squadron' a group of naval wargamers who have created a computer programme showing the different stages of the battle.

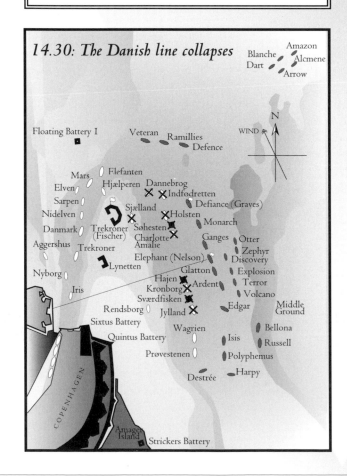

14.30: The Danish line collapses

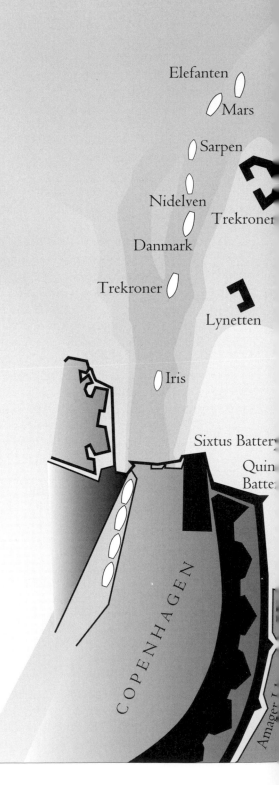

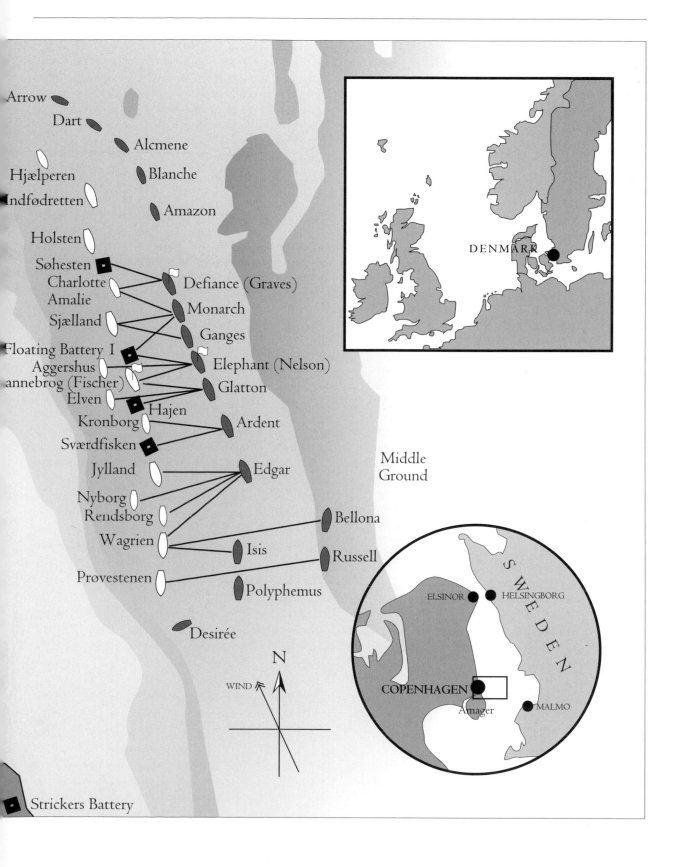

Arrow

Dart

Alcmene

Blanche

Hjælperen

Indfødretten

Amazon

Holsten

Søhesten

Charlotte   Defiance (Graves)

Amalie   Monarch

Sjælland   Ganges

Floating Battery I

Aggershus   Elephant (Nelson)

Dannebrog (Fischer)

Elven   Glatton

Kronborg   Hajen   Ardent

Sværdfisken

Jylland   Edgar

Nyborg

Rendsborg   Bellona

Wagrien   Isis

Prøvestenen   Russell

                   Polyphemus

Desirée

Middle
Ground

N

WIND

ELSINOR   HELSINGBORG

S W E D E N

COPENHAGEN

Amager   MALMO

DENMARK

Strickers Battery

fleet was formed at Great Yarmouth on the coast of Norfolk, under the overall command of Admiral Sir Hyde Parker, an experienced, if rather unimaginative, commander with good prior knowledge of the Baltic. Nelson was appointed his second. From the first, there was tension between the two men: the cautious and rather reserved Parker obviously regarding his younger and more charismatic subordinate with a certain amount of reserve.

Denmark, with its key strategic position at the entrance of the Baltic, was seen as the first target of the expedition, but Parker had been ordered to try to negotiate a settlement before beginning hostilities. So he kept the fleet at anchor off Elsinore while the diplomats made their last attempts to prevent a conflict. This pause gave the Danes time to strengthen their defences. The negotiations failed and Parker then appeared off Copenhagen itself with his entire force.

The city, and the main Danish naval arsenal, lay close to the deepwater channel and so were very vulnerable to bombardment from the sea. In an attempt to prevent this, the Danes had moored a makeshift line of old warships and floating batteries in the main channel, manned with a mixture of professional sailors, and hastily raised volunteers. At the head of the line was a newly constructed fort, the Trekroner Battery, and the line was further protected by a complex maze of shoals, made all the more confusing by the fact that the Danes had removed all the usual markers. In command of this defensive line was Commodore Olfert Fischer, flying his pendant in the old battleship *Dannebrog*.

From a distance, these defences appeared formidable but Nelson felt confident he could deal with them. Noticing that the Danish line was strongest in the north, he decided to attack instead from the south, knocking out the Danish ships in turn and then moving northwards to deal with the headmost ships. Once these had been silenced, the Trekroner Battery would be assaulted, using troops that had been specially attached to the expedition. At that point, Nelson planned to bring up his bomb-vessels and threaten the city and naval arsenal with bombardment, thus, it was hoped, inducing the Danish government to sue for peace.

Nelson prepared for the battle with his usual meticulous care. He ordered a detailed reconnaissance of the Danish line to attempt to pinpoint the shoals that surrounded it, and went himself in one of the smaller vessels of the fleet to see the situation at first hand. He then gave a dinner for some of his key captains to tell them of his plans and followed this verbal briefing with very detailed written instructions. He also experienced his usual good luck. To succeed, his plan required a northerly wind to carry his ships into their positions to start the attack and then a southerly one to carry them into action – and the wind duly obliged.

The attack began at 9.30am on the morning of 2 April and, from the start, the British encountered problems with the complex shoals. The *Agamemnon* found herself pinned against them and could not get under way at all and two more battleships went aground and were unable to take their appointed places in the attacking line. So, Nelson's attack force of twelve battleships was reduced by a quarter almost before the action had begun. Nevertheless, Nelson pressed on and, by 11.30am, all the available British ships were engaged, including the frigates under Captain Edward Riou, which gallantly took on the formidable Trekroner Battery.

They encountered a most determined resistance from the Danes and a heavy gunnery duel ensued. Almost immediately, the *Dannebrog* was set on fire by inflammable 'carcass' shot fired from the *Glatton* (commanded by Captain William Bligh of *Bounty* fame) and Commodore Fischer was forced to move his pendant to another ship. At such close range, the casualties were very heavy: both sides lost some 1000 men killed and wounded.

Meanwhile, Parker was moving in slowly, against contrary winds, with the rest of the fleet from the north. He could see that Nelson's force had been reduced and that the Danish fire still appeared unabated, even after nearly two hours of intense fighting. So, at about 1.00pm, thinking that Nelson might be forced to break off the action, he hoisted a signal ordering him to do so. Nelson, however, could see that to withdraw at that point, with the northern end of the Danish line still undefeated, would have been suicidal. So, famously, he claimed that he could not see the signal and ordered that his own signal for 'Close Action' should remain flying.

Another hour passed and still the Danish line very largely held firm. But, at around 1.45pm, Nelson began to detect that their fire was slackening and, wishing to avoid further unnecessary bloodshed, he decided on a most unusual course of action. Calling for ink, paper and sealing wax, he dashed off a hurried note, threatening to burn the prizes he had taken if the Danes did not agree to an immediate ceasefire. Instead of sending it to his immediate opponent, Olfert Fischer, he addressed it to the Danish government and it was carried ashore by Captain Frederick Thesiger (who spoke Danish) in an open boat flying a flag of truce.

The boat took about half an hour to reach the point on the shore from which the Crown Prince of Denmark was directing operations and, during that time, the whole of the centre of the Danish line suddenly collapsed. So, by the time Crown Prince Frederick received Nelson's threat, most of his defensive line had ceased to exist and, through the gap, he could see the British bomb-vessels in position, ready to start bombarding. He therefore decided to accept the opportunity Nelson had offered and

The Battle of Copenhagen, 2 April 1801. This aerial view of the battle, by Nicholas Pocock, was produced for the 'official' biography by Clarke and M'Arthur in 1809. Like all Pocock's work, it is carefully researched and so the depiction of the British ships is excellent. The Danish line, however, is not accurate.

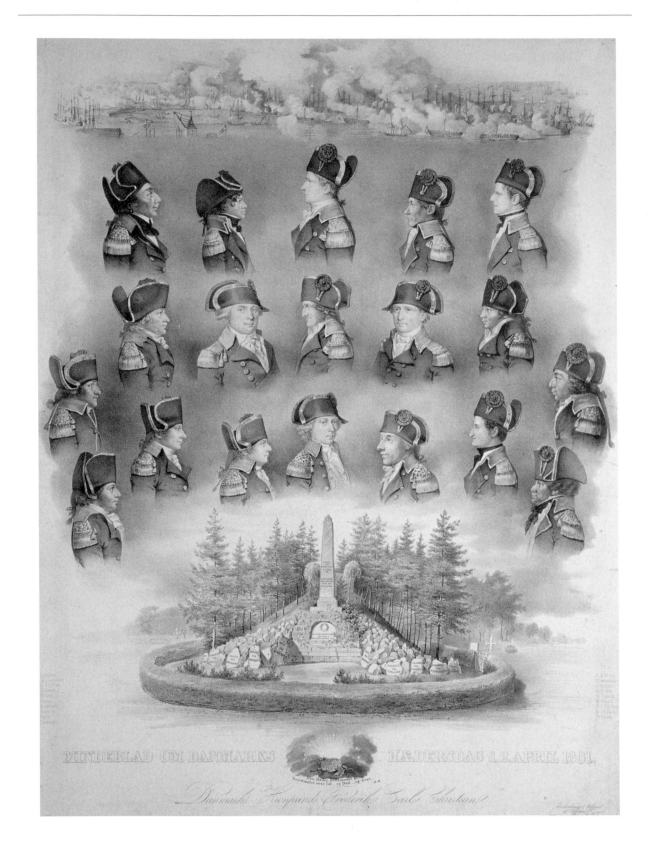

sent his aide de camp to question him more closely about his intentions. In reply, Nelson declared that his object was humanity, springing from a genuine desire to avoid any further unnecessary bloodshed, and he urged the Prince to agree to an armistice. The Prince agreed to a formal ceasefire and the battle finally ended at about 3.00pm.

Nelson's famous message has attracted much controversy and is still regarded by some Danish historians as a questionable *ruse de guerre*. But Nelson always insisted that humanity had indeed been his first object. Certainly his credentials are strong, since he was usually a humane man and famously prayed for 'humanity after victory' just before Trafalgar. But he was also conscious that the defeat of the Danes was but the first step in a much bigger campaign and, during the negotiations, frankly admitted that he wanted to gain time to move up the Baltic and deal with the Russians, whom he saw as the main foe.

In fact, no such extension of the campaign was required, since the pro-French Tsar Paul had been assassinated on 24 March. When news of the battle reached Britain, Parker was recalled and Nelson placed in chief command. Without Paul's influence, the Armed Neutrality began to dissolve and by the middle of June 1801 British trade in the Baltic was flowing freely once again.

As well as being the most hard-fought of Nelson's battles, Copenhagen was also the most controversial. Public celebrations were muted and no official medal was awarded, an omission that Nelson strove unsuccessfully to rectify for the rest of his life. In the older histories, it is usually portrayed as a hard-won, but ultimately overwhelming, victory over a gallant and determined foe. But modern Danish and British research has established that it was in fact a very close-run contest indeed. In public, Nelson always maintained that the victory had been as decisive as the other major battles of the period. But, in a private letter to his friend the Duke of Clarence, discovered only recently, he admitted that 'very untoward circumstances prevented our success from being so compleat as I intended.' (See full transcript on p268.)

SEE ALSO
Atkinson, Bligh, Blind Eye, Fischer, Hardy, Hyde Parker, Riou, Stewart, Thesiger, Thompson

LATEST RESEARCH
Ole Feldbæk, *Slaget på Reden*, Politikens (Copenhagen 2001; English translation forthcoming)
Colin White, 'The Battle from Nelson's Quarterdeck', *Proceedings of the Copenhagen 200 Conference*, The 1805 Club (Shelton 2002)

Cornwallis, Sir William (1744–1819)

Cornwallis and Nelson only served together briefly, as young men in the West Indies, but the bond that was formed between them remained strong for the rest of their lives. And in 1805, they were key players in the remarkable campaign that defeated Napoleon's ambitious plans to invade Britain.

Born on 20 February 1744, Cornwallis was a member of a distinguished military and political family and so when he entered the Royal Navy in 1755, after a brief spell at Eton, it was under the patronage of the Duke of Newcastle, then Secretary of State. Having served at the capture of Louisbourg in 1758 and the Battle of Quiberon Bay the following year, he became a lieutenant in 1761, commander in 1764 and post captain the year after, when he was just twenty-one. Like Nelson, he owed his rapid advance during these crucial early years not only to patronage but also to his own outstanding abilities.

During the peace, he became a member of parliament, first for Portsmouth and then for Eye in Suffolk and, despite long absences at sea on active service, remained an MP until 1807. When war broke out with America in 1776, he was appointed to the frigate HMS *Pallas*, eventually transferring to the 64-gun battleship HMS *Lion* in 1778. The following year, he commanded her in a sharp engagement with the French in which she was so badly damaged that he had to take her to Jamaica for a thorough refit. It was there that he first met Nelson who was waiting to take up command of his first frigate, the *Hinchinbrooke*. Despite the age gap, they quickly became friends and years later Nelson reminded his colleague of a maxim Cornwallis had taught him,

Page opposite: The Danish captains at Copenhagen. This contemporary Danish engraving includes portraits of all the Danish captains, including Commodore Olfert Fischer (top row, centre). The vignette at the top shows the battle from the Danish viewpoint.

'. . . You can always beat a Frenchman if you fight him long enough.' The friendship was further cemented the following year, when Nelson returned to Jamaica after the Nicaraguan campaign, suffering from a near-fatal combination of dysentery, malaria and tropical sprue. Cornwallis first arranged for him to be cared for by Cuba Cornwallis, formerly his servant and now a gifted nurse, and then, when Nelson had recovered sufficiently to return home to Britain, gave him passage in the *Lion* and nursed him throughout the voyage.

Thereafter, their paths diverged. Cornwallis returned to the West Indies in the 74-gun battleship *Canada* in time to serve under Sir Samuel Hood in a number of key naval actions, including the Battle of St Kitts (26 January 1782) when he thwarted a French attempt to break Hood's line by placing his ship across the path of the approaching French flagship, the massive three-decker *Ville de Paris*. Later, at the Battle of the Saintes (12 April 1782), Cornwallis captured his former opponent and would have led the pursuit of the retreating enemy but was recalled by Admiral Sir George Rodney.

His excellent war record, and influential connections, meant that Cornwallis remained employed during the peace that followed, including a spell as commander-in-chief in the East Indies, flying a commodore's pendant. When war broke out in 1793, he quickly seized all the French ships and captured most of the French trading posts in India, thus effectively destroying French power in the area. Returning home, he was promoted to rear admiral and appointed to the Channel fleet, stationed off Brest.

So began his long association with the station on which he was to make his main contribution to the war against revolutionary and Napoleonic France. In 1795, while in command of a detachment of the fleet, he made a masterly retreat in the face of a much superior French force, which increased his professional reputation still further. However, at this point he suffered a setback: appointed to command the Leeward Islands station in the West Indies he was prevented from sailing when his flagship collided with a transport. The Admiralty insisted he should, nevertheless, continue his journey in a frigate, which Cornwallis, then suffering from poor health, declined

to do. Despite much sympathy within the Navy for his position, Cornwallis was censured by a court martial and decided to strike his flag and go ashore.

There then followed five years without active service. Eventually, however, when Lord St Vincent became First Lord of the Admiralty in early 1801, he selected Cornwallis to succeed him as commander-in-chief of the Channel fleet. Cornwallis took up his command in February 1801 and remained at this post until February 1806, with only a brief break during the Peace of Amiens. He inherited a fleet that had been honed by St Vincent to a peak of efficiency but it was Cornwallis's leadership that enabled it to have such a decisive effect on the war. For, during the invasion crisis in the summer of 1805, Cornwallis not only kept in check the main French fleet, then sheltering in Brest under the command of Admiral Ganteaume, but he also detached Calder's squadron to intercept Villeneuve's fleet as it returned from the West Indies with Nelson in hot pursuit. It was Calder's fumbling action off Cape Finisterre on 22 July that finally finished Napoleon's invasion plans and it was Cornwallis who placed Calder in the right place at the right time.

By now, however, his health was beginning to give way under the strain of the long and relentless campaign and he was also deeply affected by the death of Nelson later in the year. Eventually, he hauled down his flag on 22 February 1806 and never went to sea again. He retired from Parliament in 1807 and devoted himself to his estates in Hampshire, where he died in 1819.

Because he never commanded a fleet in a major action, Cornwallis has been unfairly overlooked by earlier generations of naval historians. But, recently, his reputation has been reassessed and he has emerged as one of the great figures of the Royal Navy of his time. Highly professional, a skilled seaman and a fine leader, he resembled Nelson in many ways and he deserves to share with him in the honours of the Trafalgar campaign.

SEE ALSO
Brest, Cuba Cornwallis, Trafalgar campaign

LATEST RESEARCH
Andrew Lambert, 'Sir William Cornwallis', in Peter LeFevre and Richard Harding (eds), *Precursors of Nelson*, Chatham Publishing (London 2000)

Corsica

Throughout the early part of the war against France, one of the key aims of British naval strategy in the Mediterranean was to find a secure base and harbour for their fleet. At the outset of the war, this need was met by the great naval arsenal of Toulon on the south coast of France, which was surrendered to the British by French royalists. But when the port was recaptured by the revolutionary forces in early 1794, an alternative had to be found. The Corsicans, under the nationalist leader General Pasquale de Paoli, were in revolt against their French overlords and so the British commander-in-chief, Lord Hood, sent Captain Nelson in the *Agamemnon* with a delegation to open negotiations. Paoli agreed to accept British rule in return for assistance in driving out the French.

Hood then mounted a full combined operation, first capturing the town and bay of San Fiorenzo and then using this as a base from which to capture the rest of the island. Nelson played a key role in the campaign, landing and fighting guns ashore and assisting in the capture of the two key ports: Bastia on the northeast coast of the island and Calvi in the northwest. Eventually, in late August 1794, the last French garrison surrendered and Corsica settled down with a government of local people under a British viceroy, Sir Gilbert Elliot. It proved an excellent base from which to blockade the French fleet at nearby Toulon.

In the end, however, the British remained in the island for only two years. The entrance of Spain into the war on the French side in August 1796 meant that the British Mediterranean fleet was heavily outnumbered; while the remarkable successes of the French armies in Italy under General Napoleon Bonaparte closed the hitherto friendly ports of northern Italy to the British, thus cutting off vital sources of supply for the fleet. Eventually, in September 1796, the new British admiral, Sir John Jervis, was ordered to withdraw his fleet from the Mediterranean. Without a covering fleet, the British position in Corsica was untenable and so the island was evacuated in October.

The evacuation was carried out by Nelson. In a remarkable operation he managed to remove the viceroy, and all the defending troops, together with all their equipment and supplies, under the very nose of a French army, which had landed to recapture the island. Elliot, who had resigned himself to being captured, was greatly impressed by this achievement and became one of Nelson's closest civilian friends and a most influential supporter.

SEE ALSO
Bastia, Calvi, Elliot

LATEST RESEARCH
Robert Gardiner (ed), *Fleet Battle and Blockade*, Chatham Publishing (London 1996)
Tom Pocock, *Nelson and the Campaign in Corsica*, The 1805 Club (Shelton 1994)

Correglia, Adelaide

An opera singer in Leghorn, a seaport in Tuscany, northern Italy, she was, briefly, Nelson's mistress during 1794–1796 and, after the French occupation

Captain Horatio Nelson. A miniature painted in Leghorn in 1794 at about the time that he was courting Adelaide Correglia. Nelson's stepson Josiah Nisbet did not think it a good likeness but his mother disagreed and always treasured it, even after she had more up to date portraits of her husband in her possession. (National Maritime Museum)

of the town in June 1796, she supplied him with intelligence. Leghorn was at that time a free port and so, in the early years of the war with revolutionary France, British ships often called in for supplies and news. The British consul, John Udney, appears to have acted as a go-between, arranging liaisons for visiting naval officers; among them, Nelson and his friend Captain Thomas Fremantle. On 3 December 1794, Fremantle noted in his diary that he dined with Nelson and his 'dolly' (a slang word for mistress) and then went to the opera with Udney who introduced him to 'a very handsome Greek woman.'

Nelson's liaison with Signorina Correglia lasted for some eighteen months and it is clear that he visited her whenever the *Agamemnon* was in port. Fremantle mentions three other dinners with the couple (at least one of which was actually on board the *Agamemnon*) and a letter to her from Nelson, in execrable schoolboy French, survives in the collection in the Henry E Huntingdon Library at San Martino California: 'Ma Chere Adelaide, Je suis partant en cette moment pour la Mere, Une Vaisseau Neapolitan partir avec moi pour Livorne. Croire moi toujours Votre Chere amie Horatio Nelson. Avez vous bien successe.'

He continued to keep in touch with her even after Leghorn fell to Napoleon Bonaparte's Army of Italy in June 1796 and it has recently been established that she passed him vital information about ship movements. Papers sold at Christies, in 1989, showed that he was sending her money through an English merchant and this discovery has thrown new and revealing light on a hitherto obscure sentence in one of his intelligence reports to the viceroy of Corsica, Sir Gilbert Elliot. Writing on 3 August 1796 from off Leghorn, he said, 'One <u>old</u> lady tells me all she hears, which is what we wish,' and we can now see that the word 'old' was intended ironically. Clearly, it was a discreet, coded reference to his source of information, kept deliberately vague in case his letter was intercepted.

In passing, it is fascinating to note that this oblique mention of Adelaide in an official letter shows that Elliot obviously knew all about her. Nelson's apparent lack of shame about his relationship with her, and his willingness to reveal it to others, is an interesting

precursor of his later very public affirmation of his love for Emma Hamilton. Indeed, it seems likely that he told Emma about her as well, for in November 1798, when Nelson sailed from Naples to recapture Leghorn, she wrote to him, 'Pray . . . do not go on shore at Leghorn, their (*sic*) is no comfort their for you.'

SEE ALSO
Fremantle, Italian campaign

Cuba Cornwallis

A black woman, and former slave, who nursed Nelson back to health following his severe illness in 1780. Cuba had been freed by Nelson's contemporary and friend, Captain the Honourable William Cornwallis, and became his housekeeper in Port Royal, Jamaica. She was renowned for her success in treating naval officers who had fallen victim to the unhealthy climate of the West Indies. Using local herbal remedies, and her own brand of cheerful confidence, she nursed them devotedly during their bouts of fever and was markedly more successful than the naval and army doctors at keeping them alive.

Nelson first met her in about December 1779, when he shared quarters with Cornwallis and, in a letter dated 23 January 1780, he passed on her kind remembrances to his friend and patron Captain William Locker, whom Cuba had nursed back to health some three years before. Nelson returned to Port Royal from the Nicaraguan campaign in May 1780 badly afflicted with a potentially lethal combination of scurvy, malaria and tropical sprue, and so sick that he had to be carried ashore in his cot. Cornwallis refused to allow him to be taken to the military hospital and arranged, instead, for him to go to a lodging house managed by Cuba. He remained there about a month and her devoted nursing undoubtedly saved his life.

SEE ALSO
Cornwallis, Health

LATEST RESEARCH
Ann-Mary Hills, 'Nelson's Illnesses', *Journal of the Royal Naval Medical Service* 86 (2000)

D

Davison, Alexander (1750–1829)

Nelson's prize agent, Davison was typical of the
rather unconventional civilians with whom Nelson
tended to associate. Of Scots ancestry, he amassed a
large fortune as a government contractor and
shipowner while still a comparatively young man, in
the Canadian trade during the War of American
Independence, and he remained essentially a specu-
lator throughout his life, sometimes working on the
very edge of the law. But he was also a generous and
faithful friend, qualities that Nelson both shared and
responded to warmly in others.

They first met in Quebec in 1782 when Nelson
was a young captain in HMS *Albemarle* and Davison
was already a respected merchant and member of the
Council. It was Davison who persuaded his impetuous friend not to risk his career by disobeying orders
to set sail, so that he could continue to woo a local
beauty, Mary Simpson. He eventually returned to
Britain and purchased a large estate at Swarland Park
in Northumberland where he lived in considerable
splendour. He also bought a town house in London
and renewed his friendship with Nelson, who was at
that time at home on leave. Thereafter the two men
remained in regular correspondence.

After the Battle of the Nile, Nelson appointed
Davison agent for the sale of his prizes, even over the
head of his own brother Maurice who had, not unrea-
sonably, expected to land such a plum himself.
Davison showed his gratitude by striking medals for
all the officers and men who had served in the battle,
an act of generosity which cost him some £2000. He
also assisted the often impecunious Nelson on a
number of occasions, most notably when he
advanced him a large proportion of the purchase
price of Merton in 1801, prompting Nelson to write
to him, 'Can your offer be real? Can Davison be
uncorrupted by the depravity of the world?' Later, in
1802, he performed a much less honourable service

*The Davison Nile Medal, produced at his own expense by
Nelson's friend and agent Alexander Davison and presented
to every officer and man who had fought at the Nile. The
reverse (right) bears a splendidly executed view of the opening
stages of the battle.*

for his friend when, on Nelson's instructions, he
returned a letter to Fanny Nelson with the cruel
endorsement, 'Opened by mistake by Lord Nelson,
but not read.'

In 1803, Davison stood for Parliament as member
for Ilchester but was accused of bribery, found guilty,
and sent to prison for a short time. Four years later he
faced a much more serious charge of financial mal-
practice during his years as a government contractor.
This time he was sentenced to nearly two years'
imprisonment. He eventually died, in Brighton, in
1829.

Davison was much liked and respected by all who
knew him and, at his second trial in 1807, he was able
to call a number of senior naval officers as character
witnesses. But by then the man who might possibly
have saved him was dead, a loss which Davison
marked by erecting his own private monument in the
grounds of Swarland Place, bearing the inscription,
'to the memory of private friendship'.

SEE ALSO
HMS *Albemarle*, Frances Nelson, Nile, Mary Simpson

Death of Nelson

Like all great heroes, Nelson attracts many myths and none are more potent that those surrounding his death at the Battle of Trafalgar on 21 October 1805. Some started at once, such as the still common misconception that he was wearing a splendidly decorated full-dress uniform, which made him an easy target for the French marksmen. Others arose later, such as the tight-lipped Victorian dismissal of his touching

The Death of Nelson by Arthur Devis. Nelson is shown shortly before he took leave of Hardy (standing centre) with the famous kiss. Surgeon William Beatty, who wrote a moving account of the event, is checking Nelson's pulse and Chaplain Alexander Scott is rubbing his chest to try and relieve the very acute pain.

request for a kiss from Hardy and the inane alternative suggestion that he suddenly began talking Turkish: 'Kismet [fate], Hardy!'

In fact, the details of Nelson's last hours are very well documented by reliable witnesses and can be reconstructed with some precision. Three men were close to him as he lay dying: Surgeon William Beatty, Chaplain Alexander Scott and the purser, Walter Burke. All three wrote accounts – in Beatty's case a slim book of some one hundred pages – and they tally remarkably well (see transcript of Scott's account on p273).

Nelson was shot while pacing the quarterdeck of HMS *Victory* with Captain Thomas Hardy, at about 1.15pm. As was his invariable custom when at sea, he was dressed in a rather shabby, workaday 'undress' uniform coat. On the left breast were sewn sequin

facsimiles of his four orders of chivalry, dulled by constant exposure to the elements. In the swirl of the gunpowder smoke covering the deck, they would not have presented a particularly obvious target.

Indeed, it is even doubtful that the fatal shot was deliberately aimed at all. It is more likely that it was a stray bullet, or even a ricochet from the *Victory*'s rigging. But, whatever its source, it had a most devastating effect. Striking Nelson on the left shoulder with a force that threw him onto his knees, it smashed two ribs and tore through his left lung, severing a major artery on the way. Then, having fractured his spine, it lodged beneath his right shoulder-blade. Nelson felt death enter with it for, when the horrified Hardy bent over his stricken friend, he heard the rueful words, 'Hardy, I believe they have done it at last. My backbone is shot through.'

Hardy ordered Sergeant Secker of the Royal Marines and some sailors to lift Nelson and he was carried gently down to the orlop deck, situated below the waterline, where the surgeons carried out their operations in battle. He was laid against the ship's side and Surgeon Beatty began an examination that quickly revealed that the case was hopeless. Thinking he was going to die very soon, Nelson breathlessly gave out messages to his mistress Emma Hamilton and their daughter Horatia. In fact, he survived for almost three hours and for most of that time he was in very great pain. But he clung tenaciously to life, waiting impatiently to hear news of the battle. Finally, at about 3.30pm, Hardy was able to assure him that the British had achieved a great victory and, satisfied, he composed himself for death. He gave his last directions for the fleet, another series of loving messages to Emma and Horatia and then, finally, took his leave of Hardy.

His famous request for a kiss, which so embarrassed the Victorians (and continues to embarrass some of his less imaginative enthusiasts today) was recorded not only by Beatty but also by Scott and Burke, both of whom were within inches of him as he spoke. And Beatty records that Hardy responded not with a single kiss but with two: the first on the cheek and, after a brief reflective pause, a second on the forehead. 'Who is that?' asked Nelson. 'It is Hardy.' 'God bless you Hardy.' After Hardy had left, Nelson began to sink quickly. His breath became oppressed

and shortly afterwards he uttered his last words, 'Thank God I have done my duty.' He slipped away so quietly that no-one knew exactly when he died.

His death became the central event of the Battle of Trafalgar. Even at the time, it overshadowed the triumph of the great victory. Ordinary seamen broke down crying when the news spread through the fleet (see colour plates *XII* and *XV*) and, when the news reached England, the customary forms of rejoicing were muted by sorrow. But it was his death at the moment of victory that finally secured for Nelson the immortality he so craved.

SEE ALSO
Beatty, Hardy, 'Kiss me, Hardy', Alexander Scott, Suicide, Battle of Trafalgar, Wounds

LATEST RESEARCH
Colin White, 'The Death of Nelson', in Robert Gardiner (ed), *The Campaign of Trafalgar*, Chatham Publishing (London 1997)

Decorations and medals

By the end of his life, Nelson was entitled to wear the stars of four orders of knighthood, as well as two official gold medals. At this time, decorations and medals were not nearly so common as they are today and so some of his contemporaries felt he looked slightly ridiculous. General Sir John Moore remarked, 'he looks more like a Prince of the Opera than the Conqueror of the Nile.'

His two medals, which he wore suspended from ribbons around his neck, were the King's Naval Gold Medals for the Battles of Cape St Vincent and the Nile. Among the first British named 'campaign' medals ever issued, these were very highly prized by their recipients since only a few were awarded. His main star, or decoration, was the British Order of the Bath, awarded to him in 1797 as a reward for his exploits at the Battle of Cape St Vincent. Again, this was a most prestigious award and only a handful of admirals and captains received it.

By contrast, the three other decorations he wore were all unusual. The Order of St Ferdinand and Merit was a Neapolitan order of knighthood created specially for Nelson and his Nile captains by King Ferdinand of Naples because the existing Neapolitan orders of chivalry could be awarded only

'More like a Prince of the Opera.' This version of Lemuel Abbott's famous portrait, produced in 1799, shows Nelson wearing all his orders and decorations. Around his neck are the gold medals for St Vincent and the Nile and on his chest are the stars of his orders of knighthood. The extraordinary jewel in his hat is the 'chelengk', or plume of triumph, presented to him by the Sultan of Turkey.

to Catholics. Similarly, the Turkish Order of the Crescent was also specially created for Nelson when the Sultan of Turkey wished to reward him after the Nile but was unable to present any existing Turkish award to a Christian. The Order of St Joachim was a private German order of chivalry. When in full dress uniform, Nelson wore the stars of all four orders fastened to the left breast of his coat. When in everyday, or 'undress', uniform he wore sequin and wire facsimiles sewn directly onto the coat.

From time to time, Nelson wore other items that contributed to his unusual appearance. His friend and prize agent Alexander Davison presented all those who had fought at the Nile with a privately produced medallion and Nelson often wore a gold version of it. Additionally, he occasionally wore jewelled miniatures of the King and Queen of Naples. But his most spectacular decoration was worn in his hat. The Sultan of Turkey presented him with a 'chelengk', or plume of triumph, made of diamonds. Thirteen sprays represented the French ships at the Battle of the Nile and a large central diamond was mounted on clockwork so that it could be set turning.

Sadly, little of this splendour has survived. Most of the medals and decorations were stolen from the Painted Hall in Greenwich Hospital in 1900 and the 'chelengk' disappeared in a well-planned raid on the National Maritime Museum in 1951.

SEE ALSO
Coat of Arms, Davison, Relics

LATEST RESEARCH
John Munday, 'The Nelson Relics' in Colin White (ed), *The Nelson Companion*, Sutton and Royal Naval Museum (Stroud & Portsmouth 1995)
Richard Walker, *The Nelson Portraits*, Royal Naval Museum (Portsmouth 1997)

Descendants of Nelson

Nelson's only surviving child was his and Emma's daughter Horatia and so his most direct descendants are those who can trace their ancestry back to her. Although she and her husband Philip Ward had a

Horatia Nelson Ward. A miniature of Horatia painted in 1822 on the eve of her marriage to Rev Philip Ward. She looks remarkably like her father at the same age and passed on a number of his features – most notably his nose – to her children and their descendants.

large family, their offspring were less fruitful and, as a result, the number of people who can claim direct descent from Nelson and Emma Hamilton is not large. They tend to have the names Nelson, Ward or Suckling somewhere in their pedigree.

Nelson's English title descended to his eldest surviving male relative, his brother William, who became the first Earl Nelson and Duke of Bronte. William's only son Horace died, aged twenty, in 1808 and so when William eventually died in 1835, the title passed to his nephew Thomas, son of Susannah Bolton, Nelson's eldest sister. Thomas Bolton survived his uncle by only ten months and was succeeded by his eldest son Horatio, then aged only twelve. Since then, the title has become even more separated from the direct bloodline and so the present Earl Nelson is only distantly related to his illustrious forbear.

Moreover, the Earls Nelson are no longer Dukes of Bronte. Italian law, more enlightened in this respect than British, allows women to succeed to hereditary honours and so when Earl William died, his daughter

The title page of Nicolas' great seven-volume work. Note the reference in the central quotation to the need for a 'Literary Monument' to Nelson – most authorities agree that Nicolas supplied it with this remarkable collection of some 3500 letters

THE

DISPATCHES AND LETTERS

OF

VICE ADMIRAL

LORD VISCOUNT NELSON,

WITH NOTES BY

SIR NICHOLAS HARRIS NICOLAS, G.C.M.G.

" The Nation expected, and was entitled to expect, that while Cities vied with each other in consecrating Statues in marble and brass to the memory of our NELSON, a Literary Monument would be erected, which should record his deeds for the immortal honour of his own Country, and the admiration of the rest of the World."—QUARTERLY REVIEW.

THE FIRST VOLUME

1777 TO 1794.

LONDON:
HENRY COLBURN, PUBLISHER,
GREAT MARLBOROUGH STREET.
MDCCCXLIV.

Charlotte, who in 1810 had married Samuel Hood, later Lord Bridport, became Duchess of Bronte. The Bronte title has been linked with the Bridport family ever since.

SEE ALSO
Bronte, Family, Horatia Nelson, William Nelson

Devis, Arthur (1763–1822)

A relatively obscure artist, who specialised in portraits and historical subjects, Devis won fame with one very popular painting, *The Death of Nelson*. It has become the most familiar – indeed, the most hackneyed – image of Nelson's death scene, reproduced endlessly in engravings and popular prints and even recreated in films and waxwork tableaux.

When the news of the Battle of Trafalgar reached Britain in early November 1805, the printmaker Josiah Boydell issued an advertisement inviting artists to submit paintings of Nelson's death, and offering a prize of 500 guineas for the best one. At that time, Devis was in debtor's prison but he managed to persuade his gaolers to allow him to leave it in order to visit the *Victory*, hoping that this would give him a chance to pay off his creditors. He went on board at Portsmouth and took passage in her when she took Nelson's body round to the River Thames, ready for the state funeral.

Devis used his opportunity well. He was present when Surgeon William Beatty performed his autopsy on Nelson's body and made sketches of Nelson's face, which he later worked up into small portraits which he sold to Nelson's family and friends. He also interviewed, and sketched, those who had taken part in the famous death scene and made detailed sketches of the spot where it had occurred.

As a result, his final painting, now in the National Maritime Museum at Greenwich, has all the authenticity of a photograph (see illustration on p110). Over nine feet long, it is crowded with lifelike characters, each of whom can be identified, and the sense of mourning it conveys is very powerful. Other artists painted more heroic, or more inspiring, versions of the scene: Devis managed to capture something of the reality.

SEE ALSO
Death of Nelson, Portraits

LATEST RESEARCH
Richard Walker, *The Nelson Portraits*, Royal Naval Museum (Portsmouth 1998)

'Dispatches and Letters of Vice Admiral Lord Viscount Nelson'

Between 1844 and 1846 Sir Nicholas Harris Nicolas (1799–1848) published seven volumes of Nelson's correspondence. A massive and scholarly work, it is still widely respected and used: one of Nelson's leading modern biographers, Carola Oman, called it, 'the Bible of the Nelson student.' At the time that Nicolas was working, most of Nelson's letters were still in private hands and so he used his extensive social contacts, and his personal reputation as an antiquary and historian, to obtain permission to publish them. In this way he managed to assemble some 3500 letters which, taken together, give a remarkable insight into Nelson's character.

Moreover, Nicolas took care to arrange all his material in chronological order, adding extensive footnotes to give biographical details of almost all those who featured in the text and backing up the letters with additional documents relating to Nelson's career. As a result, the books read almost like a biography. The reader can follow Horatio Nelson from the proud young teenager writing on 14 April 1777 jokingly to his brother William, to announce his promotion to lieutenant, to the peer of the realm and commander-in-chief, penning his incomparable prayer in the half-cleared great cabin of HMS *Victory* on the morning of 21 October 1805.

There are, however, a number of important gaps. Although he had access to some of Nelson's letters to Emma Hamilton, Nicolas decided to use only a few of them and, even then, in an expurgated form, omitting any hint of impropriety. Moreover, he was unable to obtain access to Nelson's letters to his wife, or to an important series he had written to his friend the Duke of Clarence. So he had to rely on edited versions, printed in an earlier biography by James Clark and John M'Arthur, which corrected Nelson's idiosyncratic grammar and omitted his gossiping remarks about senior officers and colleagues. As a result, the private man does not appear much in Nicolas's great work: *Dispatches* remains essentially a study of Nelson the public hero.

SEE ALSO
Biographies, Letters, William IV

LATEST RESEARCH
Michael Nash, 'Building a Nelson Library', in Colin White (ed), *The Nelson Companion*, Sutton and Royal Naval Museum (Stroud & Portsmouth 1995)
Colin White, 'The Nelson Letters Project', *The Mariner's Mirror* 87 (November 2001)

Drinkwater, John (1762–1844)

An acute observer and accomplished historian, Colonel John Drinkwater played a key role in the early establishment of Nelson's reputation as a hero. In the mid 1790s, he served as aide de camp to Sir Gilbert Elliot, the viceroy of Corsica. In October 1796, Nelson evacuated Elliot and his entourage to Elba just before Corsica was recaptured by the French and the following January, he gave Elliot and Drinkwater passage in the frigate HMS *Minerve* from Elba to join Admiral Sir John Jervis's fleet off Lisbon. The viceroy and his aide were present in the *Minerve* at the Battle of Cape St Vincent on 14 February 1797 and then returned to Britain in her when she sailed home with Jervis's despatches.

Drinkwater had already written a popular history of the great siege of Gibraltar during the War of American Independence (1778–1783) at which he had been present as a junior army officer. Following Cape St Vincent, he published a very vivid account of the battle, in which he gave prominence to Nelson's exploits, thus considerably boosting Nelson's credit for the victory. Many years later, in 1840, he published a new edition of the book and extended it to include more anecdotes of Nelson both before and after the battle. Among these is a vivid account of the voyage from Elba in HMS *Minerve* that gives a fascinating pen-picture of Nelson in action. Drinkwater donated the profits from the sale of this edition to the appeal fund for the erection of Nelson's column in Trafalgar Square.

SEE ALSO
Cape St Vincent, Elliot, Gibraltar

Elba

An island off the east coast of Italy captured by Nelson in 1796. In July, a detachment of General Bonaparte's victorious Army of Italy arrived in Leghorn, then part of the independent Grand Duchy of Tuscany. The viceroy of Corsica, Sir Gilbert Elliot, and his advisors believed that the French presence on the nearby coast posed a major threat to the British in Corsica. Almost directly on the route from Leghorn to Corsica lay the Tuscan island of Elba, with its excellent harbour at Porto Ferraio, and Elliot realised that this might well be captured first by the French, to act as a base for operations against Corsica. He therefore determined on a pre-emptive strike.

By this time, Nelson had been appointed a commodore by the British commander-in-chief in the Mediterranean, Sir John Jervis, and ordered to do all in his power to hamper the French advance in Italy. He had been operating with a small squadron in the waters off Leghorn and the surrounding coast and had begun a close blockade of Leghorn itself. Jervis was far away off Toulon with the main fleet but when Elliot proposed the capture of Elba, Nelson at once agreed to help, believing that this lay within the scope of his orders.

A detachment of troops, under the command of Major John Duncan, was sent in convoy to Porto Ferraio and there Nelson met them in the battleship HMS *Captain* with the frigate HMS *Inconstant* and the sloop HMS *Peterel*. After a quick conference, Nelson and Duncan decided to land the troops about a mile to the west of the town, covered by the *Peterel*, on the night of 9 July. They marched on the town, arriving in front of its main gate at about dawn. Meanwhile, Nelson with his two other ships appeared off the port and took up positions close to the fortifications, ready to fire on them if required.

Duncan then presented the governor of the town with a letter from Elliot asking him to allow the troops to take possession of the town and promising in return that Elba would be regarded as still under the government of the Grand Duke of Tuscany and that the British would retire, and the place be restored, when peace returned. After asking for time to consult with the chief inhabitants, the governor agreed to the terms and the island was surrendered to Nelson and Duncan without bloodshed. As Nelson reported to Jervis, 'The harmony and good understanding between the Army and Navy employed on this occasion, will I trust be a further proof of what may be effected by the hearty co-operation of the two services.'

Elba remained in British hands for less than a year. In late 1796, Jervis was forced to withdraw his fleet from the Mediterranean and so both Corsica and Elba had to be abandoned. The evacuation was supervised by Nelson in January 1797.

SEE ALSO
Elliot, Italian campaign

Elliot, Sir Gilbert (Lord Minto) (1751–1814)

A cultivated, self-confident Scots aristocrat, Elliot was one of Nelson's closest civilian friends, who had a decisive influence on his career at a critical moment in 1798. Educated in Paris, Edinburgh and Cambridge, he trained as a lawyer and entered Parliament in 1776, when still only twenty-five. After an active political career, he was appointed commissioner for Toulon in 1793 when the French royalists handed the port and naval arsenal over to the British and subsequently became viceroy of Corsica when the British captured the island in 1794.

It was then that he first met Nelson and, for the next three years, the two men worked closely together. It was Elliot who ordered Nelson to capture Elba in 1796 and, when the French recaptured Corsica later that year, it was Nelson who rescued Elliot at almost the last moment. These experiences formed a bond between them that lasted until Nelson's death and, on one occasion, Elliot claimed, 'His friendship and mine is little short of that other attachment' (that is, Emma Hamilton!).

Having witnessed the Battle of Cape St Vincent in February 1797 (he was present as a passenger in one of the British frigates), Elliot returned to Britain, where he made sure that Nelson's exploits were properly reported and appreciated. A year later, he was one of those who suggested that Nelson should command the special force that was being sent into the Mediterranean, the expedition that led eventually to the Battle of the Nile (1 August 1798).

After the Nile, the balance of their relationship changed and became more a friendship of equals. Elliot, by now elevated to the House of Lords as Lord Minto, became the British minister in Vienna in 1800 and so was present when Nelson arrived there with the Hamiltons. Privately, he always deplored Nelson's relationship with Emma Hamilton but, like many of Nelson's other friends, he placed the blame firmly on Emma. 'It is hard,' he wrote, 'to condemn and ill use a hero as he is in his own element, for being foolish about a woman who has art enough to make fools of many wiser than an admiral.'

Despite this distaste, he nonetheless remained in touch with both of them and even visited them at Merton, the decoration of which he described as 'an excess of vanity which counteracts its purpose.' He was often with Nelson during his last few days in Britain in the late summer of 1805 and was actually present at the last dinner party at Merton on the eve of Nelson's departure for Portsmouth. When the news of his friend's death arrived in November, he wrote, 'My sense of his irreparable loss, as well as my sincere and deep regret for so kind a friend have hardly left room for other feelings.'

The following year, he was appointed governor-general of India and remained there until May 1814 when, having returned home in very poor health, he died the following month and was buried in Westminster Abbey.

SEE ALSO
Cape St Vincent, Corsica, Drinkwater, Elba, Merton

George Elphinstone, Lord Keith. In this portrait in oils by William Owen, Keith is shown in the undress uniform of an admiral. Note that, like Nelson, he wears a facsimile of his Bath star embroidered on the breast of his coat. (National Maritime Museum)

Elphinstone, George (Lord Keith) (1745–1823)

Although a distinguished admiral, who commanded fleets for most of the war against Napoleon, Keith is now remembered chiefly, and unfairly, as one of Nelson's professional enemies. In fact, they served together only briefly in 1799/1800, and their relations, while not exactly cordial, were for the most part polite and restrained.

Born George Elphinstone, and of noble Scots descent, on 7 January 1745, Keith first went to sea at the comparatively late age of sixteen in 1761. Having served for a time in a merchantman, he was promoted lieutenant in 1770, and post captain in 1775. He served throughout the war with America and in 1780, while commanding the 50-gun *Warwick*, captured the Dutch *Rotterdam* of similar force.

At the end of the war, he took up an active career as a member of parliament and did not serve at sea again until 1793, when he was appointed to the 74-gun battleship *Robust* and joined the Mediterranean fleet under Lord Hood. He played a key role in the capture and defence of Toulon, being among the last to leave the port when it had to be abandoned to the revolutionaries. For this service, he was made a Knight of the Bath in 1794 and later that year was promoted to rear admiral. The following year he commanded an expedition that captured the Cape of Good Hope, for which he was made a baron, taking the name of Keith as his title. In December 1798, he was appointed second in command of the Mediterranean fleet under Lord St Vincent. Soon after he arrived, St Vincent's health began to fail and so he first attempted to exercise command from ashore in Gibraltar, while Keith commanded the fleet at sea. But finally, in June 1799, the old admiral returned home to recover, leaving Keith in charge. And this meant that, for the first time, Nelson came under his direct command.

Nelson was never an easy subordinate, and at this time he was particularly difficult. For over a year, he had been acting almost entirely independently, reporting to St Vincent but exercising command over a large area in his own right. The long strain of the Nile campaign, followed by his serious head wound at the battle, had severely undermined his health; while he had allowed himself to become too closely involved in the affairs of Naples and was not, at least at that moment, capable of seeing the wider scene. So he was inclined to resent – and to resist – any attempt to control him. Keith handled him with tact and patience, although privately expressing distaste for his conduct in Naples, '. . . cutting the most absurd figure possible for folly and vanity.' For his part, Nelson remained polite and respectful and, as a result, there was never any public rift and the two men even managed to collaborate successfully in the operations that led finally to the capture of Malta from the French in September 1800. However, by the time the island finally surrendered, Nelson had gone home overland with the Hamiltons, to Keith's undisguised relief.

Keith remained in the Mediterranean until the Peace of Amiens, commanding the naval part of the successful British invasion of Egypt in early 1801. When war broke out again in 1803, he expected to be sent to the Mediterranean once more and was surprised and upset when the command was given to Nelson. Instead, he was appointed to the North Sea fleet, which meant that he had the vital task of watching Napoleon's growing invasion fleet and making plans to deal with it should it emerge. He remained in post until 1807 and then retired ashore for five years. Finally, in 1812, he took command of the Channel fleet, remaining there until the end of the war. In 1815, it was to one of his ships, HMS *Bellerophon*, that Napoleon surrendered and so it fell to Keith to convey the former emperor to Britain to learn what his fate was to be. By now a viscount, Keith retired from active service and went to live in Scotland where he eventually died on 10 March 1823.

SEE ALSO
Neapolitan campaign, Toulon

LATEST RESEARCH:
Brian Lavery, 'George Keith Elphinstone, Lord Keith', in Peter LeFevre and Richard Harding (eds), *Precursors of Nelson*, Chatham Publishing (London 2000)

'England expects'

At about 11.30am on Monday 21 October, as the British fleet was sailing into action against the Combined fleets of France and Spain, at the Battle of Trafalgar, Nelson ordered a special signal to be flown: 'England expects that every man will do his duty'. Although the most famous signal in naval history, it has been misquoted and misunderstood ever since (see colour plate *XI*).

The misquotation started immediately. A number of the British ships recorded the wording in their logs as 'England expects every man *to* do his duty' and this version has proved remarkably persistent – it even appears on the base of the Nelson column in Trafalgar Square. Then, in 1811, the tenor John Braham composed a song, *The Death of Nelson*, which was an instant 'hit' and was performed all over the British Empire throughout the nineteenth century. The signal formed part of the song's refrain and, to make the words fit the metre, Braham altered them to 'England expects that every man *this day* will do his duty.' Once again, this version has proved very persistent and still crops up today.

As for misunderstanding, the most famous example is the crotchety remark of Nelson's second in command, Vice Admiral Cuthbert Collingwood, as the strings of flags broke out in the *Victory*: 'What is Nelson signalling about? We all know what we have to do.' The signal was probably sent two words at a time, which means it would have taken at least six separate 'hoists'. Scarcely surprising, then, that Collingwood became impatient and, in any case, when the words of the signal were reported to him, he 'expressed great delight and admiration and made it known to the officers and ship's company.'

Confusion even surrounds Nelson's original wording for the signal. There is reliable evidence that he first thought of using the more trusting, and more Nelsonian, word 'confides' (that is, 'has confidence'), but that his signal lieutenant, John Pasco, persuaded him to change it to the more mandatory 'expects' because that word was in the codebook, whereas 'confides' was not. There is also a theory that he originally intended to say '*Nelson* confides' but was persuaded against it. However, close examination of the accounts of those who actually witnessed the ordering and hoisting of the signal suggests that this is unlikely.

Other navies have used their own versions of the

Hoisting 'England expects'. In this very accurate late nineteenth-century depiction of the famous scene, by Thomas Davidson, Nelson stands on the poop of HMS Victory *talking to Hardy and Blackwood while, behind him, the signalmen are hoisting his famous message.*

The Eyeshade. In this engraving of a posthumous portrait by Arthur Devis, an eyeshade can be clearly seen attached to the brim of Nelson's hat in order to cast a shadow over his good eye, thus shielding it from the glare of the sun. This is probably the origin of the myth that he wore an eyepatch over his blind eye.

famous words. Napoleon was so impressed by them that he ordered a translation, 'La France compte que chaqun fera son devoir', to be displayed in all the ships of the Imperial Navy and the great Japanese admiral, Count Heihachiro Togo, signalled at the start of the Battle of Tsushima against the Russian

fleet on 27 May 1904, 'The fate of the Empire depends upon today's battle: let every man do his utmost!' The signal is still flown by HMS *Victory* every Trafalgar Day.

SEE ALSO
Collingwood, Nelson Touch, Pasco, Battle of Trafalgar; Trafalgar Day ceremonies

LATEST RESEARCH
Colin White, 'England Expects – or was it Nelson Confides?', *The Trafalgar Chronicle* 8 (1998), The 1805 Club

Eye patch, Nelson's

A popular and persistent Nelson 'myth' is that he wore a black patch over his blind right eye. In fact, no contemporary portrait shows him with such a patch and none of the many contemporary descriptions of his appearance mention it.

The myth has probably arisen because Nelson is commonly said to have 'lost' an eye, a phrase that gives the impression there was an unsightly empty socket, which had to be hidden from public view. In fact, he lost only the *sight* of the eye, as the result of an internal injury, when he was hit in the face by gravel at the siege of Calvi in Corsica in July 1794. Once the superficial wounds had healed there was no external sign to indicate which eye was blind.

He did however, on occasion, wear an eye *shade*, which his doctors prescribed in 1801 to keep the glare of the sun out of his good left eye. Made of green felt, this was attached to the brim of his uniform hat and stuck out over his forehead, rather like the peak of a modern baseball cap. Such a shade is shown in the posthumous portraits painted from sketches made on board the *Victory* in December 1805, by Arthur Devis. Indeed, one has survived, sewn onto the brim of a uniform cocked hat supplied to Nelson by the old hatters firm of Locks and now preserved in the Undercroft Museum at Westminster Abbey.

SEE ALSO
Calvi, Devis, Wounds

LATEST RESEARCH
Colin White, 'There is but one Nelson', *The Trafalgar Chronicle* 9 (1999), The 1805 Club

Family, Nelson's

Nelson came from a long line of farmers, parsons and merchants. Originally from Lancashire, the family had moved to Norfolk in the seventeenth century to escape from persecution by royalists during the Civil War and Nelson's grandfather had been rector of Hilborough, just south of the market town of Swaffham in Norfolk. His father Edmund succeeded to the living in 1747 and then, in 1755, moved to become rector of the Burnhams, a cluster of villages on the north Norfolk coast, where he remained until his death in 1802. Edmund's portraits suggest he was rather sad and humourless but his letters reveal an altogether more attractive man: affectionate, with a whimsical sense of humour and a gentle but fixed sense of duty. All of these qualities were inherited, in varying degrees, by his son and the two men corresponded affectionately throughout their lives. Sadly, however, towards the end of Edmund's life their relations were made difficult by the old man's honourable insistence on remaining on close terms with Fanny Nelson, even when most of the rest of the family had deserted her at the behest of Emma Hamilton. As a result of this tension, Nelson was not present when his father died and did not even attend his funeral.

Unlike her husband, Nelson's mother Catherine Suckling, who married Edmund in 1749, was a member of the landed gentry. She was closely related to the influential Walpole family and was actually the great niece of the famous Sir Robert Walpole who had dominated British politics in the early part of the eighteenth century. From the few descriptions that have survived of her, it is clear that she was brighter, and more vivacious, than her somewhat ponderous husband. It would seem that Nelson was most like her – possibly even her favourite – and her early death, aged only forty-two, on Boxing Day in 1767, was clearly a psychological blow to the young boy.

Many years afterwards he wrote to one of his father's relatives, '. . . The thoughts of former days brings all my Mother to my heart which shews itself in my eyes.'

Edmund and Catherine had eleven children, of whom three died in infancy. And a number of the survivors were not very robust either, with three more dying in early adulthood. The eldest son, Maurice, was very like his father and had a worthy but unremarkable career in the Navy Office, dying when still in his forties, in 1801. The eldest daughter,

Rev Edmund Nelson. The portrait of Nelson's father used in most biographies makes him appear rather dull and ponderous. This posthumous likeness captures his gentleness – and the good humour which he passed on to his son.

Susannah, married a prosperous Norfolk merchant, Thomas Bolton, and lived for most of her life in East Anglia not far from where she had grown up. She remained in close touch with her brother throughout his life, and even tried for a while to maintain good relations with Lady Nelson after the break-up of the marriage. But Emma Hamilton would have none of this and, in 1802, Susannah was forced to write sadly to her sister-in-law, '…my dear Lady Nelson we cannot meet as I wished for everybody is known who visit you.' Thereafter, she visited her brother and Emma regularly at Merton, and was present at the last family gathering there during his brief spell of leave in September 1805. Her eldest son, Thomas, eventually became the second Earl Nelson on the death of his uncle, William.

The two siblings to whom Nelson were most close were his elder brother William, who became the first Earl Nelson in 1805, and the youngest of them all, Catherine, who was always Nelson's favourite. She alone resembled him, being vivacious, affectionate and independent; the rest of the family were remarkable only in their relationship to their extraordinary brother.

Edmund and Catherine Nelson lie side by side in the chancel of Edmund's church, All Saints at Burnham Thorpe: Edmund beneath a characteristically unostentatious slab bearing just his name and dates and Catherine under an ornately carved Latin inscription that highlights her superior pedigree. A number of their eleven children lie buried nearby, but not their most famous son, who gave directions in his will that he was to be buried beside them, unless the King decreed otherwise. His Majesty did so decree and he now lies many miles away in the crypt of St Paul's Cathedral in the centre of London.

SEE ALSO
Burnham Thorpe, Catherine Matcham, William Nelson

LATEST RESEARCH
Tom Pocock, *Nelson's Women*, André Deutsch (London 1999)

Farmer, George (1732–1779)

A fine seaman, with a distinguished fighting record, Farmer commanded the frigate HMS *Seahorse* on a commission in the East Indies, with Nelson as one of his midshipmen. Farmer himself had first gone to sea as a midshipman with Nelson's uncle, Captain Maurice Suckling, in HMS *Dreadnought* and was promoted to lieutenant in 1759. He became a post captain in 1771 and in 1773 was appointed to the *Seahorse* which, as Nelson recalled much later, 'visited almost every part of the East Indies from Bengal to Bussorah [Basrah].'

It was Nelson's first extended voyage in a man of war and, in her, he received an excellent grounding in navigation from the ship's master, Mr Surridge, whom he long after remembered as 'a very clever man.' He also first saw action, on 19 September 1775, when the frigate engaged a vessel belonging to the ruler of Mysore, Haider Ali, with whom the British were at war. Finally, he formed a lasting friendship with one of his young shipmates, Thomas Troubridge, who was to become one of the original 'Band of Brothers' and arguably the one to whom he was most close.

In December 1775, Nelson was struck down by a fever – now believed to have been an acute attack of malaria – which almost killed him and he was invalided home. The *Seahorse* remained in the East Indies for another two years and, on returning home, Farmer was appointed to the 32-gun frigate HMS *Quebec*. In her, on 6 October 1779, he encountered the larger and more heavily armed French frigate *Surveillante* off Ushant. After an action lasting nearly three and a half hours, the *Quebec* caught fire and eventually blew up, taking over two-thirds of the ship's company with her, including Farmer. The Admiralty were so impressed with his conduct that, most unusually, they recommended that a baronetcy should be conferred on his seventeen-year-old son.

SEE ALSO
Suckling, Troubridge

Films, Nelson in

Nelson has been featured on celluloid since the earliest days of films. The first on record is *The Death of Nelson*, a short, silent re-enactment of the death scene dating from 1897 and said to have been produced by the early director Philip Wolff.

The difficulties of filming naval battles realistically, and the demands of the box office, have meant that all the films featuring Nelson have tended to concentrate on his 'romance' with Emma Hamilton. The first full-length film was *Nelson*, directed by Maurice Elvey in 1918 and featuring Donald Calthorpe as Nelson and an early film star, Malvina Longfellow, as Emma. It was so successful that there was a sequel just a year later, *The Romance of Lady Hamilton*, once again starring Malvina Longfellow. She is said to have regarded Emma as her greatest screen achievement.

Since then, there have been some ten full-length films or television plays but only one of really first-rate quality, *Lady Hamilton* (known in America as *That Hamilton Woman*), directed by Alexander Korda. Released in 1941, it starred Laurence Olivier as Nelson and Vivien Leigh as Emma. Olivier suffered at the hands of contemporary critics, most of whom preferred Leigh's kittenish, vivacious, and completely inauthentic, Emma. But his performance has stood the test of time rather better and it remains by far the best portrayal of Nelson on film.

The British wartime prime minister, Winston Churchill, loved the film and once said that its effect on morale was equivalent to four army divisions. He kept his own copy, which he showed repeatedly, and cried every time. In a recent biography of his father, Korda's son has revealed that Churchill actually helped in the writing of some of the big set-piece speeches, including the climactic passage ending, 'You can't make peace with dictators!' with which Nelson harangues the Board of Admiralty after the signing of the Treaty of Amiens in 1802. With the combination of inspired writing and great acting, Nelson's aggressive spirit is admirably evoked.

SEE ALSO
Emma Hamilton

LATEST RESEARCH
John Sugden, 'Lord Nelson and the Film Industry', *The Nelson Dispatch* 2 (1985), The Nelson Society

'Lady Hamilton'. One of history's most famous love affairs portrayed by one of the cinema's most famous husband and wife teams. Vivien Leigh and Laurence Olivier pose for a publicity shot for Alexander Korda's famous wartime film.

Commodore Olfert Fischer, who commanded the Danish line of defence at Copenhagen. Taken from a Danish print commemorating all the captains who fought in the battle (see p104).

Fischer, Olfert (1747–1829)

Nelson's opponent at the Battle of Copenhagen, Fischer came from a naval family. His father, a Dutchman, became a vice admiral in the Danish Navy and his son went to sea with him. A captain by the early 1780s, he served in the West Indies in command of the frigate *Bornholme* in 1784–1787, during which time he met Captain Nelson, then commanding HMS *Boreas*.

In 1801, by then a commodore, Fischer was put in command of the Danish line of defence outside Copenhagen. But he was not a free agent: he reported to the Defence Commission, which included two admirals and a commodore. Moreover, another commodore, Steen Bille (who had also known Nelson earlier, this time in Naples), controlled a squadron of ships defending the entrance to Copenhagen harbour. Fischer and Bille could give orders only to the

ships under their immediate command and both of them were ultimately responsible to the Crown Prince, who acted as commander-in-chief.

This over-complex command structure was further complicated during the battle. Fischer's pendant ship, the *Dannebrog*, caught fire early in the action and so he was forced to move to another ship to the north of his line, the *Holsteen*. When she was eventually forced to surrender, he moved again, this time to the Trekroner Battery. His control of the battle was therefore minimal at best and this was to have a crucial effect on the outcome. For when, at about 2.00pm, Nelson decided to try to force a ceasefire on the Danes, he assumed that Fischer had already surrendered. So the boat bearing his famous note was carried first to Commodore Bille on board his pendant ship in the harbour entrance. He, in turn, did not feel able to deal with it and sent it ashore to the Crown Prince. If Fischer had still been in control of his forces, the note could have reached him in a few minutes and he may well have rejected it. As it was, the boat took over half an hour to reach the Crown Prince, and in that half-hour most of the ships in the centre of the Danish line surrendered or withdrew.

After the battle, Fischer wrote a report in which he suggested that the battle had been a very close contest, even claiming that two British ships had surrendered and then re-hoisted their colours. He also, not unnaturally, made much of the fact that it was Nelson who had sent the flag of truce, thus beginning a controversy about Nelson's motives that persists today. Nelson angrily refuted Fischer's claims in public but, in private, he admitted that the victory had not been as complete as he had hoped. Fischer remained in the Danish navy, rising to the rank of vice admiral before his death in 1829.

SEE ALSO
Copenhagen

LATEST RESEARCH
Ole Feldbæk, *Slaget på Reden*, Politikens (Copenhagen 2001; English translation forthcoming)

Foley, Thomas (1757–1833)

Although not as well known as some of the 'Band of Brothers', Foley served with Nelson on a number of occasions. Nelson admired him so much that when, in 1803, he was appointed to command in the Mediterranean, he asked Foley to serve as his captain of the fleet, or chief of staff.

Born near Narberth, South Wales, in 1757, Foley went to sea at the age of thirteen as a midshipman in HMS *Otter*. He saw much service during the War of American Independence (1778–1783), including a number of fleet actions. He was made a post captain in 1790 and, in 1793, on the outbreak of the war with revolutionary France, was sent to the Mediterranean as flag captain to Rear Admiral John Gell in HMS *St George*. During this time, he first met Nelson, who was then in command of the *Agamemnon*. In February 1797, he was flag captain to Vice Admiral Sir Charles Thompson in HMS *Britannia* at the Battle of Cape St Vincent.

Shortly afterwards, he was appointed to command the 74-gun battleship *Goliath* and, in the spring of 1798, was part of the squadron sent to join Nelson in the Mediterranean. He led the British fleet into action at the Battle of the Nile (1 August 1798) and it was he who spotted that there was room for the British ships to round the head of the French line and attack them on their undefended shore side.

Sent home in 1799, he was appointed to command the 74-gun HMS *Elephant* in the Channel. In 1801, she formed part of the special fleet assembled for the Baltic campaign under Sir Hyde Parker and Nelson. When Nelson needed a shallow-draught ship as his temporary flagship for the attack on Copenhagen on 2 April, he chose the *Elephant*. So it was on her quarterdeck that the famous incident took place when he turned a 'blind eye' to his commander-in-chief's order to withdraw from the action.

Foley was a large man, over six feet tall, with a bluff, hearty manner but he suffered from ill-health and so after Copenhagen he was forced to retire to his home in Pembrokeshire, where he was visited in 1802 by Nelson and the Hamiltons during their tour of South Wales. Continued illness forced him to decline Nelson's invitation to serve in the Mediterranean in May 1803. Promoted to rear admiral in 1808, he returned to active service as commander-in-chief in the Downs in 1811 and served finally as commander-in-chief at Portsmouth in 1830. He died there in 1833 and was buried, in a coffin made from wood from his former ship, the *Elephant*, in the Garrison Chapel on Governor's Green in Old Portsmouth.

SEE ALSO
'Band of Brothers', Blind Eye, Cape St Vincent, Nile

Foudroyant, HMS

Nelson's flagship between June 1799 and June 1800, HMS *Foudroyant* was a Third Rate battleship of 80 guns, launched at Plymouth Royal Dockyard on 31 March 1798. She was the second ship to bear the name: the first had been a French prize, captured on 28 February 1758 and taken into the Royal Navy.

As she was nearing completion, Nelson was at home in England, recovering from the loss of his arm and he was told that the fine new ship would be his flagship. However, he was ready for active service before she was and so he hoisted his flag in HMS *Vanguard* instead. The *Foudroyant* eventually reached the Mediterranean in the early summer of 1799 and Nelson transferred his flag to her on 8 June. She was his flagship throughout the campaign to recapture Naples and it was in her wardroom that the Neapolitan commodore and revolutionary leader Prince Francesco Caracciolo was tried and sentenced to death. She also took part in the capture of the two French battleships that had escaped from the Battle of the Nile: the *Généreux* on 18 February 1800 and the *Guillaume Tell* six weeks later.

This was not a happy time in Nelson's life. He was sick and drained after the exertions of the Nile campaign and in pain from his head wound. He was out of his depth in the tangled world of Neapolitan politics and he was also besotted with Emma Hamilton. Some time in early 1800 the two became lovers: indeed, it is likely that their daughter Horatia was conceived on board the *Foudroyant* in late April or early May of 1800, when Nelson took the Hamiltons and their friends on a cruise to Malta. Torn between his passion and his duty, Nelson did not live on board the *Foudroyant* continually: on a number of occasions, he remained ashore at Palermo (where Sir William and Lady Hamilton were then living) while his flagship was away on duties elsewhere. This absence from the scene of action was noted by his superiors and led eventually to a reprimand from the First Lord of the Admiralty, Lord Spencer.

The *Foudroyant*'s great cabin was often the scene of elaborate parties involving Nelson and Emma Hamilton and their friends. It was decorated with trophies from Nelson's battles: a carved coat of arms from the *San José*, the top of the mainmast of *L'Orient* and a tricoloured plume from the cap of the *Guillaume Tell*. There was also a more macabre item: a coffin made of wood from the *L'Orient* presented to Nelson by Ben Hallowell, one of his Nile captains. Far from being offended by such a bizarre gift, Nelson was delighted with it and kept it in full view in his cabin. He was eventually buried in it in 1806.

HMS Foudroyant. *This photograph was taken in 1897 when the newly-restored ship was on a cruise around Britain. Shortly after, she was wrecked at Blackpool. (National Maritime Museum, London)*

In the summer of 1800, Nelson was finally given permission to return to England to recover his health. Sir William Hamilton was recalled home at the same time and so Nelson hoped to return to Britain in the *Foudroyant* with his friends. But his commander-in-chief, Lord Keith, was not prepared to part with such a valuable ship and so Nelson's part landed at Leghorn and returned home overland instead.

The *Foudroyant* remained in the Mediterranean and was Keith's flagship during the Egyptian campaign of 1801. She was in active service throughout the rest of the war and remained in the Royal Navy until 1862, when she became a training ship. Finally, in 1892, she was sold to a German ship-breaker's firm but this caused a public outcry and she was purchased by Mr Wheatley Cobb, who wished to pre-

serve her for the nation because of her association with Nelson. He paid for her to be restored to her former appearance and proposed to send her around the country on a cruise but, on 16 June 1897, she was wrecked off Blackpool. The wreck was broken up and her wood and copper were turned into souvenirs, which still turn up regularly in sale-rooms to this day.

SEE ALSO
Caracciolo, Coffin, Keith, Naples, Neapolitan campaign

Fremantle, Sir Thomas (1765–1819)

One of Nelson's closest service friends, Fremantle served with him on a number of occasions and shared both triumph and disaster with him. The son of a Buckinghamshire squire, he joined the Navy in 1779 as a protégé of Sir Hyde Parker and, thanks to his patronage, became a captain at the early age of twenty-eight in 1793. At the outbreak of the great war with France he was sent to the Mediterranean, where he came in touch constantly with Nelson, most notably during the siege of Bastia in Corsica in 1794 and then again at the Battle of Hyères in the following year when he used his frigate HMS *Inconstant* to slow down the French battleship *Ça Ira* sufficiently to allow Nelson to catch up with her in the *Agamemnon*.

Fremantle then served in a detached squadron under Nelson's command operating off the northwest coast of Italy in 1796, when he was a disapproving witness of Nelson's liaison with the opera singer, Adelaide Correglia. In June, when Napoleon's victorious Army of Italy captured Leghorn, he evacuated British citizens from the port, including Mr and Mrs Robert Wynne and their five daughters, among them Betsey. Fremantle and Betsey fell in love and were eventually married in Naples under the approving eye of the British minister's wife, Emma Hamilton. For the next few months, Betsey accompanied her husband in his ship.

Although he missed the Battle of Cape St Vincent on 14 February 1797, having been sent on detached duty, Fremantle was present with Nelson at the abortive attack on Santa Cruz de Tenerife in July 1797 and, like Nelson, was badly wounded in the arm. The arm was saved, but Fremantle took a long time to recover fully and so he and Betsey returned home to England. Eventually, he recovered sufficiently to command the 74-gun battleship HMS *Ganges* and, in her, took part in the Battle of Copenhagen (2 April 1801) as part of Nelson's squadron.

After the brief peace following the Treaty of Amiens, Fremantle was again appointed to command the *Ganges* and remained in her until May 1805, when he transferred to the *Neptune*, a fine new Second Rate battleship of 98 guns. In her he played a major role in the Battle of Trafalgar on 21 October 1805. Lying third in Nelson's line, he was early into action and took on the massive 136-gun Spanish battleship *Santissíma Trinidad*.

He continued in active service throughout the rest of the war. Having been promoted to rear admiral in 1810, he commanded a series of small squadrons in the Mediterranean and Adriatic where, during 1813 and 1814, he captured most of the key ports and coastal towns and was made a baron of Austria for his services. In 1818, he reached the pinnacle of his career, when he was appointed commander-in-chief in the Mediterranean but he died suddenly in Naples less than eighteen months after taking up his post.

Short and stocky, about 5 feet 4 inches in height and with small rounded features and black eyes, he was not a handsome man. But he was good-natured and kind and was loved by all who knew him, including Nelson, who remained on affectionate terms with him to the end of his life.

SEE ALSO
Bastia, Copenhagen, Adelaide Correglia, Hyères, Tenerife

Funeral, Nelson's

In January 1806, Nelson's body was laid to rest in the crypt of St Paul's Cathedral in the centre of London, at the conclusion of an elaborate and colourful state funeral. The ceremonies lasted over five days and were attended by huge crowds, a vivid demonstration of the widespread affection in which the dead hero was held.

However, recent research has established that, at times, there was tension about who should be allowed to take part in the formal proceedings. Originally, there was no provision for the sailors of HMS *Victory* to participate, but pressure from the popular press forced an official change of mind.

Ticket to Nelson's funeral. This specially engraved ticket to the funeral procession from the Admiralty to St Paul's Cathedral is signed by the man responsible for the organisation of the elaborate ceremonial, Sir Isaac Heard, Garter King at Arms.

Eventually, they were allowed to carry the shot-torn colours of their ship in the procession through the streets; and, on the day, they completely stole the show. There were also tensions among some of the more prominent participants. The Prince of Wales originally indicated his intention of attending in his official capacity but the King forbade it, and so he took part as a private citizen. Even this gave rise to controversy, for the Lord Mayor of London then claimed precedence over him in the procession.

The body lay in state for three days in the Painted Hall at the Greenwich Hospital, the famous institution for sick and wounded sailors on the banks of the River Thames. Black hangings covered the vivid wall paintings, which gave the hall its name; brightly coloured heraldic devices gleamed in the rich glow from hundreds of candles in special wall sconces. The first mourner admitted was the Princess of Wales, who paid a private visit that afternoon. The following day, a Sunday, the doors were thrown open and large crowds of people pressed in to see the spectacle. There were so many of them that the authorities began to fear there might be a riot.

On Wednesday 8 January, there was a 'Grand River Procession' from Greenwich to London. A large flotilla was assembled, including eleven barges owned by the City Livery Companies, resplendent with their ornately carved and gilded decorations and distinctive banners. The coffin was placed in one of the royal barges, originally made for King Charles II, its gilding and paint shrouded in black velvet, with a large canopy erected over the stern surmounted by black ostrich plumes. It became a Nelson trophy, lovingly preserved on board HMS *Victory* and is now displayed in the Royal Naval Museum.

Slowly, the long line advanced up-river, its passage marked by the dull thuds of minute guns fired from the naval escort vessels. The weather was fine, but a strong wind was blowing from the southwest, setting up a heavy chop on the river and forcing the oarsmen to struggle to keep the unwieldy barges on station. Eventually, after passing through London, the procession arrived at Whitehall Stairs, near Westminster. The coffin was unloaded and taken to the Admiralty, where it lay overnight.

The following day, the coffin was placed on an ornate funeral car, designed to look like the *Victory* and hung with more heraldic devices and trophies. It was escorted by a huge procession made up mainly of soldiers. The only naval contingents were some Greenwich pensioners and, of course, the members of the *Victory*'s crew who proudly carried their ship's enormous battle ensigns, opening them up from time to time to display the shot holes to the admiring crowd. So, finally, the body arrived at St Paul's Cathedral. By now, the short January afternoon was drawing to its close, so a special lantern, mounted with 130 individual lamps, had been suspended from the dome.

The service that followed was striking both for simplicity and for highly charged emotion. It had been decided that the burial service would be performed within the context of evensong, said or sung daily, then as now, in churches and cathedrals throughout the land. The ceremonies began with the singing of William Croft's stark setting of the 'Burial Sentences', as the coffin was carried up the long nave, into the choir, where it was laid in front of the high altar. Immediately behind came the male members of Nelson's family, among them his young nephew George Matcham who recorded in his diary, 'it was the most aweful sight I ever saw' (see transcript on p274). Evensong was then performed. The service was read by the Dean of St Paul's who, in those pluralist days, was also Bishop of Lincoln.

At the conclusion of evensong, the cathedral organist, Thomas Attwood, played a 'Grand Dirge', composed specially for the occasion, as the coffin was carried back out into the huge space underneath the dome and set high on a catafalque for all to see (see colour plate *XIV*) . The last words were read, the familiar phrases of the Committal, 'earth to earth, ashes to ashes, dust to dust'; the last anthem sung, a special arrangement by John Page of one of Handel's choruses, 'His body is buried in peace – but his name liveth evermore!' Then the coffin began to sink slowly from sight into the crypt below.

As it disappeared, Sir Isaac Heard (who as Garter King at Arms, the Chief Herald, had been in charge of the ceremonial) read out the full titles of the deceased, ending with the unscripted words, 'The hero, who in the moment of Victory, fell covered with immortal glory.' Then, the Officers of Nelson's Household broke their white staves across their knees and handed them to Heard to be thrown into the grave. As they did so, the rubric required that the *Victory*'s sailors should reverently fold up the shot-torn colours and place them on a convenient table. But in a moment of spontaneity, which sent a *frisson* of emotion around the spectators beneath the dome, the sailors first ripped off a large portion of one of the flags and then subdivided it into smaller portions to be kept as mementos. Mrs Codrington, wife of the captain of HMS *Orion* at Trafalgar, commented, 'That was *Nelson*: the rest was so much the Herald's Office.'

SEE ALSO
Coffin, Greenwich, Lord Hood, Peter Parker

LATEST RESEARCH
Timothy Jenks, 'Contesting the Hero: The Funeral of Admiral Lord Nelson', *Journal of British Studies* 39 (October 2000)
Colin White, 'Nelson's Funeral', in Robert Gardiner (ed), *The Campaign of Trafalgar*, Chatham Publishing (London 1997)

'The Interment of Lord Nelson', *a pen and wash drawing by William Bromley. The Bishop of Lincoln (centre) reads the final prayers, watched by the Prince of Wales (with the light coat foreground) and Nelson's friend, the Duke of Clarence (centre foreground).*

G

Geographical places named after Nelson

Nelson's rise to fame coincided with a period of European expansion, when explorers were reaching, and naming, lands all over the world. As a result, his name is to be found throughout the old British Empire.

In Britain, there are two towns: one in the Colne Valley, Lancashire, and the other not far from Aberfan in South Wales. Overseas, there are towns on the South Island of New Zealand and deep in the Selkirk Mountains of British Columbia, Canada. Nelson Roads and Trafalgar Squares crop up in the street plans of mid-Victorian suburbs, including some fifty in the Greater London area alone. A Nelson River drains into Hudson Bay in Canada and a Cape Nelson overlooks Portland Bay on the south coast of Victoria, Australia. It is interesting to note that, in this respect at least, he has completely outstripped his great opponent Napoleon, who can muster only three towns in the USA.

SEE ALSO
Immortal memory

George III, King (1738–1820)

George III was King of Great Britain for almost all of Nelson's life. Born in 1738, he succeeded his grandfather, George II, in 1760 and reigned for sixty years, although for a part of that time he was prevented from carrying out his duties by severe illness and so his eldest son, the Prince of Wales, ruled as Prince Regent.

Nelson first met the King in June 1783 when, still a junior captain, he was presented at Court by his patron, Lord Hood. He had an almost mystical view of monarchy and it is clear from his writings that he saw his service in the Royal Navy as a personal service to the King. So one of the proudest days of his life was when he received the insignia of the Order of Bath on 25 September 1797 from the King's own hand at St James's Palace in London. At the reception that followed, the notoriously tactless George III suddenly exclaimed, 'You have lost your right arm!', but Nelson neatly rescued an embarrassing moment. Turning to one of his companions, he brought him forward with the words, 'But not my right hand, as I have the honour of presenting Captain Berry.'

Another encounter with the King was less happy. On his return from the Mediterranean in 1800 Nelson again attended a reception at St James's Palace. Tactlessly, he had adorned himself with all the foreign orders with which he had been presented as a reward for the Battle of the Nile; and at that time he had not been given the necessary formal permission to wear them in Britain. The King took one look at him, curtly expressed a hope that his health was improved, and then turned away to talk pointedly to an army officer for almost half an hour. It is possible that this marked snub was also meant to express the King's disapproval of Nelson's relationship with Emma Hamilton, which by then was common gossip in London.

Nonetheless, the King remained appreciative of Nelson's abilities. When the news of Trafalgar, and of Nelson's death, was brought to him at Windsor Castle in the early hours of 7 November 1805, he was so shocked that he remained silent for a full five minutes before going to St George's Chapel in the castle grounds, to give thanks for the victory. Protocol prevented him from attending Nelson's funeral but he did give orders that the procession should be re-routed so that he could watch it from a window in St James's Palace. And, when the country was awash with sentimentality over Nelson's death, it was George, with his characteristic gift for uttering simple, direct and sometimes slightly embarrassing truths, who made one of the most apt comments about it: 'It was the death he wished.'

SEE ALSO
Decorations and medals, Funeral

Germany, Nelson's journey through (July–October 1800)

In the summer of 1800, after more than two years of continuous active service in the Mediterranean, Nelson returned home to Britain. The reason he gave for his return was ill-health and, certainly, it is clear from his letters and other evidence that he was at a low ebb, both physically and emotionally. But he had been complaining about his health for some time, so it is clear that other factors influenced his decision to go when he did: chiefly, the news that Sir William Hamilton had been replaced as the British minister in Naples and was returning home with his wife. The relationship between Nelson and Emma Hamilton was then at its passionate height – Emma was already pregnant with their first child – and so a separation was unthinkable.

Nelson had hoped that he and his friends would be allowed to return in his flagship HMS *Foudroyant*. But the situation in the Mediterranean was difficult, with constant threats from the French and Spanish fleets, and so the commander-in-chief, Lord Keith, reluctant to lose the services of a fine new battleship, offered Nelson and his party a frigate instead. This was considered beneath their dignity and an alternative route was considered: overland, via Austria and the other German states.

Such a journey was not to be undertaken lightly. The terrain through which they were to travel was extremely hazardous in places, with high mountain passes and primitive roads. Additionally, in the early stages they had to pass dangerously close to the victorious French armies in northern Italy. In the end, it took them three and a half months to reach Hamburg in northern Germany. But, by then, the private journey home had become a very public triumphal progress.

At this time, the war was going very badly for the opponents of revolutionary France. Nelson's victory at the Battle of the Nile (1 August 1798) had been celebrated throughout Europe and so his name and deeds were well known. As a result, wherever he went he was acclaimed as a hero with official receptions, fireworks and excited crowds.

After crossing northern Italy from Leghorn to Ancona, they sailed to Trieste. From there, they crossed the Karawanken mountain range, arriving in Vienna on 18 August 1800. There they stayed for almost five and a half weeks, enjoying the adulation of the crowds and the patronage of the Emperor and the influential Prince Nicholas Esterhazy. They met the famous Austrian composer Franz Joseph Haydn who organised concerts for them, including a performance of his 'Nelson Mass', and sat to the court portraitist, Heinrich Füger. Nelson even found time to have a mask made of his face by the sculptor Franz Thaller. Everywhere Nelson went, Emma was at his side, sometimes wearing a dress with his name embroidered around the hem. Lady Minto, wife of the British ambassador, one of Nelson's closest civilian friends, wrote, 'He is devoted to Emma, thinks her quite an angel . . . and she leads him about like a keeper with a bear.'

Eventually, they continued their journey, passing through Prague and Dresden where they stayed a week. They then sailed down the Elbe in specially converted barges, going ashore each night to sleep and to visit places of interest, and reached Hamburg just eleven days later, a fast journey for those times. They had expected to find a frigate waiting in Hamburg to transport them to Britain but, once again, they were disappointed. So Nelson hired a mail packet, the *King George*, at his own expense and, having left Hamburg on 1 November, they arrived at Great Yarmouth on 6 November after a very stormy passage.

It was an extraordinary interlude in Nelson's life and shows how, at least in the early stages, his relationship with Emma Hamilton affected his professional judgement. Elsewhere, the war was still raging furiously. As they started their journey, Napoleon was sweeping all before him in Italy, following his remarkable victory at the Battle of Marengo in June. On 6 September, while Nelson and his friends were enjoying the hospitality of the Emperor in Vienna, the French forces in Malta finally surrendered to the British besiegers and on 5 October, when they were in Dresden, the British mounted an abortive amphibious attack on the Spanish naval base at Cádiz. Against such a background, Nelson's long, leisurely progress through Germany did him much harm with the authorities in Britain, especially since most reports of their activities highlighted his very obvious infatuation with Emma Hamilton.

SEE ALSO
Elphinstone, Emma Hamilton, William Hamilton, Malta, Masks of Nelson's face, 'Nelson Mass', Portraits of Nelson

LATEST RESEARCH
Thomas Blümel, *Nelson's Overland Journey 1800*, The Nelson Society (2000)
Otto Deutsch, *Admiral Nelson and Joseph Haydn*, The Nelson Society (2000)

Gibraltar

Standing at the very entrance to the Mediterranean and dominating the narrow straits that lie to the south of it, the Rock of Gibraltar has always been a key strategic point, and control of it was long disputed among the nations with interests in the area. Captured by the British in 1704 and heavily defended by them against constant Spanish attempts to recapture it throughout the eighteenth century, by Nelson's day Gibraltar was already seen as a vital British possession. However, because of its difficult terrain, there was no space for a large dockyard and water was always in short supply, so it tended to be used as a staging post, rather than as a major naval base.

Nelson called in there on a number of occasions throughout his naval career, usually only stopping for a few days, or even hours. His last visit was on 19 July 1805 when he went ashore briefly following his famous chase of the French fleet to the West Indies and back. As he noted in his private journal, '. . . I went on shore for the first time since the 16th of June 1803 and from having my foot out of the *Victory*, two years wanting ten days.'

HMS Victory *at Gibraltar, 28 October 1805. Nelson's battered flagship finally reached Gibraltar with his body on board after the Battle of Trafalgar. Engraving after a painting by Clarkson Stanfield.*

He did, however, return one more time in October 1805, this time in a barrel of brandy. The *Victory* had been so badly damaged at the Battle of Trafalgar (21 October 1805) that she had to put into Gibraltar for temporary repairs, arriving there on 28 October. There is a persistent local tradition that the barrel containing the body was landed at Rosia Bay while the repairs were effected but there is no record of this in any of the ship's records and so it seems likely that it remained on board.

Gibraltar still retains its character as a fortress town and some of the buildings and fortifications date back to Nelson's time and before. In the centre of the town is the small Trafalgar Cemetery, where some of those who died of wounds sustained at the battle are buried and a ceremony of remembrance is held there every year on Trafalgar Day.

SEE ALSO
Drinkwater, Trafalgar campaign

Graves, Sir Thomas (1747–1814)

Graves was third in command of the British fleet in the Baltic campaign of 1801 and took part with Nelson in the attack on Copenhagen. A man with a distinguished war record, he was already a veteran of a number of fleet actions. He went to sea with his uncle, Admiral Samuel Graves, and served throughout the Seven Years War. Promoted to post captain in 1781, he commanded the battleship HMS *Bedford* in three key battles during the War of American Independence. In January 1801, he was promoted to rear admiral and hoisted his flag in HMS *Defiance*.

Although originally opposed to a direct attack on the Danish line at Copenhagen, he was soon won over by Nelson's enthusiasm and gave him unquestioning support during the battle. For example, when Sir Hyde Parker sent his famous order to Nelson's division to discontinue the action, Graves felt bound to repeat the signal. But he made sure that it was hoisted in a position from which it could not be seen by the rest of the fleet. Later, in a letter to his brother, he explained why Nelson was right to disobey Hyde Parker's order: 'If we had discontinued the action before the enemy struck we should all have got aground and have been destroyed.'

Rear Admiral Thomas Graves. Nelson's second in command at the Battle of Copenhagen, 2 April 1801. In this engraving from The Naval Chronicle, *he is wearing the star of the Order of the Bath awarded to him for his part in the battle.*

Graves was made of Knight of the Bath as a reward for his services at Copenhagen and, since he was still on active service in the Baltic when the news of the award arrived, Nelson himself performed the investiture ceremony on the quarterdeck of his flagship HMS *St George*. Graves continued in active service, rising to the rank of full admiral before his death in Honiton, Devon, in March 1814.

SEE ALSO
Copenhagen

Admiral Don Frederico Gravina, commander-in-chief of the Spanish fleet at Trafalgar and one of the foremost Spanish admirals of his day.

Gravina, Frederico (1757–1806)

Don Frederico Gravina was the commander-in-chief of the Spanish forces at Trafalgar. A nobleman, born in Sicily (then a Spanish possession), he had joined the Royal Armada aged twelve and had seen much service in earlier wars. In particular, he had commanded the *San Cristobal*, one of the special 'battering ships' constructed by the Spanish to attack Gibraltar at the great siege during the War of American Independence (1778–1783). He subsequently commanded the *Santissíma Trinidad* in the battle with Howe off Cape Spartel in 1782. On the outbreak of war with revolutionary France, when the Spanish were allies of Britain, he had been second in command of the Spanish fleet that co-operated with Hood's Mediterranean fleet in the occupation of Toulon in 1793.

Thereafter, Gravina had pursued a diplomatic career but in 1805 he was appointed to command the main Spanish fleet, based at Cádiz. He therefore took part in the entire Trafalgar campaign, including the Battle of Cape Finisterre on 2 July 1805 where the Spanish division bore the brunt of the fighting and lost two ships to Calder's fleet. The Spanish

believed that the French had failed to support them sufficiently in the battle and this was the source of much ill-feeling between the two fleets, which led to angry scenes at the Council of War held on 1 October on board Villeneuve's flagship, the *Bucentaure*.

When the Combined fleet left Cádiz on 19 October 1805, Gravina was in command of a special 'Squadron of Observation', flying his flag in the three-decker *Principe de Asturias*. Although the original intention was for this squadron to act independently of the main body of the fleet, on the morning of the battle Villeneuve reversed course when he saw the British attack developing, so that Gravina's squadron became the rear division. Therefore it was Gravina's ships that again bore the brunt of the British attack, this time from the division led by Vice Admiral Cuthbert Collingwood.

During the battle, the *Principe* was attacked by a number of British ships in succession and succeeded in beating them all off, although she herself suffered heavy casualties in the process, including Gravina himself who was badly wounded in the arm. When it was clear that the whole of the allied line had given way at about 3.30pm, he began to rally the survivors and eventually managed to lead eleven ships back into Cádiz. But he did not recover from his wound and died in March 1806. Lord Malmesbury recorded in his memoirs that an Englishman who visited the dying man was told, 'I am going, I hope and trust, to join Nelson.'

SEE ALSO
Cádiz, Cape Finisterre, Battle of Trafalgar, Trafalgar campaign

Great Yarmouth

In Nelson's day, Great Yarmouth, on the east coast of Norfolk, was one of the main ports in East Anglia. There was a large anchorage, Yarmouth Roads, protected to the west by the shore and to the east by complex sandbanks and so it was often used by the Royal Navy to assemble fleets or convoys for the Baltic. There was a small naval depot ashore, and a hospital.

Nelson paid three main visits to Great Yarmouth. The first was in November 1800, when he returned from the Mediterranean with the Hamiltons, using the overland route through the German states. Travelling by packet boat from Hamburg, they landed at Yarmouth where Nelson was greeted as a conquering hero. They stayed at The Wrestler's Inn and the patriotic landlady asked permission to rename it The Nelson Arms. 'That would be absurd,' came the reply, 'seeing I have but one.'

Six months later, he was there again when the fleet assembled in Yarmouth Roads before the Baltic campaign of 1801. The commander-in-chief, Admiral Sir Hyde Parker, was staying at The Wrestler's Inn with his newly wed young wife and Nelson called on him there. Finally, on 1 July 1801, he landed there again when he returned from the Baltic. This time, his first call was at the naval hospital, where he visited sailors wounded in the Battle of Copenhagen (2 April 1801). Stopping at the bed of a young man who had lost an arm, he looked down at his own empty sleeve and said, 'Well Jack, you and I are spoiled for fishermen.'

The Great Yarmouth he knew has largely disappeared but The Wrestler's Arms has survived, as has the splendid parish church where he and the Hamiltons attended a thanksgiving service in November 1800. And on a spit of land overlooking the anchorage is an impressive classical column, 144 feet high, erected in his memory by the people of Norfolk in 1819.

SEE ALSO
Copenhagen, Monuments

Greenwich

Now a suburb of Greater London, in Nelson's day Greenwich was a small town in the country on the south bank of the Thames. At its centre stood the imposing palace-like Naval Hospital, built in the early part of the eighteenth century to designs by Sir

Nelson's funeral at Greenwich, 8 January 1806. The splendid buildings of the Naval Hospital provide a dramatic backdrop as Nelson's body is carried from the Painted Hall (under the dome, right background) to the barge in which it was conveyed upriver.

Christopher Wren and Nicholas Hawksmoor, to house wounded and elderly sailors.

Nelson visited there at least twice. The first occasion of which we know was in March 1797, when he was in Britain recovering from the loss of his arm. The stump was still causing him much pain and refusing to heal and so he and Fanny Nelson went to London so that he could consult some specialists. They paid a visit to Nelson's friend and former captain, William Locker, who was by then the lieutenant governor of the hospital, and stayed with him in his official residence at the river's edge. While they were there, the artist Lemuel Abbott painted the original sketch on which he based his famous series of portraits of Nelson.

The second visit was a more fleeting one on 9 September 1805, when he and Sir Sidney Smith were the guests of honour at a dinner in The Ship Tavern on the waterfront close to the main entrance to the hospital, together with a company that the newspapers reported was 'rich and fashionable'. It was in this same tavern that one of the first recorded toasts to 'The Immortal Memory' was drunk when the news of his death reached Britain in early November.

The Battle of the Gulf of Genoa, 14/15 March 1795. Nelson's first major fleet action. His 64-gun ship HMS Agamemnon *(left) lies across the bows of the large French battleship* Ça Ira, *which has just surrendered.*

Nearly two months later, in late December 1805, his body was brought to the hospital at the beginning of the elaborate state funeral and was received by the governor, Nelson's former commander and patron, Lord Hood. It lay in state in the magnificent surroundings of the Painted Hall, the principal public space of the hospital, which had been transformed for the occasion into a mortuary chapel. Black velvet hangings covered the colourful wall paintings that gave the hall its name and gilded heraldic devices gleamed in the rich glow from hundreds of candles. The body, enclosed in an elaborately decorated state coffin, lay on a catafalque under a large canopy, surrounded by captured French flags. The first mourner admitted was the Princess of Wales, who paid a private visit in the afternoon of 4 January 1806. The following day, a Sunday, the doors were thrown open and for the next three days large crowds of people pressed in to see the spectacle. There were so many of them that the authorities began to fear there might be a riot.

Eventually, on Wednesday 8 January, the body was carried out of the Painted Hall and down to the river, where a procession of barges was waiting to escort it up the Thames to the City of London, and it was finally laid to rest in St Paul's Cathedral the following day. The specially designed hearse used to carry it through the London streets was taken to Greenwich and placed on display in the Painted Hall, where it later became the centrepiece of a large display of naval paintings and memorabilia. This included many Nelson relics, among them the coat he was wearing when he was shot at Trafalgar, with the tiny bullet hole in the shoulder.

The grand hospital buildings, splendidly restored, now house the University of Greenwich and the Trinity College of Music and the residence where Nelson stayed with the Lockers and posed for Abbott has been converted into offices. But the magnificent Painted Hall is open to the public and a plaque in the floor, placed there recently by The 1805 Club, marks the spot where the coffin rested. Nearby, the National Maritime Museum now contains one of the finest Nelson collections in the country, including the Trafalgar coat.

SEE ALSO
Abbott, Funeral, Lord Hood, Locker, Museums, Relics

Gulf of Genoa, Battle of the (13/14 March 1795)

Nelson's first fleet battle was an unsatisfactory and indecisive affair but it gave him the chance to show his skills as a ship handler and his aggressive spirit. The French Mediterranean fleet had suffered a major blow as a result of the destruction wrought by the British when they briefly occupied the southern French naval arsenal of Toulon in January 1794. However, by February 1795, they had recovered sufficiently to put together a reasonably powerful squadron of fifteen battleships, including the 120-gun *Sans Culottes*. So they decided to make a determined attempt to recapture Corsica, which had fallen to the British the previous year.

At this time, the British Mediterranean fleet of thirteen battleships was commanded by the hesitant Vice Admiral William Hotham. On 13 March they intercepted the French fleet in the Gulf of Genoa. The French avoided action and, in shifting, uncertain winds, Hotham ordered a general chase, thus allowing his faster ships to draw clear of their consorts and attack the rearmost enemy ships.

In the confusion of retreat, the 80-gun *Ça Ira* collided with one of her consorts, losing her fore and main topmasts. Dropping astern of the fleet, she found herself harried first by the frigate *Inconstant*, under Captain Thomas Fremantle, and then by Captain Horatio Nelson's light and handy battleship *Agamemnon*. For three hours, Nelson skilfully tacked his ship to and fro across the Frenchman's stern, pouring in a series of murderous close-range broadsides. The French fleet turned to defend their comrade and Hotham, still too far off with the rest of the fleet to help the *Agamemnon*, was forced to order her to withdraw. The battle was rejoined the following day and this time the *Ça Ira* was captured, along with the *Censeur*, which tried to help her. Satisfied with this modest success, Hotham ended the engagement.

Nelson was thoroughly dissatisfied with the result, believing that Hotham should have followed up his success more aggressively. He even went on board the flagship to persuade his admiral to pursue the French fleet but was told, 'We must be contented. We have done very well.' 'But had we taken ten sail,' he wrote impatiently to his wife, 'and allowed the eleventh to escape if possible to have been got at, I could never call it well done.'

SEE ALSO
HMS *Agamemnon*, Fremantle, Hotham, Hyères, *L'Orient*

Gutiérrez, Antonio (1729–1799)

Nelson's opponent at Tenerife in 1797, General Antonio Gutiérrez was a distinguished and experienced regular soldier. Having seen much action – mostly against the British – in Italy, North Africa, the Falklands and Minorca, he was appointed commandant general of the Canary Islands in 1790. By 1797, he was sixty-eight years old, but he was still vigorous and efficient and had done much to improve the defences of Tenerife, and especially the main town of Santa Cruz, setting up lookout points to give early warning of attacks and reorganising the militia.

Although during the battle he had fewer than 1500 men under his command, Gutiérrez deployed them skilfully: succeeding first in outmanoeuvring Troubridge's initial landing force and then blocking Nelson's foolhardy frontal attack during the night of 25/26 July. When some of the British finally managed to get ashore, Gutiérrez kept his head and refused to be bluffed into yielding any ground to his opponents, even when they threatened to set fire to the town.

Having won his well-deserved victory, he then behaved with honour and humanity, offering food and drink to the exhausted attackers and ordering that the British wounded should be cared for in the town's hospital. Nelson, quick to recognise a kindred spirit, sent him an appreciative letter together with a barrel of English beer and cheese, to which he replied by sending Nelson some Malmsey wine.

Gutiérrez was made a Knight of the Order of Alcantara as a reward for his distinguished services and when he died, in 1799, he was buried with full honours in the Church of the Concepcion, which had

Don Antonio Gutiérrez, commandant general of the Canary Islands, the man who beat Nelson at Tenerife in July 1797. A modern portrait, based on contemporary likenesses.

been the centre of some of the fiercest fighting during the night attack.

SEE ALSO
Tenerife, Troubridge

LATEST RESEARCH
Agustín Guimerà, *Nelson and Tenerife*, The 1805 Club (Shelton 1999)
Colin White, *1797: Nelson's Year of Destiny*, Sutton and the Royal Naval Museum (Stroud & Portsmouth 1998)

H

Hallowell, Benjamin (1760–1834)

Hallowell served with Nelson on a number of occasions, and the two men clearly liked each other and worked well together. But he was never one of Nelson's inner circle of friends. A Canadian, born in 1760, he was the son of the commissioner of the American Board of Customs and joined the Royal Navy in time to serve in the War of American Independence, during which he took part in the Battle of the Saintes (12 April 1782). He reached the rank of post captain in 1793 and commanded the battleship *Courageux* in the Mediterranean, where he first met Nelson. When the two men served ashore together in Corsica at the siege of Calvi in 1794, Nelson commented on Hallowell's 'indefatigable zeal, activity and ability.'

In December 1796, the *Courageux* was wrecked in a storm while Hallowell was ashore attending a court martial. He was present as a volunteer in the *Victory* at the Battle of Cape St Vincent (14 February 1797) and famously slapped the formidable Sir John Jervis heartily on the back when the admiral announced his decision to attack the Spanish fleet, despite being heavily outnumbered. As captain of the *Swiftsure*, he was one of the squadron sent with Nelson to track down the French fleet in the Mediterranean in 1798 and was thus one of the original 'Band of Brothers'. After the Battle of the Nile, in a characteristically bluff gesture, he presented Nelson with a coffin made from the mainmast of the French flagship *L'Orient*, destroyed in the battle. Far from being offended, Nelson was delighted with the gift and made sure that it was preserved. He was duly buried in it in 1806.

After the Peace of Amiens, Hallowell again served with Nelson off Toulon, in command of HMS *Tigre*, and took part in the chase to the West Indies in 1805 in pursuit of Admiral Villeneuve, later joining Vice Admiral Collingwood in the watch on Cádiz where the French fleet under Villeneuve took shelter. In late October, his ship formed part of a squadron that was detached to Gibraltar for stores and water, thus missing the Battle of Trafalgar.

He was promoted rear admiral in 1811 and hoisted his flag in HMS *Malta* in the Mediterranean. He became a vice admiral in 1819 and a full admiral in 1830 and was knighted the following year. In 1829, under the terms of a will, he assumed the name and arms of Carew, and for the rest of his life was known as Benjamin Hallowell-Carew. He died at his home in Beddington Park in Surrey in 1834.

A large, hearty man, he was much liked by all his colleagues including Nelson. But the two men were never really close. 'His spirit is certainly more independent than almost any man's I know,' Nelson once told Emma Hamilton, adding, 'but I believe he is attached to me.' The slight hint of doubt in that last phrase is revealing.

SEE ALSO
'Band of Brothers', Coffin, Nile

Hamilton, Emma (1765?–1815)

Emma Hamilton has always been a central figure in Nelson's story. Even during his lifetime, their defiantly public affirmation of their friendship attracted much attention in the gossip columns of the newspapers, and in the correspondence of those who met them. During the nineteenth century, historians argued over whether they had been lovers and then, when there could no longer be any doubt about the matter, tended to portray Emma as a scheming adventuress who led the naïve hero astray. In the twentieth century, when there was a greater acceptance of their adultery, their love affair tended to be presented as one of history's great romances, especially by film-makers.

In fact, their relationship was often very unromantic. It is important to remember that the lovers were disgrace in 1800, at least in part because of the scandal. Frances Nelson suffered the pain of being abandoned, not only by her husband but also by most of their family and friends. And Emma herself lost her hard-won reputation for respectability and never achieved the position in British society which, as the beautiful and talented wife of the former envoy to Naples, she might have enjoyed if Nelson had not entered her life. As a result, her last years were unhappy, even tragic, with a slow descent into debt, drunkenness and death.

Emma's early history is shrouded in mystery, much of it of her own deliberate making. Even the exact date of her birth is uncertain. She always celebrated 26 April as her birthday but the year is given variously as 1763 and 1765. We do know, however, that she was christened on 12 May 1765 and that she was the daughter of Henry Lyon, the blacksmith of the village of Nesse in the Wirral, Cheshire, and his wife Mary. At an early age she moved to London to work, where her striking beauty and innocence attracted a succession of unprincipled men by whom she was used and then passed on. Eventually, in 1782, she became the mistress of Charles Greville, an earl's son and member of parliament, who installed her in a small house in Paddington Green, where he visited her over the next four years. It was during this period that she met the artist George Romney, who captured her unique combination of voluptuous beauty and girlish innocence in a remarkable series of paintings, that are still regarded as among the finest examples of late eighteenth-century portraiture.

However, in 1784, Greville wished to marry and so he sent Emma, with her mother, to visit his uncle, Sir William Hamilton, in Naples. Hamilton was a widower and it was clear that the two men had cold-bloodedly decided that Emma should become his mistress. At first she was distraught, writing

Emma Hart by George Romney. One of the many delightful portraits Romney painted of Emma as a young women. It brilliantly captures her remarkable combination of girlish innocence and mature, even voluptuous, beauty.

hardly ever alone: for most of their time together they lived with Emma's husband, Sir William Hamilton, in a remarkable, but clearly amicable, *ménage à trois*. It was also a very destructive affair. All the participants became figures of fun, lampooned, often cruelly, in newspaper reports and caricatures. Sir William and Nelson were both recalled home in anguished letters to Greville, whom she obviously genuinely loved, but Hamilton, who was an essentially humane and decent man, gradually won her over and by 1786 they had become lovers. Eventually, in 1791, he married her, which was almost certainly not what Greville (who was his uncle's heir) had intended when he packed her off on her long journey.

Marriage gave the new Lady Hamilton a place at the Neapolitan Court and she quickly developed a close friendship with the Queen, Maria Carolina. Her extraordinary beauty was much admired and she was also an accomplished singer. Moreover, under Hamilton's tutelage, she developed a striking series of poses, based on scenes on classical vases in her husband's collection, which she then put together into special solo performances, known as 'attitudes'. So, by the mid-1790s, she had became a celebrity and, rising above the squalid exploitation of her early years, had won for herself a position in society and a reputation based on her own artistic and social talents.

Then, in September 1798, Nelson came to Naples. They had met briefly before in 1793 when, as captain of HMS *Agamemnon*, he had been sent to Naples by the Mediterranean commander-in-chief Lord Hood to persuade the King of Naples to send troops to help the British hold Toulon, which had been surrendered to them by French monarchists. They obviously liked each other and he wrote of her to his wife, 'She is a young woman of amiable manners and who does honour to the station to which she has been raised.' Since then, they had corresponded from time to time, especially during the Nile campaign in 1798 when, realising the influence she had with the Queen, Nelson wrote to her about the progress of his chase of the French fleet and his urgent need for supplies. So she became personally involved in the almost unbearable tension preceding the battle and in the euphoric celebrations following it.

'Dido in Despair.' One of Gilray's cruelest caricatures of Emma Hamilton shows her a monstrous size (she was in fact eight months pregnant with Horatia at this time), bewailing Nelson's departure to sea, while a wizened Sir William slumbers peacefully in the recesses of the bed. The floor is strewn with phallic symbols, supposedly from Sir William's collection.

'Happy days at Merton.' A romanticised late Victorian view of Nelson and Emma's relationship. In fact, they were seldom able to share private moments such as this.

When Nelson arrived in Naples after the battle, he was a sick man. The strain of the campaign had undermined his health, which had in any case only recently recovered from the aftermath of the loss of his arm, and now he had been wounded again. Although not so obviously disabling, the blow to his head had given him headaches and nausea, and shortly after his arrival he collapsed. Emma and Sir William took him into their home at the Palazzo Sesa where she and her mother nursed him back to health. Close in age, with a shared impulsive enthusiasm for life, and especially in their affections, the two very quickly became close and confidential friends. This bond was further strengthened in December 1798, when they worked together in the secret, and often dangerous, operation to evacuate the King and Queen to Palermo, when Naples fell to the French army and a republic was established. Emma made most of the arrangements with the Court and, when the ships were hit by a violent storm, she rose magnificently to the occasion, dispensing help and encouragement to the terrified royal passengers. Inevitably, such courage struck chords in Nelson's heart and, thereafter, they were inseparable.

For the first time in his naval career, Nelson began to put personal considerations before his duty and was more often to be seen ashore at parties in Palermo than at sea with his fleet. Indeed, at one stage he even transferred his flag to a transport in the harbour so that he could remain close to his friends. And when close friends, such as Thomas Troubridge, tried to warn him of the gossip that was beginning to circulate, they were treated as enemies by the now increasingly infatuated couple.

At the same time, Emma's own reputation was suffering. People started to resurrect the old stories about her early life and the respectability that she had so painfully won for herself began to ebb away. The irony was that, at least at this stage, they almost certainly were not lovers. From evidence in their letters, it now appears that it was not until early in 1800 that they first started having sex together, and so when, in the early days, they protested that their relationship was pure and platonic, it seems that they were probably telling the truth. But once the sex did begin, Nelson clearly found it unlike anything he had ever experienced before, referring feverishly to 'those liberties which no woman in this world but yourself ever did . . .' (see colour plate *XIX*).

Historians have debated ever since just how much Hamilton knew about the affair. The consensus now is that he must have guessed that they were lovers but that he was content to acquiesce quietly, providing that his wife did not leave him. And his calm acceptance of the situation was crucial: without it, Emma and Nelson could never have been together as much as they were.

Eventually, in 1800, Hamilton and Nelson were recalled to Britain, both to some extent in disgrace. After an extended journey home through the German states, which turned into a triumphal progress, they arrived in Great Yarmouth in November. By now, Emma was pregnant with their first child, probably conceived onboard Nelson's flagship HMS *Foudroyant* during a visit to Malta that the friends had made together the previous May. The gossip columnists and caricaturists sniggered at how large the famous beauty had become but only a few of them seem to have guessed the true cause of her *embonpoint*. But for Nelson, who loved children, and was clearly saddened by the fact that he and Fanny Nelson had none of their own, the pregnancy bound him still closer to his lover. So when it became clear that he would have to choose between her and his wife, he parted from Fanny with cruel swiftness and, not long afterwards, told Emma in a passionate letter that she was his wife 'in my eyes and in the face of heaven' (see transcript on p267). As so often happens in such cases, Nelson's family found their loyalties painfully divided but, one by one, they deserted Fanny Nelson when it was made clear to them that any contact with her was regarded as treachery. The only one who never wavered in his support for the deserted wife was Nelson's father.

Nelson returned to active service in January 1801, which meant the lovers were apart when Emma eventually gave birth to a daughter, whom they named Horatia. Emma allowed Nelson to think that this was her first child, but in fact she had been pregnant at least twice before. They kept in touch with letters, written almost daily and, fearing that these letters might be opened, they invented an elaborate fiction. They created a sailor on board Nelson's flagship whose name was Thomson (although Nelson sometimes spelled it 'Thompson'). Thomson had a pregnant wife who was being looked after by Emma. So Nelson wrote to Mrs Thomson on the sailor's behalf and passed on messages about his love for her and the infant.

They had a pact that they would destroy all their letters, a pact that Nelson faithfully kept but that Emma did not. As a result, we have a detailed record of the progress of their affair, but only from one side. Nonetheless, it is possible to reconstruct what Emma wrote by analysing Nelson's responses and it is clear that she was often quite cruel, playing on his loneliness and jealousy, and frequently driving him almost into a frenzy. On the evidence of the letters, Nelson was not always a happy lover in 1801 and he was certainly not sure of Emma's faithfulness to him. On the other hand, Emma's situation was particularly delicate and difficult: she had to maintain her role as a faithful wife, while at the same time keeping happy the increasingly demanding and demonstrative father of her child.

For Nelson, any form of concealment was completely against his nature. Not for him a discreet affair, with clandestine and hurried meetings. He wanted to live with Emma openly; and, remarkably, with Sir William's acquiescence, he achieved this. In the autumn of 1801, Emma arranged the purchase for him of a house in Merton in Surrey and there the

three of them often lived together, until Sir William died in April 1803, supported by his wife and holding his best friend's hand. During these happy eighteen months, the relationship appears to have matured from a passionate love affair into a quasi-marriage. For when Nelson returned to sea shortly after Sir William's death, and the letters began again, they

Emma Hamilton as Britannia. In this engraving by Thomas Baxter, published shortly after Nelson's death, Emma Hamilton appears in one of her favourite roles, crowning the bust of the hero with laurel. The bust, by Thaller and Ranson, was produced in Vienna when she and Nelson visited there in 1800.

had none of the jealous anguish of the ones he had written in 1801. Instead, they resembled the letters he had once written to his wife, with complaints about Emma's inefficient packing, plans for improvements to the house and continued promises that he would be home before long, which he continually broke. Reconstructing Emma's letters to him, it would seem that they were not unlike the ones he had received from Fanny, with tit-bits of gossip about family and friends, intermingled with complaints that he was away for so long and pleas that he would not risk his life any more than was necessary.

They had one last brief time together in August and September 1805, when he came home on leave after chasing the French fleet to the West Indies and back. For the first time, they were able to have Horatia with them openly at Merton but, even so, they were hardly ever alone. The house was full of Nelson's relations and friends and he was often absent in London consulting with the politicians and the Admiralty about the next stage of the campaign. However, on the day before he left to return to active duty, they did manage to find time to go to the parish church where, in a conscious imitation of a marriage service, they received private communion and exchanged rings. And, as the *Victory* sailed into action at Trafalgar, Nelson's last private act was to write a codicil to his will, in which he implored his King and Country to provide for Emma and Horatia.

Emma was at Merton when the news of her lover's death arrived and she was prostrated by grief. Once he was gone, she was hurriedly abandoned by many of his family and friends, who had been so quick to court her when his marriage broke up, and she also found that no-one was prepared to honour her lover's last wishes and provide for her and their child. Drink, always a weakness, became an addiction. Her debts began to mount up, forcing her to sell many of her possessions, and then Merton, which Nelson had left to her, and eventually driving her into debtors' prison, where she was accompanied by Horatia, who now lived with her permanently. The final blow came in 1814 when some of Nelson's letters to her were published, opening up a public debate about the exact nature of their relationship. The blame for this indiscretion fell on her but she always denied having anything to do with the book. Modern

research suggests she was telling the truth and that the villain was probably Francis Oliver, who had been her secretary and who, it would appear, had been blackmailing her, and threatening publication.

Eventually, in July 1814, Emma crossed the Channel with Horatia to Calais to escape her creditors and six months later she died. She never acknowledged that Horatia was her daughter and, despite all the evidence, Horatia never accepted that Emma was her mother. Her verdict on the woman she had known only as her guardian was therefore emotionally detached and somewhat patronising: 'With all her faults – and she had many – she had many fine qualities which, had she been placed early in better hands, would have made her a very superior woman.'

It is Emma Hamilton's misfortune that many of her biographers have been men. Even her entry in the old *Dictionary of National Biography* was written by the naval historian John Knox Laughton, presumably on the curious grounds that he was a Nelson biographer. As a result of their Nelson-centric viewpoint, she has generally been judged harshly, with A T Mahan even going so far as to claim, 'That she ever loved him is doubtful,' which is about as cruelly unfair as it is possible to be. She was also judged harshly by the polite society that she dared to aspire to enter and many of the nasty and unkind contemporary descriptions of her accent and vulgarity are clearly influenced by snobbery. Even so, they have often been quoted by Nelson's biographers with relish, and little discernment as to their likely authenticity. More recently, however, she has been more generously treated and her latest biographer, Flora Fraser, ends her book with the delightful tale of Sir Moses Montefiore who met the couple when a youngster and, many years later, was asked for his impressions of Nelson. 'Ah, my boy,' he replied, 'I only had eyes for Lady Hamilton.'

SEE ALSO
Family, HMS *Foudroyant*, William Hamilton, Merton, Naples, Neapolitan campaign, Frances Nelson, Horatia Nelson, Nile, Francis Oliver, Palermo

LATEST RESEARCH
Flora Fraser, *Beloved Emma*, Weidenfeld and Nicolson (London 1986)
Colin White, 'Tria Juncta in Uno: Nelson and the Hamiltons', *The Trafalgar Chronicle* 6 (1996), The 1805 Club

Hamilton, Sir William (1730–1803)

Nowadays William Hamilton is remembered almost solely as the husband of Emma Hamilton who was cuckolded by his best friend, Horatio Nelson. Yet he had a long and successful career as a diplomat and was also known throughout Europe for his pioneering work in vulcanology and for his remarkable collection of paintings and classical antiquities.

Born on 13 December 1730, he was the fourth son of Lord Archibald Hamilton and grew up with the young Prince George, later King George III. After eleven years in the army and a brief spell as the member of parliament for Midhurst, he was appointed the British envoy in Naples in 1764, where he remained until his retirement in 1800. He and his first wife, Catherine, were accomplished musicians and shared a love of fine art, so their home became a salon, frequented by many of the great artists and writers of the day when they visited Naples, including Goethe and Leopold and Wolfgang Mozart. Hamilton also became fascinated by Vesuvius, which was close by, and made many ascents to the summit, sometimes at great personal danger, to study the volcano and to collect specimens of earth and minerals, which he sent home to the British Museum. Having published his findings, he was elected a fellow of the Royal Society in 1766 and went on to produce a number of important works on volcanoes.

He was also a fellow of the Society of Antiquaries and began to form a superb collection of classical vases. In 1772, they were purchased by the British Museum, then still in its formative stages, and became the basis of its classical collection. Again, Hamilton published the results of his work in a set of handsomely illustrated volumes and these in their turn influenced Josiah Wedgwood, who produced copies of the vases for his new classical collection of pottery. Having disposed of this collection, Hamilton then went on to form an even finer one and this, too, eventually found its way into the British Museum. In 1772, he was made a Knight of the Bath, as much for his services to the museum as for his diplomatic work, which was not particularly onerous until the outbreak of the great war against France in 1793.

By then, Hamilton had remarried. Catherine died in 1782 and, in 1786, the young and very beautiful

Sir William Hamilton. This engraving, after a miniature produced in 1799 by Charles Grignon (see p29), shows Sir William as the cultured connoisseur and diplomat.

Emma Hart came on a visit to Naples with her mother, sent there by Hamilton's nephew Charles Grenville whose mistress she had been. She soon became Hamilton's mistress and then, in 1791, he married her. Despite the difference in their ages it is clear that they were fond of each other and she quickly made a friend of the Queen of Naples, Maria Carolina, thus further increasing Hamilton's influence at the Court at a critical time for Britain. Already a talented actress, Emma also worked with her husband to devise an unusual form of entertainment, known as 'attitudes'. These consisted of a series of stylised poses based on scenes on the vases in Hamilton's collection and all who saw them bore witness to their dramatic power and their ability to move an audience.

When war broke out in 1793, Naples, one of the few friendly ports in the Mediterranean, became an important British ally and so Hamilton was kept busy securing aid for the British operations in the area. In this way, he first met Nelson in 1793 when the captain of the *Agamemnon* was sent by the British commander-in-chief Admiral Lord Hood to persuade Naples to lend troops for the occupation and defence of the port of Toulon, which had been handed over to the British by French royalists. The two men liked each other at once and began a regular correspondence, which continued until the British fleet retreated from the Mediterranean in December 1796.

The friends next met in September 1798, when Nelson arrived in Naples in the *Vanguard* to repair his ship and recover his own health following his severe head wound at the Battle of the Nile (1 August 1798). For the next two years, he and Hamilton worked constantly together: first in the abortive attack on Rome in the autumn of 1798, then in the evacuation of the royal family from Naples in December 1798 and, finally, in the Neapolitan campaign of July 1799 in which Hamilton was Nelson's political advisor and interpreter and as much implicated as he in the bloodbath that followed the recapture of Naples by the royalists.

At the same time, of course, Nelson was falling increasingly in love with Emma Hamilton and historians have debated ever since just how much Hamilton knew about their affair. The consensus now is that he must have guessed that they had become lovers but that he was content to look the other way as long as his wife did not abandon him. It is clear, moreover, that he was genuinely fond of Nelson, regarding him perhaps as the son he had never had. Nelson, for his part, seems to have admired the sophisticated and aristocratic man of the world. So Hamilton was far from being an unknowing cuckold; on the contrary, it is now apparent that he was a key player in what was, in a sense, a three-way relationship.

Eventually, in 1800, Hamilton and Nelson were recalled to Britain, both to some extent in disgrace as a result of official disapproval of the way in which affairs in Naples had been handled. After an extended journey home through the German states, which turned into a triumphal progress, they arrived in Great Yarmouth in November. Thereafter, Hamilton lived in retirement, his time taken up mainly with fishing expeditions, visits to the British Museum and attempts to gain a pension for himself and his wife. He and Emma lived mostly at Nelson's house in Merton and Hamilton's only flashes of ill-temper at

this arrangement came when he felt that his wife was devoting too much time to his friend and neglecting him. But their joint friendship survived even the break-up of Nelson's marriage and, when Hamilton died on 6 April 1803, Emma was holding him in her arms while Nelson held his hand. He was buried alongside Catherine Hamilton at Milford Haven. In his will he left a miniature of Emma to Nelson, '. . . in token of the great regard I have for his Lordship, the most virtuous, loyal and truly brave character I ever met with.' (See colour plate *XIX*.)

A tall, athletic man in his youth, he retained his physical and mental vigour almost to the end of his life. Sophisticated, mild mannered and cultured, he was essentially a diplomat in all his dealings and arguably his finest achievement was the way he managed to keep the companionship of his wife, and the friendship of his dear friend, despite the passion that they felt for each other. His achievements in the field of state diplomacy were perhaps not very distinguished but his genuinely impressive achievements as a vulcanologist and classical antiquarian are now much more widely recognised and in 1996 they were celebrated in a major exhibition about him entitled 'Volcanoes and Vases'. Appropriately, it was mounted by the British Museum, to the establishment of which he contributed so much.

SEE ALSO
Emma Hamilton, Naples, Neapolitan campaign, Ruffo

LATEST RESEARCH
Ian Jenkins and Kim Sloane, *Volcanoes and Vases*, British Museum (London 1996)
Colin White, 'Tria Juncta in Uno: Nelson and the Hamiltons', *The Trafalgar Chronicle* 6 (1996), The 1805 Club

Hardy, Sir Thomas Masterman (1769–1839)

Of all the 'Band of Brothers', Hardy is the man now most closely associated with Nelson. They served together for longer than any of the other members and he was the only one present at all four of Nelson's great battles. Although they were very different in temperament, it is arguable that he was Nelson's closest male friend.

Born on 5 April 1769, the son of a Dorset farmer, Hardy first went to sea briefly in 1781 and then

Captain Thomas Hardy. Most likenesses of Hardy show him in old age. This miniature, after a portrait by Lemuel Abbott, dates from about 1802/3 and so gives a better impression of what he looked like when Nelson knew him.

returned to school, followed by a spell in the merchant service, before beginning his regular naval career in 1790. Promoted lieutenant in November 1793, he was appointed to the frigate HMS *Meleager* and served in her, under the command of Captain George Cockburn, in Nelson's squadron operating off the northwest coast of Italy. When Cockburn transferred to HMS *Minerve* in August 1796, he took Hardy with him and so he was present at the capture of the Spanish frigate *Santa Sabina* in December 1796 under Nelson's command. Hardy was sent with the *Minerve*'s first lieutenant, John Culverhouse, to take possession of the prize but soon afterwards a Spanish squadron appeared and so the two lieutenants quickly hoisted English colours over the Spanish, thus diverting the enemy's attention long enough for the badly damaged *Minerve* to make her escape. The prize crew had sacrificed themselves to let their comrades escape: the sort of action that

Nelson never forgot. Culverhouse's future was assured – as first lieutenant, he would automatically be promoted as a reward for his part in the capture of the *Minerve* – but Lieutenant Hardy still had his way to make. From that moment, he was under Nelson's personal protection and became one of his inner circle of 'followers'.

That protection started immediately, for Nelson got quickly to work to secure Hardy's release from captivity with the Spaniards; with such success that he was able to rejoin the *Minerve* when she called in briefly at Gibraltar early in the following February on her way to join Sir John Jervis and his fleet off Cape St Vincent. But Hardy's reunion with his comrades was very nearly short-lived. When the *Minerve* left Gibraltar, she was chased by a Spanish squadron and, at a critical moment, a man fell overboard. Hardy went in a small boat to try and rescue him and, having failed to do so, attempted to return to the frigate, only to find that she was moving away too fast for his rowers to catch up. Nelson saw the problem and, exclaiming 'By God! I'll not lose Hardy!', ordered the ship to be hove-to to await the boat, even though the nearest Spanish battleship was gaining on him fast. Seeing the frigate apparently lying in wait and defying him, the Spanish captain hesitated long enough for Hardy and his boat's crew to be recovered. Earlier descriptions of this incident, based on the account of the landsman Colonel John Drinkwater who was a passenger in the *Minerve*, say that Nelson ordered only the mizzen topsail to be backed, but this would not have slowed the frigate sufficiently. A recently discovered account of the incident by a seafaring onlooker, watching from the ramparts of Gibraltar, confirms that '. . . in an instant she hove to in the wind all standing.'

Hardy continued in the *Minerve* and so had a grandstand view of the Battle of Cape St Vincent on 14 February 1797. Shortly after the battle, he led a cutting out operation at Santa Cruz in Tenerife in which the French brig *Mutine* was captured and was rewarded by being promoted and given command of her. He then served in her throughout the Nile campaign and at the Battle of the Nile (1 August 1798), where he assisted the 74-gun battleship HMS *Culloden*, under Captain Thomas Troubridge, when she struck the reef at the entrance to Aboukir Bay.

Following the battle, Nelson promoted Hardy to post captain and immediately gave him command of his flagship HMS *Vanguard*.

So began the first stage of Hardy's long personal association with Nelson that ended only with the admiral's death in 1805. He continued with Nelson, first in the *Vanguard* and then in the *Foudroyant*, taking part in the Neapolitan campaign of 1799 until Nelson's former flag captain, Edward Berry, returned to the Mediterranean in October of that year, whereupon Hardy returned to Britain. But Nelson had been so impressed by Hardy's efficiency that in January 1801, when he was appointed to serve in the Channel fleet, he asked for Hardy again as his flag captain in the *San Josef* and then the *St George*. They served together throughout the Baltic campaign and it was Hardy who, on the eve of the Battle of Copenhagen (2 April 1801), went in an open boat to take soundings as close as possible to the Danish line in an attempt to discover where the shoals were located.

Following Nelson's departure from the Baltic, Hardy remained there in command of the *St George* until the late summer of 1801 and it would appear from recently discovered correspondence that he then spent some time with Nelson in the Channel towards the end of his time in command there. In May 1803, he was once again Nelson's flag captain, this time in HMS *Victory*, and remained with him throughout the campaign and Battle of Trafalgar. He was pacing with Nelson on the quarterdeck when the admiral was shot and heard, and recorded, the rueful words, 'Hardy, I believe they have done it at last.' Having given orders for his friend to be taken below to the cockpit, he then continued to give orders, and to control the battle, in his name and so was able to pay only two brief visits to the cockpit to tell Nelson of the progress of the battle. Eventually, he bade him farewell with the famous kiss that has been linked with his name ever since.

Having brought the battered *Victory* home with Nelson's body on board, and having played a central role in the funeral ceremonies, Hardy was made a baronet as a reward for his part in the battle, was given command of the 74-gun battleship HMS *Triumph* and went in her to the North American station, where he served for most of the rest of the war, latterly in a command of a small squadron. After the

war, he was commander-in-chief on the South American station as a commodore and, having been promoted to rear admiral in 1825, took command of an experimental squadron that had been put together to test the sailing qualities of various designs of ship. Finally, in 1830, he became First Sea Lord and then spent his last years as governor of Greenwich Hospital. He died there on 20 September 1839 and was buried in the hospital's mausoleum with a miniature of Nelson beside him in the coffin, at his own request. There is a monument to him in the chapel of the hospital and a pillar stands above his native village of Portisham in Dorset, looking out to the sea.

A tall man, with a large, heavy frame, Hardy was an impressive figure. Reserved and unemotional, he was the perfect foil to the mercurial Nelson, who obviously found Hardy's quiet strength and dependability reassuring. Hardy, too, was his own man: alone of Nelson's close friends, he continued to visit and to correspond with Lady Nelson after the break-up of the marriage and Nelson appears to have respected him for this. He once asked Hardy why it was that they agreed so well together and Hardy replied that it was because when Nelson wished to be an admiral, Hardy would act as his flag captain but when Nelson wanted to play the captain, Hardy was content to become his first lieutenant. This adaptability, which made him such an ideal colleague and companion, also had a physical manifestation: Hardy once told a friend that he and Nelson had paced the quarterdeck so often together that he found he had, quite unconsciously, adapted his own long stride to match that of his shorter friend.

SEE ALSO
'Band of Brothers', Cape St Vincent, Copenhagen, 'Kiss me, Hardy', Nile, *Santa Sabina*, Trafalgar

Health, Nelson's

One of the most persistent myths about Nelson is that he was unusually weak and sickly. In part, this concept is derived from Captain Maurice Suckling's famous comment when Nelson asked to be allowed to go to sea with him: 'What has poor Horace done, who is so weak, that he above the rest should be sent to rough it at sea?' It is further supported by the evidence of some of the portraits, especially those painted immediately after the loss of his arm. But when Surgeon William Beatty came to examine Nelson's body during the autopsy following his death, he discovered that his internal organs were so healthy that they resembled those of a young man, rather than a man already well into middle age, and he concluded that Nelson, like his father and many of his family, would probably have survived into his seventies or eighties. It is also important to remember that Nelson not only received a number of severe wounds but also suffered many life-threatening diseases, all of which trials he survived. Arguably, therefore, the word that best describes him is not 'weak' but 'resilient'. As he himself put it, in a letter to the Duke of Clarence, during the siege of Bastia in 1794, '. . . I am here a reed among the oaks, all the prevailing disorders have attacked me but I have not the strength for them to fasten upon. I bow before the storm whilst the sturdy oak is laid low.'

Nelson's first major encounter with serious disease came in 1775 when he was struck down with malaria during his voyage to the East Indies in the frigate HMS *Seahorse*. He was so ill that his life was despaired of and he was sent home as a last desperate resort. Although he recovered from that particular attack, he suffered regular recurrences of the disease for the rest of his life; so much so that he became able to predict its arrival and referred to his 'ague day'. Five years later, when he was already weakened by scurvy, it recurred during the campaign in Nicaragua, combined with tropical sprue (an acute form of diarrhoea) in a lethal cocktail that nearly killed him. Again, he was invalided out just in time and returned to England so weak that when he went to Bath to take the waters he had to be carried to and from his bed with what he called, 'the most excruciating tortures.' At one point, he lost the use of his left arm and leg and it took him nearly nine months to recover fully. Most biographies of Nelson suggest he was suffering from yellow fever but recent medical research has established that his symptoms do not support such a diagnosis.

Thereafter, Nelson's health remained precarious. In a benign climate, when he was happy and not under too much stress, his natural robustness appears to have reasserted itself. So, in early 1796 when he was serving in the Mediterranean, he wrote to his wife, 'I fancy you will find me grown very stout and my health was never better than at this moment.' Or again, when he returned to Britain briefly in the late summer of 1805 after two strenuous but fulfilling years in the Mediterranean, friends remarked on how well he looked and how he had even grown 'plump'. But in an adverse climate – such as the Baltic in the spring of 1801, or later that year in the chilly autumn gales of the Channel – his health quickly collapsed, leaving him wracked with fever and miserable. The same applied when he was suffering from disappointment or stress: for example, in 1799 his letters from the Mediterranean complain of constant and debilitating ill-health and the descriptions of his appearance in 1800 when he returned home through the German states with the Hamiltons suggest that he was both very sick and very unhappy.

Finally, throughout his later life he suffered from regular, and often quite acute, chest pains, which he referred to as 'my dreadful spasms'. In the past, it has been suggested that this was a form of nervous palpitation known as 'Soldier's Heart and Effort Syndrome' (or 'Da Costa's Syndrome') but Beatty, who treated Nelson almost daily for over two years, believed that it was 'indigestion brought on by writing for several hours together', and modern experts tend to agree with him.

Nelson's health, and his numerous wounds, have remained a rich source of interest and debate ever since his death. In 1966, the British Orthopaedic Association held its spring meeting at the Royal Naval Hospital at Haslar in Gosport and a special temporary exhibition was mounted in the hospital library entitled, 'Nelson Chirurgiique' (Nelson and His Surgeons). The exhibition catalogue reveals that more than sixty exhibits were gathered together from collections all over the country, ranging from the tourniquet allegedly used during the amputation of his arm to the bullet that killed him at Trafalgar.

SEE ALSO
Bath, Beatty, Cuba Cornwallis, Nicaraguan campaign, Wounds

LATEST RESEARCH
Ann-Mary Hills, 'Nelson's Illnesses', *Journal of the Royal Naval Medical Service* 86 (2000)
P D Gordon Pugh, *Nelson and His Surgeons*, E & S Livingstone (London 1968)

Height, Nelson's

The popular image of Nelson is that he was an unusually small man. In fact, modern research has established that he was about 5ft 6in/5ft 7in tall (1.7/1.8 metres); in other words, around the average height for a man of his time.

Among the many relics of Nelson that have survived is a complete set of his clothes: the uniform coat, waistcoat, breeches and stockings that he was wearing at Trafalgar, now in the collection of the National Maritime Museum. When they were conserved recently, they were accurately measured and, as a result, it is now possible to calculate his height with some accuracy. The study has also established that he had a chest measurement of about 38/39 inches (96/99cm) and a waist size of about 32/33 inches (81/83cm).

The conclusion about his height is supported by contemporary descriptions. James Bagley, a Royal Marine who fought at Trafalgar, wrote, 'He is a man about five feet seven.' An American, Benjamin Silliman, who saw Nelson in September 1805, said he was 'of about middle height, or rather more.' And his nephew, George Matcham, stated categorically, 'He was not as described, a little man, but of the middle height and of a frame adapted to activity and exertion.'

So how did the myth of his smallness arise? The most likely explanation is, having heard of his deeds, people expected someone who looked more 'heroic' and so were surprised, even disappointed, when he appeared so ordinary and unremarkable. A man who saw him in Salisbury in 1801 wrote, 'As he alighted from his carriage I could not help asking myself if that one-armed, one-eyed man could really have scattered destruction among the fleets of France. I felt all my conception of what constituted a grammar-school hero utterly discomforted.'

SEE ALSO
Relics

LATEST RESEARCH
Colin White, 'What did Nelson look like?', *Alongside* 1 (1999), The Royal Naval Museum

Samuel Lord Hood. This engraving, dating from about 1795, captures the experienced and sometimes irascible old admiral under whom Nelson served in the Mediterranean in 1793/4.

Hood, Samuel Lord (1724–1816)

One of Britain's most distinguished admirals in the second half of the eighteenth century, Hood was Nelson's patron and mentor throughout most of his time as a post captain. He secured him two important ship commands and also gave him his first command of a major operation, in Corsica in 1794.

Like Nelson the son of a country parson, Hood was born in 1724 and did not go to sea until he was sixteen, which meant he received a broader education than many of his contemporaries in the Navy, giving him a more intellectual and thoughtful approach to his profession. He saw service throughout the 1740s, mostly in home waters and on the North American station, rising to lieutenant in June 1746. In 1749, he married Susannah Linzee, daughter of an influential Portsmouth apothecary and politician, and so began his long association with Portsmouth, both in naval affairs and in politics.

Promoted post captain in July 1756, he saw action on a number of occasions during the Seven Years War (1756–1763) and ended the war with a reputation for enterprise and professionalism that, together with his political connections, ensured that he remained employed during the peace. Having served as commander-in-chief in North America in the rank of commodore, he was appointed to successive Portsmouth guardships and then, in 1778, commissioner of Portsmouth Dockyard. Here he came to the attention of King George III who visited there in May 1778 and who was so impressed by what he called '. . . the Activity with which you forward the business of the dock yard' that he made Hood a baronet.

In 1780, Hood reached the rank of rear admiral and used his considerable influence to obtain an appointment as second in command in the West Indies, flying his flag in HMS *Barfleur*. So began the spell of duty that was to bring him to the forefront of his profession and to public notice. Despite strained relations with his senior, the notoriously irascible and difficult Sir George Rodney, he succeeded in transforming the ships of his division into a highly trained and motivated fighting force that enjoyed some notable successes. Chief among these was the series of encounters at St Kitts (24 January–14 February 1782) in which Hood first seized the French anchorage in a masterly manoeuvre, then repulsed a determined French counterattack and, finally, extricated his force without loss in a well-planned and tightly co-ordinated withdrawal under the cover of night. Key to his success in this and other operations was the unusual degree with which he consulted with his subordinates and relayed his intentions to them directly: a style of leadership that clearly influenced Nelson.

Later in the same year, Hood played an important role in Rodney's victory at the Battle of the Saintes (12 April 1782) where he had the honour of receiving the surrender of the disabled French flagship, the *Ville de Paris*. But Rodney, exhausted after the days of manoeuvring that had preceded the battle, failed to follow up his success as vigorously as Hood wished and so relations between them became strained to the point of breaking. Nonetheless, his conduct at the

Saintes, following so soon after St Kitts, secured Hood's fame. He was made a baron and the King entrusted to him the naval education of his son William, declaring Hood to be 'the most brilliant Officer of this war.' At the same time, Hood acquired another protégé, the young captain of HMS *Albemarle*, Horatio Nelson, who visited him on board the *Barfleur* at Sandy Hook, off New York, on 13 November, specifically to ask for his patronage. Hood, who had known Nelson's uncle Maurice Suckling when he was MP for Portsmouth, agreed and so began an association that lasted until Nelson's death.

Hood's influence immediately worked in Nelson's favour. He presented him to the King in July 1783 and the following year obtained for him a coveted, and very scarce, peacetime appointment as captain of the frigate HMS *Boreas*. Hood, in the meantime, devoted himself to a political career, standing for election as MP for Westminster in 1784. He continued in active service, including two more spells in Portsmouth as commander-in-chief and also as a member of the Board of Admiralty. When Nelson found himself without a command during his five years 'on the beach' during 1787–1793, he repeatedly asked Hood for help but was told sternly that his handling of the dispute between Prince William and Lieutenant Schomberg had led to him being 'censured' at the Admiralty. Eventually, however, in 1793, when he was appointed commander-in-chief of the Mediterranean, Hood was able to obtain for Nelson the command of the *Agamemnon* right at the outset of the long war with France.

Hood was by now over seventy but he showed little sign of his age, remaining vigorous and aggressive in his conduct of the war. When, in August 1793, French royalists offered to hand over the vital naval arsenal of Toulon, Hood seized the chance, despite the considerable risks involved, and continued even after others had despaired of success to hold on to his prize in the face of a determined counterattack by the revolutionaries. Eventually, the British and their allies had to withdraw but not before they had captured or destroyed thirteen battleships, more than in any naval action of the war, except Trafalgar.

The following year, Hood pursued a similarly aggressive policy when Corsican nationalists asked him for help in ousting the French from their island.

When his boldness, and desire for speedy action, led to strained relations with the army commanders, who favoured a much more cautious approach, Hood responded by mounting a predominantly naval operation to capture the key port of Bastia. He entrusted this to Nelson, then still one of the more junior captains in the fleet. It was Nelson's first taste of independent command and he fully justified his patron's trust by triumphantly capturing Bastia within weeks.

By now, however, Hood was worn out and, in November 1794, he went home for the winter, intending to return to the Mediterranean the following year. But he became involved in a public dispute with the First Lord of the Admiralty, Lord Spencer, over the number of ships allocated to his fleet and was so aggressive in his demands and criticisms that Spencer felt obliged to dismiss him. He was, however, raised to the rank of viscount and appointed governor of Greenwich Hospital, which post he continued to occupy until his death in 1816. It therefore fell to him, in December 1805, to receive the body of his former pupil when it was brought to the hospital to lie in state and the following month he acted as one of the supporters to the chief mourner at Nelson's funeral in St Paul's Cathedral.

Although some historians have disputed Hood's reputation as a fighting admiral, pointing out that he never commanded a fleet at a major battle, he can claim to have had a significant influence on the generation that won the great victories in the years immediately following his retirement from active service. As well as Nelson, William Cornwallis and James Saumarez served under him at crucial moments in their early careers and a number of Nelson's own protégés similarly, notably Samuel Hood the younger and George Cockburn. Moreover, there can be no doubt that Hood was highly regarded by many of his naval contemporaries, chief among whom was Nelson who once told his wife that he considered Hood's nose (a particularly prominent feature) '. . . as at least equal to four sail of the line.'

SEE ALSO

Cornwallis, Saumarez, Schomberg, William IV

LATEST RESEARCH

Michael Duffy, 'Samuel Hood, First Viscount Hood', in Peter LeFevre and Richard Harding (eds), *Precursors of Nelson*, Chatham Publishing (London 2000)

Hood, Samuel (1762–1814)

Hood served with Nelson on a number of occasions and played a key role in the Battle of the Nile. But he also had a most distinguished career in his own right and, arguably, saw more action than any other member of the 'Band of Brothers'. The son of a distinguished naval family, he first went to sea with his cousin, Samuel Hood, later Lord Hood and one of Nelson's chief patrons. He served throughout the War of American Independence and took part in the Battle of the Saintes (12 April 1782).

Promoted to post captain at the age of twenty-six, he was sent to the Mediterranean in 1793 in the frigate HMS *Aigle*, attached to Lord Hood's fleet. He later transferred to the battleship HMS *Zealous* and commanded her at the Battle of Cape St Vincent (14 February 1797). Later that year, he was one of the captains specially chosen by Lord St Vincent to accompany Nelson on the expedition to Tenerife and played a leading role in the abortive night attack on the town of Santa Cruz on 24/25 July. In 1798, he was present at the Battle of the Nile, taking the *Zealous* inshore of the French fleet in the wake of Foley's *Goliath* and knocking out the headmost French ship, the *Guerrier*. Three years later, he again distinguished himself at the Battle of the Gut of Gibraltar (12 July 1801), in command of the battleship HMS *Venerable*.

After the Peace of Amiens, Hood was appointed to command the Leeward Islands station as a commodore, and he captured the islands of St Lucia and Tobago from the French in 1803, with the help of his former Nile colleague, Ben Hallowell. Later, in September 1806, he lost his arm during a fierce action in which five large French frigates were captured. However, this did not prevent him from continuing in active service: he took part in the attack on Copenhagen in 1807 and also served in the Baltic in 1809 as a rear admiral under Sir James Saumarez, during which campaign his flagship HMS *Implacable* captured the Russian battleship *Sevelode*.

Later that year, Hood commanded the naval part of the famous withdrawal from Corunna of the British army under General Sir John Moore and was made a baronet for his services. In 1812, by now a vice admiral, he went to the East Indies as commander-in-chief and died of fever at Madras in 1816.

He bore a striking resemblance to Nelson, especially after the loss of his arm, although he was considerably taller. A colleague once said of him that 'his appearance and manners were at all times unspeakably winning' and he was genuinely loved both by his fellow officers and by his men. He was also more of an intellectual than many of Nelson's other captains, being an expert on astronomy, geography and shipbuilding.

SEE ALSO
'Band of Brothers', Lord Hood, Nile

Hoste, Sir William (1780–1828)

Although he is best known as one of Nelson's protégés and, arguably, the brightest of them all, Hoste deserves to be remembered in his own right as one of the great British frigate captains of the Napoleonic period. In his ten years of active service as a post captain, he took part in six major actions, ranging from a full-scale squadronal action to the capture of a heavily fortified port.

The son of Rev Dixon Hoste, the rector of Godwick and Tittleshall, which lie about ten miles south of Nelson's home village of Burnham Thorpe, Hoste first went to sea as a midshipman with Nelson in the *Agamemnon* in April 1793. He remained with Nelson almost continuously for the next five years, serving with him in Corsica in 1794, in Hotham's two actions against the French in 1795 and at Cape St Vincent (14 February 1797). When Nelson transferred, with Captain Ralph Miller, to the mutinous HMS *Theseus* in June 1797, Hoste was one of the hand-picked followers he took with him. Left behind in the ship during the abortive attack on Santa Cruz de Tenerife on 25 July, Hoste witnessed the return of his patron, jumping one-armed up the side of the ship and shouting orders for the surgeon to get his instruments ready 'for he knew he must lose his arm and that the sooner it was off the better.'

When Nelson returned home to Britain to recover from his wound, Hoste remained in the *Theseus*, becoming a lieutenant in February 1798, and continued in her throughout the Nile campaign. After the Battle of the Nile (1 August 1798), Nelson gave him command of the brig *Mutine* and in her he went first

Captain William Hoste. This fine portrait, attributed to Samuel Lane, dates from about 1803 and shows Hoste as a young post captain – the man whom Nelson loved as a son. (National Maritime Museum)

to Naples and then to Gibraltar and, finally, to Lord St Vincent's fleet off Cádiz, bearing the news of the victory. He then returned to Nelson and remained with his squadron for a further three years, taking part in the operations in Italy, including the capture of Rome in the autumn of 1799. When Nelson left the Mediterranean, Hoste remained there under Lord Keith and, finally, in January 1802, he was promoted post captain and appointed to the frigate HMS *Greyhound*. He heard the news at Piraeus in Greece where he had been sent with despatches for the British ambassador, Lord Elgin.

Having served continuously throughout the Peace of Amiens, Hoste returned home in April 1803 and six months later was appointed to another frigate,

HMS *Eurydice*. In her he later joined Nelson off Cádiz in September 1805 and was moved into the larger and more powerful HMS *Amphion* and sent to Algiers with presents to the Dey. So he missed Trafalgar by just a few days.

In 1807, having refitted the *Amphion* in Britain, Hoste was sent by Collingwood into the Adriatic. At first, he carried on a brisk war against enemy shipping and coastal installations almost alone but gradually his force was increased and, having established his base at Lissa (modern Vis), he was able effectively to dominate the entire Adriatic Sea with just four frigates and seriously to disrupt all the ship movements of the French and their allies. Eventually, the French sent a powerful squadron of six frigates and five smaller vessels against him under Commodore Dubourdieu but, at the Battle of Lissa (13 March 1811), Hoste and his colleagues inflicted a decisive defeat on them, capturing three of their frigates and driving a fourth on shore. As the British squadron awaited the attack, Hoste electrified his men by sending the simple telegraph signal, 'Remember Nelson!', which was greeted with loud cheers along the British line. 'Never again so long as I live shall I see so interesting or so glorious a moment,' remembered Captain Phipps Hornby of HMS *Volage*. And the name of Nelson featured frequently among the many eulogies that Hoste received when the news broke of his great victory. Lord Radstock, who had served with Nelson at Cape St Vincent, wrote, 'I look at you as the truly worthy élève of my incomparable and ever to be lamented friend the late Lord Nelson.'

Having taken the *Amphion* home for refit, Hoste was given another frigate, the *Bacchante*, and returned in her to the Adriatic in June 1812. Once again, Hoste dominated the sea and carried out a number of highly effective raids on enemy installations and shipping. Finally, in December 1813, his men took part in the capture of the supposedly impregnable fortified port of Cattaro. Establishing a battery of heavy guns and mortars on a hill dominating the town – very much as he had seen Nelson do twenty years before in Corsica – Hoste succeeded in forcing the French garrison to surrender. He then repeated the operation at the neighbouring town of Ragusa.

By now, however, Hoste's health – already undermined by a severe bout of malaria in 1802 – was failing and he was obliged to return home. He was made a baronet as a reward for his remarkable exploits and, later, in 1815 received the KCB. He never really recovered his health and his only other appointments were to home-based ships, including a spell as captain of the royal yacht *Royal Sovereign* in 1825. He eventually died in London on 6 December 1828.

A friendly, affectionate man, Hoste was much loved by all those with whom he came into contact, including Nelson who once told his father, 'his worth as a man and an officer exceeds all which the most sincere friend can say of him. I pray God to bless my dear William.' Hoste always acknowledged how much he owed his patron and repaid him with devotion, writing, 'Him I look upon as almost a second father, a sheet anchor whom I shall always have to trust to.'

SEE ALSO
HMS *Agamemnon*, Tenerife, Weatherhead

LATEST RESEARCH
Tom Pocock, *Remember Nelson*, Collins (London 1977)

Hotham, William Lord (1736–1813)

Hotham was commander-in-chief in the Mediterranean for a brief spell in 1795 during which time he commanded the fleet at two indecisive engagements with the French at which Nelson was present. He started his naval career at the newly established Naval Academy in Portsmouth in 1748 and entered the Royal Navy three years later, rising to lieutenant in 1754. He became a post captain in 1757 and served throughout the Seven Years War (1756–1763), including taking part in the capture of Belleisle in April 1761. During the war against America, he served as a commodore under Rodney and also took part in the relief of Gibraltar under Howe in 1782.

Promoted to rear admiral in 1787 and to vice admiral in 1793, he was appointed second in command of the Mediterranean fleet under Lord Hood and was present with him in the capture of Toulon and the campaign in Corsica. When Hood went home in late 1794, Hotham succeeded him although, since Hood was expected to return after a spell of leave, it was assumed it would be only a temporary appointment. In fact, it lasted the best part of a year, during which

Commodore William Hotham. This watercolour miniature dates from about 1780 and shows Hotham before he became the rather unadventurous admiral who so exasperated Nelson with his half-hearted approach to battle in 1795.

time the fleet twice encountered the French: at the Battles of Genoa (14/15 March 1795) and Hyères (13 July 1795). At both engagements, Hotham displayed hesitation and a disinclination to take risks that infuriated some of his young captains, including Nelson, then commanding the battleship HMS *Agamemnon*.

Hotham was a good officer and had been an excellent subordinate commander but he was clearly not suited for the top post, a failing that was seen all too clearly by his associates. 'I can entre nous perceive,' wrote Sir William Hamilton to Nelson, 'that my old friend Hotham is not quite awake enough for such a command as that of the King's Fleet in the Mediterranean.' The Admiralty agreed and, when Hotham returned to Britain in late 1795, he was not employed at sea again. Raised to the peerage in 1797, he died on 2 May 1813.

SEE ALSO
Genoa, Hyères

Hyères, Battle of (13 July 1795)

Throughout 1795, the French made a number of attempts to recapture Corsica from the British. Despite its losses at the Battle of the Gulf of Genoa in March, the French Mediterranean fleet tried again in July. Their approach was discovered on 7 July by Nelson who was on detached duty on the French coast in the *Agamemnon*, with three frigates. The French chased him and Nelson led them south to San Fiorenzo, on the southwest coast of Corsica, where he knew the British commander-in-chief, Vice Admiral William Hotham, was based with the rest of the British fleet.

Hotham had twenty-two battleships, while the French had only seventeen; so when they sighted the British fleet, they turned and retreated north towards their nearest base at Toulon. Hotham followed and, after four days of searching, succeeded in coming up with them on 13 July off Hyères Island on the south coast of France, close to Toulon. After wasting some four hours in a favourable wind making small adjustments to his line, Hotham realised that he could not catch the French with his slower ships and signalled a general chase. The fastest-sailing British ships then forged ahead and managed to catch up with the rearmost French ships and a partial action ensued in which one French ship was set on fire and blew up. Other British ships were now arriving on the scene, among them the *Agamemnon*, and a decisive battle seemed imminent. But the wind was becoming fitful and by now Hotham himself was some eight miles astern and unable to see clearly what was going on. So he hoisted the signal of recall, allowing the French to escape back into Toulon.

Nelson was very disappointed at this tame result. 'Had Lord Hood been here,' he told his wife, 'he would never have called us out of action but Hotham leaves nothing to chance.' He was also very critical of the time Hotham wasted earlier in the day getting his fleet into line of battle: 'what might not have been expected had our whole fleet engaged?' he wrote to his brother William. In this frustration, we can see the beginnings of the tactical ideas that were to bear fruit in his famous battle plan before Trafalgar in 1805.

SEE ALSO
HMS *Agamemnon*, Fremantle, Battle of Gulf of Genoa, Hotham, Nelson Touch

I

'Immortal Memory, The'

Every year, Nelson is remembered in a special toast, drunk after the Loyal Toast at Trafalgar Night dinners: 'The Immortal Memory'. As with all such customs, its exact origins are hard to trace and it probably evolved gradually, rather than being specifically introduced on any particular occasion.

The word 'immortal' was often applied to Nelson even when he was alive. But it was most in use during the months immediately following his death and a number of private toasts to his memory were drunk when the news of Trafalgar arrived in England in early November, for example at a dinner at The Ship tavern in Greenwich. One of the first printed records of it occurs in a caricature of two sailors drinking Nelson's health, published in December 1805 (see colour plate *XVI*).

However, the first recorded public event at which it was used was not until 1811, when a dinner was held on Trafalgar Day at The Green Man public house at Blackheath, near Greenwich. And in 1813, Emma Hamilton wrote to her friend Thomas Lewis inviting him to come to dinner on the anniversary of the Battle of the Nile: 'If you come,' she promised, 'we will drink to his Immortal Memory.'

Certainly, the toast was in general use by Trafalgar Day 1846. According to a report in *The Times*, Captain John Pasco (who had supervised the hoisting of Nelson's signal 'England expects' in 1805) presided at a dinner on board his old ship HMS *Victory* and proposed a toast to 'The immortal memory of Nelson and those who fell with him.' Sadly, the second part of Pasco's toast no longer forms part of the traditional Trafalgar Night ritual. Yet it is clear that it was common practice in the earliest days. In 1867, John Yule, son of one of the *Victory*'s Trafalgar lieutenants, recalled his father's own private annual commemoration: 'I have yet a pleasing & lively recollection of my Father wearing his Trafalgar shirt & surrounded by his seven Sons and four Daughters proposing after dinner, "The Immortal Memory of Lord Nelson" and then of those whom "England expected (not in vain) that they would do their duty".'

SEE ALSO
Pasco, Trafalgar Day ceremonies

LATEST RESEARCH
Colin White, 'The Immortal Memory', in his *The Nelson Companion*, Sutton and Royal Naval Museum (Stroud & Portsmouth 1995)

Italian campaign (1795/6)

For just over a year, between August 1795 and August 1796, Nelson, then a commodore, commanded a small squadron off the northwest coast of Italy. His main task was to act in support of the Austrians, who were attempting to defend their possessions on the Italian peninsula from the armies of revolutionary France. Operating out of Vado Bay, near Genoa, where the Austrian commander-in-chief, General de Vins, had his headquarters, Nelson imposed a close blockade of the coast, thus preventing supplies from reaching the French by sea. He also carried out a series of closely targeted raids on key French-held ports to capture and destroy their shipping.

However, in March 1796, Napoleon Bonaparte took command of the French Army of Italy and began the brilliant campaign which first established his reputation. Nelson continued to harry the French coastal supply route, and even succeeded in capturing Napoleon's siege train at Oneglia on 30 May. But the French advance was inexorable and, in June, the port of Leghorn fell to their victorious armies. Thereafter, there was little that the British could do to assist their allies and they concentrated their attention on securing Corsica from attack, a task in which Nelson played a key role by capturing the islands of Elba (10 July 1796) and Capraia (18

September 1796). However, the entry of Spain into the war on the side of France, in the autumn of 1796, meant that even Corsica had to be abandoned and, eventually, in December, the British commander-in-chief, Sir John Jervis, withdrew his fleet altogether from the Mediterranean.

Although the campaign itself ended in failure, Nelson's active and efficient role in it had drawn attention to his abilities and had attracted the notice of some influential people. Chief among them were Sir John Jervis – who, Nelson told his wife, 'seems at present to consider me as an assistant more than a subordinate' – and the First Lord of the Admiralty, Lord Spencer.

SEE ALSO
Adelaide Correglia, Jervis, Napoleon

Nelson, in HMS Agamemnon, *in action on the coast of Italy, in the autumn of 1795. An engraving from* The Naval Chronicle.

J

John Jervis, Lord St Vincent. Although this engraving dates from about 1805 and shows St Vincent in old age, it still captures the alertness and intelligence that made him such a successful fighting admiral.

Jervis, John (Lord St Vincent) (1735–1823)

John Jervis dominated the Royal Navy throughout Nelson's final years. A brilliant administrator and trainer of officers and men, he more than any other created the efficient fighting machine that Nelson and his colleagues used to such effect. Indeed, it is arguable that, without Jervis's careful preparatory work, Nelson could never have been as successful as he was.

The son of a lawyer, Jervis ran away to sea at the age of thirteen. Although forced to return home, his wish to serve in the Navy was granted and he was first entered on the books of the 50-gun battleship HMS *Gloucester* in January 1749. Promoted to lieutenant in 1755, he served in the West Indies in a fleet commanded by one of the great mid eighteenth-century admirals, Edward Boscawen. It was probably from him that he first learned the importance of actively maintaining the good health of sailors: a lesson he put into such striking practice when he commanded fleets himself. The following year, he moved to the Mediterranean and served under another great admiral, Edward Hawke, who three years later won one of the most remarkable naval victories of the century at Quiberon Bay (20 November 1759). Finally, in late 1756, he transferred to the flagship of Charles Saunders and served with him at the capture of Quebec in 1759, where he met and became friends with the brilliant young general James Wolfe. So, within the space of just four years, he had come under the influence of some of the key military leaders of his time and these early influences can be seen both in his later career and in the precepts he passed on to his own pupils.

Promoted commander in 1759, he finally became a post captain in 1760. During the peace following the Seven Years War, he travelled in France to learn the language and to study the coast around the great western French port and naval arsenal of Brest and also to Russia where he visited and studied the naval dockyard at Cronstadt. During the war with America, he saw distinguished service in command of the fine 80-gun battleship HMS *Foudroyant*, culminating in the capture of the French 74-gun *Pégase* in April 1779. For this exploit he was made a Knight of Bath, a rare honour for a post captain.

During the next peace he became a member of parliament, first for Launceston and then for Chipping Wycombe, and was actively involved in the politics of the time, supporting the modest reform of Parliament and religious tolerance. Although originally opposed to Prime Minister William Pitt's policies when they seemed to be leading to war, he eventually resigned his seat in 1794 and offered himself for active service. Having been promoted to rear admiral in 1787, he was now a vice admiral and so he was offered command of the West Indies squadron. Despite early successes, it was not a happy tenure of office and when he returned home, in 1795, it was to face a motion of censure in the House of Commons. Then, in the autumn of 1795, Jervis was offered the command of the Mediterranean fleet. The former commander-in-chief, Lord Hood, had quarrelled with the Admiralty and his two successors, William Hotham and Sir Hyde Parker, had proved hesitant and inefficient. Clearly, a man of determination and experience was needed and Jervis was generally believed to be the right candidate.

So began a remarkable period of active service that led him to the very peak of his profession. Jervis set about transforming the Mediterranean fleet with regular exercises, strict discipline and insistence on the high standards of health and hygiene that he had learned under Boscawen. Although forced by the general strategic situation to abandon the Mediterranean in December 1796, he nonetheless went on resoundingly to defeat the Spanish fleet at the Battle of Cape St Vincent on 14 February 1797 and then bottled it up in Cádiz, enforcing a tight blockade, despite the fact that at one point his fleet was seething with discontent following the great mutinies at Spithead and the Nore. In achieving all this, he always acknowledged that he had the support of a fine body of younger officers, among whom he rated Thomas Troubridge highest, followed closely by Horatio Nelson.

Nelson admired Jervis from the time of their first official meeting in December 1795 and Jervis quickly recognised the worth of his younger subordinate, giving him a succession of independent commands, culminating in the squadron with which he eventually won the Battle of the Nile on 1 August 1798. But he was not an uncritical friend, writing to Sir Gilbert Elliot in 1796, 'his zeal does now and then – not often – outrun his discretion.' And he was also very good at handling Nelson, using a deft mixture of firmness and flattery to persuade him to follow orders and supporting him loyally against the attacks of jealous rivals. Nelson responded by treating him almost like a father: 'We look up to you as we have always found you, as to our Father, under whose fostering care we have always been led to fame.'

Sadly, however, this highly productive professional relationship eventually became soured. First Nelson and St Vincent (as he became when he was made an earl in 1797) became embroiled in a legal battle over prize money and then, in the late summer of 1801, Nelson began to suspect (almost certainly wrongly) that his old mentor was deliberately keeping him at sea in the Channel long after it was really necessary, in order to separate him from Emma Hamilton. Although they continued to correspond in polite public letters, their friendship never really recovered its old trust and intimacy.

Meanwhile, St Vincent was coming increasingly to dominate naval affairs. After a period in command of the Channel fleet in 1800/1 during which he ruthlessly enforced the same standards of discipline as he had insisted upon in the Mediterranean, he became First Lord of the Admiralty in February 1801. Once the war with France was ended by the Treaty of Amiens, he set about applying the same rigour to the royal dockyards, which he saw as hotbeds of corruption. The short-term results were disastrous: when war broke out again, Britain's naval mobilisation was seriously affected and St Vincent found himself embroiled in a fierce political battle which led to his own resignation, and that of the government of which he was part, in May 1804.

Having retired briefly in high dudgeon, he was eventually persuaded on a change of government to resume command of the Channel fleet. He took over in March 1806, at the age of seventy-one, but served for little more than a year before resigning in April 1807. He never saw active service again, although he remained keenly and actively involved in naval affairs until his death in 1823.

Although a handsome man, he had a stocky build and a big head set low on his shoulders that gave him an aggressive, bull-like appearance. He was short-tempered and irascible, given to flashes of rage, and fond of expressing himself in sometimes violent hyperbole. But he could also be kindly and he retained to old age an impish sense of humour. He hated all forms of parade and displays of emotion and so he often found Nelson intensely irritating; he made his feelings clear in exasperated remarks, that have sometimes been quoted out of context, to suggest that he saw his brilliant protégé as little more than an instinctive fighter. But his true attitude is probably best reflected in the fact that he selected Nelson for a commander-in-chief's post on three separate occasions: the Baltic and the Channel in 1801 and the Mediterranean in 1803. Although ill-health, and his deep-seated dislike of excessive show, meant that he did not attend Nelson's funeral, he nonetheless felt his death keenly, remarking to a friend that he had been 'prepared for anything great from Nelson, but not for his loss.'

SEE ALSO
Cape St Vincent, Channel Command, Italian campaign, Troubridge

LATEST RESEARCH
Pat Crimmin, 'John Jervis, Earl of St Vincent', in Peter LeFevre and Richard Harding (eds), *Precursors of Nelson*, Chatham Publishing (London 2000)

I. Nelson by Heinrich Füger (1800). Produced in Vienna by the Court painter of Austria, this fine oil portrait captures Nelson's ruthlessness and is now agreed to be one of the best likenesses of him. See **Portraits**

II. Nelson in October 1805. This new figure, commissioned in 1999 by the Royal Naval Museum, is based on all the latest research into Nelson's appearance. See **Portraits**

III. Nelson by Henry Bone after the portrait in oils by John Hoppner. (The Royal Collection © 2002, Her Majesty Queen Elizabeth II)

IV. Nelson by John Hoppner (1800). Discovered recently, this raw, unfinished preliminary oil sketch for a full-length portrait was painted at the time of the break-up of Nelson's marriage. See **Portraits**

Right: *V. Nelson and the polar
bear. A famous incident in
Nelson's early life depicted by
Edward Orme. In fact, Nelson
and the bear were separated by
a large chasm in the ice. See*
Arctic Expedition

Below: *VI. Nelson at the Battle
of Cape St Vincent, 1797.
Daniel Orme's sanitised
representation of the moment
when Nelson received the
Spanish surrender. The Spanish
admiral (lying left) was in fact
dying below of his wounds and
Nelson's uniform was in tatters
and his face blackened with
gunsmoke. See* **Cape St
Vincent, Battle of**

Above: *VII. The destruction of* L'Orient *at the Battle of the Nile (1798). The French flagship exploded at the height of the battle. See* **L'Orient**

Left: *VIII. 'The extirpation of the plagues of the Nile', a caricature by Gilray. The crocodiles represent the French ships captured or destroyed. Note that Nelson is shown with a hook. See* **Nile, Battle of the**

Right: *XII. 'The Death of Nelson', a superb caricature by Gilray mocking the overblown way in which Nelson's death was commemorated by contemporary artists while, at the same time, paying its own personal tribute. The figure of Britannia supporting Nelson is a caricature of Emma Hamilton. See* 'Immortal Memory', **The**

Below: *XIII. The* Victory *at Spithead, 4 December 1805, an oil painting by J W Carmichael. With her flags at half mast, the* Victory *arrives in England with Nelson's body on board. See* **Victory,** HMS

Left: *XIV. The funeral service in St Paul's Cathedral, 9 January 1806. This coloured engraving, based on drawings made on the spot by Augustus Pugin, shows the final act of the state funeral, when Nelson's coffin was lowered into the crypt of St Paul's. See* **Funeral, Nelson's**

Below: *XV. The Immortal Memory. This painting on glass shows the body of the Hero being borne home in a sea-chariot drawn by Tritons, while Neptune looks on. See* **'Immortal Memory, The'**

XVI. 'The Immortal
Memory.' In this
affectionate caricature
by Rowlandson, dating
from December 1805,
two sailors mourn
Nelson and drink to
'The Immortal Memory
of the Hero of the Nile'
– one of the first records
of this famous toast.
See **'Immortal
Memory, The'**

XVII. Staffordshire pottery group 'The Death of
Nelson'. A typical example, dating from the mid
nineteenth century, of the many cheap and popular items
that were produced to commemorate Nelson. See
Commemorative material

XVIII. Nelson Commemorated. A collection of enamel patch boxes
commemorating the Battle of the Nile (top) and the Battle of
Trafalgar and Nelson's death. See **Commemorative material**

Left: *XIX.*
Miniature of
Emma Hamilton
worn by Nelson.
See **Hamilton,**
Emma

Right: *XX.*
Miniature of
Nelson worn by
Emma Hamilton.
It is based on the
portrait by Simon
de Koster, which
Nelson once said
was 'the most like
me.' See **Portraits**

XXI. Frances, Lady Nelson. A watercolour by Henry Edridge, painted in about 1807, captures Fanny's quiet, genteel beauty and commemorates her undying devotion to her husband. In front of the bust on the table is a casket containing a miniature of him, painted in Leghorn in 1794, which she always kept with her. See **Nelson, Frances Lady**

XXII. Horatia Nelson aged about four. This naïve but charming portrait shows Horatia as she appeared when Nelson saw her for the last time in the autumn of 1805. See **Nelson Ward, Horatia**

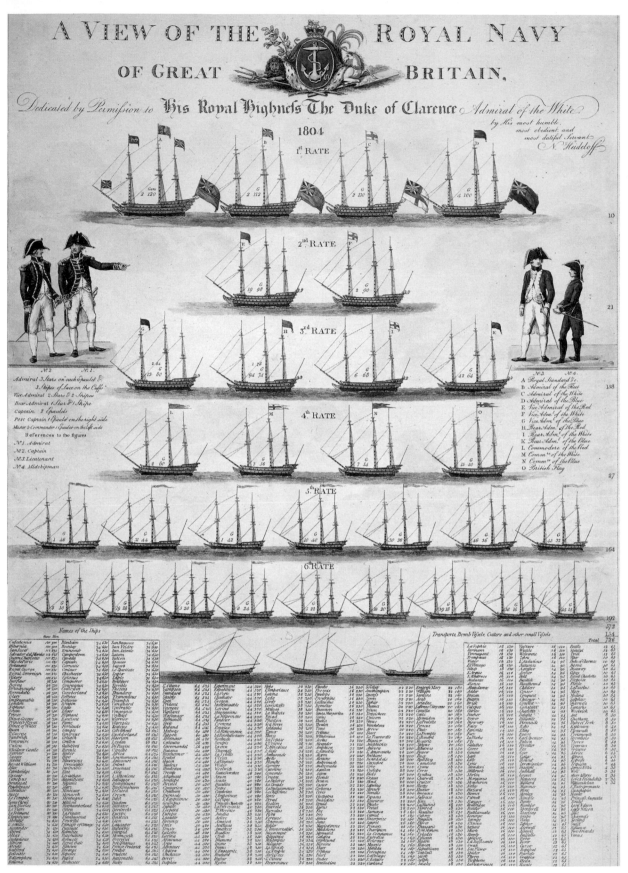

XXIII. *The ships of the Royal Navy, 1804. Every type of ship in which Nelson served is depicted here: Top row: First Rates (such as* Victory *and* San Josef). *Second row: Second Rates (such as* St George). *Third row: Third Rates (such as* Vanguard *and* Agamemnon). *Fourth row: Fourth Rates (such as* Bristol). *Fifth row: Fifth Rates (such as* Lowestoffe *and* La Minerve). *Sixth row: Sixth Rates (such as* Albemarle *and* Boreas). *Bottom row: Smaller, unrated vessels (such as* Badger *and* Carcass)

Keats, Sir Richard (1757–1834)

Keats was not one of the original 'Band of Brothers' and served with Nelson only once, in the Mediterranean between 1803 and 1805. But Nelson valued him highly. Keats became one of his inner circle and was one of those with whom he first shared the battle plan with which he later won Trafalgar (see p236).

Like Nelson the son of a clergyman, Keats was born at Chalton in Hampshire on 16 January 1757. Entering the Royal Navy in 1770, he served with his patron, Captain (later Admiral) James Montagu, until he was promoted to lieutenant in 1777. In 1779, he served in HMS *Prince George* where he first met Prince William Henry, later the Duke of Clarence and King William IV, with whom he became close friends. He became a post captain in 1783 and, when the war against revolutionary France broke out, was appointed to command the frigate HMS *Galatea*. In her, he saw much active service off the French coast.

In 1801, he was appointed to the 74-gun battleship HMS *Superb* and remained in her for nearly nine years, first as her captain and then as an admiral. Later that year, he played a leading role at the Battle of the Gut of Gibraltar (12 July 1801) when a British squadron under Rear Admiral Sir James Saumarez chased and defeated a superior Franco-Spanish force in a fast-moving night action. Keats in the *Superb* first attacked two large Spanish First Rate battleships, setting fire to both, and then went on to capture a French battleship.

Having remained in the Mediterranean throughout the Peace of Amiens, Keats then served under Nelson throughout the long watch outside Toulon and the famous chase to the West Indies and back in July and August 1805. By then, however, the *Superb* was badly in need of repair and tended to lag behind the rest of the fleet, prompting a characteristic letter of reassurance from Nelson: '. . . I know and feel that the *Superb* does all which is possible for a Ship to accomplish.' However, she was in such bad condition

Captain Sir Richard Keats. This fine portrait in oils of Keats dates from towards the end of the war with France and shows him wearing his gold medal for the Battle of San Domingo, 1806. (National Maritime Museum)

that after the long voyage she had to return to Britain for an extensive refit and, as a result, Keats missed Trafalgar. While on leave, he called on Nelson at Merton and was given a résumé of Nelson's new plan of battle. When asked what he thought of it, Keats was so stunned he could not immediately reply. 'I'll tell you what I think of it,' said Nelson, excitedly, 'I think it will surprise and confound the enemy!'

In 1806, Keats took the *Superb*, now flying the flag of Vice Admiral Sir John Duckworth, to the West Indies where he played a key role in the Battle of San Domingo (6 February 1806). As she sailed into action, the *Superb*'s band played the popular song 'Nelson of the Nile' as well as the more usual patriotic tunes and Keats apparently hung a portrait of Nelson on the mizzen stay, where it remained throughout the battle.

Promoted rear admiral in 1807, he again served under Saumarez, this time in the Baltic, for which campaign he received the Order of the Bath, and he then remained almost continuously in active service thereafter until his health finally gave way in 1812. He was appointed governor of Greenwich Hospital in 1821 and remained there until his death in 1834. He was buried in the hospital's mausoleum alongside a number of Nelson's closest associates, including Hardy.

Although he was never the commander-in-chief in any major action, Keats was widely recognised by his contemporaries as one of the leading lights of the Royal Navy of his day. Among his warmest admirers was Nelson who, just three days after their first meeting, wrote of him, 'I esteem his person alone as equal to one French 74 and the *Superb* and her Captain equal to two 74-gun Ships.'

SEE ALSO
'Band of Brothers', Nelson Touch, Trafalgar campaign

Keith, Lord *see: Elphinstone, George*

'Kiss me, Hardy'

As he lay dying in the cockpit of HMS *Victory* during the Battle of Trafalgar on 21 October 1805, Nelson was twice visited by his close friend and flag captain, Thomas Hardy. When the moment came for the two men to part for the last time, Nelson, then very close to death, asked Hardy to kiss him. Hardy kissed him on the cheek. 'Now I am satisfied,' said Nelson, 'Thank God I have done my duty.' Hardy stood up and then, having spent a few moments looking down silently at his friend, knelt and kissed him again on the forehead. 'Who is that?' asked Nelson, now barely able to see. 'It is Hardy.' 'God bless you, Hardy.'

This touching request, so wholly in keeping with Nelson's character, and indeed with the spirit of the age in which he lived, was misunderstood by later generations, who found it embarrassing. As a result, the ludicrous legend was invented, and persists to this day, that Nelson *actually* said 'Kismet Hardy', which is Turkish for 'fate'.

The famous request for the kiss, and the other words uttered at the same time, were recorded by Surgeon William Beatty in his meticulous and very detailed account of Nelson's death, published in 1807. That in itself should have been sufficient to scotch the 'Kismet' theory; but it has proved remarkably persistent, with its supporters straining credibility further by suggesting that perhaps Beatty misheard. Even if he did, this of course does not explain why Hardy kissed Nelson twice. In fact, Beatty's recollection is supported by the written testimony of two other eyewitnesses: Rev Alexander Scott, the *Victory*'s chaplain, who was sitting next to Nelson, rubbing his chest to relieve the pain, and Walter Burke, the purser, who was supporting the bed under him, both heard and recorded his words (see Scott's account of Nelson's death on p273).

The request for the kiss, and the fact that the normally unemotional and undemonstrative Hardy complied with it, are both key pieces in the complex jigsaw of Nelson's personality and there is no need to try to explain them away, or to view them with inappropriate embarrassment.

SEE ALSO
Beatty, Death, Hardy, Wounds

L

Lapenotiere, John (1770–1834)

Lapenotiere is best known as the man who brought home the news of the Battle of Trafalgar to Britain in late 1805. But he had a most interesting and varied career both before and after his brief moment of glory. Born in Ilfracombe in Devon, in 1770, Lapenotiere was the son of a naval officer and first went to sea with his father Frederick at the age of ten. After peace was declared in 1783, he took part in two trading voyages with the King George's Sound Company: first to the west coast of America in 1785–1788 and then in the South Pacific in 1791–1793. When war broke out again, he rejoined the Navy and served in the battleship HMS *Boyne*, flagship of Admiral Sir John Jervis, in the West Indies. He so distinguished himself in various actions that Jervis promoted him to lieutenant in 1794 and gave him command of the schooner *Berbice*.

In 1802, he was given command of the schooner HMS *Pickle* and served in her at the Battle of Trafalgar (21 October 1805). After the battle, on 26 October 1805, Vice Admiral Cuthbert Collingwood, who had succeeded to the command of the fleet after the death of Nelson, ordered Lapenotiere to return to Britain with his official despatches. Despite high winds and heavy seas, the *Pickle* made the voyage of more than a thousand miles in just over eight days, reaching Falmouth on the morning of Monday 4 November. From there, Lapenotiere took a fast coach to London, arriving at the Admiralty in Whitehall at 1.00am on Wednesday 6 November, less than eleven days after he had left Collingwood. Most of the officials had long since retired for the night, but the Secretary to the Board, William Marsden, was on his way to his private apartments, having just finished work in the Board Room. Lapenotiere handed over the despatches with the simple words, 'Sir, we have gained a great victory. But we have lost Lord Nelson.'

As was customary, Lapenotiere was rewarded for being the bearer of the news of victory with promotion to the rank of commander and was presented with a sword of honour, valued at one hundred guineas, by the Patriotic Fund at Lloyds. He continued in active service throughout the rest of the war, taking part in the second Battle of Copenhagen in 1807 and rising to the rank of captain in 1811. His famous feat in bringing home the Trafalgar despatches in such record time is honoured to this day by the Royal Navy with 'Pickle Night' dinners, traditionally held on, or near, 6 November. And the first arrival of the news of Trafalgar in Britain is celebrated each year by a special service in the church at Madron, near Penzance in Cornwall.

SEE ALSO
Admiralty, Collingwood, Jervis, Battle of Trafalgar, Trafalgar Day ceremonies

Latouche Tréville, Louis de (1745–1804)

Latouche was one of the most effective French admirals of the Napoleonic period and the only one who could boast that he had defeated Nelson. Born into an old naval family in 1745, he first saw service as a cadet during the Seven Years War (1756–1763), rising to the rank of captain during the War of American Independence (1778–1783), when he distinguished himself in a number of actions.

At the outbreak of the Revolutionary War, Captain Latouche, like many former officers of the Marine Royale, volunteered for active service and was promoted to rear admiral the following year. But his royalist links told against him and, after a year in prison, he spent a further six in poverty ashore until finally he was recalled to service after Napoleon seized executive power in November 1799.

Recognising Latouche's worth, Napoleon placed him in command of the Channel flotilla in March

Admiral Louis de Latouche Tréville, one of France's most successful admirals, who beat Nelson at Boulogne in 1801 and later was opposed to him in the Mediterranean in 1804.

1801. By then, all the other major European powers having been eliminated, only Britain remained at war with France and Napoleon hoped to force her into a peace by threatening invasion. Latouche concentrated his forces at Boulogne. There he established his headquarters in a tower on the hills overlooking the town, from where he had a clear view of the Channel and the opposing British ships. On 29 July, he heard that those ships were now commanded by Nelson and, anticipating an immediate attack, made his preparations accordingly.

As expected, Nelson launched almost immediately into aggressive action with a distant bombardment by bomb-vessels on 4 August, followed eleven days later by a major night attack by boats. But he was up against a determined and experienced opponent, who had prepared his defences carefully, and so the gallant attempt met with a bloody repulse.

This important propaganda success confirmed Latouche as Napoleon's favourite admiral and so, during the brief European peace, following the Treaty of Amiens in 1802, he was sent to the French-occupied island of San Domingo in the West Indies to deal with an uprising. There, he caught yellow fever and would have died had he not managed to escape back to Europe. Now aged fifty-eight, his health was dangerously undermined and his next appointment was to give him little respite.

In January 1804, he took command of the French Mediterranean fleet in the naval base of Toulon on the south coast of France, finding himself opposed once more to Nelson. As at Boulogne, he established his command headquarters in a tower, this time at the summit of Cape Cepet, the promontory overlooking the approaches to Toulon harbour. Nelson was maintaining a very loose blockade, trying to tempt the French out. Latouche kept his forces trained, and in a good state of morale, by making regular, teasing sorties, without ever intending to emerge permanently. On one such occasion, on 14 June, when Nelson was present with his battlefleet, Latouche took his own fleet to sea but avoided a direct battle. His subsequent official account of this minor encounter, which made it sound as if Nelson had run away, was seized on by the propaganda-conscious Napoleon and published in the *Moniteur*, the French government newspaper. Latouche was rewarded with a promotion within the order of the Légion d'Honneur.

Latouche's claim incensed Nelson, who vowed he would make him eat his letter when he captured him. But shortly afterwards, during the night of 18/19 August, Latouche died on board his flagship, the *Bucentaure*, having refused to be transferred to a hospital. One of his officers wrote later, 'he possessed a superior will, capable of transforming men and of dominating events.' It is fascinating to speculate what might have happened had he lived to command the Combined fleet at Trafalgar.

SEE ALSO
Boulogne, *Bucentaure*, Channel Command, Toulon

LATEST RESEARCH
Rémi Monaque, 'Latouche-Tréville: The admiral who defied Nelson', *The Mariner's Mirror* 86 (August 2000)

Editing Nelson's letters. This letter, written to Emma Hamilton on 1 October 1805, has never been fully published. At some stage, someone has obliterated some phrases (probably referring to Horatia) and the passage at the top of the right-hand page, with loving messages to Emma and Horatia, was edited out of the printed version published in 1814.

Letters, Nelson's

Nelson was a prolific letter writer. Although, in his later years, he had the help of secretaries, he still wrote a large number of his letters himself and many of them have survived: at the last count, some 5000. They give us a vivid picture of him, especially when seen in the original autograph. The words pour off his pen, with scant attention to punctuation, and with an eager and wholly unpolished style, almost as if he is speaking. Like the diaries of Samuel Pepys, with which they have sometimes been compared, Nelson's letters give us a clear window into the soul of the man who wrote them.

The letters fall into three distinct types. First, there are the official despatches and reports he wrote to senior officers and politicians. Although inevitably more formal than the rest of his correspondence, they still contain traces of Nelson's engaging earnestness and directness. Then there are his letters to family and close friends: chatty, even gossipy at times, and often very frank about his own feelings and ambitions. He was a most faithful correspondent throughout his life, always good at keeping in touch with old friends and keen to acknowledge kindnesses and to repay them, if it lay within his power. Finally, there are his letters to Emma Hamilton which fall into a category all of their own, ranging from frenzied and excited, through explicit and lustful, to tearful and maudlin.

A large proportion of the surviving letters are in public repositories: chiefly, the British Library, the National Maritime Museum and the Nelson Museum in Monmouth. But there are many others scattered in public and private collections all over the world and Nelson letters still regularly appear in the sale-rooms, where they always fetch high prices.

Many of them have been published: most comprehensively in Sir Nicholas Harris Nicolas's monumental seven-volume collection, published during 1844–1846. But Nicolas deliberately omitted most of Nelson's letters to Emma Hamilton and many were later published separately, by Thomas Pettigrew in 1849, and by Alfred Morrison in 1893/4. Additionally, Nicolas was not able to gain access to Nelson's letters to his wife and so these were not published until George Naish's scholarly edition of 1958.

In all these published collections, with the honourable exception of Naish's, the letters are heavily edited. Nelson's grammar and punctuation is 'corrected', and all traces of impropriety expurgated, so that he speaks in a stilted, nineteenth-century manner and not at all with the eager directness of the originals. Moreover, there are still many of his letters that remain unpublished: at the last count, over 550. A new, complete and unexpurgated collected edition is urgently required.

SEE ALSO
Biographies, 'The Dispatches and Letters of Vice Admiral Lord Nelson', Signatures, 'Thomson' Letters

LATEST RESEARCH
Felix Pryor, 'Nelson the letter-writer', in Colin White (ed), *The Nelson Companion*, Sutton and Royal Naval Museum (Stroud & Portsmouth 1995)
Colin White, 'The Nelson Letters Project', *The Mariner's Mirror* 87 (November 2001)

Locker, William (1732–1800)

Locker was one of Nelson's early captains and arguably the one, after Maurice Suckling, who had the most important influence on his development and career. The son of a naval family, he first went to sea in 1746 during the War of the Austrian Succession (1739–1747). When peace came, he served at sea with the East India Company until returning to the Royal Navy in 1756 and took service under Admiral Edward Hawke, becoming a lieutenant shortly afterwards in HMS *Experiment*. In her, he took part in a bloody action with a French privateer in the Mediterranean during which he was wounded in the leg by a splinter while leading a boarding party, leaving him with a slight limp for the rest of his life. His success in this battle obviously made a deep impression on Locker: years later, Nelson was to remind him, '. . . it is you who taught me to board a Frenchman by your conduct in the *Experiment*. It is you who always told me "Lay a Frenchman close and you will beat him".'

In 1758, he served in the frigate HMS *Sapphire* and was present at Hawke's great victory on 20 November 1759, one of the most dramatic naval battles of the sailing era. In the teeth of a fierce Atlantic storm, Hawke's ships chased a retreating French fleet into

Captain William Locker. This engraving, after a portrait by Lemuel Abbott, captures the genial and fatherly man who helped Nelson at a critical moment of his career and with whom he remained on close and affectionate terms.

the dangerous rock-strewn waters of Quiberon Bay, on the west coast of France, capturing or destroying a third of their force. In many ways, Nelson was Hawke's tactical heir and, although the two men never served together, Locker provided a direct personal link.

Locker eventually became a post captain in 1768 and, when war broke out with America, was appointed to command the frigate HMS *Lowestoffe* in 1777. With him, as second lieutenant, went the newly promoted Lieutenant Horatio Nelson and so began an association that lasted to the end of Locker's life. He carefully preserved all of Nelson's letters and, from them, it is clear that the two men quickly became close friends. Nelson nursed the older man when he fell ill in the West Indies – prompting Locker to present his protégé with a prayer book as a mark of his gratitude – and Locker persuaded Nelson to have a portrait painted by Francis Rigaud, which he then hung in his home. As well as impressing on him his own maxim of close action, he also gave him his first

command, the schooner *Little Lucy*, captured by the *Lowestoffe* in the spring of 1778, became the frigate's tender with nineteen-year-old Lieutenant Nelson as her proud captain. In her, as he later remembered, '. . . I made myself a complete pilot for all the passages through the Keys Islands.'

In July 1778, Nelson was transferred to HMS *Bristol*, flagship of Sir Peter Parker, and thereafter, he and Locker never served together again. Locker's health gave way in 1779 and he was not able to serve again until 1790, when he commanded the battleship HMS *Cambridge*. In 1792, he was appointed commander-in-chief at the Nore, with the rank of commodore, and the following year became lieutenant governor of Greenwich Hospital, where he remained until his death in 1800. He and Nelson remained in touch and Nelson and his wife stayed with the Lockers at Greenwich in October 1797, when Nelson was on leave in Britain recovering from the loss of his arm. While he was there, Locker persuaded him to sit for another portrait, this time by Lemuel Abbott.

Although Nelson and Locker served together for little more than a year, it is clear that Locker made a strong impression on his young pupil. After his death he wrote of him, '. . . he has left us a character for honour and honesty which none can surpass and very very few attain.'

SEE ALSO
Abbott, Greenwich, Jervis, Portraits

L'Orient

The flagship of Vice Admiral Brueys at the Battle of the Nile (1 August 1798), *L'Orient* was one of the largest ships in the world at that time. Her destruction in a series of massive explosions marked the climax of the battle and remains its most enduring image.

Originally named the *Dauphin Royal*, she was completed in Brest in 1791 and renamed *Sans Culottes* in a burst of revolutionary fervour ('Sans Culottes' – literally, 'without breeches' – was the nickname given to the supporters of the French Revolution who wore trousers instead of the more aristocratic knee-breeches). Designed by one of France's leading naval architects, J N Sané, she was over 200 feet long and mounted 124 guns on three decks. She took part in a

The Battle of the Nile, 1 August 1798. As the battle reaches its height, the French flagship L'Orient *(centre) blazes furiously. At about 10.00pm she blew up with a huge detonation. (National Maritime Museum, London)*

number of operations in the Mediterranean and was actually engaged briefly by Nelson during his fight with the *Ça Ira* during the Battle of Hyères in March 1795.

In 1798, she was selected as the flagship for Napoleon Bonaparte's Eastern expedition and renamed *L'Orient*. Napoleon sailed in her, with his naval commander, Vice Admiral François de Brueys, first to Malta and then to Alexandria. De Brueys then took his fleet to Aboukir Bay where he was attacked by Nelson's fleet on the night of 1/2 August.

L'Orient was stationed in the centre of the French line and succeeded in driving off the first of her attackers, the 74-gun HMS *Bellerophon*, with heavy damage. But other British ships gathered around her

and subjected her to overwhelming broadsides and she caught fire, eventually blowing up at about 10.00pm. The noise was so loud that contemporary accounts mention only one detonation. But modern research, based on close examination of her remains on the seabed at Aboukir Bay, has established that there were in fact two separate explosions. First, the fire reached her main magazine and blew off her stern, driving her forwards in the water, and then, seconds later, her smaller forward magazine blew up, shattering her bows. She sank in a few minutes, taking many hundreds of her officers and men with her.

It was a cataclysmic event, so shocking that all fighting ceased for a time while men stood dazed by the noise and glare. It has become the most familiar image of the battle, featured in almost every painting or print of the action (see colour plate *VII*). The *L'Orient*'s shattered remains were eventually discovered in 1983 by the French diver Jacques Dumas and they have since been excavated, and minutely recorded, by his compatriot, Franck Goddio.

SEE ALSO
HMS *Bellerophon*, de Brueys, Hyères, Napoleon, Nile

LATEST RESEARCH
Michelle Battesti, *La Bataille d'Aboukir*, Economica (Paris 1998)
Laura Foreman and Ellen Blue Phillips, *Napoleon's Lost Fleet*, Discovery Books (London 1999)

Louis, Sir Thomas (1759–1807)

Although he is now among the least-known of the 'Band of Brothers', Louis was in fact close to Nelson and served with him on a number of occasions. A Devonian from Exeter, he entered the Navy in 1770 and served as a lieutenant in the battleship *Bienfaisant* in the Battle of Ushant (27 July 1778). In 1780, he fought in Rodney's action off Cape Finisterre (8 January 1780) and was made prizemaster of the captured Spanish flagship. Promoted to post captain in 1783, he was given command of the battleship HMS *Minotaur* at the beginning of the Revolutionary War and served in her at the Battle of the Nile (1 August 1798).

He remained with Nelson after the battle and took part in the operations in Italy in 1798, including the capture of Rome in November 1798. On that occasion, he was rowed up the Tiber in his barge and raised the English colours on Fort Sant' Angelo, after the French had been driven out of the city. In 1801, still in command of the *Minotaur*, he took part in the Egyptian campaign under Lord Keith.

Promoted to rear admiral in 1804, he at first served under Keith again in the Channel but he was not happy and begged Emma Hamilton, with whom he was on friendly terms, to persuade Nelson to ask for his services. This, Nelson duly did and so Louis joined him in the Mediterranean in early 1805, flying his flag in HMS *Canopus* with one of Jane Austen's brothers, Francis Austen, as his captain. He took part in the famous chase of the French fleet to the West Indies in the summer of 1805 but missed Trafalgar when Nelson sent him into Gibraltar for supplies a few days before the battle.

On 6 February 1806, he took part in the action off St Domingo under Sir John Duckworth, and was made a baronet as a reward for his conduct. Having taken part in the unsuccessful Dardanelles campaign of 1807, he died suddenly on 17 May on board the *Canopus* while on active service in Egypt and was buried in Malta.

SEE ALSO
'Band of Brothers', Nile

Lutwidge, Skeffington (?1740–1814)

Skeffington Lutwidge was one of Nelson's earliest commanders, with whom he remained in affectionate touch to the end of his life. Joining the Navy in time to see active service as a young man throughout the Seven Years War, Lutwidge became a lieutenant in 1759. Promoted to post captain in 1773, he was appointed to command the exploration vessel HMS *Carcass* on an expedition to the Arctic commanded by Captain the Honourable Constantine Phipps. With him, as captain's coxswain, went the young Horatio Nelson. It was Lutwidge who, many years afterwards, told the famous story of Nelson's encounter with a polar bear; recalling that when he reprimanded the boy, and asked him what motive he had for putting his life in such danger, Nelson '. . . pouting his lip as he was wont to do when agitated, replied, "Sir I wished to kill the bear that I might carry its skin to my father".'

In 1794, Lutwidge met up with Nelson again in the Mediterranean, when he commanded the battleship HMS *Terrible* at the capture of Toulon. Promoted to rear admiral, he became commander-in-chief at the Nore in 1798 and then moved to the Downs in 1800. When Nelson was placed in command of the specially created anti-invasion force in the Channel in July 1801, his relationship with the Downs commander could have been awkward but Lutwidge made no difficulties: on the contrary, he welcomed Nelson and supported him loyally. He and his wife also befriended Emma Hamilton when she and Sir William visited Nelson at Deal, and Emma remained in regular touch thereafter with Mrs Lutwidge, once signing a letter 'Emma Hamilton – I would say Nelson – how pretty it sounds!'

After the Peace of Amiens, Lutwidge did not serve again but he continued to rise in the Navy, becoming an Admiral of the Red before his death in 1814.

SEE ALSO
Arctic, Channel Command

M

Maddalena Islands, Sardinia
See: Agincourt Sound

Malta

A small island in the centre of the Mediterranean, Malta commands the relatively narrow channel between the southernmost tip of Sicily and North Africa, and so it has long been regarded as a key strategic position. After being occupied for more than 300 years by the Knights of St John of Malta, it was seized in June 1798 by a special French expeditionary force, under General Napoleon Bonaparte, on its way to the conquest of Egypt. The Maltese rose in arms against their new overlords and appealed to the British for assistance. Nelson responded by sending a small detachment of his fleet under the command of Captain Alexander Ball.

Nelson's sweeping victory at the Battle of the Nile (1 August 1798) had temporarily eliminated the French as an effective naval force in the Mediterranean and had given the British control of the sea. So Ball was able to cut off the French forces from all help of aid and supplies and, at the same time, reinforce and supply the Maltese forces ashore. The French were forced to retreat into the massive fortress of Valetta, where they managed to hold out for almost two years. Eventually, however, they surrendered on 5 September 1800 and the British took control, with Ball being appointed civil commissioner in 1801. By the terms of the Treaty of Amiens (1802), Malta was to be returned to the Knights but, realising the strategic importance of the island and fearing the return of French influence, the British delayed the transfer. When war broke out again in 1803, Malta was still in British hands and so it remained until it gained independence in 1963.

Nelson visited Malta on a number of occasions. He went there first in October 1798 to inspect the blockade instituted by Ball. He returned in February 1800 as part of a fleet under the command of Lord Keith, by then commander-in-chief of the Mediterranean, and so was present at the capture of the French battleship *Le Généreux*. One of only two battleships to escape from the Nile, she was intercepted by Nelson's flagship *Foudroyant*, while attempting to escort a relief convoy into Malta. Three months later, he was back again in the *Foudroyant* but this visit was much less warlike. The Hamiltons were on board, together with a number of their friends, and the voyage had the air almost of a yachting party, with dinners and concerts in the flagship's great cabin. Indeed, it has been suggested that Emma's and Nelson's daughter Horatia, who was born in late January 1801, may well have been conceived during this voyage.

His last visit was three years later, when he called in briefly in June 1803 while on a tour of his new command, following his appointment as commander-in-chief in the Mediterranean. Realising that the voyage between Malta and his station off Toulon was far too long, he looked around for another more convenient base, which he eventually located at Agincourt Sound in the Maddalena Islands on the north coast of Sardinia. Thereafter, he never visited Malta again, preferring to have the essential supplies of victuals and naval stores for his fleet shipped from there to Maddalena.

Much of the Malta that Nelson saw on these various visits has been obliterated by later building and bombing in the Second World War. However, Grand Harbour, where he landed in 1803, still has many traces of the older fortifications erected by the Knights during their long rule and the San Anton Palace, where he visited his old friend Alexander Ball, is still standing and is now the official residence of the President of Malta. Ball's monument, an elegant Grecian temple, stands in the Lower Barracca Gardens overlooking Grand Harbour. And in the Upper Barracca Gardens is a monument to Thomas

Fremantle, who died in Malta while commander-in-chief of the Mediterranean in 1819.

SEE ALSO
Agincourt Sound, Ball, Elphinstone, *Foudroyant*

Masks of Nelson's face

For many years, two masks of Nelson's face have been displayed in the collections at the Royal Naval and National Maritime Museums. Originally believed to be death masks, taken when Nelson's body arrived in England after the Battle of Trafalgar, recent research has established that they are in fact *life* masks, taken some five years earlier in Vienna, Austria.

Mask of Nelson's face. As the original caption shows, this was formerly believed to be a death mask, taken from Nelson's face after his body arrived in England in 1805. It is now known that it was taken in Vienna when he was visiting there with the Hamiltons in 1800.

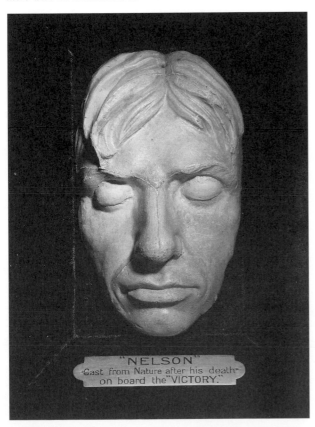

In August 1800, Nelson and Sir William and Lady Hamilton stopped for a month in the Austrian capital, during their long overland trip home to England from the Mediterranean. Their journey had turned into a triumphal progress, with excited crowds turning out to acclaim the 'Hero of the Nile', and in Vienna Nelson was approached by the sculptor Franz Thaller, who wished to make a bust of the man of the moment. However, because Nelson was busy, and his movements uncertain, Thaller persuaded him to allow his colleague, Matthias Ranson, to make a cast of his face.

The resulting mask was then used as a model for a striking bust of Nelson, generally agreed to be one of the best likenesses of him. And, now they are known to have been taken from the life, the surviving masks provide us with excellent yardsticks against which to judge all the many other portraits and busts of Nelson.

SEE ALSO
Nelson's tour of Germany, Portraits

LATEST RESEARCH
Michael Nash (ed), *The Nelson Masks*, Marine Books (Hoylake 1993)
Richard Walker, *The Nelson Portraits*, Royal Naval Museum (Portsmouth 1998)

Matcham, Catherine (1767–1842)

Nelson's youngest sister, Catherine (always known in the family as Kate), was born on 19 March 1767. Her mother died on Boxing Day the same year: as Susannah, the eldest sister, later poignantly remarked, 'she had bred herself to death.'

Like Horatio, Catherine resembled her mother, especially in her vivacity and sense of fun, and so the two shared a closer bond than they had with their more dull and worthy siblings. At one time, Nelson even considered setting up home with her and wrote to their brother William, 'she shall never want a protector and sincere friend while I exist.' However, Kate was well able to look after herself: clever and strikingly pretty, with a delightful mane of curly, light-coloured hair, she managed to attract a most eligible suitor, George Matcham, a much-travelled and intelligent man who had served overseas with the East India Company and had written a book about his experiences. They married in 1787 and went to live in a fine and spacious house in Norfolk, Barton Hall.

The Matchams remained on friendly and affectionate terms with Nelson. They never treated him with the exaggerated respect that the rest of the family tended to adopt; nor did they expect him to make careers for them or their children. When their eldest son George dared to hint that his uncle might do more for them, he was treated to a stern lecture from his father on the need to rise by one's own endeavours. They were with Nelson at Merton during his last leave in Britain in August/September 1805 and there is a strong family tradition that Catherine even travelled to Portsmouth to bid him farewell.

After Nelson's death, they honoured his memory by keeping in touch with Emma Hamilton and Horatia, and when Emma died in poverty in Calais in 1815, they rescued Horatia and welcomed her into their home and family, the first happy home the poor girl had experienced. Later, when young George married a Wiltshire heiress, they moved to Newhouse, on the boundaries of the splendid estate purchased by the new Earl Nelson with the money voted to him by a grateful nation. After George Matcham senior's death, Catherine continued to live there until her own death in 1842.

SEE ALSO
Family, Horatia Nelson

Mediterranean Command (1803–1805)

Having been appointed commander-in-chief in the Mediterranean in May 1803, Nelson arrived at Gibraltar on 3 June and, after making a quick tour of his command, joined the fleet off Toulon on 8 July. From then, until he left the Mediterranean on 6 May 1805, in pursuit of the French Toulon fleet under Villeneuve, his whole attention was taken up with the conflicting demands of this most complex of commands and he carried out his duty without relief and with no breaks for leave. A remarkable achievement, both of personal stamina and professional ability, it has usually been dealt with in the past as if it was simply a long and rather tedious prelude to the more dramatic and exciting Trafalgar campaign. In fact, it was one of the most important periods in his

professional career, during which he demonstrated his abilities as an all-round commander better than at any other time.

His main object, as he himself put it, was '. . . to keep the French fleet in check and if they put to sea to annihilate them.' To do this, he had only a small fleet – nine battleships to begin with and most of them in urgent need of refit – and the nearest base was many miles away from Toulon at Malta. So his first priority was to find a way of keeping his ships in fighting trim without weakening his force by detaching them and he achieved this by making use of the fine anchorage at Agincourt Sound in the Maddalena Islands on the north coast of Sardinia and arranging for all his supplies to be sent to him there. In addition to well-equipped ships, he also needed healthy crews and so much of his time was taken up with organising a regular supply of fresh food and in keeping his men amused and their morale high. As a result of his efforts, when Dr Gillespie arrived on board HMS *Victory* in January 1805, after she had been constantly at sea for over eighteen months, he found only one man sick out of a ship's company of 840.

As well as being a good administrator, the Mediterranean commander had also to be a diplomat: and here Nelson showed a much surer touch than he had displayed during his previous time in the Mediterranean. Urgent invitations from the Queen of Naples to go ashore and recover his health in the city were politely rebuffed and he never again allowed himself to become embroiled with the affairs of any one state, as in 1799. Instead, he maintained a voluminous correspondence with British ministers in all the main ports and with the rulers of the many states that came within his area. His efforts won him the approval of some of the leading politicians back in Britain, and it was during this period that he consolidated his reputation among them for dependability, and for wisdom in public affairs, that led them to rely on his advice so much during the crisis of 1805 (see transcript on p270).

All this work created a large amount of paper, most of which passed through Nelson's hands. The administration of the fleet was in the capable hands of George Murray, captain of the fleet, and Nelson was also assisted by two secretaries: John Scott who looked after his public correspondence and fleet orders and the *Victory*'s chaplain Rev Alexander Scott, who handled his foreign correspondence and also from time to time undertook intelligence operations ashore. But, even with their help, Nelson still spent long hours at his desk, often writing his letters himself. He also insisted on having every newspaper that reached the *Victory* read aloud to him so that he could keep in touch with the progress of the war. Apparently, he needed very little sleep and would sometimes snatch just a short nap in a chair rather than retiring to bed.

A significant amount of this paperwork has survived but only Nelson's letters have been published: by Nicolas, where they take up two of his seven thickly packed volumes. There is still a large amount of untapped material in all the main Nelson archives and, until that has been properly researched and written up, this fascinating period in his career can never be fully appreciated or accurately evaluated. But even the comparatively small amount currently available demonstrates that, as well as being a great fighting admiral, Nelson was also, at least in his latter years, a thorough administrator and a sagacious diplomat.

SEE ALSO
Agincourt Sound, Murray, Alexander Scott, John Scott, Toulon

Merton Place

In 1801, Nelson bought Merton Place, a house and estate in the village of Merton in Surrey, to the southwest of London and close to the main road to Portsmouth. He lived there whenever he was in England on leave, sharing it with Sir William and Lady Hamilton.

Always a countryman at heart, Nelson had dreamed of buying a 'cottage' and had often discussed the possibility with his wife. In 1798, they purchased a house called Roundwood, near Ipswich in Suffolk, but Nelson himself never lived there. When he returned to Britain with the Hamiltons in 1800, he revived the dream, but this time he wanted to share it with Emma.

Emma did the house-hunting while Nelson was at sea commanding the anti-invasion forces in the Channel. Despite a very discouraging surveyor's

Merton Place, Surrey – 'Paradise Merton' as Emma Hamilton called it – where she and Nelson and Sir William lived happily together. In the foreground is an ornamental canal, which was christened 'the Nile'. Emma is shown in the foreground talking to a gardener and Sir William is fishing underneath the tree on the right.

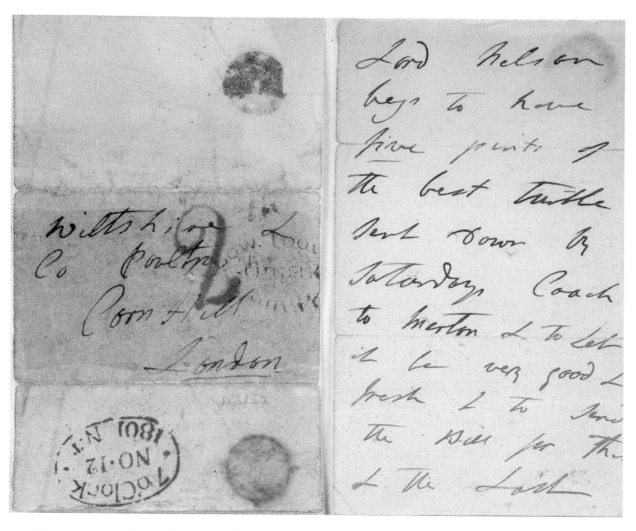

Turtle Soup for Merton. Emma Hamilton orders 'Five Pints of the best turtle' to be delivered to Merton and asks that the bill should be sent to Lord Nelson.

report, Merton Place seemed ideal and Nelson bought it for £9000 with the help of a loan from his agent and friend Alexander Davison. He first saw his new home in the early morning of Friday 23 October 1801 and was enchanted with what he found there: a modest but handsome red-brick house, with a secluded garden and an ornamental canal (immediately dubbed 'The Nile') spanned by an ornate Italianate bridge. Emma had decorated the interior with mirrors to make the rooms look larger and, according to Nelson's friend Lord Minto, 'the whole house, staircase and all [is] covered with nothing but

pictures of her and him, of all sizes and sorts, and representations of his naval actions, coats of arms, pieces of plate in his honour, the flagstaff of *L'Orient* etc. – an excess of vanity that counteracts its own purpose.'

Excess of vanity it may have been, but Nelson was happy there: first, between 1801 and 1803 with both of the Hamiltons then, briefly, in the autumn of 1805 with Emma and their beloved Horatia, and other members of his family, during his all too short spell of leave before the Battle of Trafalgar. He revelled in his role as village squire, attending the local parish church of St Mary and dispensing charity to the poor. His letters to Emma are full of plans for extensions and improvements and he dreamed of retiring there. Sadly, the house has not survived. It was sold in 1823, finally pulled down in 1846 and the site built over.

SEE ALSO
Emma Hamilton, William Hamilton, Elliot

LATEST RESEARCH
Peter Warwick, 'Here was Paradise', *The Trafalgar Chronicle* 4 (1994), The 1805 Club

Middleton, Charles (Lord Barham) (1726–1813)

One of the finest naval administrators of his day, Barham was First Lord of the Admiralty in the climatic years of the naval war with France, 1805/6. It was he who masterminded the complex series of fleet deployments which so decisively countered Napoleon's invasion plans and culminated in Nelson's great victory at the Battle of Trafalgar on 21 October 1805.

Barham saw very little active service at sea. His main contribution to Britain's success was as a long-serving naval administrator: first as Comptroller of the Navy 1778–1790, when he was responsible for the design and building of many of the ships which fought in the long war with France, and then as an ordinary member of the Admiralty Board.

In May 1805, he was appointed First Lord by Prime Minister William Pitt at a critical moment in the war, when a French invasion of Britain seemed a very real threat. Although nearly eighty, Barham worked tirelessly, deploying his forces with remarkable skill and keeping a steady nerve when many around him were despairing. It was his careful positioning of the various British fleets that prevented the French and Spanish fleets from entering the Channel in early August 1805 and so defeated Napoleon's over-ambitious invasion plans. Trafalgar, fought over two months later, merely confirmed this verdict.

Nelson played a key role in this complex campaign. Although he allowed the French Mediterranean fleet to escape from Toulon, he chased it resolutely to the West Indies and back, driving it into the arms of the forces Barham had assembled. Barham did not know Nelson well and was, at first, inclined to be critical of him for allowing the French to escape. But when the two men met in late August 1805, during Nelson's brief spell of home leave, Barham very quickly changed his mind. Deciding that he was the right man to take command of the fleet then being assembled outside Cádiz to deal finally with the combined Franco-Spanish fleet, he gave him a completely free hand in assembling and deploying it. He was, therefore, in a very real sense, one of the main architects of the great victory at Trafalgar.

SEE ALSO
Admiralty, Cape Finisterre, Napoleon, Battle of Trafalgar, Trafalgar campaign

LATEST RESEARCH
Roger Morriss, 'Charles Middleton, Lord Barham', in Peter LeFevre and Richard Harding (eds), *Precursors of Nelson*, Chatham Publishing (London 2000)

Miller, Ralph (c1760–1799)

Miller was undoubtedly one of the bright stars of the Nelsonian navy: 'an officer of the first merit,' as his obituary in *The Naval Chronicle* put it. He was highly regarded by Nelson, who once described him as 'a most exceeding good officer and worthy man,' and

Charles Middleton, Lord Barham. This engraving, dating from 1806, shows the newly ennobled lord proudly wearing his peers' robes.

the two men served together during two of the most important years in Nelson's career.

Born in New England, USA, the young Ralph was sent to Britain to be educated at the Naval Academy in Portsmouth. He first went to sea in 1778 and saw much service in the American war, including a number of the key fleet actions. In 1781, he was personally promoted by Admiral Rodney and married the girl he always called 'my beloved Nancy'.

When war broke out again in 1793, Miller was appointed a lieutenant in the 98-gun battleship HMS *Windsor Castle* in the Mediterranean fleet under Lord Hood. When the Royalist-held port of Toulon had to be evacuated in January 1794, he volunteered to help in the destruction of the shipping and the arsenal and played a very active role in both operations. Later that year, he took part in the sieges of Bastia and Calvi which led afterwards to the capture of Corsica. It was there that he first met Nelson.

When Sir John Jervis took command in the Mediterranean in December 1795, he quickly recognised Miller's worth and appointed him to command the frigate *Mignonne*, thus giving him his all-important step to the rank of post captain. But he did not remain in frigates for long for, when Nelson moved to HMS *Captain* as commodore in June 1796, he asked for Miller as his captain. This rapid promotion showed how highly he was regarded by his peers.

Miller commanded the *Captain* with Nelson's pendant flying in her, at the Battle of Cape St Vincent (14 February 1797), and on the morning after the battle Nelson presented him with a sword and a ring with the words, 'Miller I am under the greatest obligations to you.' 'And indeed,' wrote Miller to his father, 'I feel satisfied that our friendship will last as long as ourselves.' In fact, that friendship had only two more years to run.

After Cape St Vincent, Nelson and Miller moved to the *Theseus* and served together in the blockade of Cádiz, where Miller showed great ingenuity in planning the attacks on the Spanish, and again at Tenerife in July 1797. There, Miller took part in both the abortive landings and was lucky to escape unharmed in an action in which so many other senior officers were killed or wounded.

Nelson left the *Theseus* to recover from the loss of his arm in August 1797 but Miller continued in command. In June 1798, he was one of the carefully chosen band that Lord St Vincent sent into the Mediterranean to join Nelson for the campaign that culminated in the Battle of the Nile (1 August 1798). The *Theseus* was relatively undamaged in the battle and so she was left by Nelson to patrol in the eastern Mediterranean. Miller and his men took part in the Siege of Acre in 1799, where Sir Sidney Smith, with a small force of British sailors and their Turkish allies, checked the advance of Napoleon and his Army of the East. But, sadly, one of the casualties was Miller, killed in a tragic accident on 14 May, when a captured French shell was mishandled. His death was keenly felt among his friends and professional colleagues. Nelson organised a subscription for a public monument, which was erected in St Paul's Cathedral.

Miller left a number of accounts of the actions in which he was involved, most of which have been published. They are not only vivid and detailed but also extremely frank, so they are invaluable cross-references to the often rather sanitised official accounts.

SEE ALSO
Cape St Vincent, Nile, Tenerife

LATEST RESEARCH
Kirstie Buckland, *The Miller Papers*, The 1805 Club (Shelton 1999)

Minto *see: Elliot, Gilbert*

Monuments to Nelson

Nelson is commemorated by over twenty monuments in Britain and overseas. The first were erected as soon as the news of his death arrived in November 1805. At Castletownshend, near Cork in Ireland, Captain Joshua Rowley Watson and 200 men from his division of the Sea Fencibles (a maritime volunteer reserve force), helped by eight masons, erected a memorial arch in less than five hours. In Taynuilt, near Loch Etive in Argyllshire, Scotland, some workers from the local ironworks erected a 12 foot high granite standing stone. At the same time, Vice Admiral Cuthbert Collingwood, Nelson's second in command at Trafalgar, was organising a collection among the officers who had fought at Trafalgar. The money was used to erect a simple granite obelisk on the top of Portsdown Hill overlooking Portsmouth Harbour, the foundation stone of which was laid on 4 July 1807. At the top, in a niche, is a large bust of Nelson and an inscription records that it was erected 'by the zealous attachment of all those who fought at Trafalgar to perpetuate his triumph and their regret.'

In the years following Trafalgar, key towns and cities in Britain vied with each other to produce a memorial to Nelson. In 1806, Hereford erected a simple column and Glasgow a massive obelisk. Statues of the hero were set up in Birmingham and Dublin in 1809 and Liverpool in 1813. The first monument in Nelson's native Norfolk was a superb column on the sands at Great Yarmouth, erected in 1819. A cottage was built nearby for a keeper and the first man appointed was James Sherman, who had served in the *Victory*. Later, in 1829, he rescued a drowning sailor from a ship wrecked on the beach nearby. The newspaper report of his deed was seen by the novelist Charles Dickens, who visited Great Yarmouth, and found in Sherman the model for the character of Ham Peggotty in *David Copperfield*.

Overseas, in Montreal, Canada, the news of the Battle of Trafalgar arrived during an Assembly Ball in the Exchange House when a waiter rushed in, carrying a copy of a New York paper in which Collingwood's famous despatch was printed. A resolution was immediately proposed to erect a monument and a superb coadestone statue by Joseph Panzetta was produced by the firm of Coade & Sealey in Lambeth, London, and transported out to Canada in 1808 by the packet ship *Eweretta*. A more modest statue by the leading sculptor Westmacott was erected the following year in Barbados.

The news of the battle arrived in London just a few days before the traditional Lord Mayor's Banquet on 9 November 1805, when Prime Minister William Pitt made his ringing claim, 'England has saved herself by her exertions and will, as I trust save Europe by her example.' The mayor and his guests sat under an illuminated arch bearing the words 'Nelson and Victory' with behind them a portrait of Nelson and, in the emotion of the moment, the Common Council of the City of London voted to erect a monument to Nelson in the Guildhall itself. An open competition was held to select the best

The Nelson monument on Portsdown Hill, overlooking Portsmouth Harbour. Erected in 1807, it was the first public monument to Nelson and was paid for by the officers and men who fought with him at Trafalgar.

design and, eventually, after much debate and controversy, an allegorical composition by an unknown sculptor James Smith was chosen.

At the same time, another competition was being held to decide who should produce a statue for St Paul's Cathedral in the City of London. This time, the commission went to a well-known sculptor, John Flaxman. He produced a striking likeness of Nelson, showing him in full dress uniform and wearing all his orders and medals.

Despite all these monuments and memorials, there was still a strong feeling in the country that Nelson should be honoured with a national monument. In 1830, a suitable site finally became available when the area in front of the National Gallery in central London was levelled and turned into a square. A national subscription was launched to raise money and yet another competition was held to decide on the design. Eventually, the commission went to William Railton who proposed a column, based on Trajan's Column in Rome, surmounted by a massive statue. The column was completed in 1843 and a banquet for some of the subscribers was held on its flat top on 3 November, before the huge 17 foot high statue by Edward Hodges Bailey was hoisted into place. For a time, the base of the column was left plain but eventually, in 1854, four bas-reliefs depicting Nelson's victories were added. And in 1867 came the final touch, the installation of the four great lions designed by Landseer and sculpted by Baron Marochetti.

Nelson's Column quickly became a popular London landmark. The square offered a superb amphitheatre for large popular gatherings and political rallies and it is still one of the main places where Londoners celebrate the arrival of the New Year. Towards the end of the nineteenth century, the Navy League began the custom of holding a special service there on Trafalgar Day. Nelson's last signal was suspended from the top of the column and the lions were decorated with laurel wreaths. So powerful a symbol did the column become that, in 1940, Adolf Hitler declared that once the invasion of England had been accomplished, he would remove it from Trafalgar Square and re-erect it in Berlin. 'Ever since the Battle of Trafalgar,' he claimed, 'the Nelson column has represented for England a symbol of British naval might and world dominion. It would be an impressive way of underlining the German victory if the Nelson column were to be transferred to Berlin.'

There have also been a number of private monuments. Alexander Davison, Nelson's prize agent, erected an obelisk in his estate in Northumberland 'to the memory of private friendship.' Sir William Paxton built a tower overlooking Carmarthen in the Towy Valley in Wales, with stained-glass windows based on the illustrations in the *Life of Admiral Lord Nelson* published by Clark and M'Arthur in 1809. At Birchin Edge on the Derbyshire Moors stands a sim-

ple obelisk surmounted by a ball commissioned by Mr John Brightman, and Lord Feversham set up some ceremonial gates on his estate at Duncombe Park in Yorkshire. More recently, in 1951, a statue of Nelson was erected on Southsea Common in Portsmouth, close to the spot where he left England for the last time on 14 September 1805. And, in 1994, a simple monument was erected in memory of Emma Hamilton, close to the spot in Calais where she was buried in 1815.

All these monuments require constant care and attention. Some remain in the hands of public authorities but some now have no-one to look after them. So, in 1990 a group of enthusiasts founded The 1805 Club, whose main aim is to restore and maintain monuments and graves associated with Nelson, his family and those who served with him.

SEE ALSO
Pitt, Trafalgar Day ceremonies

LATEST RESEARCH
Flora Fraser, 'If you seek his monument', in Colin White (ed) *The Nelson Companion*, Sutton and Royal Naval Museum (Stroud & Portsmouth 1995)

Moutray, Mary (1752–1843)

The first married woman with whom Nelson became emotionally involved, Mary Moutray (née Pemble), was a Scot and the daughter of a naval captain. In 1772, she married Captain John Moutray, then a widower aged forty-nine. In 1780, Moutray was court-martialled for losing a valuable convoy to a Franco-Spanish squadron. Denied any further chance of active service afloat, he accepted the post of commissioner to the dockyard at English Harbour, Antigua, in the West Indies, and his wife went out there with him.

Nelson arrived in Antigua on 28 July 1784, in command of the frigate HMS *Boreas*. His close friend Cuthbert Collingwood was already friendly with the Moutrays and introduced Nelson to them. Mary was vivacious and witty but, at the same time, sympathetic and almost motherly, the sort of woman that Nelson always found irresistible. And, characteristically, he was quite unable to hide his affection, writing of her as 'my sweet amiable friend' and 'a treasure of a woman.'

However, Mary Moutray was well able to deal with her ardent admirer and managed to keep him at a distance without losing his friendship. He remained in touch with her to the end of his life and when her son James died of a fever, while serving as a lieutenant in HMS *Victory* during the campaign in Corsica ten years later, he paid for a memorial tablet to be placed in the church at San Fiorenzo.

SEE ALSO
Antigua, Collingwood

LATEST RESEARCH
Tom Pocock, *Nelson's Women*, André Deutsch (London 1999)

Mary Moutray. A delightful miniature watercolour by John Downland, dating from 1781, showing one of Nelson's early loves in the full panoply of a late eighteenth-century lady of fashion. (Courtesy Clive Richards)

Murray, George (1759–1819)

Although not one of the original 'Band of Brothers', Murray was one of Nelson's close associates in his later years and served with him for over two years as his captain of the fleet in the Mediterranean. Murray was born in Chichester in West Sussex in 1759, and entered the Royal Navy aged just eleven. He served for a time with Nelson's patron Sir Peter Parker in HMS *Bristol*, in which ship he first met Nelson who was briefly one of her lieutenants. Promoted to lieutenant in 1777, he was wrecked in HMS *Arethusa* off Ushant and spent two years as a prisoner of war in France. Having been exchanged in 1781, he served in the Indian Ocean, seeing action in the battles between the fleets of Admirals Suffren and Hughes. He was promoted for his gallant conduct, becoming a post captain in 1782, still aged only twenty-three.

When war with France broke out again he was appointed first to frigates and then, in 1797, to the 74-gun battleship HMS *Colossus*. He commanded her at the Battle of Cape St Vincent (14 February 1797) but was unfortunately shipwrecked again not long afterwards. In 1801, he commanded the *Edgar* in the Baltic campaign where the gallant way in which he led the British line into action won him a special mention in Nelson's despatch, referring to Murray's '. . . noble example of intrepidity which was well followed up by every Captain, Officer and Man in the Squadron.'

Like so many before him, Murray quickly fell under Nelson's spell and, less than two months after the battle, was intimate enough with his admiral to be one of those who nursed him when he fell ill with the strain of the campaign and the cold of the Baltic. Later, in 1803, having failed to persuade the ailing Thomas Foley to become his captain of the fleet, Nelson turned to Murray who was, at first, also inclined to refuse. The captain of the fleet was chief staff officer to the commander-in-chief and Murray feared that such a role could often lead to tension. Nelson's reply was characteristic: if there were any disagreements he would waive his rank as admiral and speak to Murray as a friend. Murray duly went with Nelson to the Mediterranean and it was very much due to his hard work and administrative skill that the fleet remained in such good order, and good health, throughout the long taxing campaign that followed.

When Nelson returned to England in the *Victory* in the late summer of 1805, Murray, by now a rear admiral, applied for leave to clear up some family affairs following the death of his father-in-law and so missed Trafalgar. His career, thereafter, was unremarkable and he died in Chichester on 28 February 1819.

SEE ALSO
Copenhagen, Mediterranean Command

Museums with Nelson Collections

Nelson's remarkable, and continuing, popularity is reflected in the large number of collections of his personal relics and memorabilia that are available in museums. Although some notable private collections of Nelson memorabilia still exist, the trend since 1900 has been towards a concentration of material, so that most of the main Nelson relics can now be seen by visiting the three Nelson centres at Monmouth, Portsmouth and Greenwich.

The Nelson Collection at Monmouth was assembled by Lady Llangattock, Georgiana Shelley Rolls, mother of Charles Rolls who, in partnership with Henry Royce, produced the famous car. Lady Llangattock was a dedicated Nelson enthusiast and spent most of her life acquiring items at sales and from dealers of varying reliability. On her death, her collection was bequeathed to the town of Monmouth, which Nelson visited during his tour of Wales and the Midlands with the Hamiltons in 1802.

The collection includes a wide selection of silver and china, together with the only sword that can be confidently attributed to Nelson. It also includes a fine collection of original letters, including most of those he wrote to his wife. But the collection is also well known (and, indeed, appreciated) for its special collection of Nelson fakes. Among the swords with 'H.N.' engraved on them, or standard pieces of silver with coats of arms of a design dating from twenty-five years after Trafalgar, there is also Nelson's glass eye. He, of course, lost the *sight* of his right eye, not the eye itself.

Then there is the collection at Portsmouth, housed in the Lambert McCarthy Gallery of the Royal Naval Museum, with windows looking out onto HMS *Victory*. Named after another notable Nelsonian lady, and American citizen, Mrs Lily Lambert McCarthy, CBE, the gallery houses her pre-eminent collection of Nelson commemorative material together with the museum's own collection of Nelson's possessions. At the core of the latter is a large group of material donated by the descendants of his daughter Horatia, including some of the most personal and intimate relics in existence. There is the locket containing Emma Hamilton's portrait and hair that Nelson wore round his neck, the locket of him that she wore and the rings they exchanged in a quasi-marriage service in September 1805. Over the years, the museum has added individual relics to this collection by donation and purchase, including items that had hitherto not appeared in public, such as a prayer book given to Nelson by Captain William Locker and later presented by him to Emma Hamilton.

Finally, the most comprehensive collection of all is the one at the National Maritime Museum at Greenwich. There is much material from Nelson's family, some important portraits and battle paintings, all of Nelson's surviving uniform coats, including the one he was wearing when he was shot at Trafalgar, and furniture and relics from Merton Place, the house he shared with the Hamiltons. The museum also houses an important collection of Nelson letters, together with the relics and papers of key members of his family and close naval colleagues.

But the true Nelson enthusiast should not stop there. For Nelson relics crop up everywhere. They can be found enshrined in a special room inside the self-consciously modern office buildings of Lloyds of London; in a medieval Essex church at Southminster; in a grand castle in Norwich, a converted town house in Great Yarmouth and a humble village pub in his birthplace at Burnham Thorpe, Norfolk. And they can also be found, more conventionally housed, in numerous smaller museums throughout Britain and, indeed, throughout the world.

SEE ALSO
Burnham Thorpe, Greenwich, Portsmouth, Relics

Naples

Naples is a large city and port on the southwest coast of Italy. In Nelson's day, it was the capital of the independent 'Kingdom of the Two Sicilies' comprising the Neapolitan mainland and the island of Sicily. King Ferdinand was an ally of Britain throughout most of the war with France and so Nelson often visited there. The first occasion was in 1793 when he was sent there by Lord Hood in HMS *Agamemnon* to ask the King of Naples for assistance with the defence of Toulon and he often called there in subsequent years for information and supplies. However, these were fleeting visits. Between 1798 and 1800, it became one of the main centres of his operations, and arguably his obsession. It was also the

Naples – The Villa Emma. An engraving dating from about 1790 of the delightful seaside villa at Posillipo (right), on the edge of the Bay of Naples, where Nelson was entertained by the Hamiltons in the autumn of 1798.

scene of the deeds for which he has been most con-
sistently criticised, when he became closely involved
with the bloody campaign to restore the Neapolitan
monarchy in 1799.

He returned only once, in 1803, when, having
been appointed commander-in-chief of the Mediterranean, he called there briefly during a tour of his
new command. In the years that followed, he often
received invitations to go ashore there to rest and
recover his health; but he had learned his lesson and
never again allowed himself to become so embroiled
in the affairs of one country that he overlooked the
needs of his wider command.

Naples has, of course, changed greatly since his
day: but the spectacular Palazzo Reale, where he was
received by the King and Queen, still survives, as
does the Palazzo Sesa where he lodged with the
Hamiltons during his stay there in 1798.

SEE ALSO
William Hamilton, Emma Hamilton, Neapolitan
campaign, Palermo

Napoleon I, Emperor (1769–1821)

Napoleon Bonaparte dominated European affairs
throughout the latter part of Nelson's life, first as one
of the most successful generals of the revolutionary
armies and then as the French head of state and thus
the personification of all that Britain was fighting
against. Although Nelson and Napoleon never
directly met in combat, their careers overlapped on a
number of occasions and each was very conscious of
the other.

The first overlap was at Toulon in 1793, when
Nelson was still a relatively unknown battleship captain and Napoleon a junior general. It was
Napoleon's brilliant use of artillery that was very
largely responsible for driving the British out of
Toulon, but by the time that his guns began to have
their effect, Nelson had been sent off on detached
duty and so the two men did not actually exchange
fire.

Their next encounter was during the Italian campaign of 1795/6 when Nelson commanded a small
squadron off the northwest coast of Italy, attempting
to hold up the advance of the victorious French
armies under Napoleon by combined operations with

*Napoleon Bonaparte. This engraving shows Napoleon on
board the British battleship HMS Bellerophon, following his
defeat at Waterloo in June 1815. He surrendered to her
commanding officer, Captain Maitland and was brought in
her to Britain.*

the defending Austrian armies. Again, there was no
direct contact between them, although by now
Nelson, in common with most of his colleagues, had
heard the name of Bonaparte and had begun to
respect him as a formidable opponent.

Their closest encounter came in 1798, when
Nelson commanded the squadron sent into the
Mediterranean by Lord St Vincent to discover and
destroy the French expedition that eventually captured Egypt. We now know that, at one point in the
famous chase down the Mediterranean before the
Battle of the Nile, Nelson's fleet was within a few
miles of Napoleon's armada and it is fascinating to
speculate what course history might have taken if the
British had sighted the French fleet and a full-scale
naval battle had ensued.

It was at this point that Nelson began to feel an

almost personal rivalry with Napoleon. This feeling was intensified after the Battle of the Nile (1 August 1798) when he captured some of Bonaparte's personal correspondence which, Nelson realised, showed that 'he does want, and will strive to be, the [George] Washington of France', a perceptive remark considering that Bonaparte's seizure of executive power was then more than a year away. Napoleon seems to have developed a similar personal feeling: apparently, during the Peace of Amiens, he placed a bust of Nelson on his dressing table, presumably as a reminder of the man who had caused him and France the most trouble during the preceding war. But the ultimate tribute came after Trafalgar. On being told of Nelson's famous 'England expects' signal, Napoleon apparently ordered that a French translation should be placed prominently in all his ships, 'La France compte que chacun fera son devoir.'

SEE ALSO
Brueys, Channel Command, 'England expects', Italian campaign, Latouche Tréville, Nile, Trafalgar campaign

Navy Board, The

In Nelson's day, the Navy Board handled all the technical and financial aspects of the Royal Navy. Run separately from, but in parallel with, the Admiralty (which was responsible for all operational matters), the Board was housed in the splendid surroundings of Somerset House on the Strand in central London, and it was there that Nelson underwent his *viva voce* examination for lieutenant in 1777.

First established by King Henry VIII in 1546, the Navy Board's main responsibility was for the building, maintenance, fitting out and supplying of ships. So its chief officers tended to be men of practical experience. The head was a senior captain called the comptroller, an office held by Nelson's maternal uncle Captain Maurice Suckling between 1775 and 1778. He was assisted by surveyors, who were responsible for ship design and building, and other specialists in victualling, storekeeping and finance. The administration of the Board was handled by the clerk of the acts (a post once held by the famous diarist, Samuel Pepys) assisted by secretaries. Nelson's elder brother Maurice worked there as a clerk from 1762 until his death in 1801.

Eventually, in 1832, the separation of functions was found to be unsatisfactory and the Navy Board and Admiralty were merged into a single organisation responsible for every aspect of naval affairs. Somerset House, magnificently restored, is now open to the public and houses displays telling the story of the Navy Board and of its work.

SEE ALSO
Admiralty, Family, Suckling

LATEST RESEARCH
Brian Lavery, *Nelson's Navy*, Conway Maritime Press (London 1989)

Neapolitan campaign (1799)

Following the Battle of the Nile (1 August 1798), Nelson went in HMS *Vanguard* to Naples, then one of Britain's few allies in the Mediterranean basin. He arrived on 22 September 1798 to a rapturous welcome. His stunning victory appeared to have changed the course of the war. The invincible French had received their first major check and the Mediterranean had been transformed into an English lake by the elimination of the French fleet. Later in the year, urged on by Nelson, King Ferdinand of Naples entered Rome in triumph at the head of his army, having driven out the French occupying forces. Feeling that his task in the Mediterranean was complete, Nelson began to talk of returning home to England.

But his sense of completion was premature. The French quickly struck back. Within a week, Ferdinand had been forced to leave Rome and, by the middle of December, the French army was threatening Naples itself. Ferdinand fled, with all his court and treasure, in Nelson's flagship HMS *Vanguard*, to his second capital of Palermo in Sicily, leaving his Neapolitan subjects to their fate. On 27 January 1799, the French armies entered Naples and the Parthenopean Republic was proclaimed. Although supported by the educated middle classes and liberal aristocracy, the new republic was bitterly disliked by the ordinary Neapolitans, most of whom remained fiercely loyal to their monarch. And so the seeds of a bloody civil war were sown.

Nelson's hopes of a triumphant return home to England were shattered by these events. Ferdinand

and his anglophile queen, Maria Carolina, saw Nelson as their only hope of salvation and made emotional appeals to him not to desert them. These pleas were supported by Emma Hamilton, with whom he was already deeply involved emotionally. She, and her husband Sir William Hamilton, the British ambassador to Naples, were passionate in their commitment to the King and Queen and added their persuasive voices to the royal requests that Nelson should remain and help Ferdinand to regain his throne. This was Nelson's first encounter with the complexities of international diplomacy and Court intrigue and he was, quite simply, out of his depth. He allowed himself to become too closely involved with one particular aspect of the campaign; a more experienced commander would have remained aloof, giving himself greater flexibility.

In Naples itself, a counter-revolution had already begun, led by Cardinal Fabrizio Ruffo. One by one, the revolutionary-held towns fell to his army and everywhere there were scenes of terror and slaughter as the victorious monarchists took their revenge on the people they saw as rebels. Nelson supported Ruffo's campaign by sending Captain Thomas Troubridge with a small squadron to blockade Naples from the sea. By the end of April, it looked as if the war in Italy was once again going the allies' way.

But, at this crucial moment, the French made a bold strategic move, which threatened the whole delicate balance. Twenty-five battleships, under Admiral Bruix, escaped from Brest and entered the Mediterranean, accompanied by seventeen Spanish ships from Cádiz. This powerful fleet represented a major threat to all British operations in the area and so the commander-in-chief, Lord Keith, ordered his scattered forces to concentrate off Minorca. Nelson was torn in two by this order. All his sense of duty, and a lifetime's training, required him to obey his senior officer's order and sail to Minorca; emotion, and his infatuation with Emma, tied him to Palermo. At first, he compromised by sending ten of his ships to Minorca, while remaining himself at Palermo. But then came the news that the Combined fleet was sailing eastwards and might be heading for Naples itself to assist the rebels in their fight. This finally galvanised Nelson into action and he concentrated

his fleet off the island of Marettimo, on the west coast of Sicily.

In the meantime, Cardinal Ruffo's forces had reached the gates of Naples. Nelson had left a frigate, HMS *Seahorse*, commanded by Captain Edward Foote, to maintain the blockade and so it was Foote who now established contact with Ruffo as the reconquest of Naples entered its last stages. The rebels withdrew to the great forts defending the port, from which only a major assault would dislodge them. Knowing that the French fleet was at large, and fearing that it might arrive and relieve the forts, Ruffo decided, with Foote's reluctant agreement, to make terms, agreeing to allow the revolutionaries free passage to France in return for surrendering the forts without further resistance.

No sooner had the terms of the truce been agreed than sails were sighted on the horizon. The first thought was that the French had, after all, managed to come to the rescue of their beleaguered colleges. But, in fact, it was Nelson. Learning that the Combined fleet had retired eastwards to Toulon, and that the campaign in Naples was reaching a climax, he had brought his whole fleet with him to finish the business.

When Nelson was told of the truce, he angrily repudiated it. Ruffo's orders from Ferdinand had been specific. There were to be no negotiations with the rebels: unconditional surrender was required. An angry scene between him and Ruffo ensued on board the *Foudroyant*, with Sir William Hamilton acting as interpreter and arbiter between the two leaders, and eventually Nelson appeared to give way. The republicans embarked in vessels that were supposed to be taking them to France, only to find themselves escorted to the British fleet and then handed over to their opponents ashore. In the end, most of them were eventually allowed to continue their journey to France but not before about a hundred had been tried and sentenced to summary execution.

Nelson's apparent treachery has never been satisfactorily explained. To the end of his life, he claimed that he believed the republicans had come out of the castles fully understanding that their surrender was unconditional. Some historians have written off this claim as a direct lie and have suggested that Nelson cynically tricked the republicans into emerging from

King Ferdinand of Naples by an unknown artist. This miniature, which belonged to Nelson and passed to his daughter Horatia, captures the essential stupidity of this unattractive monarch. But it fails to show the underlying cruelty, which led him to wreak such a savage revenge on his rebellious subjects.

the safety of their castles, but such deviousness was not in character. Recently, it has been suggested that Sir William Hamilton allowed Nelson (who spoke no French or Italian and who was thus unable to converse directly with Ruffo and his colleagues) to think that the surrender was unconditional. This certainly sounds more plausible, since Hamilton was a wily diplomat who, moreover, had strong personal reasons for disliking the leaders of the Neapolitan republicans.

Among the first to be executed was Commodore Prince Francesco Caracciolo, who had commanded the Neapolitan naval forces during the short-lived republic. He argued, in his defence, that the King had deserted his people, leaving loyal subjects like himself in an impossible position. But he knew he was doomed. Even his pleas to be shot as befitted an officer and gentleman, and for a stay of execution to

allow time to prepare himself for death, were turned down by an implacable Nelson, now acting on the King's behalf, and the unfortunate Caracciolo was hanged from the yardarm of his former flagship, the *Minerva*.

For the rest of the ringleaders, the end was considerably less dignified: a hangman's noose in the large central square in front of a jeering crowd. Of course, Nelson himself played no part in this bloodbath: it was the inevitable end of the sharp internal divisions in Naples, revealed by the civil war. But his presence, along with his fleet, in support of King Ferdinand's savage revenge, left an unpleasant memory in Naples that has never been erased.

Nelson's close personal involvement in these events was controversial at the time and historians still argue over whether his behaviour represents a blot on his reputation, or another example of his ability to act decisively in a complex situation. Certainly, the successful reconquest of Naples marked an important turning point in the war and secured a valuable ally and friendly port for Britain. But it had been a thoroughly vicious and bloody conflict, as civil wars so often are, with much bitterness and cruelty on both sides and, as one of the key players, Nelson must bear some of the responsibility.

SEE ALSO
Francesco Caracciolo, William Hamilton, Emma Hamilton, Naples, Palermo

LATEST RESEARCH
Carlo Knight, 'The British at Naples', *The Trafalgar Chronicle* 11 (2001), The 1805 Club

'Nelson's Blood'

This is a popular nickname for rum. It originates from a very long-standing tradition in the Royal Navy that Nelson's body was preserved in a barrel of rum and the macabre suggestion that, after the body had been removed, the rum was then issued to the *Victory*'s sailors. But this is a classic sailors' tall story. Nelson was, indeed, preserved in spirits but Surgeon William Beatty in fact used brandy and spirits of wine. And there is no evidence at all to support the claim that this liquor was then 'recycled'!

The usual method of disposing of the bodies of those killed in naval battles was to bury them at sea but Nelson's officers knew that his country would wish to do honour to his remains. A method, therefore, had to be devised of preserving the body so that it could be transported home to England. So Surgeon William Beatty arranged for a large wooden storage cask, known as a 'leaguer', to be filled with brandy and the body, dressed only in a shirt, was placed in it. As a result, the body was still in a reasonable condition when the *Victory* eventually reached England some six weeks after the battle.

Frances Nelson. This charming miniature by Daniel Orme, produced in 1798, shows what a very attractive woman Fanny Nelson was. It dates from one of the happiest periods in her marriage, when she was devotedly nursing her husband back to health after the loss of his arm. (National Maitime Museum).

SEE ALSO
Beatty, Death

LATEST RESEARCH
A J Pack, *Nelson's Blood: the story of rum*, Kenneth Mason (Emsworth 1982)

Nelson, Frances Lady (1761–1831)

In the past, Frances Nelson has been often portrayed as a cold and rather colourless woman. Certainly, she suffers from comparison with the earthy and rumbustious Emma Hamilton and the high romance and drama of Nelson's relationship with Emma makes his marriage to Frances appear very ordinary. But, in fact, they were happily married for over ten years and Lady Spencer, the wife of the First Lord of the Admiralty, later remembered Nelson telling her in 1797, apparently with all the eagerness of a newly married husband, '. . . that he was convinced I must like her. That she was beautiful accomplished; but above all that her angelic tenderness towards him was beyond imagination.'

Frances Woolward was born on the West Indian island of Nevis in 1761. Nevis was then a rich sugar island and she was closely related to the island's governing élite: her father was the senior judge and her uncle John Herbert was President of the Council. In 1779, she married a doctor, Josiah Nisbet, and the couple moved to England, where a son, also named Josiah, was born. But Nisbet was in delicate health, both physically and mentally, and in 1781 he died. Frances returned to Nevis with her son, where she became her uncle's hostess.

In 1785, Nelson visited Nevis while in command of the frigate HMS *Boreas* and so became acquainted with Fanny (as he always called her). Apparently, on one occasion very early in their acquaintance, he was found playing happily under the table with young Josiah, which must have endeared him to the young widow, and it is clear from his surviving letters that he was quickly attracted to the beautiful and accomplished young woman (see transcript on p264). A long but affectionate courtship ensued and they were eventually married at Montpelier, John Herbert's estate, on 11 March 1787. Nelson's friend Prince William Henry gave the bride away.

The Nelsons then returned to Britain and, after some months spent in London, Bath and visiting relations, they travelled to Nelson's parental home in Burnham Thorpe, arriving in December 1788, in the middle of one of the coldest winters on record. Fanny, used to the warmth and luxuries of the West Indies, was prostrated by the chill and spent much of her time in bed and their problems were made worse by Nelson's growing frustration at his inability to obtain another command and his obvious dissatisfaction with a tame life as a farmer. Additionally, as the years passed, it also became clear that there were to be no offspring, a fact that Nelson, who particularly loved children, obviously found extremely difficult to accept happily. All in all, then, the marriage did not have a very auspicious start.

Nelson finally went back to sea in early 1793 and Fanny did not see him again for over four years. They corresponded regularly and affectionately but it is clear from their letters, most of which have been preserved, that neither was able fully to sympathise with the other. Fanny has often been criticised by Nelson's male biographers for failing to support her spouse: filling her letters with fears about his safety and longings for him to return home. But these are natural feelings for the partner of a man constantly in the front line and, to be fair, it is clear that Emma Hamilton wrote to him in very similar terms when her turn came to wait at home for long periods without news. On the other hand, Nelson did not try to meet Fanny halfway: his letters are always full of his warlike deeds and his longings for yet more glory, which can have done little to allay her fears.

In the end, of course, he did come home to her, in July 1797; but he was wholly altered from the vigorous still-young man to whom she had said goodbye. White-haired, haggard with pain and with one arm missing, the first sight of him must have been an appalling shock. And yet she nursed him devotedly, wrote his letters for him and even learned how to dress his unpleasant wound. Ironically, it was probably their happiest time together and it was during this period that he described her to Lady Spencer in the enthusiastic terms quoted earlier. He also told another friend that she was 'everything which is valuable in a wife.'

Having recovered from his wound, he went off again on active service in April 1797 but not before they had seen and purchased a handsome home together at Roundwood, just outside Ipswich. She divided her time between there and Bath for another three years of separation, while he went on to win the Battle of the Nile and to fall in love with Emma Hamilton. The lovers made no secret of their infatuation and so rumours of the affair reached Britain long before Nelson and the Hamiltons eventually returned in late 1800.

What happened then has never been definitely established. There are accounts that Fanny received her husband coldly and there is even a harrowing story of an argument so bitter that Nelson was forced to leave the house and wander the streets of London distractedly until finally he fetched up at the Hamiltons' house in the early hours of the morning. But such stories mostly derive from sources that were strongly influenced by Emma and there is an alternative, and rather more plausible, tradition that the end of the marriage was reasonably dignified, and that Nelson declared Fanny was entirely innocent of all blame in the matter. Certainly, having separated, he treated her generously, allocating to her half of his income. However, when she tried to bring about a reconciliation he responded cruelly, ordering her last letter to be returned to her with a blunt endorsement by his agent Alexander Davison, 'Opened by mistake by Lord Nelson but not read.'

They never met again. As so often happens in such cases, Nelson's family found their loyalties painfully divided but, one by one, they deserted Fanny when it was made very clear to them that any contact with her was regarded as treachery. The only one who never wavered in his support was old Edmund Nelson who continued to write to her and visit her and she responded by nursing him in his final illness in 1802.

As Nelson received rewards for his victories, so Fanny found herself elevated, becoming Baroness Nelson in 1798 and Viscountess Nelson in 1801. After his death, she was awarded a generous pension and she also received a number of special gifts, including a splendid silver vase from Lloyds. She remained unswerving in her devotion to her husband (see colour plate *XXI*) and one of her granddaughters remembered that she once showed her a miniature painted in Leghorn in 1795, depicting Nelson as a young captain, and said, 'When you are older little Fan, you may know what it is to have a broken heart.' Her heart was further broken when her son Josiah died of pleurisy in 1830 and she followed him shortly after, dying on 6 May 1831. She was buried beside Josiah in the churchyard at Littleham, near Exmouth, where they had lived together for some years.

Almost everyone who knew Fanny Nelson loved and respected her. Lord St Vincent remained in touch with her to the end of his life and Nelson's truest friends – for example, Thomas Hardy – also refused to drop her. She has been unfairly blamed in the past for the break-up of the marriage and has been particularly criticised for failing to give Nelson the adulation and encouragement he craved. But such judgements have tended to be based on a few brief, and heavily edited, extracts from her letters to him published by Sir Nicholas Harris Nicolas as footnotes in his 'Dispatches and Letters'. When, in 1958, the letters were finally published in full by the Navy Records Society, it became clear that Fanny had been much more supportive than had hitherto been supposed. As a result, she is now, increasingly, seen as the innocent victim of a love affair that was extremely destructive, as well as highly romantic.

SEE ALSO
Nevis, Josiah Nisbet, Family, Roundwood

LATEST RESEARCH
Tom Pocock, *Nelson's Women*, André Deutsch (London 1999)

Nelson Ward, Horatia (1801–1881)

The only surviving child of Emma Hamilton and Horatio Nelson, Horatia was born at the end of January 1801. Nelson was away at sea at the time and, to preserve the proprieties, Emma's confinement had to be disguised as a stomach complaint, so the exact date is hard to establish. Moreover, it would appear from hints in Nelson's letters that Horatia had a twin sister and, recently, there has been speculation that Emma may have placed this other girl in a foundling hospital. However, it now appears more likely that the twin, if there was one, died at birth, or soon after.

The little girl's early years were shrouded in secrecy. As long as Sir William Hamilton was alive, Emma could not have her living with her and so she was lodged with a wet nurse, Mrs Mary Gibson. Emma visited her regularly and Mrs Gibson's own daughter later remembered seeing Nelson playing on the floor with his child on one of his rare visits while on leave. He was always fond of children and later, when he returned to sea after the Peace of Amiens, he began writing to her and sending her presents (see transcript on p269). To start with, he referred to her as his 'goddaughter' but in his last letter, written just before Trafalgar, he abandoned all pretence and wrote, 'Receive my dearest Horatia the affectionate parental blessing of your Father'. He also had a delightful watercolour of her hanging on the bulkhead of his cabin in the *Victory* alongside a fine portrait of Emma, which was hardly a discreet gesture. However, the only extended time he was able to spend with her was during his brief spell of leave in the late summer of 1805, by when she was living openly at Merton as his 'adopted' daughter. His last act before leaving the house to begin his last journey to Portsmouth was to kneel in prayer at her bedside and, one of his last acts before the Battle of Trafalgar was to write a codicil to his will in which he committed her, and Emma Hamilton, to the care of his country (see colour plate *XXII*).

The question of Horatia's parentage remained a hotly debated question for the rest of her life. She came to accept, and even to glory in, the fact that she was Nelson's daughter; but she never accepted that Emma was her mother, even when letters were found that proved her parentage beyond question. Partly, no doubt, this was because Emma herself denied she was her mother, but it must also have been because their last years together were not happy ones. As Emma became increasingly embroiled in debt, and more and more the slave of drink, it is clear that she sometimes behaved very cruelly to her daughter. Some of her letters have survived castigating Horatia for ingratitude in terms that must have been very distressing to a teenage girl. But Horatia was always ready to defend Emma and stayed by her loyally until she died in Calais in January 1815.

She was then taken in first by the Matchams and then by the Boltons and so, for the first time, experi-

Horatia Nelson aged about three. This delightful watercolour, attributed to Henry Edridge, was taken by Nelson to sea and hung in his cabin in HMS Victory.

Silver gilt cup given by Nelson to Horatia during his last visit to England in 1805. As Emma Hamilton later recorded, 'She used it till I thought it proper for her to lay it by as a sacred relic.'

enced a happy family life with her cousins. In 1822, she married a curate, Philip Ward, and they enjoyed a contented marriage that produced ten children before Philip died in 1859.

Throughout her life, Horatia bore a striking resemblance to her father. A miniature produced in 1822 on the occasion of her marriage, when she was just twenty-one, looks remarkably like the portrait of Nelson at the same age by Francis Rigaud (see p113). Moreover, photographs of her taken in old age show a face that had aged in a very similar way to Nelson's and with his very distinctive nose, which she passed on to most of her descendants. She gradually amassed a large collection of personal Nelson relics and letters and after her death these were distributed among her children. Most of this material has been presented by her descendants to the National Maritime and Royal

Naval Museums and so is now available to the public.

Tall, intelligent and witty, with a delightful smile (another reminder of her father) and a love of thunder and lightning, she inherited the longevity of her Nelson ancestors and lived to the age of eighty, dying eventually on 6 March 1881 in Pinner. Even in death, discretion ruled and the inscription on her gravestone originally stated that she was 'the Adopted Daughter of Vice Admiral Lord Nelson,' though some time later the words were altered to 'the Beloved Daughter.'

SEE ALSO
Emma Hamilton, Catherine Matcham, 'Thompson' letters

LATEST RESEARCH
Tom Pocock, *Nelson's Women*, André Deutsch (London 1999)

'Nelson Mass', The

In August 1798, Josef Haydn, Kappellmeister to Prince Nikolaus Esterházy in Austria, composed the third of his six great masses, commissioned by the Prince to celebrate the name day of his wife, Princess Marie. At that time, the whole of Europe was in the grip of war and the French, against whom the Austrians were opposed, in alliance with Prussia and England, seemed to be successful everywhere. So Haydn named his new work *Missa in angustiis* ('Mass in straightened times') and some of the musical pas-

William, Earl Nelson. Although this engraving of Nelson's elder brother shows him in old age, around 1820, it gives a good impression of this rather unattractive man.

sages certainly seemed to express a sense of tension and anxiety.

About two weeks after Haydn had completed work on the mass, the news arrived in Vienna of Nelson's astounding victory over the common enemy, the French, at the Battle of the Nile on 1 August. So, by the time that the mass received its first performance on 23 September 1798, Nelson's name was on everyone's lips. Now, some passages in the mass, notably the jubilant *Gloria in excelsis Deo* ('Glory to God in the highest'), seemed to reflect the general mood of rejoicing and so the new mass acquired a new name, the 'Nelson Mass'.

Almost exactly two years later, in September 1800, Nelson visited Prince Nikolaus's palace at Esterháza, just outside Vienna, during his triumphant tour of the German states with the Hamiltons. He and Haydn liked each other at once and Nelson gave the composer a watch in return for the pen with which his scores were written. A concert was held at which Emma Hamilton sang a Haydn cantata, accompanied on the piano by the composer, and it would appear that the 'Nelson Mass' was also performed at a special thanksgiving service.

Haydn's *Missa in angustiis* is generally regarded as the finest of his late masses and it has been closely associated with Nelson ever since: so much so, that some authorities have claimed that it was composed in celebration of Nelson's victory. But, attractive as this idea may be, the chronology does not support it.

See also
Nelson's tour of Germany, Nile

Latest research
Otto Deutsch, *Admiral Nelson and Joseph Haydn*, The Nelson Society (2000)

Nelson, William Lord (1757–1835)

Nelson's eldest surviving brother, William, was born at Burnham Thorpe on 20 April 1757 and, having graduated from Cambridge in 1781, followed their father into the Church in the same year. In 1784, he became rector of Brandon and, apart from a brief spell as a naval chaplain in his brother's frigate HMS *Boreas* during 1784–1786, he remained there until, in 1797, he moved to one of his father's former parishes at Hilborough in Norfolk.

After 1798, William reaped the rewards of his younger brother's growing fame: being awarded an honorary doctorate by Oxford in 1802 and a prebend's stall at Canterbury the following year. But the greatest reward of all came after Trafalgar in 1805 when, as his brother's closest living male relation, he was suddenly elevated to the peerage as the first Earl Nelson, and granted a pension of £5000 and a lump sum of £90,000 to provide him with an estate worthy of his new rank. This he used to purchase Stanlynch Park, near Salisbury in Wiltshire, where he lived until his death on 28 February 1828. His only son, Horatio, had died in 1808 and so, to his great disappointment, the title passed to his eldest nephew, Thomas Bolton, son of his sister Susannah. However, the Italian title of Bronte, which he had also inherited from his brother, passed to his daughter Charlotte.

Loud and boisterous, with a large heavy body, he was as unlike his brother in character as he was physically, being graceless, mean and essentially unattractive. He was perfectly content to enjoy benefits for which he had given no service at all and, indeed, appears to have regarded them as his right. Having assiduously cultivated Emma Hamilton's friendship when it was clear that this was the only way of remaining in favour with his brother, he hurriedly abandoned her after his brother's death. He failed even to make any provision for Nelson's beloved daughter Horatia, despite being well aware of the moving plea in the famous last codicil to his brother's will.

SEE ALSO
Bronte, Descendants, Family

Nevis

One of the northernmost of the Leeward Islands in the West Indies, Nevis was the scene of Nelson's wedding, to Mrs Frances Nisbet, in March 1787. A single volcanic cone, rising to 3000 feet, it was then a rich sugar island, with a wealthy, cultured expatriate English community who regarded themselves as a social élite. Nelson first visited in 1785 when he was serving in the area in command of the frigate HMS *Boreas*. He had seized four American merchantmen off the island, which he claimed were trading illegally, and had been sued by the shipowners. Somewhat

to his surprise, the influential President of Nevis, John Herbert, supported him, and even agreed to stand bail for him if he was arrested.

Herbert invited Nelson to visit his estate, Montpelier, where he lived in style in an elegant mansion surrounded by a large sugar plantation. There, Nelson met Herbert's niece, Frances Nisbet, and began courting her. Eventually, they were married at Montpelier on 11 March 1787. Shortly afterwards, the couple sailed home to Britain and Nelson never visited the island again.

The house at Montpelier where the Nelsons were married has disappeared, although some gateposts remain, marking the old entrance to the plantation. The local church, where the marriage was registered, is still standing and many of the buildings in the island's capital at Charlestown date from the period. There is even a small Nelson Museum, which includes a number of Nelson relics in its collections.

SEE ALSO
HMS *Boreas*, Frances Nelson, Nisbet, William IV

New York

In the late autumn of 1782, Nelson spent a few days in the vicinity of New York in North America, which was at that time still in British hands. His ship first lay at anchor off Sandy Hook, at the mouth of the Hudson River, and later moved up into the East River. It would appear from his letters that Nelson went ashore on at least two occasions. The short while he spent in the area proved to be a pivotal period in his life, when he met two men who were to become close friends and, in their respective ways, influential in his future career.

He arrived at Sandy Hook in his frigate, HMS *Albemarle*, on 13 November. He was at a low ebb emotionally, having recently parted from Mary Simpson, a young Quebecoise with whom he had been very much in love. Moreover, the naval war with America and her allies was clearly approaching a climax in the West Indies – which he described in a letter to his father as 'the Grand Theatre of Actions' – whereas he was attached to the North American squadron, and his duties were mainly routine: escorting convoys and harrying enemy trade.

At Sandy Hook, he found a detachment of the

West Indies fleet under the command of Rear Admiral Lord Hood. Having recently taken part in Admiral Sir George Rodney's decisive defeat of the French fleet at the Battle of the Saintes (12 April 1782) in the West Indies the previous April, the ships had come north to refit. Nelson was introduced to Hood, who had been a friend of his uncle Maurice Suckling, and Hood was clearly impressed with the young captain, for he immediately arranged for the *Albemarle* to be transferred to his fleet. It was the beginning of a professional friendship that was to last to the end of Nelson's life. And it had a decisive effect on his future career, for it was Hood who introduced him to key public figures in England and who later gave him his first opportunities to distinguish himself in the Mediterranean during 1793–1795.

When Nelson called upon Hood in his flagship, HMS *Barfleur*, the admiral introduced him to one of his midshipmen, Prince William Henry, the son of King George III, who was on active service in the Royal Navy. The prince's first impressions were not particularly favourable. Many years later, he recalled that Nelson had appeared 'the merest boy of a captain I ever beheld.' However, like so many others after him, Prince William found that his first impressions were quickly challenged for, when Nelson started speaking, 'There was something irresistibly pleasing in his address and conversation; and an enthusiasm when speaking on professional subjects that showed he was no common being.' The two men became friends and continued to correspond regularly on service matters, even after the Prince had been removed from the Navy.

SEE ALSO
HMS *Albemarle*, Lord Hood, Mary Simpson, William IV

Nicaraguan campaign (1780)

In 1780, when he was just twenty-one and a newly promoted post captain in the frigate HMS *Hinchinbrooke*, Nelson commanded the naval contingent in an amphibious campaign in Central America. The War of American Independence was at its height and Spain had entered the war on the French side. An expedition was sent up the San Juan River to attack Spanish possessions in Nicaragua from the rear. Originally, Nelson's role was simply escort duty but,

when the small expeditionary force attempted to land at the mouth of the river, it quickly became apparent that the military forces had no experience of boatwork. Nelson therefore volunteered to accompany them with two of his ship's boats and fifty sailors.

In the end, however, he did not confine himself to manning the boats. When the first Spanish outpost was encountered, he personally led a frontal assault with his sailors, while the soldiers attacked it in the rear: 'I boarded, if I may be allowed the expression, an outpost of the enemy,' he later wrote in his autobiographical *Sketch of My Life*. And when the expedition eventually reached its chief objective, the Castillo de la Imaculada Concepcíon, guarding the approaches to Nicaragua, he constructed a battery using the small cannon from his boats. Although the castle was eventually captured, the British force was decimated by dysentery and malaria and the expedition came to a floundering halt.

Nelson himself was taken so ill that he was forced to leave the expedition before the castle fell. It has always been supposed in the past that he was suffering from yellow fever, but recent research has established that it was more likely a severe attack of tropical sprue, when he was already weak from scurvy and malaria. So ill was he that, after an initial recovery in Jamaica, he was forced to return home to England, 'reduced quite to a skeleton' in the graphic words of his medical report.

However, Nelson's drive and professional skill during the early stages of the campaign had been noted and reported back to London in glowing terms by the expedition commander, Colonel Polson: 'I want words to express what I owe to that gentleman. He was the first on service by night or by day.' It was a small but significant first step on his rise to fame.

SEE ALSO
Cuba Cornwallis, Health

Nile, Battle of the (1 August 1798)

The first of Nelson's three great victories, fought against the French in the Bay of Aboukir on the Mediterranean coast of Egypt during the night of 1/2 August 1798, the Battle of the Nile was a victory so complete that it was unique in the annals of naval

Fort San Juan, Nicaragua, 1780. A drawing done on the spot by a member of the expedition. The battery in which Nelson mounted his guns is to the left of the Spanish fort, underneath the Union flag.

warfare under sail. Out of a French fleet of thirteen battleships, eleven were captured or destroyed. French naval power in the Mediterranean was eliminated overnight and Nelson became a household name throughout Europe.

In December 1796, the British, under Sir John Jervis, were forced to abandon the Mediterranean because of the lack of any secure bases and ports from which supplies could be obtained. Left in full control of the Inland Sea, the French used the opportunity to plan a bold and imaginative stroke that they hoped might win the war for them: an invasion of Egypt, followed by an overland attack on British trade in India. In overall command was the brilliant young General Napoleon Bonaparte, fresh from his recent conquest of Italy.

Sailing on 19 May 1798 with 35,000 troops in 400 transports, escorted by thirteen battleships, the French went first to Malta, which was surrendered without a fight, and from there to Egypt, where they arrived on 1 July. The army was landed without

opposition and, by the end of the month, Egypt was under French control.

The British knew that an expedition was being prepared but they did not know where it was heading. So, in April 1797, Lord St Vincent sent Nelson into the Mediterranean to try and discover the French force and, when found, to destroy it. With him, Nelson had a force of fourteen battleships commanded by some of the most distinguished captains of the fleet. Mostly the same age as their admiral, and old comrades, they formed an élite team which worked together superbly: a 'Band of Brothers' as Nelson later termed them (quoting from his favourite Shakespeare play, *Henry V*).

But they could not find the French. They had no

THE NILE
1 August 1798

1. Most plans of the Battle of the Nile make Aboukir Bay look as if it is a small cove on the west coast of Britain, with the French ships usually shown quite close inshore. In fact it is a large open roadstead and the French fleet was anchored right in the middle of it, at a great distance from the shore.

2. The new plan is based on the results of a survey of the bay recently carried out by the French marine archaeologist, Franck Goddio, which has established the exact location of the wreck of *L'Orient*, and the discarded anchors of some of the British ships. For more details see, Laura Foreman, *Napoleon's Lost Fleet*, Discovery Books (London 1999).

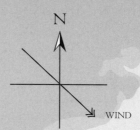

WIND

NELSON ISLAND

4 6-pounder guns
2 carronades

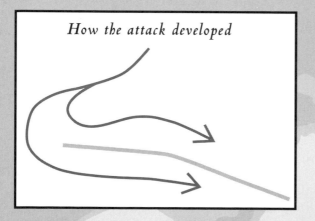

How the attack developed

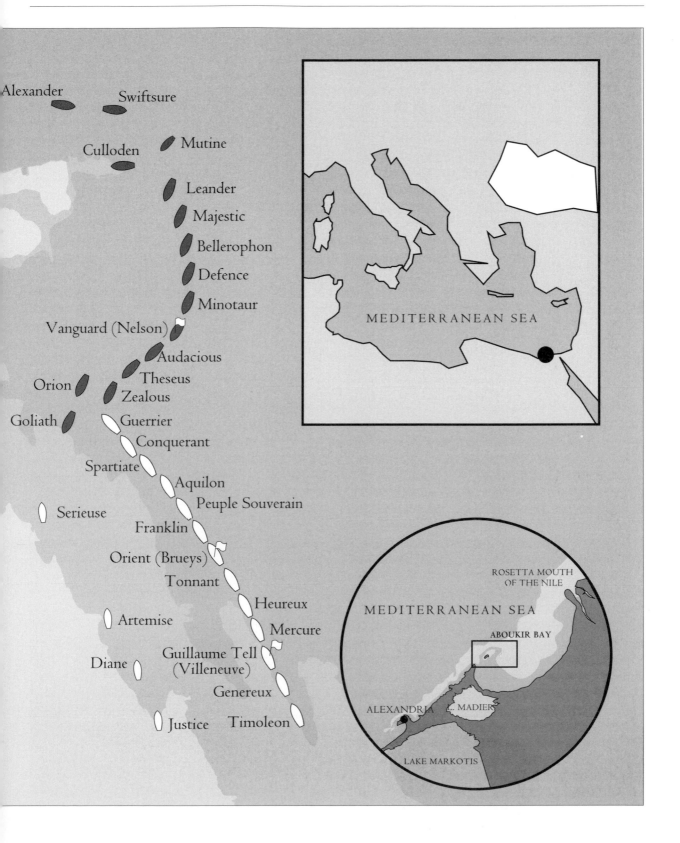

Alexander

Swiftsure

Culloden

Mutine

Leander

Majestic

Bellerophon

Defence

Minotaur

Vanguard (Nelson)

Audacious

Orion

Theseus

Zealous

Goliath

Guerrier

Conquerant

Spartiate

Aquilon

Peuple Souverain

Serieuse

Franklin

Orient (Brueys)

Tonnant

Heureux

Artemise

Mercure

Guillaume Tell
(Villeneuve)

Diane

Genereux

Justice

Timoleon

MEDITERRANEAN SEA

MEDITERRANEAN SEA

ROSETTA MOUTH
OF THE NILE

ABOUKIR BAY

ALEXANDRIA

L. MADIER

LAKE MARKOTIS

scouting vessels and, as a result, on one occasion they passed within a few miles of Napoleon's huge convoy without sighting it. Hearing that the French might be heading for Egypt, they raced there but their fast-sailing ships outstripped their slower quarry. They found the harbour at Alexandria empty and sailed away again. Two days later, the French arrived and began landing. Distracted with worry, Nelson combed the Eastern Mediterranean, desperately searching for clues. Then, finally, on 28 July, he heard that the French had landed in Egypt. Another rapid voyage followed and, on 1 August, the British came in sight of Alexandria again. There they found the transports, but still no warships.

Then, just as they were beginning to despair of ever tracking down their elusive opponent, the news came that the French battlefleet had been sighted in the Bay of Aboukir a few miles down the coast. The French naval commander, Vice Admiral François Brueys, had anchored his battleships in a strong defensive line, inside the bay, with its head defended by batteries on a promontory. Expecting an attack on his centre and rear, he had placed his strongest

ships there, including his own flagship, the massive 120-gun three-decker *L'Orient*, and three large 80-gun two-deckers, the *Franklin*, *Tonnant* and *Guillaume Tell*. In the van, he placed his oldest and weakest ships, out of harm's way.

Aboukir is not really a 'bay' at all, more an open roadstead, with a complex maze of sandbanks and, to strengthen his position still further, Brueys had placed his line as close as possible to the shoals. However, his four large ships drew more water than their smaller comrades and so he was forced to place his line further out than if he had a fleet of only 74-gun ships. Even so, the French seem to have assumed that an attack from the landward was impossible and did not bother to prepare their ships for action on that side. However, modern archaeological

The Battle of the Nile, 1 August 1798. In this engraving, produced for the 'official' biography by Clarke and M'Arthur in 1809, Pocock captures the moment when Captain Foley, in HMS Zealous, *rounded the head of the French line. However, Aboukir Bay is an open roadstead, not an enclosed bay, and the French ships were much further out from the shore.*

surveys have established that the gap between the French line and the nearest shoals was in fact extremely wide, certainly more than wide enough for the British 74-gun battleships, which drew less water than their larger French opponents.

Thanks to recently published French research, we also now know that Brueys's fleet was decimated by disease. Moreover, his ships were all very short of water and supplies and so large numbers of men were scattered ashore foraging. However, the afternoon was already well advanced when the British were sighted, so Brueys expected to have the night to recall his forces and to strengthen his position further. But he had reckoned without his opponents. The British pressed on, forming their battle line as they went, and, contrary to all expectations, attacked the weak French van first. Nelson and his colleagues had often discussed how they would tackle their opponents and so hardly any signals were necessary: each captain acted on his own initiative.

As he led the way into the bay, Captain Thomas Foley of HMS *Goliath* noted that the French had left enough room between the shoals and their vanmost ship for him to slip through and so he pushed round onto the landward side of his opponent, followed by the ships immediately astern of him. Nelson, flying his flag in the centre of the British line, in HMS *Vanguard*, took the rest of his force down the outside of the French line. So, right from the outset, the French van was overwhelmed and crushed on both sides by superior numbers and firepower. And since the wind was blowing directly down their line, the rearmost ships were unable to do anything to help their comrades. Instead, they were forced to wait as the tide of battle rolled relentlessly towards them.

Eventually, the battle reached *L'Orient* in the centre and, at about 9.00pm, she was seen to be on fire. Despite the heroic efforts of her crew, it was soon out of control. The admiral was already mortally wounded and his flag captain, Commodore Casa Bianca, was also badly hurt. With him was his young son, who refused to leave his father, thus inspiring the famous poem by Mrs Hemams, 'The boy stood on the burning deck / whence all but he had fled.'

Just after 10.00pm, the fire reached *L'Orient*'s magazines and she blew up with a noise that was heard by the French troops in Rosetta ten miles away. For a

'Nelson triumphant'. A popular print shows the wounded Nelson being presented with captured French flags on the morning after the battle.

moment, all fighting stopped and there was a stunned silence in the bay. Contemporary accounts refer to only a single massive explosion. But, recently, a French archaeological expedition has found and surveyed the shattered remains of the great ship and it is now clear that there were two detonations. First, the main magazine went up, blowing off her stern and propelling her forwards in the water, and then her foremost magazine blew, showering the bay with debris. Divers swimming today among her shattered timbers can still smell traces of gunpowder and they have found a two-ton cannon hurled over 400 yards by the force of the explosion (see colour plate *VII*).

By now, all the ships of the French van had been eliminated and the British were beginning to move towards the French rear. Nelson himself had been badly wounded some time earlier: a piece of shrapnel had struck him on the forehead, causing a flap of skin to fall over his good eye. Not for the first time in his life, he thought it was a mortal wound and reeled into his flag captain Berry's arms saying, 'I am killed. Remember me to my wife.' In fact, the gash, though messy and very painful, was not life threatening and within an hour he had begun penning his victory despatch.

Meanwhile, the battle was beginning to die away. The British were exhausted and their ships badly damaged, so they were not able to push home the attack on the French rear with the same ferocity with which they had hit the unfortunate van. And they were now dealing with bigger, more heavily armed ships and without the advantage of surprise. Even so, only two French battleships escaped, the *Guillaume Tell*, flagship of Rear Admiral Pierre de Villeneuve, and the *Généreux*. As dawn broke on 2 August they managed to slip out of the bay, leaving behind a scene of destruction almost unparalleled in naval history. 'Victory,' wrote Nelson later, 'is not a name strong enough for such a scene.'

This spectacular victory gave new heart to all the opponents of revolutionary France. At last, the apparently invincible French had been checked and all Europe heaved a sigh of relief. Nelson became an international hero (see colour plate *VIII*) and many rewards were lavished on him and on his men. But perhaps the most important result of the battle was that it showed the world what a truly professional force the Royal Navy had become. The importance of Nelson's leadership should not be underestimated but, as he was the first to point out, the battle had been won by the remarkable teamwork of his well-trained and highly motivated force.

SEE ALSO
Brueys, Foley, *L'Orient*, Malta, Napoleon, HMS *Vanguard*, Villeneuve, Wounds

LATEST RESEARCH
Michelle Battesti, *La Bataille d'Aboukir*, Economica (Paris 1997)
Laura Foreman, *Napoleon's Lost Fleet*, Discovery Books (London 1999)
Robert Gardiner (ed), *Nelson against Napoleon*, Chatham Publishing (London 1997)
Brian Lavery, *Nelson and the Nile*, Chatham Publishing (London 1998)

Nisbet, Josiah (1780–1830)

When Nelson married the young widow Fanny Nisbet (née Woolward) in 1787, one of the bonds between them was his affection for her son Josiah. On one occasion early in their acquaintance, he was found playing happily under a table with the child and this bond remained strong for some years afterwards.

In 1793, Nelson took Josiah to sea with him in HMS *Agamemnon* and his letters home to Fanny are full of proud references to the boy's progress. Josiah seems to have been rather headstrong, and not particularly clever, but he was undoubtedly brave and, in February 1797, he fought at his stepfather's side at the Battle of Cape St Vincent. Later, in July that year, he saved Nelson's life at the attack on Santa Cruz de Tenerife. When Nelson was hit in the arm, it was Josiah who stanched the flow of blood, applied a tourniquet and then managed to get his stepfather back to his ship for treatment. Nelson afterwards acknowledged, 'Ten minutes and I was no more.'

Sadly, this was to be the high point of their relationship. In 1798, Josiah sailed with Nelson in the *Vanguard*, took part in the Battle of the Nile (1 August 1798) and went with him to Naples afterwards. There, still aged only eighteen, he became infatuated with Emma Hamilton and, when Nelson's own love for her became too obvious to be ignored, a combination of jealousy and understandable anger on his mother's behalf, soured the young man's relationship with his stepfather forever. Always prone to heavy drinking, he became quarrelsome and argumentative and on more than one occasion berated Nelson publicly for his infidelity.

Nelson continued to try to further his career and, wholly because of his influence, Josiah was made a post captain at the early age of twenty. But it was clear to all, himself included, that he was not fit for naval service and shortly afterwards, in 1802, he went on half pay and never served at sea again. He became a successful businessman and, after the war ended, lived and worked in Paris. He died suddenly from pleurisy in 1830 and was buried in the churchyard at Littleham, near Exmouth in Devon, where, just eleven months later, his mother was laid beside him.

SEE ALSO
Frances Nelson, Tenerife

Oliver, Francis

Originally a secretary to Sir William Hamilton when he was the British envoy to Naples, Oliver later became a confidential assistant to Nelson, as well as to the Hamiltons, when they re-encountered him in Vienna in 1800 during their triumphal tour through Europe. An accomplished linguist, he agreed to remain in their employ, to help them with their travel arrangements. He also appears to have acted as confidential courier between Emma Hamilton and Nelson, carrying the intimate private letters about their relationship and Horatia that they did not dare to entrust to the public post.

Later, after Nelson's death, he assisted Emma as her secretary and it is clear from the surviving correspondence that they had a bitter quarrel. It is very likely – although impossible to prove – that he stole from her some of Nelson's letters, which she had lovingly preserved. Published anonymously, in 1814, they revealed, for the first time, that the famous relationship had been very far from the pure and platonic friendship that the lovers had claimed it was.

SEE ALSO
Emma Hamilton, Letters

Orde, Sir John (1751–1824)

Orde is now usually remembered as one of Nelson's professional enemies although, in fact, his quarrel was more with Lord St Vincent than with Nelson, and he never attacked Nelson personally. He was born on 22 December 1751 and entered the Royal Navy in 1766. Promoted to lieutenant in 1774, he served throughout the war with America, being promoted to post captain on 19 May 1778: which meant he was senior to Nelson, by less than a month.

After a spell as governor of the West Indies island

Sir John Orde. An engraving from The Naval Chronicle.

of Dominica, he returned to service in the Royal Navy and was made a baronet for his services. Promoted to rear admiral in 1795, he joined Lord St Vincent off Cádiz in early 1798 as third in command of the Mediterranean fleet. But then, just when his career appeared to be flourishing, he suffered a significant setback. In May 1798, St Vincent, acting on his own initiative but with the full support of the First Lord of the Admiralty, Lord Spencer, appointed Nelson to command a special squadron that was sent into the Mediterranean to look for the French fleet. Orde, who was of course Nelson's senior, felt he had been unfairly passed over and he made the fatal mistake of questioning St Vincent's decision in language so strong that the old admiral peremptorily ordered him home. Orde applied for a court martial and when this was refused even went so far as to challenge St Vincent to a duel in 1800 but the two men were bound over to keep the peace. Nelson, not unnaturally, took St Vincent's side in the quarrel and regarded Orde as a personal enemy, although Orde always protested that it was the principle of the appointment he was contesting and not the man who had been chosen.

Unfortunately for Orde, St Vincent now became First Lord of the Admiralty and so long as he controlled appointments, Orde was left on shore. However, in 1804, St Vincent left the Admiralty and Orde was offered command of a squadron off Cádiz, which Nelson, by then commander-in-chief in the Mediterranean, and never one to forgive a slight easily, saw as a deliberate diminution of his authority. In April 1805, Orde was watching Cádiz when Villeneuve arrived with the Toulon fleet to unite with the Spanish fleet, before sailing for the West Indies in accordance with Napoleon's ambitious plans for the invasion of Britain. Greatly outnumbered, Orde retired to the north and fell back on the main British fleet off Brest, an act for which he was condemned at the time, not least by Nelson.

Historians have been more lenient, pointing out that Orde acted in accordance with long-established British strategy of concentrating in the mouth of the Channel in times of crisis. However, such cautious conduct, although technically correct, was not in accordance with the mood of the country at that time and so, when he returned to home waters, Orde was ordered to strike his flag and never served at sea again. In 1807, he became member of parliament for Yarmouth in the Isle of Wight and continued to serve until his death on 19 February 1824.

In January 1806, Orde acted as one of the pall-bearers at Nelson's funeral. This may, at first sight, appear hypocritical but he always expressed warm regard for Nelson personally and appears not to have reciprocated the animosity that Nelson felt for him. Like Sir Robert Calder, whom in many ways he resembled, he was a careful and competent officer who had the misfortune to be overshadowed by his more brilliant contemporary.

SEE ALSO
Jervis, Spencer, Trafalgar campaign

Orient see L'Orient

Palermo

A major city and port on the north coast of the island of Sicily, in Nelson's day Palermo was the second capital of the King of Naples and Sicily. When the Neapolitan royal family had to leave Naples in December 1798, following a French invasion, Nelson conveyed them to Palermo in his flagship, HMS *Vanguard*. The Hamiltons rented a comfortable palazzo near the waterfront and Nelson established his headquarters there so as to be near them, even going to the length of shifting his flag to a transport lying at anchor in the harbour. Although it appears from his surviving letters that Nelson and Emma's sexual relationship did not begin until early 1800, their intimacy was noticed long before then and the rumours began circulating. As one critical observer remarked, 'He is now completely managed by Lady Hamilton.'

The part of the city where Nelson and the Hamiltons lived was largely destroyed by bombing in the Second World War. But some of the royal palaces where they paraded their friendship have survived, most notably the Palazzina Cinese in the royal hunting park of La Favorita, where some English prints which they presented to their royal patrons can still be seen on display.

SEE ALSO
Emma Hamilton, William Hamilton, Naples, Neapolitan campaign

Parker, Edward (c1778–1801)

Parker was one of Nelson's favourite young protégés, whom he often referred to as his son, and yet little is known about him. Most accounts state that they first met in the Baltic in 1801 but recent research has established that Parker first served with Nelson as a lieutenant in HMS *Foudroyant* in the Mediterranean in 1799 and there is a suggestion that he was person-ally recommended by Lord St Vincent. It would seem that Parker also met Emma Hamilton around this time and may even have acted as a go-between for the lovers, since both she and Nelson refer to him affectionately in their letters to each other.

In October 1799, Parker was promoted to commander by Nelson and given command of the sloop HMS *Amaranthe*, in which he served in the Baltic campaign. He was at Nelson's side on board the *Elephant* during the Battle of Copenhagen (2 April 1801) and later accompanied him during the negotiations ashore. By now, he was clearly very close to Nelson, who usually referred to him as 'little Parker'. In early May, when Nelson expected to be recalled home, Parker returned to Britain taking some of his patron's belongings with him. When Nelson was, instead, appointed commander-in-chief in the Baltic in place of Sir Hyde Parker, Parker returned to the Baltic, bringing letters from Emma and news of their daughter Horatia.

When Nelson finally left the Baltic in late June, Parker returned with him and accompanied him on a brief holiday, at Staines, with the Hamiltons and members of his family. He appears to have acted as an unofficial aide de camp, a role which was formalised shortly afterwards in late July, when Nelson was appointed to command the anti-invasion forces in the Channel. The first order he signed named Parker as his aide and, thereafter, Parker wrote out most of Nelson's daily orders and often signed them on his behalf.

Parker played a central role both in the planning and in the execution of the abortive attack on the French line of defence outside Boulogne on 15 August, during which his thigh was shattered. He was taken ashore to lodgings at Deal and given the best medical attention, all paid for by Nelson. In the end, the leg had to be amputated but even this could not save him and eventually he died on 27 September. Grief-stricken, Nelson ordered a funeral with full military honours, which he attended as chief mourner. At the end of the ceremony, after the body had been lowered into a grave in the churchyard at St George's, Deal, he was seen leaning against a tree, weeping inconsolably.

Nelson had a number of other young protégés during his life – notably John Weatherhead and William Hoste – but none were as close to him as Parker, whom he often called his 'dear son and friend'. Parker returned this affection wholeheartedly. Writing to Emma Hamilton shortly after his wound, he described Nelson as '. . . my Friend, my Nurse, My Attendant, my Patron, my Protector, nay him who the world cannot find Words sufficient to praise.'

SEE ALSO
Boulogne, Channel Command, Hoste, Weatherhead

Parker, Sir Hyde (1739–1807)

It is Parker's misfortune that he is mainly remembered as the over-anxious commander-in-chief who ordered Nelson to withdraw at the height of the Battle of Copenhagen (2 April 1801). But his earlier career was much more distinguished and he deserves to be honoured as an effective, although not a front-rank, naval officer.

The second son of Vice Admiral Sir Hyde Parker, he entered the Royal Navy in his father's ship, the battleship HMS *Vanguard*, in 1751. Promoted lieutenant in 1757, he served throughout the Seven Years War (1757–1763), rising to the rank of post captain in 1763. In 1776, while in command of the frigate HMS *Phoenix*, he led a gallant operation to occupy the North River in America which had been closed by blockships and defences designed by Benjamin Franklin. He succeeded in forcing his way through them and was knighted for his services in 1779. The following year, the *Phoenix* foundered in a hurricane off the West Indian island of Cuba but Parker managed to save almost all her ship's company, together with guns and equipment. In the following October, he served under his father's command at the Battle of Dogger Bank and in 1782 under Howe at the Relief of Gibraltar.

Promoted to rear admiral in 1793, Parker was first appointed Hood's captain of the fleet in the Mediter-

Vice Admiral Sir Hyde Parker. This engraving dates from about 1785 and shows Parker as a younger and more vigorous man than the admiral who ordered Nelson to discontinue the engagement at the Battle of Copenhagen in 1801.

ranean, then third in command and even commanded the whole fleet briefly in late 1795 before handing over to Sir John Jervis. He was then appointed commander-in-chief in the West Indies, where he remained until 1800, when he returned to Britain and was appointed second in command of the Channel fleet.

So when, in 1801, a special fleet was assembled to be sent into the Baltic, Parker seemed an ideal choice to command it: an admiral of wide experience and proven courage who also happened to have a good knowledge of the Baltic, having previously served there in 1790. Indeed, Lord St Vincent himself recommended him to the First Lord of the Admiralty, Lord Spencer: 'Should the Northern Powers continue this menacing posture Sir Hyde Parker is the only man you have to face them.'

Unfortunately, Parker was no longer the man who

had forced the North River in 1776. Now over sixty, he had become over-cautious and appears to have been overwhelmed by the heavy responsibility of his new command. Recent research has revealed that he was so anxious in the days before the Battle of Copenhagen that he hardly slept at all and he certainly conducted the opening stages of the campaign very hesitantly. Although Nelson was his second in command, Parker at first consulted very little with him, and only began to involve him in the decision-making when it became clear that offensive action would have to be taken. It is probable that he was rather suspicious of his energetic and much younger subordinate, having known him as a somewhat bumptious captain in the Mediterranean. However, Parker soon came to appreciate Nelson's qualities as a strategist and tactician and effectively handed over the planning of the campaign to him.

At the Battle of Copenhagen, Parker played a subordinate role, threatening the northern end of the Danish line of defence with the heavier ships of the squadron. But the responsibilities of command still weighed heavily on him, which led him to make the crucial mistake for which he is now remembered. Seeing that three of Nelson's ships were out of the battle, having encountered difficulties with the shoals, and realising that the Danes were putting up a much stouter resistance than Nelson had anticipated, he decided to signal Nelson's squadron to discontinue the action. There has been much debate over whether this signal was a direct order or was intended to be discretionary but Nelson's incredulous reaction – as faithfully recorded by Colonel William Stewart – shows that it was as unexpected as it was ill-judged.

Following the battle and the difficult negotiations that followed – in which Nelson again took the lead – Parker showed great hesitation when the decision had to be taken about what the fleet should do next. Nelson was all for moving on directly to deal with the Swedish and Russian fleets but Parker procrastinated. In the meantime, the first reactions to the news of the battle were gratifying. Parker received the thanks of both Houses of Parliament and there was even talk of a peerage. Then abruptly, and cruelly, the mood changed and he was peremptorily summoned home. He never fully understood this sudden change in

fortune and asked for an enquiry to clear his name. But it is now clear that St Vincent had been told privately of the notorious signal by Colonel Stewart and acted with his characteristic ruthlessness to remove a man who was now seen as a liability. Parker did not serve at sea again and died on 16 March 1807.

SEE ALSO
Copenhagen, Stewart

LATEST RESEARCH
Peter Lefevre, 'Little merit will be given to me: Sir Hyde Parker', *Proceedings of the Copenhagen 200 Conference*, The 1805 Club (Shelton 2002)
Clive Wilkinson, 'Admiral Sir Hyde Parker', *The Nelson Dispatch*, 7 (April 2001), The Nelson Society

Parker, Sir Peter (1721–1811)

One of Nelson's patrons, Parker had an important influence on his young protégé's early career. It was largely thanks to him that Nelson received such rapid promotion to post captain, which in turn meant that he became an admiral when still comparatively young.

Parker was the son of Rear Admiral Christopher Parker and first went to sea with his father in the 1730s. Promoted to post captain in 1747, he served throughout the Seven Years War (1756–1763) and commanded the battleship HMS *Buckingham* at the capture of Belleisle in 1761. Knighted in 1772, he was appointed a commodore on the American station in 1775 and served there throughout the war with America, becoming commander-in-chief in Jamaica in 1778, having been promoted to rear admiral the previous year.

It was during his time in Jamaica that he first met Nelson, then still a lieutenant, revelling his first independent command: a small schooner named *Little Lucy*. Nelson's captain, William Locker, who was an old friend of Parker, recommended the young man to him and so Parker took Nelson into his flagship, HMS *Bristol*, as third lieutenant.

Nelson probably owed this first step to the fact that he was the nephew of the influential Comptroller of the Navy, Captain Maurice Suckling, but it would seem that he quickly impressed Parker with his own abilities. Within a few months, he had been promoted to first lieutenant and, before the end of

Admiral of the Fleet Sir Peter Parker. This engraving of Nelson's patron and lifelong friend, taken from The Naval Chronicle, *includes Parker's coat of arms.*

1778, Parker had made him a commander and given him the brig HMS *Badger*. Then, less than six months later, came the all-important step to post captain, when Nelson was still only twenty. Thereafter, promotion came only by seniority and so, theoretically, all Nelson had to do to become an admiral was to stay alive long enough.

It is clear, too, that Nelson quickly won Parker's friendship, and also that of his wife Margaret, who had accompanied her husband to Jamaica. The couple remained in close touch with Nelson for the rest of their lives and Margaret Parker once told him that she and her husband had always looked upon him as a son. They also became friends with Fanny Nelson, and remained loyal to her even after the break-up of the Nelson marriage.

In 1782, Parker returned to Britain and entered Parliament as MP for the borough of Maldon in 1787. He did not see active service again but held a number of shore appointments during the war with revolutionary France, including commander-in-chief at Portsmouth. While there, he and Lady Parker looked after Nelson briefly on his return home in 1797 to recover from the loss of his arm.

In 1799, on the death of Lord Howe, Parker became admiral of the fleet: then the most senior rank in the Royal Navy. As a result, it was he who acted as chief mourner at Nelson's state funeral in January 1806. By then, he was so frail that Lady Nelson (who had always kept in touch with the Parkers) wrote to the Herald's Office to ask for special permission for his servant to stand close by him during the long and tiring ceremony, ready to support him if he felt faint. It was his last public engagement and he died in 1811.

SEE ALSO
Funeral, Locker

Pasco, John (1774–1853)

Pasco was the signal lieutenant of HMS *Victory* at the Battle of Trafalgar (21 October 1805) and so was responsible for sending Nelson's famous signal, 'England expects'. Indeed, it was he who suggested the final wording. He joined the Navy in 1784 and was promoted to lieutenant in 1795. He was appointed to the *Victory* in April 1803 and, by the autumn of 1805, was her senior lieutenant. But Nelson attached such importance to signalling that he asked Pasco to act as signal officer, rather than as first lieutenant, as was his right. It was usual for the first lieutenant of a ship involved in a successful battle to be promoted so this was a considerable sacrifice on Pasco's part, and one that he was to regret.

He was severely wounded in the right arm early in the battle and in fact spent much of the time in the cockpit, close to the dying Nelson. He received a pension for his wound of £250 a year from the Patriotic Fund but he did indeed miss his promotion. He was not made a post captain until 1811 and, following the end of the war with France, he remained unemployed for almost thirty years. Eventually, however, in 1846, he was appointed captain of HMS *Victory*, by then preserved at moorings in Portsmouth

Lieutenant John Pasco. This contemporary miniature shows Pasco in about 1805, when he was signal lieutenant of HMS Victory *at the Battle of Trafalgar.*

Harbour. While in command he began the custom, which is still continued, of celebrating Trafalgar Day with a special dinner on board. He died, a rear admiral, in Plymouth in 1853.

SEE ALSO
'England expects', Trafalgar Day ceremonies, HMS *Victory*

Pitt, William (1759–1806)

Having become the youngest prime minister in British history in 1784, Pitt dominated politics throughout most of Nelson's adult life. The son of the great war leader William Pitt, first Earl of Chatham, the Younger Pitt always admitted his ignorance of military affairs and his whole policy during the great war with France was directed towards keeping Britain

'The Plum Pudding in Danger'. This splendid caricature by Gilray sums up the war against France. Napoleon (right) carves up Europe, oblivious to the fact that his great opponent, William Pitt, is helping himself to a generous slice of the rest of the world – including the ocean.

out of direct military involvement on the continent of Europe. He preferred instead to combat the French by forming a series of alliances with key European nations, which he supported with subsidies.

Although Nelson was related through his mother to the great Whig family of the Walpoles, and had once considered entering Parliament as a Whig, he tended to be a Tory in politics. Like the majority of country gentlemen, he preferred Pitt's more unassuming friend and colleague Henry Addington, who was prime minister between 1801 and 1804. But he also acknowledged that, at a time of crisis, Pitt was the right man to lead the nation, calling him, 'the greatest Minister this country ever had.' In the autumn of 1805, he was flattered when Pitt consulted him during the hectic days of planning before Trafalgar and recalled proudly that, at the conclusion of one of their meetings, the prime minister had personally escorted him to his carriage.

For his part, Pitt obviously admired, and indeed liked, Nelson. When he was wakened in the early hours of 7 November to be told of the victory at Trafalgar, and of Nelson's death, he found that, for the only time in his life, he was unable to go back to sleep, so intense were the emotions aroused by the news. Less than three months later, he too was dead.

SEE ALSO
Addington, Trafalgar campaign

Plymouth

In Nelson's day, Plymouth, in Devon, was one of the three great naval bases in Britain. Although a long way from London, it was well sited, close to the entrance of the Channel and thus conveniently situated for watching the key French base of Brest. It boasted a large and well-equipped dockyard on the eastern bank of the River Tamar, together with a victualling yard, marine barracks and hospital. Its main drawback was that, unlike Chatham and Portsmouth, it had no sheltered anchorage nearby: at that time, Plymouth Sound was completely open to southerly winds and consequently very dangerous. So it was usual for large fleets to anchor instead in Torbay, several miles away to the southwest.

Nelson did not visit Plymouth very often. His most extended stay in the area was in the early part of 1801

when he was, briefly, attached to the Channel fleet, flying his flag in HMS *San Josef*. It was not a happy time for him. He had recently returned home overland with the Hamiltons following his long spell in the Mediterranean and, after a few very painful weeks, had separated from his wife. Now, Emma Hamilton was about to give birth to their first child and he was anxiously waiting for news.

Plymouth is still a major naval base and many of the buildings that Nelson knew have survived in the Historic Dockyard, parts of which are open to the public.

SEE ALSO
Chatham, Portsmouth, *San José*

LATEST RESEARCH
Jonathan Coad, *The Royal Dockyards, 1690–1850*, Scholar Press (Aldershot 1989)
Roger Morriss, *The Royal Dockyards during the Revolutionary and Napoleonic Wars*, Leicester University Press (Leicester 1983)

Sir Home Riggs Popham. An engraving from The Naval Chronicle.

Popham, Sir Home Riggs (1762–1820)

Although Popham and Nelson never served together, it was Popham who devised the telegraphic code that enabled Nelson to send his famous signal 'England expects' at the Battle of Trafalgar. Born on 12 October 1762, Popham entered the Royal Navy in 1778, becoming a lieutenant in 1783. Having served throughout the peace in the merchant service, he rejoined the Royal Navy when war broke out and was eventually, in 1795, given special promotion to post captain as a reward for his services in the abortive expedition to Flanders the previous year.

A brilliant, eccentric man, he had a tempestuous naval career, and was often involved in controversy with his immediate superiors or the Admiralty: as, for example, when in 1804, he took a squadron from the Cape of Good Hope without orders to attack Buenos Ayres in South America. Promoted to rear admiral in 1814, he served as commander-in-chief in the West Indies from 1817 to 1820 and died on 10 September only shortly after returning home.

Although Popham's military services were distinguished, they did not win him much popular recognition and he is best remembered today for the major breakthrough he made in signalling by the invention of his telegraphic code in 1803. Before, admirals had been constrained in what they could say to their fleets by the phrases that were already in the signal book. Using Popham's system, where the numeral flags meant single words rather than complete phrases, admirals could almost literally 'talk' to their subordinates for the first time. Nelson made a particular study of signalling, always seeking ways of improving his communications with his subordinates and, quick to see the advantages of Popham's code, he took copies of the new signal book, then hot off the press, with him when he rejoined his fleet just before Trafalgar.

SEE ALSO
Blackwood, 'England expects'

Sir Horatio Nelson by Daniel Orme (1797). Nelson as Byronic hero. This small engraving was extremely popular and the first edition sold out in a few days.

Portraits of Nelson

There are over thirty contemporary portraits of Nelson and each of them shows a different side to his character. The most famous likeness is undoubtedly the portrait by Lemuel Abbott for which Nelson sat during the winter of 1797/8 when he was at home in England, recovering from the loss of his arm (see p112). Abbott painted over forty versions of it for various clients. It was much reproduced at the time in engravings and prints, and it has been reproduced in almost every biography since, so it has become almost hackneyed. It is largely responsible for the common myth that he was unusually thin and emaciated, because it shows him when he was still in severe pain from his wound and taking regular doses of opium to relieve it. As a result, he had lost weight, his hair, normally a light sandy brown, had turned white with shock and his face was gaunt and lined with suffering. Indeed, in most versions of the painting, ribbons can be seen in the left sleeve of his coat. These closed a slit in the sleeve through which his wife or valet could insert their hand to help him to ease the very painful stump through the tight arm-hole.

Other surviving portraits show a more robust and healthy man: for example, the splendid 'state' portrait by William Beechey painted for the City of Norwich in 1800/1 (see p64). Here Nelson is depicted as The Hero, standing on his quarterdeck, surrounded by trophies of his battles. He looks about six feet tall and has a barrel chest and leonine mane of hair. Similar in style is the portrait painted in Vienna in 1800 by Heinrich Füger who captured some of Nelson's ruthlessness and capacity for concentration (see colour plate *I*). An early portrait, painted by Francis Rigaud in 1777, shows him before illness and wounds prematurely aged him: a striking young man with an elegant, slender figure, fresh complexion and bright, penetrating eyes, carrying himself with an attractive poise and self-assurance.

Vice Admiral Lord Nelson by John Hoppner (1800). This engraving is based on one of the best likenesses of Nelson, now in the Royal Collection. Hoppner captured Nelson's sensitivity and the vulnerability that made him so much loved.

On the other hand, there are other portraits which support Abbott's view: most striking of all, the almost bizarre likeness by the obscure Neapolitan artist Leonardo Guzzardi, who painted Nelson while he was in Palermo, Sicily, in early 1799. At that time, Nelson was still recovering from the painful head-wound he had received at the Battle of the Nile and so he wears his hat pushed back on his head to avoid the scar and, once again, he appears ill and emaciated.

So which portrait is the best likeness? Nelson was once asked that question and replied that he thought that an unassuming study of his left profile by Simon de Koster was 'the most like me'. It was not even a formal portrait, being based on a pencil sketch drawn hastily at a dinner party in 1800, but Emma Hamilton agreed with his judgement and had a small miniature copy made, which she wore round her neck (see colour plate *XX*).

As it happens, we now have a good yardstick against which to judge the surviving portraits. In 1800, while in Vienna, a mask was made of Nelson's face by the sculptor Franz Thaller, which he then used as the basis for a bust and copies have been identified in the collections of the Royal Naval and National Maritime Museums (see p171). When compared with these, the portrait that appears to capture Nelson most closely is a fine full-length by John Hoppner, principal portrait painter to the Prince of Wales (see colour plate *III*). It shows Nelson in full dress uniform, leaning against a rock while the Battle of Copenhagen rages behind him. The face, which matches well with the features of the mask, is full of character and sensitivity and the figure is slim and wiry. It was later used as the basis for a life-sized wax effigy made for Westminster Abbey, of which Emma Hamilton said, 'the likeness was so great it was impossible for anyone who had known him to doubt about or mistake it.'

Recently, much research has been done on Nelson's appearance by various experts and their findings have been brought together in another very striking life-sized figure, commissioned by the Royal Naval Museum (see colour plate *II*). Based on the Vienna mask and the Hoppner and de Koster portraits, it shows Nelson as he may have looked on the eve of Trafalgar. Rather taller than many people expect, at 5 feet 6 inches, with a full head of 'pepper

and salt' hair and a countenance bronzed by months at sea, this Nelson is far removed from the sickly, emaciated image made popular by Abbott's famous likeness.

SEE ALSO
Abbott, Beechey, Height, Nelson's tour of Germany, Masks, Museums

LATEST RESEARCH
Richard Walker, *The Nelson Portraits*, Royal Naval Museum (Portsmouth 1998)

Portsmouth

In Nelson's time, as now, Portsmouth was the premier British naval base. Strategically placed in Hampshire, at the half-way point of the English Channel, it was equally convenient for ships operating in the North Sea as for those heading westwards for the Atlantic and further afield. It offered a large stretch of protected inland water, with a long expanse of foreshore ideally suited for naval installations; together with a spacious, sheltered deep-water anchorage close by at Spithead, where large fleets could assemble in safety.

Warships had been based at Portsmouth since the 1200s but the naval dockyard was really founded by King Henry VIII in 1540. By 1800, the Royal Dockyard had expanded to become one of the largest industrial complexes in the country, employing over a thousand men to build and repair warships and to manufacture all the equipment needed to keep them afloat and in fighting trim. In addition, there were facilities for producing food and brewing beer and a large arsenal for guns and ammunition.

Nelson visited Portsmouth on a number of occasions during his naval career: the first time in 1776, when he was just seventeen, on his way to take up an appointment as a lieutenant in HMS *Worcester*. Nearly thirty years later, he ate his last meal in England at the George Hotel in the town centre before embarking in HMS *Victory* on his way to the Battle of Trafalgar (21 October 1805). But, generally, his memories of Portsmouth tended to be of unhappy returns – as in 1797 when he came back a pain-racked invalid after losing his arm at Tenerife (July 1797) – and of emotional partings, particularly from Emma Hamilton in 1803 and again in 1805.

The Royal Dockyard at Portsmouth, c1790. Portsmouth as Nelson knew it, seen from the harbour mouth. On the right are the Great Storehouses which now house the Royal Naval Museum, where many of the country's key Nelson relics are displayed.

Portsmouth is now one of the principal centres in Britain for Nelsonian studies. His great flagship HMS *Victory* lies in a drydock at the very centre of the old eighteenth-century yard that he knew, that has been miraculously preserved from both German bombers and modern developers. Alongside, many of his relics are displayed in the Royal Naval Museum, housed in the three Great Storehouses built in the mid eighteenth century to contain the spare gear of the ships in which he served. In nearby Old Portsmouth, it is still possible to trace the route of the last walk he took on English soil from the George Hotel in the High Street to the beach at Southsea.

SEE ALSO
Chatham, Plymouth, Museums, HMS *Victory*

LATEST RESEARCH
Jonathan Coad, *The Royal Dockyards, 1690–1850*, Scholar Press (Aldershot 1989)
Roger Morriss, *The Royal Dockyards during the Revolutionary and Napoleonic Wars*, Leicester University Press (Leicester 1983)

R

Raisonnable, HMS

Nelson's first ship, HMS *Raisonnable*, was a 64-gun Third Rate battleship. Launched in 1768, she was first commissioned in 1770 under the command of Nelson's uncle, Captain Maurice Suckling. Nelson, then aged twelve, saw an announcement of his uncle's appointment in a newspaper and begged to be allowed to go to sea with him. Suckling agreed, with some amusement, asking, 'What has poor Horace done, who is so weak, that he, above all the rest, should be sent to rough it out at sea?' and so the boy was sent to join the ship at Chatham in March 1771.

The *Raisonnable* had been brought into active service because war with Spain seemed likely, but the crisis passed and, realising that his ship would probably remain in harbour for long periods, Suckling sent his nephew to sea in the merchantman *Mary Ann*, commanded by one of his former lieutenants, John Rathbone, to learn his trade. So the young Nelson spent very little time in his first warship.

But it was not the last time he saw her, for the *Raisonnable* was present at the Battle of Copenhagen (2 April 1801), although she did not take part in the actual fighting. She was also involved in the complex manoeuvres in the summer of 1805 that finally defeated Napoleon's invasion plans and took part in the Battle of Cape Finisterre (22 July 1805). She was finally broken up in 1815.

SEE ALSO
Cape Finisterre, Chatham, Suckling

Relics of Nelson

A large number of relics of Nelson have survived, and they offer a striking demonstration of his popularity. So, for example, the complete set of clothes that he was wearing when he was shot at Trafalgar – coat, waistcoat, shirt, breeches and stockings – is pre-

The ultimate Nelson relic. The bullet that killed him, extracted by Dr Beatty, together with a piece of epaulette, shirt and uniform coat and placed in a locket. Now in the Royal Collection.

served at the National Maritime Museum. The French musket ball that killed him is displayed in a specially made locket in the Royal Collection at Windsor Castle. Pieces from the splendid collections of silver tableware presented to commemorate his victories at the Nile and Copenhagen are in the Nelson Collection at Lloyds of London. And in the Royal Naval Museum are some of the most intimate

Nelson at prayer. In a moment of repose before the Battle of Trafalgar, Nelson kneels in prayer, as he had done every morning and night of his life. This mid nineteenth-century engraving wrongly shows Nelson in full dress uniform. He was actually wearing his rather threadbare everyday 'undress' coat.

relics of all: the rings he and Emma exchanged in their quasi-marriage service just before he left for Trafalgar and the miniatures which each wore of the other. Most macabre to modern taste, much of his hair has survived. It was cut off after death at his own request and distributed to his family and friends who had it made into rings and bracelets, and placed small locks in lockets and albums.

Moreover, his name gave value to many otherwise humble items. During his lifetime, men who served with him, and casual acquaintances, cherished scraps of his handwriting, and ordinary possessions that he discarded casually, or perhaps gave as mementoes, were lovingly preserved. After his death, his personal property – from small everyday articles to large pieces of his furniture – was distributed to friends and relations as keepsakes. So the main Nelson collections also contain many ordinary artefacts made extraordinary by their association with him: toothpicks, handkerchiefs, shoe buckles, even a clasp that fastened his boat cloak.

Where such things are so much sought after, there are always those who are keen to supply the demand. So, ever since 1805, there has been a steady trade in Nelson 'fakes'. Swords and pieces of silver have appeared engraved with his coat of arms, forgeries of his letters abound, and the Nelson Museum at Monmouth even has a glass eye that was supposed to have been his.

SEE ALSO
Death, Museums

LATEST RESEARCH
John Munday, 'The Nelson Relics', in Colin White (ed), *The Nelson Companion*, Sutton and Royal Naval Museum (Stroud & Portsmouth 1995)

Religious faith, Nelson's

Nelson was a naturally religious man. His father was an English parish priest and the records of the church at Burnham Thorpe show that young Horatio sometimes assisted his father, for example by standing as godfather to children from the village at their baptism. He remained constant in his private religious practice throughout his life. In 1791, he wrote in his private journal, 'When I lay me down to sleep I recommend myself to the care of Almighty

God, and when I awaken I give myself up to His direction amidst all the evils that threaten me.' On 21 October 1805, as the *Victory* was sailing into action at Trafalgar, Lieutenant Pasco found him in his cabin on his knees at prayer (see transcript of prayer on p273).

He also made sure that religion was practised publicly in all his ships. He obtained bibles and prayer books for his sailors from the Society for the Promotion of Christian Knowledge (SPCK) and paid careful attention to the appointment of chaplains. Rev Alexander Scott, who was his chaplain in the *Victory* during 1803–1805, recorded that Nelson always listened attentively to his sermons and occasionally suggested subjects or lent Scott books of sermons from his own library. He ordered public services of thanksgiving in his ships after his victories and even asked for special prayers of thanksgiving to be said in his local church following his recovery from the loss of his arm in early 1798.

Nelson's faith was essentially 'patristic' and 'monotheist'. He seldom mentioned Jesus Christ, preferring instead to address all his petitions directly to God. Like many of his contemporaries, he believed firmly in predestination. In 1801, shortly after the Battle of Copenhagen (2 April 1801), he wrote to Emma Hamilton, 'I own myself a <u>Believer in God</u>, and if I have any merit in not fearing death, it is because I feel that His power can shield me when he pleases and that I must fall whenever it is His good pleasure.'

Revealingly, that passage came at the end of a letter in which he had told Emma that she was his 'guardian angel' and that he had just celebrated the birthday of 'Santa Emma' at a special dinner party with all his officers. His sense of having a direct line to God came in very useful when he had to square his adultery with Emma with his Christian faith. He did so by deciding that God *intended* her to be his wife: 'Now my own dear wife,' he wrote to her in March 1801, 'for such you are in my eyes and in the face of heaven.' And they acted out this belief on 13 September 1805 when, in a moving ceremony in the parish church at Merton, the couple took Holy Communion together privately and then exchanged rings.

SEE ALSO
Comyn, Alexander Scott

LATEST RESEARCH
Ann-Mary Hills, 'Nelson's Religion', *The Nelson Dispatch* 7 (July 2001), The Nelson Society

Riou, Captain Edward (c1758–1801)

One of the leading frigate captains of Nelson's day, Riou commanded a squadron of frigates attached to Nelson's attacking force during the Battle of Copenhagen (2 April 1801). He already had a considerable reputation for gallantry. In 1789, he commanded HMS *Guardian* on a voyage to Australia with stores and convicts for the penal settlement in New South Wales. The ship hit an iceberg and holed herself badly. Putting as many of her crew as possible into the boats, he ordered them to make for the nearest land at the Cape of Good Hope, while he remained on board the stricken ship with a skeleton crew. By extraordinary seamanship, he managed eventually to bring her safely to the Cape.

Before the Battle of Copenhagen, Riou was chiefly responsible for surveying and buoying the channel, so that Nelson's ships could make their approach in safety. Even so, three of the battleships grounded, which meant there were not enough ships to tackle the great Trekroner Battery defending the head of the Danish line. Riou attempted to fill the gap with his frigates but they were badly mauled by heavy and accurate Danish fire. When Sir Hyde Parker made his notorious signal to Nelson ordering him to withdraw from the action, Riou, who was closest to the commander-in-chief, felt obliged to obey and hauled off with the words, 'What will Nelson think of us?' Almost at that moment, he was cut nearly in two by a Danish shot.

SEE ALSO
'Band of Brothers', Copenhagen

Roundwood

During the early part of their married life, Nelson and his wife Fanny lived either with Nelson's father at the rectory in Burnham Thorpe, Norfolk, or in rented accommodation. But they always dreamed of a place of their own in the country, or 'cottage' as Nelson often referred to it in his letters to Fanny. Eventually, when Nelson was fortunate with prize money in 1796 and 1797, they were able to realise their dream, although 'cottage' is scarcely an appropriate word to describe the large and handsome house they purchased.

Roundwood was a spacious, four-bedroomed house situated just outside the market town and port of Ipswich in the county of Suffolk. According to the agent's description, it had two 'genteel parlours', a dressing room and spacious wine vaults and was surrounded by fifty acres of grounds in which were a barn, dairy, stables, cowhouse and a 'well-planted garden'. The Nelsons bought it for £2000 on 13 November 1797 after paying a flying visit to inspect it. However, the legal business took some time to conclude and before they could take formal possession Nelson was back at sea and on his way in HMS *Vanguard* to the campaign which would culminate in the Battle of the Nile (1 August 1798).

Fanny Nelson moved into the house in May 1798 and lived there happily for over two years, making modest improvements and planting the garden with 'Admiral Nelson' carnations. But Nelson only visited there very briefly on one occasion, in 1800. Having landed at Great Yarmouth in Norfolk with Sir William and Lady Hamilton, after their triumphant tour of Germany, he called there en route to London, expecting to find Fanny waiting to greet him and his friends. But she had gone on ahead to London and the house was shut up. Embarrassed and angry, he continued his journey to London and, only a few weeks later, separated from his wife. Neither of them ever lived at Roundwood again and it was sold less than a year later, the deed of sale being the last document that they signed together. It remained standing until 1961, when it was finally demolished to make way for a new school.

SEE ALSO
Frances Nelson

Ruffo, Cardinal Fabrizio (1744–1827)

Ruffo was the leader of the Neapolitan monarchist forces that recaptured Naples from the republicans and their French allies in July 1799, but who then found himself in dispute with Nelson over the fate of the republicans he had captured. Of noble birth, he had served Pope Pius VI as treasurer and war minis-

ter, and was rewarded with a cardinal's hat, although he was only in minor orders. When the republicans took over Naples, he made an offer to King Ferdinand to go to Calabria, where he had been born, raise an army there and declare a holy war against the French. In this he was so successful that he soon had more than 20,000 men in his 'Christian Army of the Holy Faith' and after only a few weeks of campaigning he had driven the French forces back to the gates of Naples. Nelson supported him by blockading Naples from the sea with a small squadron under Troubridge's command.

Once Ruffo's forces broke into Naples, there was widespread murder and plundering and the leading Neapolitan republicans took refuge in the massive castles that defended the city. Anxious to avoid further bloodshed, Ruffo agreed to surrender terms, under which those who wished would be allowed to go to France, while a general amnesty would be offered to the rest. In making this offer, he exceeded his orders from King Ferdinand, who had demanded unconditional surrender.

Nelson arrived the next day with his fleet and, acting in the name of the King, repudiated the surrender terms. An angry scene between him and Ruffo ensued on board Nelson's flagship, the *Foudroyant*, with Sir William Hamilton acting as interpreter and mediator, and eventually Nelson appeared to give way. The republicans embarked in vessels that were supposed to be taking them to France, only to find themselves escorted to the British fleet and then handed over to their opponents ashore. In the end, most of them were eventually allowed to continue their journey to France but not before about a hundred had been tried and sentenced to summary execution.

Ruffo played no further part in the restoration of the monarchy. He lived in retirement in Naples during the second French occupation under Joseph Bonaparte and Joachim Murat and then, when King Ferdinand was finally restored in 1814, he served for a time as a minister. He died in 1827.

SEE ALSO
Naples, Neapolitan campaign

LATEST RESEARCH
Carlo Knight, 'The British at Naples', *The Trafalgar Chronicle* 11 (2001), The 1805 Club

S

Santa Sabina

The *Santa Sabina* was a Spanish frigate captured by Nelson in December 1796 while he was en route to Elba to evacuate the British forces there, following the British withdrawal from the Mediterranean the previous month. Nelson, then a commodore, was flying his pendant in the frigate HMS *Minerve* and another frigate, HMS *Blanche*, was in company. On Tuesday 19 December, they encountered two Spanish frigates, *Santa Sabina* and *Ceres*, off Cartagena on the southeast coast of Spain. Clearing for action, they set off together to investigate, diverging as they went to take on both opponents.

As Nelson was a commodore, it would have been usual for the *Minerve*'s captain, George Cockburn, to have conned the ship during the battle but it is clear from the log that Nelson took personal command and fought the ship himself. Placing her across the stern of the *Santa Sabina* in a raking position, he hailed her and called on her captain to surrender. To his surprise, the answer came back in excellent English, 'This is a Spanish frigate and you may begin as soon as you please,' and a furious gun battle erupted. The two foes were fairly evenly matched: but the darkness gave the edge to the ship with superior training and gunnery and so, finally, after refusing several other invitations to surrender, the Spanish commander admitted defeat. When he was brought across to the *Minerve* to hand over his sword, the reason for his excellent English was revealed: he was Don Jacobo Stuart, great grandson of King James II. In the meantime, the *Blanche* had tackled the *Ceres*, which had put up a much less spirited resistance, surrendering after only seven or eight broadsides.

The battle over, the hard work of repairing damage and securing the prize began. The *Minerve*'s first lieutenant, John Culverhouse, took a party across to the *Santa Sabina*, including one of the junior lieutenants, the young Dorset man Thomas Hardy, and a

tow rope was secured. Amidst all this noise and bustle, Nelson sat down to write his official report to Jervis. At long last, he had won the headline-catching victory for which he longed: he had beaten a powerful enemy in fair fight. It had been a classic single-ship contest, the sort of action that usually received a separate entry in *The London Gazette*, and was commemorated with a popular print. Moreover, the glamour of Don Jacobo's name would give an extra touch of personal interest to the story.

Scarcely had he finished his letter, than he was interrupted. Another Spanish frigate hove into sight and about half an hour later ranged up alongside the *Santa Sabina* and fired a broadside into her. The *Minerve* cast off her prize, the better to engage this new opponent, which hauled off after a sharp half-hour engagement. More ships were then seen approaching and the growing daylight revealed that they were a Spanish squadron of two battleships, accompanied by two frigates.

By now, the *Minerve* was badly crippled, with all her masts shot through and her rigging and shrouds slashed. It took all Nelson's and Cockburn's combined skill to escape, helped considerably by the prize crew in the *Santa Sabina* who diverted the attention of the Spanish squadron by hoisting English colours over Spanish. The Spaniards took the bait, abandoned their chase of the *Minerve* and set about recapturing their former colleague.

Nelson was left with a problem: he had on his desk a despatch reporting a decisive victory but his prize had been recaptured, which meant that the victory was now incomplete. With the natural instinct for good public relations he was to display repeatedly during his career, he proceeded to make the best of the situation. Instead of tearing up his first letter and starting again, he let the stirring account of the victory stand and wrote a second, and completely separate, letter reporting the recapture of the *Santa Sabina*. The two letters were eventually published together in *The London Gazette* but, as he expected, the letter reporting the victory received the most attention.

SEE ALSO
Cockburn, Elba, Hardy

LATEST RESEARCH
Colin White, *1797: Nelson's Year of Destiny*, Sutton and Royal Naval Museum (Stroud & Portsmouth 1998)

San José (*also:* HMS *San Josef*)

The *San José* was a three-decker Spanish First Rate battleship of 120 guns, built in the northern Spanish port of Ferrol to the designs of the French-born naval architect Franciso Gautier in 1783. On 14 February 1797, she formed part of the Spanish fleet at the Battle of Cape St Vincent, when she flew the flag of Rear Admiral Don Francisco Winthuysen. She was in the thick of the fighting and suffered badly from the heavy British broadsides, losing over 150 of her crew killed and wounded, including her admiral who lost both legs and was carried below to die.

At the height of the action, the *San José* was rammed by her next astern, the 80-gun *San Nicolas*, and the two ships became locked together. It was at this point that Nelson made his famous move, leading a boarding party onto the *San Nicolas* and carrying her by storm. Seeing the plight of their comrades, the Spanish in the *San José* tried to help them by firing on Nelson's men, only to find themselves assailed in their turn. This further blow was too much for an already demoralised crew and, moments later, a dazed Nelson found himself receiving the surrender of all the Spanish officers on the quarterdeck of the *San José*. He handed their swords one by one to one of his barge's crew, William Fearney, 'who put them with the greatest sang froid under his arm.'

The three other Spanish ships captured at Cape St Vincent were used only as hulks but the *San José* actually enjoyed a long active service in the Royal Navy as HMS *San Josef*, the only foreign First Rate battleship ever to do so. Her first service was as Nelson's flagship in the Channel in January 1801. Some of Nelson's biographers have suggested that this was done as a special compliment to him, and he certainly asked to have her if she was available. But the most likely explanation is that she was brought into service hurriedly as a replacement for the British First Rate *Queen Charlotte*, which had been accidentally destroyed by fire the previous year.

In any case, Nelson served in her for only a few weeks and it was in her that he received the news that he was a father, when Emma Hamilton gave birth to Horatia at the end of January. In February, Nelson was appointed second in command of the fleet that was assembling at Great Yarmouth in Norfolk for the campaign against Denmark and transferred his flag to the Second Rate battleship *St George* which, being smaller, and with a shallower draught, was more suitable for service in the Baltic. The *San Josef* remained in active service and, after Nelson's death, her association with 'The Hero' meant that she was preserved long after her useful life was over. She lasted until 1849 and, when she was finally broken up, much of her wood was made into furniture and other relics.

SEE ALSO
Cape St Vincent

LATEST RESEARCH
Robert Gardiner, *Warships of the Napoleonic Era*, Chatham Publishing (London 1999)

Santissíma Trinidad

The most famous Spanish warship of her day, the *Santissíma Trinidad* played a central role in two of Nelson's battles. With her four gundecks mounting a total of 136 guns, she was spoken of at the time as the largest ship in the world, a claim often repeated subsequently by historians. Modern research has established that she was actually appreciably smaller than the impressive French three-deckers launched just before the war.

Built in Havana in 1769, to the designs of the Irish naval architect Matthew Mullan, the *Trinidad* was originally a standard three-decker battleship, mounting 116 guns. However, in 1795, her forecastle was joined to her quarterdeck, and a light battery of eight-pounder guns mounted, thus creating her distinctive 'four-decker' appearance. But although this change made her look most impressive, it also considerably worsened her sailing qualities and her stability. So she tended to be a liability in battle, rather than an advantage.

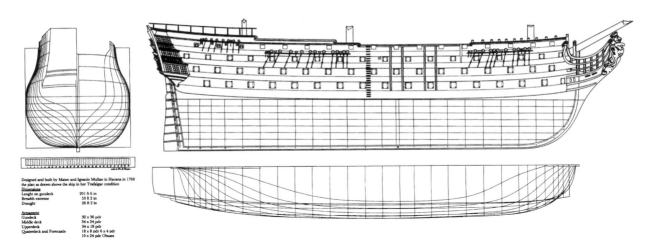

Designed and built by Mateo and Ignacio Mullan in Havana in 1769
the plan as drawn shows the ship in her Trafalgar condition
Dimensions
Lenght on gundeck   201 ft 6 in
Breadth extreme   53 ft 2 in
Draught   26 ft 2 in

Armament
Gundeck   32 x 36 pdr
Middle deck   34 x 24 pdr
Upperdeck   34 x 18 pdr
Quarterdeck and Forecastle 18 x 8 pdr 6 x 4 pdr
                         10 x 24 pdr Obuses

The Santíssima Trinidad, *renowned as the only four-decked battleship in the world. But, as this drawing of her lines clearly shows the fourth 'gundeck' was really only a light battery of small guns mounted on her forecastle, waist and quarterdeck.*

She was also an obvious 'trophy' and the British made very determined attempts to capture her. At the Battle of Cape St Vincent (14 February 1797), where she was the flagship of the Spanish commander-in-chief, Teniente General José de Córdoba, she came under attack from at least five British battleships including, briefly, Commodore Nelson in HMS *Captain*. After a heroic defence, in which she was totally dismasted and suffered over 300 casualties, she surrendered. But, before the British could take possession of her, the British commander-in-chief, Admiral Sir John Jervis, was forced by the arrival of fresh Spanish ships to break off the action. The *Trinidad*'s crew managed to rig jury masts and bring their battered ship safely into Cádiz harbour, despite a gallant attempt to recapture her by the British frigate HMS *Terpischore* under Captain Richard Bowen.

Eight years later, however, she was less fortunate. At Trafalgar (21 October 1805), flying the flag of Rear Admiral Don Baltazar de Cisneros, she was once again set upon by a concentration of British ships and eventually surrendered to HMS *Neptune*, commanded by Nelson's close friend Captain Thomas Fremantle. HMS *Prince* took her in tow, but she had been so badly damaged that she sank in the great storm that followed the battle.

SEE ALSO
Bowen, Battle of Cape St Vincent, Fremantle, Battle of Trafalgar

LATEST RESEARCH
Robert Gardiner, *Warships of the Napoleonic Era*, Chatham Publishing (London 1999)
José Gonzales-Aller, 'The Spanish Navy in the Eighteenth Century', in Stephen Howarth (ed), *Battle of Cape St Vincent 200 Years*, The 1805 Club (Shelton 1998)

Saumarez, James Lord (1757–1836)

Saumarez and Nelson served together briefly during 1797 and 1798 and he was Nelson's second in command during the Nile campaign. But they were very different in temperament and so relations between them were never close: indeed, at times they became quite strained. Yet Saumarez was very like Nelson in his fighting abilities, and his instinct for seizing tactical opportunities was very similar to that of his more famous colleague. He is now generally regarded as one of the most distinguished naval leaders of the period.

A Guernseyman, Saumarez was born at St Peter Port on 11 March 1757. He joined the Royal Navy in 1770 on board the battleship HMS *Montreal* and served in the Mediterranean before transferring to the 50-gun HMS *Bristol* in 1775 for service in North American waters. The *Bristol* was the pendant ship of Commodore Peter Parker, who was shortly afterwards to become Nelson's patron, and under Parker Saumarez distinguished himself in operations in America, becoming a lieutenant in 1778. He subsequently served in HMS *Victory* and *Fortitude* and was present at the Battle of the Dogger Bank on 5 August 1781. The same year, he was promoted to commander and appointed to the fireship *Tisiphone*. Having sailed in her to the West Indies in 1782 with despatches for Samuel Hood, he was present in the closing stages of Hood's brilliant operations against de Grasse at St Kitts (25/26 January 1782) and then, having trans-

Rear Admiral Sir James Saumarez. Dating from about 1802, this engraving shows Saumarez at the time of his remarkable victory at the Gut of Gibraltar. He is wearing the medal for the Battle of Cape St Vincent in his lapel.

ferred to the battleship *Russell*, commanded her at Rodney's great victory over the French at the Battle of the Saintes (12 April 1782). In an act that foreshadowed Nelson's more famous manoeuvre at Cape St Vincent, he took his ship out of the line of battle to assist in the capture of de Grasse's flagship *Ville de Paris*, earning the approval of Admiral Rodney himself, who commented that the *Russell*'s captain was 'a fine fellow, whoever he is.'

Following the end of the war, Saumarez then spent eleven years ashore and it was not until 1793 that he returned to sea, in command of the frigate HMS *Crescent*. In her, he captured the French frigate *La Reunion* in one of the first major single ship actions of the war and then in 1795 was appointed to command HMS *Orion* in the Channel fleet. She was one of the ships sent to reinforce Sir John Jervis in February 1797, arriving just in time to take part in the Battle of Cape St Vincent. There, all Saumarez's earlier experience of fleet actions came into play. During the early stages, he helped to repel a determined Spanish attack on the British line, covering the retreat of HMS *Colossus* when she was forced to drop out of the action. When the battle became a general mêlée he forced the three-decker *Salvador del Mundo* to surrender and then moved on to attack the huge Spanish flagship *Santissíma Trinidad*, with the help of Cuthbert Collingwood in the *Excellent*. He was convinced she had surrendered, when the approach of the remainder of the Spanish fleet forced Jervis to break off the action, allowing the three-decker to escape. After the battle, Nelson, already the hero of the hour following his remarkable boarding exploits, tried to reassure Saumarez by telling him that the Spanish had confirmed that the *Trinidad* had surrendered, only to receive the stiff reply, 'Whoever doubted it sir? I hope there is no need for such evidence to establish the truth of a report of a British officer.' It was probably their first encounter and already the austere and reserved Guernseyman was obviously irritated by his flamboyant and enthusiastic colleague.

Following the battle, Saumarez remained with Jervis's fleet off Cádiz until May 1798, when the *Orion* formed part of Nelson's squadron, sent into the Mediterranean to track down and destroy the French expedition under Napoleon. Saumarez was the senior captain in the squadron and so technically the second in command, but Nelson obviously preferred to consult his old friend Troubridge, often leaving Saumarez in the dark. At the Battle of the Nile, Saumarez distinguished himself once more, attacking first the *Peuple Souverain* and then the powerful 80-gun *Franklin*, both of which surrendered. But amidst all the euphoria after the extraordinary victory, Saumarez again clashed with Nelson when he dared to suggest, in a conversation on the *Vanguard*'s quarterdeck, that the tactic of doubling the French line had been dangerous, resulting in damage and casualties in the British ships from what would now be termed 'friendly fire'. As Saumarez began his remarks, Nelson cut him short and went below angrily. Although he later wrote to Saumarez, reassuring him that 'I could have formed no opinion of the *Orion* that was not favourable to her gallant and Excellent Commander and her Crew,' the awkwardness remained. So it was with some relief that Saumarez learned that Nelson had decided he should escort the French prizes home. They never served together again.

Saumarez's subsequent career was as distinguished as his earlier years. Promoted rear admiral in January 1801, he commanded a British squadron in the Mediterranean where he defeated a superior Franco-Spanish force at the Battle of the Gut of Gibraltar (12 July 1801) having, only a few days before, suffered a reverse at the Battle of Algeciras (6 July). For this he was made a Knight of the Bath and, when the House of Lords debated a motion to send him a vote of thanks, it was seconded by Nelson, in one of his few parliamentary speeches. During the Peace of Amiens, Saumarez lived happily with his growing family in Guernsey and during the Trafalgar campaign commanded the naval forces defending the Channel Islands. Then, in 1808, he was appointed commander-in-chief in the Baltic, with his flag in HMS *Victory*, and so began an important four-year period of service when he and his fleet played a key role in hampering the French land operations in that area, especially during the great campaign between France and Russia in 1812. Following the end of the war, he retired finally to Guernsey, where he eventually died on 8 October 1836. Just a few years before his death he had, very belatedly, been made a baron.

SEE ALSO
Cape St Vincent, Lord Hood, Nile, Peter Parker

LATEST RESEARCH
David Greenwood, 'A study of the life and career of James Admiral Lord de Saumarez, Bt, GCB' (unpublished manuscript)

Schomberg, Isaac (1753–1813)

Schomberg and Nelson served together only twice, and then only briefly. Even so, he unwittingly had a significant effect on Nelson's career, for it has recently been established that an earlier encounter between them was one of the main reasons why Nelson was left on half pay for five years between 1787 and 1793.

Like Nelson a Norfolkman with a naval captain for an uncle, Schomberg was born at Great Yarmouth on 27 March 1753 and entered the Royal Navy in 1770. Promoted to lieutenant in 1777 he served on the North American station in the battleship HMS *Canada*, rising to be her first lieutenant. In her, he took part in Hood's battles at St Kitts (25/26 January 1782) and Dominica and obviously attracted the admiral's attention for when, in 1786, King George III was looking for an experienced officer to serve as first lieutenant to his second son Prince William when he was appointed captain of the frigate HMS *Pegasus*, for service in the West Indies, Hood recommended Schomberg.

In fact, the choice was not a particularly happy one. By now thirty-three, Schomberg was much older than his charge and not a tactful subordinate. For his part, the Prince was determined to assert his authority and impatient with having someone who was so obviously a 'minder'. The two men clashed frequently, usually over very minor matters, and eventually when Schomberg sent a boat on shore without William's permission, the Prince reprimanded him in writing for neglect of duty. Schomberg asked for a court martial to clear his name and this request arrived on Nelson's desk as the senior officer on the station.

It was an awkward situation, requiring tact and diplomacy, neither of which were Nelson's strong suits at that time in his life. Moreover, he always tended to defer too readily to royalty and the Prince was already showing him very flattering attention by insisting that he would attend his forthcoming wedding to Frances Nisbet and give the bride away. He decided to agree to Schomberg's request for a trial and placed him under arrest until sufficient post captains could be assembled to form a court. As a result, the affair dragged on for six months during which what had started as a trivial incident developed into a major issue and, in the end, it was only resolved when Commodore Alan Gardner did what Nelson should have done in the first place. First, he persuaded the Prince that he did not have enough evidence for a conviction and then persuaded Schomberg to withdraw his request for a court martial. Schomberg returned home and was soon after appointed first lieutenant of Hood's flagship HMS *Barfleur*, then the guardship at Portsmouth: a clear indication that he was regarded as a wronged man. Nelson's clumsy handling of the matter was noted both by Hood and by the Admiralty and even the King was apparently annoyed with him for not finding a way to defuse the incident. As a result, he found that all his requests for another ship during the next few years were turned down. Years later, in the 'Sketch' of his life, which he wrote in 1799, he said that this impasse was 'due to a prejudice evidently against me at the Admiralty which I can neither guess at or in the least account for' and until recently his biographers have shared his apparent mystification. But a letter from Hood to Nelson, dating from November 1790, has recently been discovered in which Hood states quite plainly that the Schomberg affair was one of the main reasons why his protégé was being 'censured'.

In 1788, Schomberg sailed for the East Indies in the battleship HMS *Crown*, flying the pendant of Commodore William Cornwallis. But, even there, he managed to get into trouble by writing a letter to the governor of Madras complaining of some comparatively minor infringement of the elaborate rules for salutes and the paying of courtesies. Again, a court martial was threatened and, again, Schomberg was allowed to return home quietly. Promoted to post captain in 1790, he was given command of the 74-gun battleship *Culloden* and in her played a prominent role in the Battle of the Glorious First of June in 1794, capturing the French battleship *Vengeur*. However, that was his last service at sea and, thereafter, he served only in shore appointments.

He and Nelson did have one further encounter. Schomberg was appointed to the Sea Fencibles, a sea-going reserve force made up of fishermen and other men in 'protected' trades. In 1801, he commanded the Essex division and so came under the overall command of Nelson when he was appointed commander-in-chief of the anti-invasion forces in July of that year. They met at Harwich in early August when Nelson went there to inspect the Fencibles and a number of letters from Schomberg have recently been discovered among Nelson's papers, including a detailed chart of the defences of the Thames Estuary. So it would seem that the two men were able to forget their former differences and to work closely together.

Schomberg continued in the Sea Fencibles until 1808 and then became a commissioner on the Navy Board. He rose finally to deputy controller of the Navy, which office he continued to hold until his death on 20 January 1813.

SEE ALSO
Channel Command, Lord Hood, William IV

Schools, Nelson's

Before he went to sea at the age of twelve, Nelson attended two schools in Norfolk. He went first to the Royal Grammar School in the Cathedral Close in Norwich. The records of this period in his life are scanty but it is supposed that he boarded there from about the age of nine and there is a family tradition that he spent the school half-holidays with his great aunt, Mrs Henley, who lived in the town. He was then moved, with his elder brother William, to the Paston School in North Walsham, where he remained until he left Norfolk to join his uncle, Captain Maurice Suckling, on board HMS *Raisonnable* in early 1771.

The Paston School was then a comparatively new foundation with attractive modern buildings and a more liberal curriculum than was usual in most schools of the day. As well as the classics, the boys were taught French by an elderly master known as 'Jemmy Moisson' and it would seem that Shakespeare's plays were studied too, since in later life Nelson was able to quote reasonably accurately from a number of them.

Both schools still thrive today. A statue of Nelson, erected in 1847, stands outside the Grammar School in Norwich and, at the Paston School, the gracious red-brick schoolhouse that he knew has survived and now houses a small private Nelson museum.

SEE ALSO
Shakespeare, Nelson and

Scott, Alexander (1768–1840)

Scott was chaplain of HMS *Victory* at the Battle of Trafalgar and Nelson's confidential secretary. The son of a naval lieutenant, he first went to sea with his uncle, Commander Alexander Scott, in HMS *Lynx* on a voyage to the West Indies in 1772. He returned to Britain in 1777, graduated from St John's College Cambridge in 1791 and in 1792 was ordained priest. The following year, beset by debt, he accepted the offer of the post of chaplain of the battleship HMS *Berwick*, commanded by Captain Sir John Collins, an old friend of his father.

The *Berwick* formed part of Lord Hood's fleet in the Mediterranean and so Scott was present throughout the campaigns in which Nelson first made his name in the Royal Navy. A gifted linguist, and already a fluent French speaker, he set himself to learn Italian and Spanish, in which endeavour he was so successful that, in 1795, Vice Admiral Sir Hyde Parker invited him to be his confidential secretary on board his flagship HMS *St George*. The two men became friends and when Parker was posted to the West Indies, in 1796, Scott accompanied him. In 1800, he returned to Britain with his patron and went with him to the Baltic, where his gift for languages made him very useful in the delicate negotiations following the Battle of Copenhagen (2 April 1801). Already a good German speaker, he quickly picked up Danish and even began to learn Russian.

These remarkable gifts soon attracted Nelson's attention, so much so that when Hyde Parker was recalled home, he asked Scott to stay in the Baltic to assist him; but Scott honourably refused to abandon his old patron in his moment of distress. However, in May 1803, he agreed to accompany Nelson when he was appointed commander-in-chief of the Mediterranean and remained with him throughout the long campaign that culminated in the Battle of Trafalgar (21 October 1805). Although officially the chaplain of HMS *Victory*, Scott chiefly acted as Nelson's private secretary and interpreter, translating his foreign letters for him and writing the replies in fluent French, Italian or Spanish as required. He also frequently undertook intelligence missions ashore in Spain and Italy, liaising with the agents who sent Nelson information and negotiating concessions on supplies with local officials. It was largely thanks to his efforts, for example, that Nelson was able to use the excellent anchorage at Agincourt Sound in the Maddalena Islands in the north of Sardinia to water and supply his ships. Scott kept in close touch with the local officials and population, even on one occasion purchasing a set of silver candelabra and a crucifix for Nelson to present to the village church, where they are proudly displayed to this day.

At the Battle of Trafalgar, Scott's action station was in the *Victory*'s cockpit, where the wounded were treated, and so he was present throughout Nelson's long death agony, rubbing his chest in an attempt to relieve the pain and trying to comfort him with fragments of prayers. Already a very nervous man after being struck by lightning some years before, the trauma of Nelson's death almost unhinged him and he refused to leave the body, remaining doggedly beside it until it was finally laid to rest in St Paul's Cathedral.

After the funeral, he retired to Southminster in Essex, of which parish he had been the absentee rector since 1802, moving to Catterick in Yorkshire in 1816 where he finally died in 1840. Although Nelson always called him 'Doctor' to distinguish him from his other secretary, John Scott, he did not in fact become a Doctor of Divinity until 1806, which honour he received by royal mandate as a reward for his services at Trafalgar.

Nelson was clearly very fond of Scott and admired his abilities, although he was constantly amused by his odd manner, once remarking that 'absolutely too much learning has turned his head.' Scott returned that admiration with hero-worship, summing Nelson up after his death with the famous phrase, 'when I think, setting aside his greatness, what an affectionate, fascinating little fellow he was, how kind and condescending his manners, I become stupid with grief for what I have lost.'

SEE ALSO
Agincourt Sound, Death, Mediterranean Command, Hyde Parker, Religious faith, John Scott

Scott, John (d1805)

Formerly the purser of the battleship HMS *Royal Sovereign*, John Scott transferred to the *Victory* at Nelson's request in May 1803 and served with him throughout the long campaign that followed. He acted as Nelson's principal secretary and handled most of his public correspondence, helped by a small team of clerks and by the *Victory*'s chaplain, the Rev Alexander Scott, who dealt with the foreign and confidential correspondence.

Scott is a shadowy figure, about whom very little is known. He clearly knew Emma Hamilton, for he corresponded with her and gave her news of Nelson. She in turn appears to have taken Scott's wife under her protection and it was from Emma that he learned that she had safely given birth to their first child, shortly after he left England. He also visited Nelson and Emma at Merton in August 1805, during Nelson's brief spell of leave before Trafalgar.

At Trafalgar, his action station was at Nelson's side on the quarterdeck, ready to take notes as the battle progressed. However, one of the first enemy shots to reach the *Victory* cut him in two, killing him instantly. His body was hurriedly disposed of over the side, as was customary in the heat of battle, but a pool of his blood was left behind on the deck: on the very spot where Nelson fell about an hour and a half later, when he was struck by the bullet fired from the *Redoutable*. So it is Scott's blood – and not, as is usually supposed, Nelson's – which so dramatically stains the breeches and stockings that are now displayed alongside Nelson's Trafalgar coat at the National Maritime Museum in Greenwich.

Nelson clearly liked Scott and valued him highly. In August 1805, he wrote him a glowing testimonial, which included the words, '. . . as a Secretary for ability, punctuality and regularity I believe your superior is not to be met with.' Scott returned this admiration fully, writing to his wife, '. . . his penetration is quick, judgement clear, wisdom great and his decisions correct and decided.'

SEE ALSO
Alexander Scott, Mediterranean Command

Shakespeare, Nelson and

Nelson often quoted Shakespeare in his letters and it would seem that he knew a number of the plays well: indeed, he may even have learned some key passages by heart. By far the most famous of his Shakespearean quotations was the phrase he used to describe his captains at the Nile: 'a Band of Brothers'. It comes, of course, from the famous Agincourt speech in Shakespeare's great history play, *Henry V*, when the King, rallying his greatly outnumbered troops before battle, refers to,

> We few, we happy few, we band of brothers
> For he today that sheds his blood with me
> Shall be my brother; be he ne'er so vile
> This day shall gentle his condition.
> (*Henry V, IV, 3*)

Nelson was clearly familiar with the Agincourt speech, so much so that it seems likely he had learnt it. Another of his favourite quotations was,

> But if it be a sin to covet honour
> I am the most offending soul alive.

He used it a number of times (although he always used the word 'glory' instead of 'honour'). He even knew the whole scene in *Henry V* well enough to be able to quote another phrase from later on, when King Henry defies the French herald:

> We are but warriors for the working day . . .
> But by the mass our hearts are in the trim!

Writing to his wife Fanny on 22 October 1798, he said, 'Our hearts are in the trim and God is with us, of whom then shall we be afraid?' The second part of that passage is a reference to the Bible (Romans, Chapter 8, verse 31), 'If God be for us, who can be against us?' This ability to bring together passages from two completely different sources and then mould them into a vivid phrase of his own is a striking demonstration of Nelson's highly intelligent mind.

Another of the passages he knew well, and quoted throughout his life, was the great patriotic boast from *King John*:

> This England never did, nor never shall
> Lie at the proud foot of a conqueror . . .
> Come the three corners of the world in arms
> And we shall shock 'em
> Nought shall make us rue
> If England to herself do rest but true.
> *(King John*, V, 7)

He quoted from it in a letter to his wife on 13 October 1796, when Sir John Jervis's fleet was preparing to abandon the Mediterranean: ' I lament in sackcloth and ashes our present orders, so dishonourable to the dignity of England whose fleets are equal to meet the world in arms.' On 24 August 1803, he reassured his friend and prize agent, Alexander Davison, about the French invasion threat: 'I hope my dear Davison that Old England will be taken care of. If we are true to ourselves we need not mind Bonaparte.'

Another of his favourite quotations was from *Julius Caesar*. Caesar's arrogant boast to Calpurnia,

> Cowards die many times before their deaths
> The valiant never taste of death but once.
> *(Julius Caesar*, II, 2)

He wrote from the siege of Bastia to Fanny Nelson on 1 May 1794, 'all my joys of victory are twofold to me knowing how you must partake of them, only recollect a brave man dies but once, a coward all his life long.' Later, writing to Emma, he managed to get a little closer to the original: 'Cowards die ten thousand times before their death: a brave man only once.'

To sum up, references in Nelson's letters suggest that he had a fairly thorough knowledge of *Henry V, Henry IV Part One, Hamlet* and *King John* and at least some acquaintance with five other plays: *Julius Caesar, Macbeth, Othello, Two Gentlemen of Verona* and *Much Ado About Nothing*.

Where did he acquire this knowledge? It may have been at home, or simply from his own reading. But the fact that he appears to have learned some key passages by heart suggests strongly that he learned his Shakespeare at school. If so, the most likely candidate is the Paston School at North Walsham, which is known to have had a more liberal approach to the curriculum than the more traditional grammar schools of the day.

SEE ALSO
'Band of Brothers', Letters, Schools

LATEST RESEARCH
Colin White, 'Nelson and Shakespeare', *The Nelson Dispatch* 7 (July 2000), The Nelson Society

Ships named after Nelson

As might be expected, a number of warships have been named after Nelson, or in honour of his victories. The first major vessel to bear his name was a 120-gun First Rate battleship, launched in 1814. She was followed by a Victorian sail and steam frigate in 1876 and by an Edwardian battleship of 1907, the *Lord Nelson*. There was even a sailing frigate christened HMS *Horatio* in 1807.

Most famous of all was the huge 35,000-ton battleship of 1925, with her bridge superstructure placed well aft, giving her a distinctive, slipper-like profile. She saw distinguished service in the Second World War, including the Malta Convoys, the invasion of Sicily and the D-day landings in Normandy, France. In peacetime, she carried a number of Nelson relics on board, including one of his uniform coats. When these were sent ashore for safe keeping in September 1939, a lock of his hair was retained and displayed prominently in a small picture frame.

Interestingly, at least four figureheads representing Nelson have survived, including two at Portsmouth from the sailing battleships HMS *Nile* (launched in 1839 and later the famous training ship *Conway*) and HMS *Trafalgar* (1841). The figurehead from HMS *Horatio* is preserved at the National Maritime Museum in Greenwich, with a very obviously blinded eye, which makes Nelson look as if he has recently emerged from a boxing match. The huge figurehead of the 1814 battleship found its way to Australia, when the ship was handed over to the

HMS Nelson, *c1935. This splendid view of the great Second World War battleship, preparing to leave Portsmouth Harbour, captures her striking appearance and power.*

New South Wales government. It is now the centre-piece of the Navy section of the splendid Australian National Maritime Museum in Sydney.

SEE ALSO
Relics

Signatures, Nelson's

Nelson's signature changed often during his life, reflecting the many changes in his personal circumstances. As a boy, he signed himself 'Horace Nelson',

using the anglicised version of his Christian name, but he seems to have settled on 'Horatio' shortly after he went to sea in 1771.

In 1797 came the first, and most dramatic, change when he suddenly had to learn to write left-handed, following the amputation of his right arm when he was wounded during the failed attack on Santa Cruz de Tenerife (July 1797). Until then, his handwriting had been a fairly conventional (and not very legible) cursive, sloping to the right. Now, once he had mastered the new way of writing, it became squarer, with a tendency to slope to the left, and much easier to read.

Following his elevation to peerage as Baron Nelson, as a reward for his victory at the Battle of the Nile (1 August 1798), he began signing himself sim-

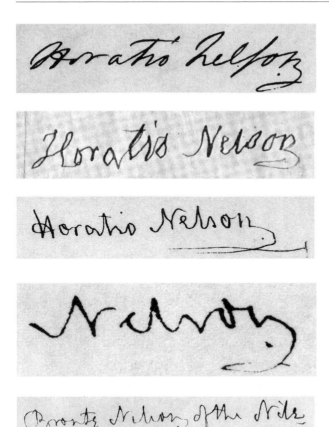

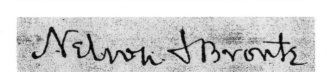

Nelson's signatures. (From top to bottom): *right-handed signature; second attempt at left-handed signature, 26 July 1797; left-handed signature, April 1798; signature after being created Baron Nelson; signature after being created Duke of Bronte; final signature.*

ply, 'Nelson', as was customary. Then, on 13 August 1799, he was created Duke of Bronte by the King of Naples and changed his signature again to 'Bronte Nelson'. Finally, on 21 March 1800, he learned that his full English title included the words 'of the Nile' and so he started using his most extended signature, 'Bronte Nelson of the Nile'.

He must have found this a laborious way of signing his letters and, in any case, when he returned to England in November 1800, it was pointed out to

him that it was tactless to use a foreign title in precedence to his English one. There then followed a brief period of uncertainty, during which he tried, 'Nelson of the Nile' and even reverted to the simple 'Nelson' until, finally, in January 1801, he was granted official permission to use his Neapolitan title. Thereafter, he settled on 'Nelson & Bronte' (always using the ampersand) and never changed his signature again.

Nelson's use of his Neapolitan title had a fascinating literary side effect. One of his admirers was an Irish clergyman called Patrick Brunty and, inspired by Nelson's famous double signature, he decided to change his name to Brontë. The fame of his daughters, Charlotte and Emily Brontë, has led many of Nelson's biographers to add their dieresis to the last letter of his name but, in fact, he never used it: or, indeed, any other accent.

SEE ALSO
Bronte, Letters

LATEST RESEARCH
Felix Pryor, 'Nelson the Letter Writer', in Colin White (ed), *The Nelson Companion*, Sutton and Royal Naval Museum (Stroud & Portsmouth 1995)

Simpson, Mary (1766–?)

The first great love of Nelson's life, Mary Simpson was the daughter of Colonel Saunders Simpson, a former soldier in the army of General James Wolfe, which had captured Quebec from the French in 1759. Simpson settled in Canada and raised a family there. By the time that the young Captain Horatio Nelson visited the city in September 1782, while in command of the frigate HMS *Albemarle*, the sixteen-year-old Mary was a renowned beauty and much wooed by the dashing young army officers of the locality.

Nelson arrived in Quebec after a punishing period on patrol during which he and his crew had become seriously ill with scurvy. He remained there for over a month recovering and, eventually, was able to write to his father, 'Health that greatest of blessings is what I never truly enjoyed until I saw fair Canada.' He also saw fair Mary and fell violently in love with her. She seems to have returned his affection but in a less intense, more flirtatious way. She was said to have told one of her other suitors, Robert Matthews, an army captain, 'I cannot think of accepting anyone belonging to the Army whose rank was below that of colonel after having been sought by a captain of the Royal Navy!'

Nelson obviously believed his suit was proceeding well but then, in October, he received orders to escort a convoy of transport ships south to New York. As was to happen again later, and more dramatically, with Emma Hamilton, he risked his career by deciding to disobey his orders and return to Quebec, apparently intending to beg Mary Simpson to marry him. However, he was met on the quayside by one of his new friends in Canada, the Scots victualling agent Alexander Davison, who eventually persuaded him to return to his ship. Mary Simpson married her army suitor, who not long afterwards was promoted to major.

SEE ALSO
HMS *Albemarle*, Davison

LATEST RESEARCH
Tom Pocock, *Nelson's Women*, André Deutsch (London 1999)

Spencer, George, Lord (1758–1834)

Spencer was First Lord of the Admiralty throughout most of the war with revolutionary France and had an important influence on Nelson's career at a key moment in its development. Born on 1 September 1758, the son of the first Earl Spencer, he was educated at Harrow and Cambridge and entered the House of Commons in 1780 as the member for Northampton. In 1783, he succeeded his father as earl and, the following year, became a warm supporter of the young prime minister, William Pitt. For the next twenty years, his political fortunes were tied to Pitt's.

Appointed First Lord of the Admiralty on 11 June 1794, he remained in office for over six years and it was under his leadership that the Royal Navy won some of its most famous victories. He deserves to share in the credit for those successes, for he was an accomplished administrator and also an excellent judge of men, who handled his often difficult senior naval colleagues with both tact and firmness. His achievement is the more remarkable when it is remembered that he had no previous experience of

naval affairs and that, at the time, he was still only in his late thirties and early forties.

Spencer first noticed Nelson when he was still a relatively unknown senior captain in the Mediterranean. Writing to Nelson in March 1797 to tell him he had been awarded the Order of the Bath for his 'distinguished conduct' at the Battle of Cape St Vincent (14 February 1797), he also specifically mentioned 'your successful and gallant exertions on several occasions during the course of the present war in the Mediterranean.' This delighted Nelson, who felt that those earlier services had been unfairly ignored.

The two men first met the following autumn, when Nelson returned home to recover from the loss of his arm and was entertained at Admiralty House by Lord and Lady Spencer. Spencer was so impressed with him that, when in the following year it was decided that a squadron should be sent into the Mediterranean to discover and destroy the French fleet, he suggested to Lord St Vincent that Nelson was the right man to command it, even though he was still a very junior rear admiral. St Vincent had in fact anticipated the suggestion and, by the time Spencer's letter arrived, Nelson had already departed on the mission that would lead him to the Battle of the Nile and fame. When this appointment met with angry protest from some of Nelson's more senior colleagues, Spencer loyally supported St Vincent's decision.

There now began a long semi-official correspondence between Nelson and Spencer lasting two years, during which Spencer skilfully nurtured and encouraged his brilliant protégé, while at the same time trying to curb his more obvious excesses. However, by the summer of 1800, it had become clear that Nelson had become too closely tied to the court of Naples, and so Spencer was forced to recall him, remarking bluntly, '. . . you will be more likely to recover your health and strength in England than in an inactive situation at a foreign Court.' However, he added, in a characteristically emollient touch, '. . . I trust that you will take in good part what I have taken the liberty to write as a friend.'

Despite this embarrassment, he continued to value Nelson's qualities as a fighting admiral and almost his last act in office was to appoint him second in command of the Baltic fleet in February 1801.

When Pitt resigned shortly afterwards, Spencer went with him, receiving the Order of the Garter as a reward for his services. Apart from a short spell as home secretary in 1806/7, he took no further part in active politics, devoting himself instead to his home county of Northamptonshire and intellectual pursuits, such as his trusteeship of the British Museum and the development of his own superb library at Althorp. He died there on 10 April 1834.

SEE ALSO
Admiralty, Italian campaign

St Vincent, Lord *See: Jervis, John*

Stewart, Sir William (1774–1827)

Stewart is best known as a distinguished soldier and one of the founders of the famous Rifle Brigade. But he also served briefly with Nelson at the Battle of Copenhagen and the two men became friends. Born on 10 January 1774, Stewart joined the army in 1786 and became a lieutenant colonel in 1795. In 1800, he proposed the formation of a corps of riflemen and became its second in command, being largely responsible for the training and organisation of the new force.

In February 1801, when a special Baltic fleet was assembled under the command of Sir Hyde Parker and Nelson, Stewart and his riflemen were attached to it, to serve as marines and also for land service if necessary. When Nelson put together his plans for the attack on the Danish defences at Copenhagen, he anticipated that a landing force would be needed to storm the large Trekroner Battery, once the Danish ships had been eliminated, and so Stewart's riflemen were transferred to the attacking ships. In the event, they played only a minor role since Nelson stopped the battle with his flag of truce before any attempt at a landing was made.

Stewart himself was stationed on board Nelson's temporary flagship HMS *Elephant*, and so was an interested and perceptive witness of Nelson's conduct during the battle. He wrote a detailed account of his experiences and it is to him we owe the story of Nelson's famous gesture, when he put the telescope to his blind eye and claimed he could not see Hyde Parker's signal to discontinue the engagement.

Shortly after the battle, Stewart was sent home to Britain with despatches. Prior to his arrival, Sir Hyde Parker had been officially congratulated on the victory at Copenhagen and there was even talk of a peerage for him. However, on 21 April Stewart met with the First Lord of the Admiralty, Lord St Vincent, and the very next day Parker was summarily recalled and Nelson was appointed commander-in-chief in his place. Recent research has established that Stewart had told St Vincent the truth about Hyde Parker's conduct of the campaign and, in particular, had mentioned the unfortunate signal.

Stewart returned to the Baltic and served with Nelson for the rest of the campaign. The two men remained in touch, writing to each other regularly, and Nelson stood godfather to Stewart's first son, Horatio. Stewart continued to serve throughout the war with France, including four years with Wellington's army in the Peninsula. After the war, he settled at Cumloden in Kirkudbrightshire, Scotland, and died there on 27 January 1827.

SEE ALSO
Copenhagen, Hyde Parker

Suckling, Maurice (1725–1778)

Nelson's maternal uncle, Maurice Suckling, was a distinguished naval officer in his own right and, had he lived, might well have risen to the top of his profession. However, he is now remembered mainly as the man who assisted the early career of his nephew, overseeing his initial training and, thereafter, using his influence to win the young man promotion and key postings.

Suckling was born into a well-connected Norfolk family in 1725 and joined the Royal Navy at a very early age, becoming a lieutenant by the time he was twenty-two. At the outbreak of the Seven Years War, in 1757, he was a captain in command of the Fourth Rate battleship *Dreadnought* of 60 guns. On 21 October, the *Dreadnought*, together with three other British battleships, fought a spirited action against a larger French squadron, and succeeded in forcing them to retreat. As the *Victory* sailed into battle at Trafalgar, exactly forty-eight years later, Nelson remarked to his officers that the 21st had always been regarded as a 'fortunate day' by his family.

In 1764, Suckling married Mary Walpole, daughter of the first Lord Walpole, thus allying himself to one of the most powerful political families in Britain. As a result, his career continued to flourish, even in peacetime. In 1775, he was appointed comptroller of the Navy, the senior officer of the Navy Board, which was responsible for all the technical and financial aspects of the Navy, and held this influential post until his early death in 1778.

In 1770, when he was appointed captain of the battleship HMS *Raisonnable*, Suckling took his nephew to sea with him. Having at first been doubtful about the frail young Horatio's ability to stand up to the rigours of naval life, he soon recognised the boy's special qualities and set about fostering his career. But it would be a mistake to suppose that Nelson owed his rapid early rise solely to his uncle's influence. Suckling clearly delighted in his talented relative and was content to let him win his own laurels. When Nelson sat his examination as lieutenant in 1777, Suckling was one of the examining board. He concealed his relationship from his colleagues until the teenager had passed with flying colours and only then introduced him as his nephew. When his colleagues expressed surprise he replied, 'I did not wish the younker to be favoured. I felt convinced he would pass a good examination and you see, gentlemen, I have not been disappointed.'

SEE ALSO
Navy Board, HMS *Raisonnable*

Suicide, Nelson and

One of the more recent, and fanciful, myths surrounding Nelson's death is the notion that he deliberately sought his fate in a quasi-suicidal manner. The theory is based on the undisputed fact that he wore the stars of his orders of knighthood on his uniform coat at Trafalgar, thus apparently presenting a perfect target to the French sharpshooters, and on contemporary accounts that make it clear he actually resisted his officers' attempts to persuade him to change into a less conspicuous costume. It is also based on a double misunderstanding—on the one hand of the type of coat that he wore and on the other of eighteenth century leadership style.

A common misconception is that Nelson wore a full dress, or highly decorated, coat on 21 October 1805. In fact his 'Trafalgar' coat was preserved as a relic and so we can see for ourselves that it was unremarkable. A standard 'undress' vice admiral's uniform - in other words an everyday coat - it is very plain, with only two thin gold rings on the sleeves and epaulettes on the shoulders to single the wearer out as a senior officer. Although the left breast certainly is adorned with the stars of Nelson's four orders of chivalry, these are not the showy gold and silver stars he would have worn on full dress occasions, but smaller and much less gaudy wire facsimiles. It is by no means clear that these would have presented a particularly obvious target in the smoke and confusion of battle.

Moreover, modern examination of the actual course of the bullet that killed Nelson has led to the suggestion that it may not have been deliberately aimed at all. It entered his body at his left shoulder and lodged under his right shoulder blade, which means that it hit him at an angle of about 30 degrees from the horizontal—far too shallow for it to have been fired from the fighting top of the *Redoutable*, as the traditional accounts suggest. In addition, although fired from a distance of no more than 50 feet, it did not pass through him but remained lodged in his body, which suggests that it was partially spent by the time it hit him. Taking these two pieces of evidence together it is more than likely that it was a ricochet.

As for leadership style: for Nelson, as for all senior officers of this period, his main role once battle was actually joined was to set a conspicuous example of courage and coolness under fire. The coat he donned on the morning of 21 October was the same pattern as those he had worn day after day during the long campaign in the Mediterranean and the dramatic chase the West Indies that followed. What sort of message would it have sent to his men if the admiral had suddenly appeared in a plain coat and without his distinctive stars? No wonder then that when his officers begged him to change, he replied sharply, 'This is no time to be shifting a coat.'

Nelson was not the suicidal type—indeed in October 1805 he had everything to live for. He had just spent a tantalizingly short period with Emma Hamilton and their beloved daughter Horatia and had glimpsed briefly the domestic happiness that was at last within his reach. He had also enjoyed the adulation of the crowds and the admiration and respect of some of the leading figures of the establishment. So, both the glory and the personal happiness he had craved in almost equal measure throughout his life had been granted him and it is clear from his letters to Emma at this time that he was longing to return home and savour them more fully. The very last words he wrote to her were, '. . . May God Almighty give us success over these fellows and enable us to get a Peace.'

But Nelson also knew that the 'pell-mell' battle he was planning involved a high degree of risk. So his mood as he faced his destiny was one of resignation. As he put it in a prayer that he wrote on the road to Portsmouth on 13 September, '. . . May the Great God whom I adore enable me to fulfill the expectations of my Country and if it is His good pleasure that I should return my thanks will never cease being offered up to the Throne of His Mercy. If it is His good providence to Cut short my days upon Earth I bow with the greatest Submission . . .'

SEE ALSO
Death of Nelson, Relics

LATEST RESEARCH
Colin White, 'The Death of Nelson', in Robert Gardiner (ed), *The Campaign of Trafalgar*, Chatham Publishing (London 1997)

Sykes, John

A Lincolnshire man, Sykes was one of the crew that Nelson took to sea with him in 1793 in HMS *Agamemnon*. He eventually became Nelson's coxswain and transferred with him to HMS *Captain*, serving with him at the Battle of Cape St Vincent in February 1797 and in the daring attacks on Cádiz

later in the same year. As coxswain, he was the senior member of the crew of Nelson's barge, and in charge of it. The post was always given to an experienced and reliable sailor and coxswains often became very close to the officers for whom they worked.

Sykes showed exceptional devotion to Nelson. At Cape St Vincent, he fought alongside him in the boarding party that captured first the *San Nicolas* and then the *San José*. Six months later, on 4 July 1797, he was at his side again when Nelson and the crew of his barge became involved in a bloody little skirmish with a larger Spanish boat outside the harbour of Cádiz. In the confused, hand-to-hand, fighting Sykes managed to save Nelson on at least two occasions by deflecting blows aimed at him.

But then came a blow that even he could not parry: a deadly descending sweep of a sabre that could have severed Nelson's head. Reaching up, Sykes put his own hand in the path of the blow. At that moment, the Spaniards were attacked from the other side by another British boat and forced to surrender. As the fighting died down, Nelson was found cradling his rescuer in his arms. 'Sykes', he was heard to say, 'I cannot forget this.' 'Thank God, sir, you are safe,' came the reply.

Nelson was as good as his word. He mentioned Sykes by name in his official despatch – at that time a most unusual honour for a seaman – and he also tried to get him made a lieutenant. But Sykes had not served long enough as a petty officer to qualify for promotion and so he had to be satisfied with a gunner's warrant. Unfortunately, he was killed by a bursting cannon in October 1799 before he could reach commissioned rank.

SEE ALSO
Cádiz, Cape St Vincent, HMS *Captain*

LATEST RESEARCH
Colin White, *1797: Nelson's Year of Destiny*, Sutton and Royal Naval Museum (Stroud & Portsmouth 1998)

T

Tenerife, The attack on (22–25 July 1797)

Tenerife was one of the worst defeats suffered by Nelson in the course of his career. He was repulsed in two successive attacks and lost over 250 men killed and wounded out of a total force of just over a thousand. He himself lost his right arm: a *stigmata* that he carried to his grave as a constant reminder of his failure. In the immediate aftermath of the defeat, he even thought his naval career was ended.

In the summer of 1797, the main Spanish fleet was penned in Cádiz, on the southwest coast of Spain, following its defeat by the British under Sir John Jervis, at the Battle of Cape St Vincent (14 February 1797). Repeated attempts to drive it out, by starvation through close blockade, or through bombardment, had failed and so Jervis and his officers were searching for other ways to bring the war closer to the ordinary Spanish population and thus, it was hoped, to persuade Spain to sue for peace. Tenerife, one of the main islands in the group known as the Canaries, lying off the west coast of Africa, appeared to offer an ideal target. It was a long way from the mainland and thus unlikely to be reinforced and recent reconnaissance had suggested that the defences were weak. Moreover, according to intelligence, a richly laden Spanish treasure ship, bringing a cargo of gold from Havana, was sheltering in the main port of Santa Cruz.

In early July 1797, Jervis – by now ennobled as Lord St Vincent – sent his energetic young protégé, Rear Admiral Sir Horatio Nelson, to Tenerife with a squadron of battleships and frigates. He was ordered to take possession of Santa Cruz 'by a sudden and vigorous assault' and then to demand the surrender of the treasure ship.

The attack on Tenerife, July 1797. A watercolour painted on the spot by Lieutenant William Webly of HMS Zealous. *The British squadron is on the right. In the centre, at the foot of the conical hill, is the Castillo de Paso Alto, the objective of the first attack. The town of Santa Cruz, where the night attack was made, is on the left.*

This was Nelson's first major operation in independent command and he straight away demonstrated two key qualities that were to make him so successful later in his career. First, he paid meticulous attention to detailed planning. Second, he discussed his plans openly beforehand with all his captains and backed up these pre-battle conferences with detailed written orders.

In fact, the first assault, on 22 July, was defeated by the one factor for which Nelson could not plan: the weather. He had decided to land a large force of sailors and Royal Marines under the cover of night to the north of Santa Cruz, where they would take possession of one of the outlying forts and turn its guns on the town. However, the boats bearing the landing force were caught in adverse currents and winds and could not reach their target before daybreak. The force commander, Captain Thomas Troubridge, did not feel confident enough to press on with the plan on his own initiative and returned to Nelson's flagship, HMS *Theseus*, to consult with his admiral, thus forfeiting all possibility of surprise. A second attempt, at a different location later in the day, was countered by the Spanish defenders, who had by now had time to rally, and eventually Nelson was forced to re-embark his men without having achieved anything.

It is arguable that, at this point, Nelson should have accepted defeat and withdrawn. But, as he himself later admitted to a friend, 'my pride suffered' and, just as he was considering what he should do, a deserter from the shore brought news that the defences were very lightly manned and that the defenders were in a state of high alarm. Nelson then called a Council of War at which a third attack was eagerly agreed for the night of 24/25 July.

This time, however, there was to be no feinting. Instead, Nelson now ordered a concentrated attack on the town itself by all his available men, crammed into small boats and vessels. He himself regarded it as a 'forlorn hope' and apparently spent the eve of the battle rereading, and then burning, many of his wife's letters.

In fact, the attack went disastrously wrong almost from the outset. Far from being in a state of panic, the defenders were thoroughly on the alert and had been carefully positioned by their experienced commander, General Antonio Gutiérrez. As a result, the attacking force was discovered as soon as it approached the town and a heavy cannonade started. This cut down large numbers of attackers, including Nelson himself, who was struck in the upper right arm by a musket ball as he was preparing to land from his barge. He fell back into the bottom of the boat where his stepson, Josiah Nisbet, quickly applied a tourniquet, thus preventing him from bleeding speedily to death. Refloating the heavy boat, Nisbet and some sailors rowed Nelson back to his flagship where the arm was amputated.

In the meantime, a number of small parties of British sailors and Royal Marines had managed to struggle ashore through breaking surf. Most of their ammunition was wet and they found themselves in a confusing maze of dark narrow streets in which the defenders, although very thinly spread, nonetheless had the considerable advantage of local knowledge. Eventually, however, Captains Troubridge and Hood managed to concentrate about 350 men outside a convent in the centre of the town, which they seized and barricaded. They then sent messages to General Gutiérrez threatening to burn the town if the treasure ship was not surrendered to them. Gutiérrez refused to respond to this bluff and, in the end, the British commanders agreed to surrender. They were permitted to re-embark with their arms and full honours of war. The British squadron returned to Cádiz and Nelson returned home to England to recover from the loss of his arm, in constant pain and deeply depressed, believing that his naval career was at an end: '. . . a left handed admiral will never again be considered as useful.'

In an attempt to make sure that the British did not attack again, Gutiérrez ordered a rumour to be spread that there were 8000 defenders on the island and Nelson and Troubridge, not unnaturally, seized on this figure to explain their defeat. As a result, in traditional British accounts, Nelson's failure at Tenerife is usually presented as a gallant fight against impossible odds. But modern Spanish research has established that Gutiérrez, in fact, had fewer than 1500 men at his disposal, of whom rather more than half were untrained militiamen, many of them armed only with sickles.

Nelson failed at Tenerife because he was inexperienced. His original plan was carefully calculated and could well have succeeded had the weather conditions not prevented it. But the impetuous night attack, carried out against an alert foe, had all the hallmarks of a young commander who still felt happiest leading aggressively from the front, rather than remaining detached and able to make objective decisions. Tenerife also showed that Nelson's shock tactics were not infallible: they could be countered by firm, experienced leadership and a highly motivated force fighting on home ground.

SEE ALSO
Gutiérrez, Samuel Hood, Thompson, Troubridge

LATEST RESEARCH
Kirstie Buckland, *The Miller Papers*, The 1805 Club (Shelton 1998)
Agustín Guimerà, *Nelson and Tenerife*, The 1805 Club (Shelton 1999)
Colin White, *1797: Nelson's Year of Destiny*, Sutton and Royal Naval Museum (Stroud & Portsmouth 1998)

Temeraire, HMS

Although Nelson never served in the *Temeraire*, her name is closely linked with his: a striking example of the way in which the 'Nelson Legend', in its remarkable development, has absorbed many otherwise peripheral stories.

The *Temeraire* was a 98-gun Second Rate battleship, launched in 1798 at Chatham and named after her predecessor, a French ship captured by Admiral Boscawen at the Battle of Lagos in 1760 and added to the Royal Navy without a change in name. At Trafalgar, commanded by Captain Eliab Harvey, she was the *Victory*'s next astern as the British fleet sailed into battle. Indeed, at one point it appeared that she might

The 'Fighting Temeraire'. *As the Battle of Trafalgar comes to a close, the* Temeraire *(centre, with the large stern) lies alongside her prize, the smaller French 74-gun* Redoutable. *(National Maritime Museum, London)*

overtake the flagship, upon which Nelson hailed her impatiently, 'I'll thank you Captain Harvey to keep your proper station, which is astern of the *Victory*!'

During the battle she was in the thick of the fighting around the *Victory* and it was to her that Captain Lucas's *Redoutable* eventually surrendered after a very gallant defence. Collingwood made a special mention of her exploits in his despatch and, as a result, her name became inextricably linked with Trafalgar and the death of Nelson.

The rest of her career was much less distinguished but her fame saved her from destruction until 1838, when she was finally sold for breaking up, long after most of the other Trafalgar ships had gone. The news of her demise caused much sadness and nostalgia, an emotion brilliantly captured by the great artist J M W Turner in his famous painting 'The Fighting *Temeraire*', which shows the grand old ship being towed to the breakers' yard against a lurid sunset. The nickname – in fact, Turner's own invention – stuck and, in its turn, inspired a number of poems, the most famous of which is Henry Newbolt's emotional lament for her passing.

Now the sunset breezes shiver
Temeraire! Temeraire!
And she's fading down the river
Temeraire! Temeraire!
Now the sunset breezes shiver
And she's fading down the river
But in England's song forever
She's the fighting Temeraire.

SEE ALSO
Battle of Trafalgar

Thesiger, Sir Frederick (d1805)

A former officer in the Russian navy, Thesiger served in the British fleet as a special advisor during the Baltic campaign in 1801 and was present in Nelson's flagship HMS *Elephant* during the Battle of Copenhagen (2 April 1801). It was he who, at the height of the battle, carried ashore Nelson's famous letter to the Danish government.

The son of a German who had settled in England, Thesiger first served in the Honourable East India Company, transferring to the Royal Navy during the War of American Independence. He was promoted to lieutenant in 1782 and served on board HMS *Formidable*, the flagship of Admiral Rodney, at the great British victory at the Battle of the Saintes in April of that year. During the long peace that followed the end of the war, Thesiger, like so many of his colleagues, was unemployed and so, in 1789, he transferred to service in the Russian navy with the rank of full captain. He took part in a number of battles in the war against Sweden and was knighted by the Empress Catherine, remaining in Russian service until 1800. At that time Russia, under Tsar Paul, became more hostile to Britain and so Thesiger returned home and resumed his Royal Navy rank of lieutenant, just as the special fleet was being assembled for service in the Baltic against the League of Armed Neutrality. In recognition of his expertise, he was promoted to commander and attached to Sir Hyde Parker's staff in HMS *London*.

When the decision was made to attack the Danish line defending Copenhagen, Thesiger transferred to HMS *Elephant* to act as aide de camp to Nelson. At the height of the battle, sensing that the Danish fire was beginning to slacken, and wishing to avoid further bloodshed, Nelson sent a letter ashore to the Danish government threatening to burn all his prizes unless there was an immediate ceasefire. Since Thesiger was known by some of the key Danes, and also understood Danish, he was the obvious choice for such a mission and so he went in a small open boat, carrying a flag of truce attached to an oar, through the thick of the fire to the shore, where the Danish Crown Prince had set up his command centre. He delivered Nelson's letter and opened the negotiations with the Prince, which led eventually to an armistice.

Following the battle, Sir Hyde Parker was recalled to England and Nelson assumed command of the fleet, taking Thesiger with him into his flagship HMS *St George*. He remained with Nelson throughout the rest of the campaign and helped with the delicate negotiations with Russia following the assassination of Tsar Paul and the accession of the more pro-British Tsar Alexander.

Thesiger's services in the Baltic were rewarded by promotion to post captain and he was also given formal permission to wear his Russian order of knighthood. But he did not live long to enjoy these honours, dying in August 1805 at Gosport, Hampshire, where he was serving as agent for prisoners of war.

SEE ALSO
Copenhagen

'Thomson' Letters, The

In late January 1801, Emma Hamilton gave birth to twin girls, fathered by Nelson. One died almost at once, but the other, named Horatia, survived. Nelson was at this time serving at sea in the Channel fleet and, while he was anxious to receive news of the child, and her mother, he was concerned that his letters might be opened in the post. So he devised an elaborate charade to enable him to write to Emma openly about their child.

He invented a sailor on board his flagship whose name was Thomson (although Nelson sometimes spelled it 'Thompson'). Thomson had a pregnant wife who was being looked after by Emma. So Nelson wrote to Mrs Thomson on the sailor's behalf and passed on messages about his love for her and the infant.

The letters make very strange reading. Sometimes Nelson writes as Thomson; sometimes on behalf of Thomson. Sometimes the letter is addressed to Mrs Thomson, sometimes to Lady Hamilton. Often, Nelson drops in and out of role a number of times in the same letter. Occasionally, he stops taking the fiction seriously and drops clues that even the densest reader can unpick. For example, when talking about arrangements for the baby's baptism, he writes: 'Its name will be Horatia, daughter of Johem and Morata Etnorb. If you read the surname backwards and take the letters of the other names it will make, very extraordinary, the names of your real and affectionate friends Lady Hamilton and myself.'

However transparent the 'Thomson' story may seem today, it appears to have served its purpose at the time. Nelson's intimate friend Captain Thomas Hardy went to his grave convinced that Thomson had been a sailmaker on board HMS *Elephant*. Sir Nicholas Harris Nicolas, the compiler of the collection of Nelson's letters and despatches, devoted a voluminous appendix in his great work to proving that Emma Hamilton was *not* the mysterious 'Mrs Thomson'!

SEE ALSO
Emma Hamilton, Horatia Nelson, Letters

LATEST RESEARCH
Flora Fraser, *Beloved Emma*, Weidenfeld and Nicolson (London 1986)

Thompson, Sir Thomas Boulden (1766?–1828)

One of the original 'Band of Brothers', Thompson served with Nelson in three of his actions and was wounded three times. Born in Barham in Kent, he first went to sea in 1778 with his uncle Captain Edward Thompson and reached the rank of lieutenant in 1782. Eventually, he became a commander in 1786 and a post captain in 1790 but then remained unemployed until 1796. In that year, however, he was appointed to command the 50-gun HMS *Leander* and in her he took part in Nelson's abortive attack on

Sir Thomas Thompson. An engraving from The Naval Chronicle.

Tenerife in July 1797. Thompson had visited Santa Cruz before and his first-hand knowledge of the layout of the town was one of the factors that persuaded Nelson to undertake his risky frontal attack on the night of 25/26 July. Thompson went with Nelson in the first wave and, like him, was wounded in the arm in the attack on the mole. However, his wound was not as severe as Nelson's and he was able to continue in active service.

The following year, the *Leander* was one of the ships sent by Lord St Vincent to reinforce Nelson in the Mediterranean and so Thompson took part in the Battle of the Nile and the great chase that preceded it. Although 50-gun ships were generally regarded as too small to serve in the line of battle, in the fighting Thompson distinguished himself by placing the *Leander* neatly between the *Peuple Souverain* and the *Franklin* in a position where her guns could rake them both without suffering serious damage himself. After the battle, in the absence of the frigates that would normally have performed the duty, Nelson ordered him to carry Edward Berry with his despatches to Lord St Vincent at Cádiz, but the *Leander* had the misfortune to encounter the 74-gun *Généreux*, one of three French ships that had escaped from the Nile. After a most gallant defence against overwhelming odds in which both Thompson and Berry were wounded, the *Leander* was forced to surrender. Having been exchanged, Thompson returned home to face court martial but was honourably acquitted and knighted for his services.

In 1799, he was appointed to the 74-gun battleship HMS *Bellona* and, having served in both the Channel and the Mediterranean, was attached to the special fleet assembled under Sir Hyde Parker and Nelson for the Baltic campaign of 1801. The *Bellona* was in Nelson's squadron at the Battle of Copenhagen (2 April 1801) but on the morning of the battle, her experienced master, Alexander Briarly, volunteered to guide the British through the complex shoals and was transferred to the lead ship HMS *Edgar*. Left without a pilot, Thompson was forced to conn his ship himself and, going too close to the shoals, he grounded on an unmarked spur. At almost the same moment, he was struck by a Danish cannonball, which took off his leg, so he was unable to play any further part in the battle. A few days afterwards, he received a comfort-

ing letter from Nelson, '. . . patience My Dear fellow is a Virtue (I know it) but I never profest it in my life yet I can admire it in others.'

This third and most serious wound finished Thompson's sea-going career. He was given a pension and command of the yacht *Mary*: essentially a sinecure designed to enable him to remain on full pay. He remained in regular touch with Nelson and one of the last letters Nelson wrote in England in September 1805 was a request to Prime Minister William Pitt to make special arrangements for Thompson's widow to continue to receive his pension after his death since, '. . . Sir Thomas has scarcely anything but what dies with him.' In fact, Thompson survived for another twenty-three years until 1828, becoming comptroller of the Navy in 1806, a rear admiral in 1809 and a vice admiral in 1814. He also served as MP for Rochester from 1807 to 1818.

Thompson's correspondence with Nelson, from which the above quotations have been taken, has only recently been discovered in the British Library and it has now become clear that the two men were rather closer than has hitherto been supposed. In his 1805 testimonial to Pitt, Nelson wrote of his friend, '. . . A more gallant active and Zealous Sea Officer is not in the Service.'

SEE ALSO
'Band of Brothers', Copenhagen, Nile, Tenerife

Touch, The Nelson

Before Trafalgar, Nelson devised a comprehensive battle plan based on his own long experience of war, and on the tactical experiments of his predecessors, which he called 'The Nelson Touch'. When he explained it to his captains shortly after his arrival in the fleet of Cádiz in late September 1805, it caused great excitement: '. . . it was like an electric shock,' Nelson wrote to Emma Hamilton, 'Some shed tears, all approved – It was new, it was singular, it was simple.' (See transcript on p271.)

The plan's simplicity was its main strength. Nelson's aim was annihilation: he wanted to bring about what he called a 'pell-mell battle', or a mêlée,

Continued on page 238

The Nelson Touch – A new discovery

During his brief period of leave in Britain in August and September 1805, Nelson discussed his ideas for the tactics he would use in his next battle on a number of occasions. For example, he told Captain Richard Keats, who had served with him in the Mediterranean in HMS *Superb*, that his object was to 'surprise and confound the enemy' by forming the fleet into three divisions and then attacking them 'at once' with two divisions, while the third acted as a reserve to contain part of the enemy force, thus preventing them from turning to help their comrades. He also described a similar plan to his friend Lord Sidmouth (formerly Prime Minister Henry Addington) and illustrated his ideas by sketching them out on the surface of a small table, with a finger dipped in wine.

Now, thanks to a very recent discovery in the Nelson papers held by the National Maritime Museum, we can see Nelson's plan for ourselves – almost certainly drawn by him. During routine research for the 'Nelson Letters Project' a set of rough notes in Nelson's handwriting was examined (below), which refer to promotions and appointments that he was hoping to obtain for some of his protégés and for men who had served with him in the *Victory* during the 1803-1805 campaign in the Mediterranean (NMM: CRO/15). Although the paper is undated these names, together with analysis of the handwriting, show that the notes must have been written in 1805 and it is a fair assumption that they were jotted down as an *aide memoire* prior to one of Nelson's meetings at the Admiralty during his leave period.

On the reverse of the paper (below) is a very rough sketch and the evidence would appear strongly to suggest that it is a diagram demonstrating the tactics that Nelson described to Keats.

In the lower half of the sketch, the enemy line is represented by the continuous diagonal line. The British fleet can be seen first forming into three divisions on the left of the page and then cutting the enemy line in two places, while the third division 'contains' part of the enemy line by ranging alongside it. It is even possible to catch an echo of the excitement with which Nelson has demonstrated the cutting of the enemy line – his pen has dug deeply into the paper and the ink has flowed thickly.

The upper diagram is less easy to interpret. One theory is that it may be intended to show how an attack by ships only in a single line (represented by the diagonal row of dots) could easily be countered by the enemy if they simply altered their course, so as to take their attackers between two fires.

A number of sketches by Nelson of his earlier battles have survived, but each of these was drawn after the event. This is the only known example of one of his pre-battle demonstrations of his tactics.

(For a full analysis of the diagrams, and of the evidence for the provenance of the plan, see Colin White, 'Nelson's 1805 Battle Plan', *Journal of Maritime Research*, April 2001.)

at very close quarters in which the superior gunnery and training of his crews would have maximum, and devastating, effect. To achieve this, he planned to attack in three divisions, instead of a single line, as was customary. The larger part of his fleet would concentrate on one section of the enemy's line, crushing it with sheer weight of numbers and rapid, accurate gunfire. In the meantime, the rest of his ships would cut off the rest of the enemy by breaking through their line and preventing them from coming to the aid of their comrades.

Some older accounts of Trafalgar suggest that Nelson's plan was revolutionary. But, in fact, none of the individual components was new: each had been tried in earlier battles. For example, Admiral Sir George Rodney had broken through the French line in two places at the Battle of the Saintes in the West Indies (2 April 1782). Admiral Adam Duncan had attacked the Dutch fleet in two divisions at the

Battle of Camperdown off the Dutch coast (11 October 1797). Concentration on one part of an enemy force was a very old tactic and Nelson himself had used it with devastating success at the Battle of the Nile in 1798.

What *was* new was the way in which Nelson brought the different elements into a single, coherent plan, which he then presented to his captains, well in advance of the battle. First, he held what we would now call 'briefings' round the dining table in his quarters in HMS *Victory* and then he issued a reminder of what he had said in the form of a memorandum (see transcript on page 271). Moreover, central to his thinking was the idea that, once battle was joined, he was prepared to trust his captains to use their own judgement in carrying out the plan, rather than relying on him for instructions: '. . . something must be left to chance,' he wrote, 'nothing is sure in a seafight above all others . . . But in case Signals can neither be seen or perfectly understood, no Captain can do very wrong if he places his Ship alongside that of an Enemy.' This was indeed revolutionary, and it is no wonder that his captains were so excited.

Another of his own innovations was the idea that

The Nelson Touch. Nelson explains his plan of attack to his excited captains. This engraving of the famous scene was produced by Edward Orme in 1806.

'the Order of Sailing is to be the Order of Battle.' Having watched in frustration at the Battle of Hyères in July 1795 while Admiral Hotham wasted four hours arranging his fleet in line, and then lost the French fleet when the wind died away, Nelson was determined his fleet would be able attack at once, as soon as the Combined fleet was sighted.

With his characteristic gift for the telling phrase, Nelson dubbed his plan, 'The Nelson Touch' and the phrase has perplexed historians ever since. There are a number of theories of how he came by it but the most plausible would seem to be that it is derived from a speech in his favourite Shakespeare play *King Henry V*. One of the play's choruses describes the warrior king's sensitive way of dealing with his frightened men on the eve of battle as 'a little touch of Harry in the night'. Writing to Emma Hamilton just before his arrival with the fleet of Cádiz, Nelson reminded her about the 'Nelson Touch', 'which, *we* say, is warranted never to fail.' Seen in this context, it

The destruction of Toulon, 1793. As the British abandon Toulon, following the successful counterattack by French revolutionary forces, ships and shore installations are destroyed.

seems most likely that the famous phrase originated as a lovers' sexual joke.

SEE ALSO
Hyères, Nelson and Shakespeare, Battle of Trafalgar

Toulon

The main French naval base in the Mediterranean, Toulon is situated on the south coast of France, in Provence. There has been a port there at least since Roman times but the first naval dockyard was established in the sixteenth century and then greatly enlarged in the late seventeenth century during the major expansion of the French Marine Royale under King Louis XIV and his minister Colbert. By

Nelson's time, there were two large ship basins, each with its own set of docks and supporting buildings, while outside the harbour was a large anchorage, the 'Grande Rade', where fleets could take shelter. To the north, the town was dominated by high hills on which batteries and forts were erected, thus creating a formidably strong arsenal and base.

Nelson first visited Toulon in 1793, when it was handed over by French royalists to the British Mediterranean fleet under Lord Hood. However, his stay was only brief, as he was sent on a mission to Naples to persuade the King to send Neapolitan troops to assist with the occupation. It was on this occasion that he first met Sir William and Lady Hamilton. In the end, the British occupation was short-lived and they were forced to evacuate the port by a republican army, whose artillery was commanded by the rising young general Napoleon Bonaparte.

Thereafter, Nelson visited Toulon only to watch it from the sea, most memorably during 1803–1805 when he spent almost two years constantly afloat in the area. Unlike his colleagues at Brest, whose object was always to keep the French in port, Nelson tried constantly to tempt his opponents to emerge by keeping most of his ships out of sight over the horizon. On one occasion, when the City of London passed a resolution congratulating him and the officers and men of his fleet for their remarkable feat in blockading Toulon for so long, Nelson replied, 'I beg to inform your Lordship that the Ports of Toulon has never been blockaded by me: quite the reverse –

The Battle of Trafalgar, 21 October 1805. Nicholas Pocock's superb aerial view of the battle captures the moment when the Victory *(centre) broke through the Franco-Spanish line astern of Villeneuve's flagship* Bucentaure.

every opportunity has been offered the Enemy to put to sea.'

Toulon remains one of the main French naval dockyards and a number of the buildings and docks that Nelson knew have survived.

SEE ALSO
HMS *Agamemnon*, Lord Hood, Latouche Tréville, Mediterranean Command, Napoleon I

Trafalgar, Battle of (21 October 1805)

Trafalgar is the best known of Nelson's great victories and has acquired a symbolic significance that far exceeds its actual importance in the conduct of the great war against France of 1793–1815. A number of myths have gathered around it, the most persistent of which is that it saved Britain from invasion. In fact, by the time the battle was fought, Napoleon's over-ambitious invasion plan had already been thwarted by the skilful strategic moves of the First Lord of the Admiralty, Lord Barham. Hearing that the Combined Franco-Spanish fleet under Vice Admiral Pierre Villeneuve had retreated southwards to Cádiz

'Truth and Falsehood.' This caricature, published in late 1805, portrays the propaganda battle after the Battle of Trafalgar. Napoleon (left) tries to play down his defeat while John Bull (right) loudly trumpets the great victory.

after its confused encounter with Calder's squadron off Cape Finisterre (22 July 1805), Napoleon turned his 'Army of England' about and marched on Austria, which had just declared war. He directed the fleets to sail into the Mediterranean in support of his operations, and so when, on 19 October, Villeneuve left Cádiz with thirty-three battleships, he was starting a completely new campaign.

Waiting out of sight over the horizon was a British fleet of twenty-seven battleships, commanded by Nelson. Following his epic chase of Villeneuve's fleet to the West Indies and back in the previous summer, Nelson had gone on leave to Britain, hoping for a rest. But he found that his reputation had been so enhanced by his recent exploits that everyone from Prime Minister William Pitt down wanted to consult him. 'I am now set up for a *conjurer*,' he commented ruefully, 'and God knows they will very soon

TRAFALGAR
21 October 1805

1. The Battle of Trafalgar was a confusing mêlée—as Nelson had intended. So contemporary plans, based on the reminiscences of those who took part, tended to reflect this confusion and, as a result, contradicted each other.

2. In an attempt to resolve this confusion, the Admiralty appointed a committee of historians and naval officers to examine the logs of the ships involved to prepare an accurate plan and track chart. The plan shown here is based on the committee's findings, published in 1913.

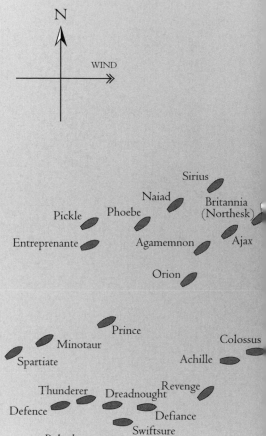

N

WIND

Sirius
Naiad
Britannia (Northesk)
Pickle   Phoebe
Entreprenante   Agamemnon   Ajax
Orion

Prince
Minotaur   Colossus
Spartiate   Achille
Thunderer   Dreadnought   Revenge
Defence   Defiance
Polyphemus   Swiftsure

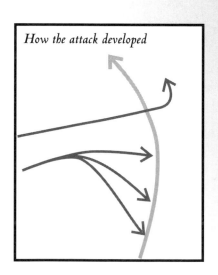

How the attack developed

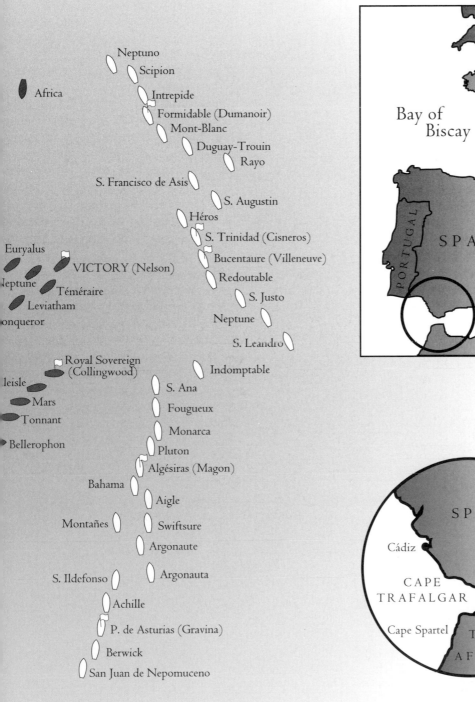

Africa

Neptuno
Scipion
Intrepide
Formidable (Dumanoir)
Mont-Blanc
Duguay-Trouin
Rayo
S. Francisco de Asis
S. Augustin
Héros
S. Trinidad (Cisneros)
Bucentaure (Villeneuve)
Redoutable
S. Justo
Neptune
S. Leandro

Euryalus
VICTORY (Nelson)
Neptune
Téméraire
Leviatham
Conqueror

Royal Sovereign
(Collingwood)
Indomptable
leisle
S. Ana
Mars
Fougueux
Tonnant
Monarca
Bellerophon
Pluton
Algésiras (Magon)
Bahama
Aigle
Montañes
Swiftsure
Argonaute
Argonauta
S. Ildefonso
Achille
P. de Asturias (Gravina)
Berwick
San Juan de Nepomuceno

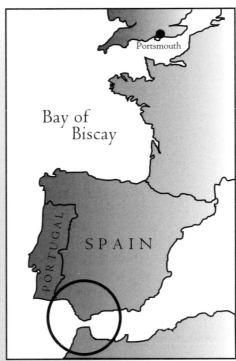

Portsmouth

Bay of
Biscay

PORTUGAL

SPAIN

SPAIN

Cádiz

CAPE
TRAFALGAR

Gibraltar

Cape Spartel

Tetuan

AFRICA

Britannia Triumphant.

THE MOST DECISIVE AND GLORIOUS
NAVAL VICTORY
THAT EVER WAS OBTAINED SINCE THE CREATION OF THE WORLD!!
THE VICTORIOUS *BRITISH* FLEET
Was commanded by the most renowned, most gallant, and ever-to-be-lamented Hero,
Admiral Lord Viscount NELSON;
AND THE VANQUISHED FLEETS OF FRANCE AND SPAIN
By the Admirals VILLENEUVE and GRAVINA.

This memorable Action was fought off Cape Trafalgar, near the Entrance of the Streights of Gibraltar, on the 21st of October, 1805.

The ENGLISH FLEET consisted of TWENTY-SEVEN Ships of the Line.

The Combined Fleets of FRANCE and SPAIN consisted of 33 Ships of the Line.

The Combined Fleets superior in Guns 474, in Men 8,153.

LONDON: PRINTED BY R. EDWARDS, CRANE-COURT, FLEET-STREET.   SOLD BY E. KENT AND SON, 116, HIGH-HOLBORN.   PRICE TWO-PENCE.

Celebrating Trafalgar. A contemporary British engraving celebrates the battle and lists the ships and men involved – and the fates of the French and Spanish ships.

find out I am far from being one.' He also found that everyone expected him to return to complete the work he had begun by defeating the Combined French and Spanish fleet and so, after only twenty-five days with Emma Hamilton and their daughter Horatia at Merton, he sailed from Portsmouth in the *Victory* on 14 September.

By then, the British had assembled a large fleet off Cádiz, where Villeneuve had taken refuge. As soon as he arrived, on 28 September, Nelson set about moulding his captains, most of whom had never served with him before, into a single fighting unit.

He held dinner parties at which he explained his battle plan and then issued a memorandum summing up his tactical ideas (see transcript on page 271). His plan, which he called 'The Nelson Touch', was very simple. He planned to concentrate one part of his force on the enemy rear, crushing it with superior gunfire. In the meantime, the rest of his ships would prevent the remaining enemy ships from coming to the aid of their comrades. This, he hoped, would bring 'a pell-mell battle', in which the superior gunnery and ship-handling of his crews would have maximum advantage.

Another Trafalgar myth is that this plan was completely new and the product of Nelson's personal tactical genius. In fact, none of the individual elements was particularly revolutionary: Nelson was building on years of tactical experiment in the Royal Navy. What *was* new, however, was the way in which he was prepared to discuss his plans in advance and then, having done so, to delegate responsibility to individual captains. As he wrote in his famous memorandum, 'No captain can do very wrong if he places his ship alongside that of an enemy.'

As the Combined fleet emerged, heading south for the Straits of Gibraltar, it was expertly shadowed by British frigates under Captain Henry Blackwood, who kept in close touch with Nelson, using a new telegraphic signal system devised by Sir Home Riggs Popham. As a result, Nelson was able to choose both the precise moment and the direction of his attack.

The two fleets sighted each other at about 6.00am on 21 October but the wind was light and so the first shots were not fired until mid-day. As planned, the British fleet split into two divisions. One, led by Vice Admiral Cuthbert Collingwood in HMS *Royal Sovereign*, headed for the rear of the Franco-Spanish line; while Nelson in HMS *Victory* aimed his division directly at their centre. Scarcely any operational signals were required: a tribute to the thoroughness of Nelson's pre-battle briefings. Indeed, when the flags were hoisted with his famous message of encouragement, 'England expects that every man will do his duty', Collingwood's first reaction was to remark crossly, 'I do wish Nelson would stop signalling. We all know what we have to do!'

Collingwood was first into action, firing a broadside into one of the Spanish flagships, the *Santa Anna*, as he passed under her stern at about 12.20pm. He was followed by the ships of his division, which approached in a slanting line abreast, thus spreading the force of the impact and enveloping the allied rear, as Nelson had intended. Nelson, meanwhile, was heading towards the great *Santíssima Trinidad*, easily recognisable with her four tiers of guns. But, spotting that Villeneuve was flying his flag in the ship next astern, the *Bucentaure*, he ordered Hardy to attack her first. So the *Victory* passed under her stern, firing a murderous broadside as she went that gave the French vessel a knockout blow right at the start of the contest. As the *Victory* moved on, she became entangled with the *Redoutable*, whose captain, Jean Lucas, had been gallantly trying to help his comrades, and the two ships drifted away, locked in a deadly close-quarters struggle. This created a large gap in the allied line through which the ships of Nelson's division then poured, thus splitting the enemy fleet in two: again, exactly as Nelson had intended (see colour plate *IX*).

Thereafter, the battle developed into a ferocious pounding match. The French and Spanish ships fought with great bravery but they were isolated and leaderless, while the British were working to a single pre-concerted plan and with the advantage that they were much better trained in delivering rapid, accurate gunnery. Collingwood's ships gradually subdued the allied rear, while Nelson's division first captured most of their centre and then fought off a belated counterattack by the van under Rear Admiral Dumanoir. When the battle finally ended at about 4.30pm, seventeen allied ships had been captured and another was a blazing wreck. Four ships escaped with Dumanoir, but were captured a few weeks later at the Battle of Cape Ortegal (4 November 1805), and only eleven managed to struggle back into Cádiz, under the command of the Spanish senior admiral, Gravina, who was himself badly wounded.

For the British, triumph at this extraordinary result was overshadowed by the news that Nelson was dead. Shot on his quarterdeck at about 1.15pm, he was carried down to the *Victory*'s cockpit where, having been told of his great victory, he died at about 4.30pm. The triumph was further dissipated by a fierce storm that blew up after the battle, forcing the British to scuttle most of their hard-won prizes. A daring sortie from Cádiz on 23 October by some of the survivors of the allied fleet under Commodore Cosmao-Kerjulien succeeded in wresting two of the prizes from their British captors but the allies lost a further three ships in the process.

News of Trafalgar reached London about a fortnight after the battle in the early hours of 6 November, carried home in the schooner *Pickle* by Lieutenant John Lapenotiere. Public rejoicing for the victory was muted by widespread sorrow for the death of Nelson: as the poet laureate Robert Southey later remembered in his biography of Nelson, published in 1813, 'The victory of Trafalgar was celebrated, indeed, with the usual forms of rejoicing, but they were without joy.' Collingwood was made a baron, all the captains received the King's Naval

Gold Medal and a special grant of money was made by the government to all those who had taken part to compensate them for the prize money they had lost when their captures sank in the storm. And Nelson's body was brought home to Britain and buried in St Paul's Cathedral with the elaborate ceremonial of a full state funeral.

Because it was so decisive, and because there were no other great set-piece fleet actions in the rest of the war, Trafalgar has acquired a reputation for completeness that it does not really deserve. True, the Spanish fleet had been dealt a mortal blow from which it never really recovered, losing over a quarter of its effective battleships (eight out of thirty) and, perhaps more important, suffering serious casualties among its high command. The French, however, had lost a smaller proportion of their effective fleet (thirteen out of seventy) and these were later replaced in an extensive building programme. Moreover, Trafalgar had little immediate effect on the overall course of the war. The day before, Napoleon had defeated the Austrians at Ulm and, six weeks later, he was to confirm his ascendancy over Europe with an even more decisive victory over the Austrians and Russians at Austerlitz (2 December 1805). Arguably, therefore, Nelson's victory at the Nile in 1798 was much more decisive than Trafalgar: in that battle, almost the entire French Mediterranean fleet had been eliminated and a completely new phase in the war began.

On the other hand, the psychological effect of Trafalgar was immeasurable. It demonstrated that the Royal Navy had a superiority in training, professionalism and expertise in naval tactics that set it apart from any of its rivals. Above all, it gave the Royal Navy an unmatched tradition of victory that is still potent even 200 years later.

SEE ALSO
Bucentaure, Blackwood, Cape Ortegal, Collingwood, Death, 'England expects', Funeral, Lapenotiere, Popham, 'The Nelson Touch', Trafalgar campaign, *Santissíma Trinidad*, HMS *Temeraire*, HMS *Victory*, Villeneuve

LATEST RESEARCH
Robert Gardiner (ed), *The Campaign of Trafalgar*, Chatham Publishing (London 1997)
Alan Shom, *Trafalgar: Countdown to Battle*, Michael Joseph (London 1990)

Trafalgar campaign (March–October 1805)

The Battle of Trafalgar, fought on 21 October 1805, was preceded by arguably the largest-scale naval campaign ever mounted in the Age of Sail. Involving the fleets of Britain, France and Spain, amounting in total to over a hundred battleships and many more smaller vessels, together with the armies of France, Britain and Austria, it lasted eight months and covered a vast area bounded by the Channel in the north to the Mediterranean in the south and at one point extending even to the West Indies.

When war between France and Britain broke out again in 1803, following the brief Peace of Amiens, Napoleon immediately revived plans for an invasion of Britain, concentrating an army around Boulogne and Calais in northeastern France and building a large flotilla of specially designed boats to carry the troops across the Channel. The British responded by organising a three-tiered defence. First, there were squadrons of small vessels operating right on the French coast to harry the invasion forces as they emerged from port; then there were larger vessels, stationed in the Channel itself under Vice Admiral Lord Keith; and, finally, there was a major system of land defences involving specially constructed fortifications and a large force of militia and volunteers. It soon became clear that the French invasion flotilla could not hope to reach Britain unless it was protected by a large fleet.

To achieve this, Napoleon devised an ambitious strategy that he hoped would draw the British away from their usual blockading stations and enable him to concentrate a significant force of ships in the Channel. He ordered his admirals at Brest, Rochefort and Toulon to emerge from port and rendezvous in the West Indies, where they were to attack the rich British islands, thus forcing the British to divert ships for their defence. They were then to return swiftly to the mouth of the Channel in a concentrated force large enough to sweep aside the remaining British defenders and, finally, to move into a position that would enable them to cover the invasion flotilla as it made its hazardous crossing.

It was essentially a soldier's plan, devised by someone who was used to being able to synchronise fairly exactly the movements of different groups of his forces and who had little understanding of the problems of winds and tides. In practice, however, it worked surprisingly well and it is arguable that the great fleet movements of the summer of 1805 gave the British government more cause for concern than all the warlike preparations on the other side of the Channel.

After a number of false starts, the campaign got under way in earnest on 30 March 1805, when Vice Admiral Pierre de Villeneuve left Toulon in southern France with eleven battleships and some 3000 troops on board. He was being watched by Nelson, then commander-in-chief in the Mediterranean, but, at the time that he left, Nelson was refitting and resupplying his ships at Palma Bay in Sardinia. So the French managed to get clean away: sailing first to Carthagena and Cádiz to collect Spanish ships that were stationed there and then beginning the long Atlantic crossing.

Villeneuve arrived in the West Indies in mid-May and began the wait for his colleagues. But, at this stage, the plan began to go wrong. Another, smaller fleet under Rear Admiral Missiessy had already sailed for the West Indies in January but, having waited for nearly three months, had now begun its voyage home. Moreover, the main French fleet, stationed at Brest under Vice Admiral Ganteaume, was unable to leave port because of the tight blockade imposed by the British Channel fleet under Vice Admiral William Cornwallis. Finally, as the French intentions began to become clear, the various British squadrons responded by falling back northwards on the Channel fleet. As a result, by mid-June 1805, far from being dispersed as Napoleon had intended, the Royal Navy was very largely concentrated in the mouth of the Channel.

The one exception to this was the Mediterranean fleet under Nelson. Having first searched for Villeneuve in the Mediterranean, he eventually passed through the Straits of Gibraltar in early May and, having established that the combined French and Spanish fleet, now numbering seventeen battleships, had sailed for the West Indies, he resolved to go after them with his ten battleships. He made a remarkably quick passage and arrived at Barbados on 4 June. But, misled by false information, he sailed first for Trinidad and then to Grenada. Four days later, Villeneuve learned that his opponent had arrived and, immediately abandoning his plans for further operations in the West Indies, began the voyage home on 10 June. Nelson learned of this two days later and at once set sail himself, sending the fast brig *Curieux* ahead to warn the Admiralty of Villeneuve's movements. On the 19th, she sighted the Combined fleet briefly and so was able to carry accurate information about their course, which appeared to be heading for northern Spain, rather than the Mediterranean or the Channel. This news reached Lord Barham at the Admiralty on 8 July and so he was able to order Cornwallis to send a detachment from his fleet, under Vice Admiral Sir Robert Calder, to intercept the approaching enemy.

So it was that when Villeneuve eventually arrived off Cape Finisterre on 22 July, he found a British fleet waiting for him in the mist. In the ensuing battle he lost two Spanish ships but was able to escape, first into Vigo and then into Ferrol where he collected more Spanish reinforcements, bringing his force to twenty-nine battleships. But he had clearly been unnerved by the way that his every move had been countered by the British and so, when he emerged again in early August, he did not sail northwards as Napoleon had intended to join with Ganteaume off Brest. Instead, he went south and took refuge in Cádiz. When the news of this retreat was brought to a furious Napoleon, he abandoned his plans to invade Britain and, turning his army around, marched on Austria, which had by then agreed to enter the war on the British side.

So, by the end of August 1805, the immediate threat of invasion was over. Nelson took his fleet to join with Cornwallis off Brest and then returned home in the *Victory* for a long overdue rest. His role in the campaign has not always been fully understood and it has even been suggested that his chase to the West Indies was foolhardy and risky and that he should, instead, have followed his fellow admirals northwards to the Channel. But such criticism is misplaced. Far from dashing impetuously after Villeneuve, Nelson spent almost a week in the mouth of the Straits of Gibraltar gathering information before he set off. By the time he began his voyage, he had established that the rest of the British fleets had gone northwards and he knew that the West Indies were defended by only a few ships. His decision to pursue Villeneuve was therefore based on a careful assessment of the risks. And his assessment was supported by Lord Barham, far away in London. Just a few days after Nelson had sailed, the First Lord sent orders to Collingwood to pursue the enemy, providing Nelson had not already done so. It was this sort of mutual understanding about the right course to follow, shared instinctively by the key British naval leaders, that thwarted Napoleon's ambitious scheme in 1805, rather than any great battle.

SEE ALSO
Calder, Cape Finisterre, Middleton, Toulon, Trafalgar, Villeneuve

LATEST RESEARCH
Robert Gardiner (ed), *The Campaign of Trafalgar*, Chatham Publishing (London 1997)
Alan Shom, *Trafalgar: Countdown to Battle*, Michael Joseph (London 1990)

Celebrating Trafalgar. Trafalgar veterans from the Naval Hospital at Greenwich (the buildings of which can be seen in the middle distance) gather to celebrate the anniversary of the battle.

Trafalgar Day ceremonies

The tradition of marking Trafalgar Day with special ceremonies and celebrations is a long-established one. By the 1840s, it had become the custom to decorate HMS *Victory*, then at anchor in Portsmouth Harbour serving as the flagship of the admiral superintendent of Portsmouth Dockyard, with laurel wreaths at her mastheads and another surrounding the plaque on the quarterdeck marking the spot where Nelson fell. In 1846, John Pasco, who as a lieutenant had supervised the hoisting of Nelson's famous signal, 'England expects', was appointed her captain. He held a special Trafalgar Dinner on board at which a toast was drunk, 'To the immortal memory of Nelson and those who fell with him.' Later in the nineteenth century, it became the practice to fly the 'England expects' signal from all the *Victory*'s available masts and yards. For many years, however, the flags were taken from the wrong codebook and it was not until 1908 that the mistake was noted and the correct flags substituted.

Similar customs were to be found elsewhere in Britain. In 1895, the Navy League – a patriotic pressure group formed explicitly to campaign for a stronger Navy – began the custom of holding a spe-

cial commemorative service in Trafalgar Square for which the column and lions were festooned with flags and laurel. In Penzance in Cornwall, which still vies with the neighbouring port of Falmouth for the honour of being the first place in Britain where the victory of Trafalgar was proclaimed in November 1805, a service was held in the old parish church to commemorate the arrival of the news.

Many of these traditions are continued today. A special service of remembrance is still held every Trafalgar Day on board HMS *Victory*, which is still decorated with laurel wreaths and the flags of 'England expects'. In the evening, a formal dinner is held in Nelson's cabin and the main toast after the meal is still 'The Immortal Memory'. Indeed, recently, Trafalgar Night dinners have become more common than ever before. They are now major annual events, not just in naval ships and establishments but in many sea-related organisations as well, and overseas as well as in Britain.

SEE ALSO
'England expects', 'Immortal Memory', Pasco, HMS *Victory*

LATEST RESEARCH
Colin White, 'The Immortal Memory', in his *The Nelson Companion*, Sutton and Royal Naval Museum (Stroud & Portsmouth 1995)

Troubridge, Sir Thomas (1758–1807)

Thomas Troubridge was one of Nelson's closest service friends, having known him since they were both fifteen, and they served together on a number of occasions. They were much alike, both in their gifts and in their temperaments, and this led eventually to friction between them. But, in 1797/8, they formed a remarkable fighting partnership that was directly responsible for two notable naval victories.

Although a Londoner by birth, and educated at St Paul's School, Troubridge was an Irishman by descent and always spoke with a touch of the brogue. He joined the Royal Navy in 1773 as an able seaman in the frigate HMS *Seahorse* under Captain George Farmer, in which he sailed to the East Indies. In her, he met the young Horatio Nelson and they served together for over two years, during which time they lived alongside each other in the gunroom. After Nelson had been invalided home in 1775, Trou-

Rear Admiral Sir Thomas Troubridge. This engraving, based on a portrait commissioned and owned by Lord St Vincent, shows Troubridge wearing his gold medals for the Battles of Cape St Vincent and the Nile and the Neapolitan order of St Ferdinand and Merit presented by the King of Naples for his part in the restoration of the monarchy in 1799.

bridge remained out in the east for another ten years, taking part in a number of naval actions and rising to lieutenant in 1781, commander in 1782 and post captain in 1783. He was given command of the frigate HMS *Active* and served in her at the Battle of Cuddalore (20 June 1783). Finally, he became flag captain to the commander-in-chief, Admiral Sir Edward Hughes, and returned home to Britain with him in 1785. It was a remarkable period of continuous active service that meant he was far more experienced in fleet actions, and the administration of large fleets, than his friend.

He then, like Nelson, had to endure five years of half pay but in 1790 he was sent out again to the East Indies in the frigate HMS *Thames* and then served in the Channel fleet in the frigate HMS *Castor*. In her, he was captured by a French squadron in May 1794 and, having been placed as prisoner in the French battleship *Sans Pareil*, was present on the French side during the Battle of the Glorious First of June. The *Sans Pareil* was captured and so Troubridge was able to return home, where he was rewarded with the command of the 74-gun battleship *Culloden* and sent out to join the Mediterranean fleet.

There he met up again with Nelson and so began their remarkable partnership that was to lead them to both triumph and defeat. Having been present at the unsatisfactory action with the French at Hyères (13/14 March 1795), under Admiral William Hotham, Troubridge then led the British fleet into action at Cape St Vincent (14 February 1797), driving his ship relentlessly into the gap between the two Spanish divisions and then joining with Nelson in the onslaught on the Spanish centre division that led eventually to the capture of four ships. The skill and gallantry that he displayed on that day confirmed him in Sir John Jervis's mind as one of the brightest of all his officers and from then on Jervis tended to regard, and to speak of, Nelson and Troubridge as equals.

The following year, Troubridge and Nelson served once more together at the abortive attack on Santa Cruz in Tenerife. Nelson treated Troubridge as his partner in the enterprise, entrusting the first landing to him and consulting with him regularly during the careful planning that preceded the attack. In the event, Troubridge's initial assault was frustrated by adverse winds and currents and, in a rare failure of nerve, he returned to Nelson for orders instead of acting on his own initiative. A recently discovered account of the attack suggests that he was actually very unwell at the time, which would account for his uncharacteristic hesitation.

In 1798, Troubridge served with Nelson for a fourth time, in the Nile campaign. Although James Saumarez was technically Nelson's second in command, it was Troubridge whom he consulted most and who was summoned most often to the flagship to discuss the pursuit of the French fleet, and the tactics to be used in any ensuing battle. So it was a cruel irony that, on the night of the battle itself, Troubridge's *Culloden* went aground on a reef at the entrance to Aboukir Bay and was not able to play any part in the fighting. Troubridge was distraught and Nelson (always good at supporting a comrade in misfortune) made sure that he was included in all the praise and rewards that were showered on the victorious captains.

Saumarez returned with the captured French ships to Britain and so Troubridge became Nelson's undisputed deputy. They collaborated again in the Neapolitan campaign of 1799, with Troubridge commanding the squadron that blockaded the city as Ruffo's force attacked from the land. Troubridge was more closely involved with fighting ashore than Nelson and appears to have shown a similar unattractive ruthlessness: on one occasion, regretting that he was unable to send his commander the head of one of the rebels because it was already decaying in the heat. Once Naples had been returned to the royalists, he led the attack on Rome and then, the following year, transferred to Malta where he assisted in the siege of the French in Valetta. In all these operations, he collaborated closely with Nelson, writing to him regularly and, on many occasions, acting as his official representative.

At the same time, the first traces of strain began to appear in their relationship. Troubridge dared to warn Nelson about the rumours that were beginning to circulate about him and Emma Hamilton and, as a result, he was seen by Emma – and so, inevitably, by Nelson – as one of those who opposed their friendship. The strain was increased further when, having returned home to recover from an attack of jaundice in 1800, Troubridge became St Vincent's captain of the fleet and then followed his patron to the Admiralty, as one of the Admiralty Board, when St Vincent became First Lord in February 1801. Nelson clearly was jealous, although he was not averse to using Troubridge as an unofficial contact and wrote him a number of private letters during the Baltic campaign, most of them highly critical of his senior officer, Sir Hyde Parker.

The final blow to their friendship came later that year when Nelson was given command of the special anti-invasion fleet in the Channel. As the war began to wind down and the opportunities for action became correspondingly few, Nelson was anxious to go on leave to join Emma, who was looking for a house for him, and he pestered the Admiralty and Prime Minister Henry Addington for his release. But St Vincent refused to let him go and gradually Nelson began to suspect that the old admiral and Troubridge were deliberately contriving to keep him away from Emma. In his frustration, he became very bitter, accusing Troubridge of ingratitude.

Previous accounts have suggested that the rift was never healed and certainly few letters have survived from Nelson to Troubridge dating from after 1800. However, Nelson did take Troubridge's son Edward into the *Victory* as a midshipman in July 1803, which suggests that some sort of rapprochement was reached. Troubridge himself was finally promoted to rear admiral in April 1804 and the following year was appointed commander-in-chief in his old station, the East Indies, hoisting his flag in an elderly battleship, HMS *Blenheim*. When the ship foundered in a gale off Madagascar in February 1807, there were no survivors and so it is presumed that he was drowned with the rest of his ship's company.

Like Nelson, Troubridge was an emotional man, much given to mood swings according to his circumstances, and this shared trait probably helped both to heighten their friendship and to exaggerate the rift when it occurred. But, essentially, each man admired the other greatly. Nelson wrote to St Vincent in 1798, '. . . I know he is my superior and I so often want his advice and assistance.' And in 1800, Troubridge wrote to Nelson, 'There is not a man on earth I love, honour or more esteem than your Lordship.'

SEE ALSO
'Band of Brothers', Cape St Vincent, Nile, Tenerife, Trafalgar

Turk's Island, Nelson's attack on (8 March 1783)

In 13 February 1783, as the War of American Independence (1778–1783) was nearing its close, about 150 French troops, supported by three warships, captured the small Turk's Island at the south-eastern extremity of the Bahamas. Nelson, then captain of the frigate HMS *Albemarle*, received news of the capture a fortnight later from Captain James King of the frigate HMS *Resistance* and, as senior officer, immediately decided to attempt to recapture the island. It was the first time he was in independent command of an operation and, like some of his later amphibious attempts, it ended in failure.

To start with, Nelson had a strong force with him, of three frigates and three smaller warships, so he felt confident that he could muster sufficient men to overwhelm the small French contingent. By the time he arrived off Turk's Island, one of his frigates and one of the smaller ships had parted company, thus reducing his force to parity with the French. Even so, he still sent in a flag of truce to demand the surrender of the island, receiving a contemptuous answer in reply.

Nelson now ordered a landing by 160 sailors and marines, under the command of Captain Charles Dixon, and ordered his smaller ships to cover them by bombarding the enemy's positions. But he had made the fundamental mistake of failing to reconnoitre the defences properly before ordering his attack and so he was unaware that the French had made very good use of their weeks ashore. Their troops were well entrenched, with covering fire from carefully placed field guns, and when the bombarding ships got close to the entrenchments, they suddenly found themselves under heavy fire from a hitherto unnoticed small battery. Faced with this unexpected opposition, the landing party's attack halted almost as soon as it had struggled ashore and Dixon sent to Nelson for further orders. Realising that the position was far too strong to be taken by the small force at his disposal, Nelson was forced to order an ignominious retreat.

It was a small incident, and is barely mentioned in most biographies of Nelson. But it showed that, in 1783, he still had much to learn about warfare. One of those who had taken part, Lieutenant James Trevenen, wrote scathingly, 'It was a ridiculous expedition, undertaken by a young man merely from the hope of seeing his name in the papers, ill depicted at first, carried on without a plan afterwards...'

SEE ALSO
Lord Hood

Vanguard, HMS

Nelson's flagship at the Battle of the Nile on 1 August 1798, HMS *Vanguard* was the fifth of ten Royal Navy ships that have borne the name. A Third Rate battleship, she was built at the Royal Dockyard at Deptford on the River Thames and launched on 6 March 1787. She was 168 feet long and carried 74 guns on two gun decks. 'Seventy-fours', as they were commonly called, were the backbone of the fleet at this time: for example, all but one of Nelson's fourteen battleships at the Battle of the Nile were of this type.

The *Vanguard* saw much active service in the Channel and the West Indies in the early part of the war with revolutionary France and then, in 1797, she was taken into Chatham Dockyard in Kent for an extensive refit. Nelson was in England at that time, recovering from the loss of his arm. He had been promised a new ship, HMS *Foudroyant*, as his next flagship but when he was pronounced fit for active service she was not ready and so the *Vanguard* was allocated to him instead, with his old friend Edward Berry as her captain. He hoisted his flag on board her at St Helen's, the anchorage off the eastern tip of the Isle of Wight, on 28 March 1798 and sailed a fortnight later for Cádiz.

Nelson was then sent in the *Vanguard* into the Mediterranean by the British commander-in-chief, Admiral Lord St Vincent, to discover, and if possible to destroy, the massive expeditionary force which the French were known to be assembling at their naval arsenal at Toulon on the south coast of France. Before he could do so, however, Nelson's small force was hit by a violent storm off Sardinia. The *Vanguard* lost her foretopmast and would have been wrecked had not Captain Alexander Ball in HMS *Alexander* managed to tow her out of danger.

The *Vanguard*'s crew effected temporary repairs and so she was still able to take part in the remarkable chase of the French fleet that ensued, culminating in the Battle of the Nile on the night of 1/2 August 1798.

She took a key role in the battle, capturing the *Spartiate*, the third ship in the French line. But she suffered a great deal of damage and so, after the battle, Nelson, who had himself been badly injured, decided to go in her to Naples where he could recover and his ship could be refitted. The *Vanguard* remained at Naples and it in was in her that Nelson evacuated the Neapolitan Royal family to Palermo in Sicily when Naples fell to the advancing French armies in December 1798. Eventually, in the summer of 1799, the *Foudroyant* arrived in the Mediterranean and Nelson transferred his flag to her on 9 June.

The *Vanguard* returned to England for an extensive refit. She saw service later in the Caribbean, and at the second battle of Copenhagen in 1807 and was converted into a receiving ship for housing men newly recruited or press-ganged into the Navy in 1812. She was finally broken up in 1821 after a career lasting forty-four years.

SEE ALSO
Ball, Berry, HMS *Foudroyant*, Naples, Nile

LATEST RESEARCH
The Nelson Society, HMS *Vanguard at the Nile*, The Nelson Society (1998)

Victory, HMS

Now the last surviving example of a ship of the line of the sailing era, the *Victory* owes her survival mainly to her close association with Nelson and the Battle of Trafalgar. But he served in her for only just over two years and, by that time, she was already a distinguished ship in her own right, with more than twenty years of active service to her credit and a number of battle honours.

The orders for the building of a new First Rate were given by the Board of Admiralty on 13 December 1758 and her keel was laid in Number Two Dock at Chatham Dockyard on 23 July 1759. She was designed by Sir Thomas Slade, surveyor of the Navy, a particularly able naval architect who was

'*The Flagship of Maritime Britain*'. *Nelson's great flagship* HMS Victory, *lovingly restored to her appearance at the time of Trafalgar and now open to the public in the Historic Dockyard at Portsmouth.*

responsible for some of the most successful ships of the Royal Navy of that period. Over 2000 oak trees were used in the construction of her hull – equivalent to some 60 acres of forest – and the final cost was £63,176 (over £50 million today).

The proposal to name her *Victory* was not universally

popular. The previous ship of that name had sunk with all hands off the Scillies in 1744 and so sailors believed that the name was unlucky. But the new ship was begun at the height of the Seven Years War (1756–1763) and 1759 saw such a remarkable series of British victories on land and sea that the year was nicknamed the *annus mirabilis* ('wonderful year'). Suddenly, the name seemed appropriate after all.

Building proceeded very slowly, so she was not launched until Tuesday 7 May 1765 and even then the hull remained at moorings 'in ordinary' (reserve) without being fitted out. This long period of weathering meant that her hull timbers were very well seasoned, which was one of the main reasons why she survived for so long. Finally, however, when war with America broke out, she was completed and prepared for active service, being commissioned for the first time in March 1778. Fitted for the first time with a full set of masts, she was given some 27 miles of rigging and four acres of sail. She was also equipped for the first time with guns: 104 in all.

She quickly proved a most successful ship. The excellent design of her underwater lines made her easily manoeuvrable despite her size and, in the right conditions, she could sail faster than many of her smaller consorts. These qualities made her a popular ship and she was constantly asked for by admirals: Augustus Keppel under whom she first saw action in an indecisive encounter off Cape Ushant in July 1778; Richard Kempenfelt and Lord Howe under whom she took part in the relief of Gibraltar in 1782.

Following a refit, and a period in ordinary during the peace, she was recommissioned in 1793 as the flagship of Lord Hood in the Mediterranean and took part in the capture of Toulon in 1793 and of Corsica in 1794. After another refit during the winter of 1794/5, she returned to the Mediterranean and, on 3 December 1795, became the flagship of the new commander-in-chief, Sir John Jervis. Under him, she was present at the Battle of Cape St Vincent (14 February 1797) and played a major part in the opening stages of the battle, when her broadsides repulsed a determined Spanish attack on the British line of battle. Badly battered in the action, and in any case now quite an elderly vessel, she was sent home at the end of 1797 and converted into a hospital ship. It seemed that her active service days were over.

However, when war broke out in 1803, following the brief Peace of Amiens, there was an urgent need for First Rate battleships and so the *Victory* was given a major repair and fitted out as Nelson's flagship, in which role she served throughout the long campaign that eventually culminated at Trafalgar in October 1805. During those two years she was never docked. All necessary repairs were carried out by her own ship's company, either at sea or in the sheltered waters of Agincourt Sound in the Maddalena Islands in Sardinia.

At Trafalgar, the *Victory* led Nelson's line into battle, coming under the concentrated broadsides of six French and Spanish ships during the long, slow approach. She was badly damaged, both in her masts and in her hull, so when she returned to Britain with Nelson's body on board, in December 1805 (see colour plate *XIII*), she was again given a major refit. Then, in 1808, she was commissioned as the flagship of Rear Admiral Sir James Saumarez for service in the Baltic, continuing in this role until November 1812, when she returned to Portsmouth and was again placed in ordinary.

After a period when her future seemed uncertain, the *Victory* was recommissioned in 1823 as the flagship of the port admiral at Portsmouth, lying permanently at anchor in the harbour. Sentiment played a key role in ensuring her survival and her association with Nelson was emphasised in a number of ways. A plaque on the quarterdeck marked the spot where he fell; the words of his famous signal were inscribed around the ship's wheel; and the cockpit where he died was arranged as a shrine. There was even a collection of Nelson relics on board, including the royal barge in which his body had been conveyed up the River Thames in the state funeral procession. She became a tourist attraction: visitors were rowed out to her by watermen and then conducted around the ship by old sailors. At around the same time, the custom grew of marking Trafalgar Day with special ceremonies on board and a dinner in the evening at which the toast to 'The Immortal Memory' was drunk. Later, in the mid-1890s, the custom began of flying the flags for 'England expects' from all her masts and yards on Trafalgar Day, although, to begin with, the flags were taken from the wrong signal code book. The mistake was only spotted, and rectified, in 1908.

HMS Victory, *c1890. For almost a hundred years, the* Victory *lay at anchor in Portsmouth Harbour. Even then, she was visited by tourists who were rowed out to her by watermen and then conducted around the ship by old sailors.*

Time was taking its toll and by the early 1920s she was in such poor condition that she was in danger of sinking. By now, too, successive refits and repairs had changed her appearance so much that she bore little resemblance to the ship that Nelson had known. So, the decision was taken to move her to a permanent home in drydock in Portsmouth Dockyard and to restore her to her condition at the time of the Battle of Trafalgar. Eventually, after six years of careful research and restoration, led by the Society for Nautical Research, she was opened to the public by King George V on 17 July 1928. However, she retained her status as a fully commissioned ship in the Royal Navy and, to this day, continues to serve as the flagship of the Second Sea Lord.

She has long been one of the main symbols of Britain's maritime heritage, celebrated in great paint-ings and poetry and in popular art and ephemera. She has been refitted and repaired so many times that, over the years, large amounts of wood have been taken out of her, much of which has been made into souvenirs. So there are now many pieces of the *Victory*, in many different forms, in national and private collections all over the world. However, perhaps the poignant relic of all is her 1805 foretopsail, peppered with shot holes of many sizes from the furious cannonade that enveloped her as she led the British fleet into action at Trafalgar.

SEE ALSO
Cape St Vincent, Hardy, Jervis, Mediterranean campaign, Portsmouth, Battle of Trafalgar, Trafalgar campaign, Trafalgar Day ceremonies, Saumarez

LATEST RESEARCH
Peter Goodwin, *Countdown to Victory*, Manuscript Press (Portsmouth 2000)
Alan McGowan, *HMS Victory: her construction, career and restoration*, Chatham Publishing (London 1999)

Villeneuve, Pierre, Comte de (1763–1806)

Villeneuve was twice opposed to Nelson: at the Battle of the Nile (1 August 1798) where he commanded the French rear division, and at Trafalgar (21 October 1805) when he was the commander-in-chief of the allied Franco-Spanish fleet. Born in 1763, he joined the French Royal Navy in 1778 and served throughout the American war. Despite his noble rank, he managed to remain in the Navy when many of his brother-nobles were removed and received rapid promotion, to captain in 1793 and rear admiral in 1796.

In 1797, he was third in command of the French fleet that escorted Napoleon's expedition to Egypt and managed to escape from the destruction of the Battle of the Nile with two battleships and two frigates. Following the death of Latouche Tréville in 1804, Villeneuve, by now a vice admiral, took command of the French Mediterranean fleet. In April 1805, he managed to elude Nelson's watching frigates and, escaping out of the Mediterranean, joined up with the Spanish fleet at Cádiz. He then led the combined force to the West Indies to play his part in Napoleon's masterplan for the invasion of Britain. In the event, however, no other French fleet was able to join him and, learning that Nelson was close behind, he returned to European waters. There, he was intercepted off Cape Finisterre by a British fleet under Sir Robert Calder, losing two ships before seeking shelter in the port of Ferrol on the northern Spanish coast.

Napoleon's plan now required that Villeneuve should appear off Brest and release the large French fleet there but, unnerved by Nelson's headlong pursuit, and by the way in which he had been so efficiently intercepted by Calder, Villeneuve felt unable to carry out his orders. He sailed instead for Cádiz, thus effectively ending Napoleon's hopes of invading Britain.

Napoleon's attention now transferred to Austria and, turning his so-called 'Army of England' around, he marched to attack her armies before they could be fully mobilised. To tie down some of the Austrian forces, he ordered his fleet to sail to Italy to create a diversion by attacking Austrian possessions there and, when Villeneuve continued to hesitate, ordered that he was to be replaced by Admiral Rosily. Hearing that Rosily was on his way, Villeneuve took his fleet to sea on 19 October 1805 in an attempt to retrieve his reputation.

Villeneuve knew that Nelson was in command of the British fleet outside Cádiz and he had, of course, seen Nelson in action before. So, before sailing, he issued battle orders to his fleet that showed an almost uncanny preknowledge of the tactics Nelson would use. He was, however, unable to suggest any way of countering them, contenting himself with exhorting his captains to rely on their 'love of glory' to see them through. He also added, 'The captain who is not in action, is not at his post', a striking echo of a phrase Nelson used in his own famous memorandum, 'No captain can do very wrong if he places his ship alongside that of any enemy.'

In the event, there was little that Villeneuve could do to prevent the disaster that overtook him and his comrades. Very early in the action, as Nelson had planned, his flagship the *Bucentaure* was knocked out of the fight, dismasted by the leading ships of Nelson's line, most of which sailed across her defenceless stern, pouring in their devastating broadsides. Unable to control his fleet by signal, Villeneuve attempted to move to another ship to continue the battle but found that all the *Bucentaure*'s boats were

shattered. He was therefore forced to surrender, less than two hours after the first shots had been fired.

After the battle, he was taken on board the frigate HMS *Euryalus*, in which Vice Admiral Collingwood was flying his flag, impressing his captors with the dignified way in which he accepted his fate. He was taken to Britain, where he was placed in open confinement in Bishop's Waltham in Hampshire. His captivity was not very arduous and he was even allowed up to London to witness Nelson's funeral in January 1806. Later that year, he was allowed to return to France, having been formally 'exchanged', but only a few days after his arrival, on 22 April, he was found dead in his hotel room in Rennes, stabbed through the heart. The official story was that he had committed suicide but the suspicion has always lurked that he had been murdered on the orders of Napoleon.

SEE ALSO
Bucentaure, Cape Finisterre, Trafalgar campaign, Battle of Trafalgar

LATEST RESEARCH
David Howarth, 'The man who lost Trafalgar', *The Trafalgar Chronicle* 9 (1999), The 1805 Club

Vice Admiral Pierre de Villeneuve. A French engraving, dating from about 1804.

Wales and the Midlands, Nelson's tour of (July/August 1802)

In the summer of 1802, when Britain was at peace following the Treaty of Amiens, Nelson and Sir William and Lady Hamilton travelled to Sir William's estates in Milford Haven in southwest Wales. Originally planned as a private visit, it quickly turned into a triumphant progress, in which Nelson was fêted and acclaimed wherever he went.

Leaving the house they shared at Merton on 21 July, the three friends, accompanied by their servants and members of Nelson's family, went first to Oxford where Nelson was given an Honorary Doctorate in Civil Law by the university. They then travelled west, via Gloucester, Ross-on-Wye, Monmouth, Llandovery and Carmarthen. The journey began badly when they called on the Duke of Marlborough at Blenheim Palace, only to be crudely snubbed and refused admission. However, thereafter the mood was very different: at each of their main stops there were enthusiastic crowds and hastily contrived civic ceremonies.

Having reached their destination and inspected Sir William's estates, they then returned via Swansea and Newport to Monmouth, arriving there on 18 August. Forewarned of their approach, the small town had arranged a series of events culminating in a grand banquet at which Nelson made one of his rare public speeches. Thanking his hosts for their hospitality and for the praise they had lavished on him, he said, 'In my own person I have received an overflowing measure of the Nation's gratitude, far more than I either merited or expected; because the same success would have crowned the efforts of any other British admiral who had under his command such distinguished officers and such gallant crews.' (see transcript on page 269.)

From Monmouth, the most direct way home lay back along the route they had come but, instead, Nelson and his party now decided to prolong their journey by visiting the Midlands. So they went on to Hereford, Worcester, Birmingham and Warwick before ending their tour with a formal call on Lord Spencer, formerly the First Lord of the Admiralty, at his grand house at Althorp. Again, wherever they went, crowds gathered – often removing the horses from Nelson's carriage to drag it through the streets – and special ceremonies were arranged. By the end of the tour, Nelson had been made a freeman of half a dozen towns and he had repeated his Monmouth speech as many times, always to great acclaim. It is clear from all the accounts that he was perfectly relaxed amid all the excitement and was good at 'working' a crowd, always appearing natural and approachable. For example, he frequently recognised former shipmates in the crush and singled them out for personal attention.

Even making allowances for the fact that many of the formal ceremonies were organised by local officials keen to capitalise on Nelson's fame, the tour was nonetheless a remarkable demonstration of spontaneous affection. Nelson had already enjoyed the adulation of the crowds in London, and in the naval ports, but this was the first time that he had experienced at first hand how popular he was with the population at large. It clearly affected him deeply. Shortly after his return, he wrote to Alexander Davison, '…the reward of general approbation and gratitude for my Services is an ample reward for all I have done.'

SEE ALSO
Amiens, Emma Hamilton, William Hamilton

LATEST RESEARCH
Edward Gill, *Nelson and the Hamiltons on tour*, Suttons (Stroud 1987)

Weatherhead, John (c1777–1797)

The son of the Reverend Thomas Weatherhead, rector of Sedgeford in Norfolk, John Weatherhead was one of a number of Norfolk boys who went to sea as midshipmen with Nelson in HMS *Agamemnon* in 1793. A handsome and friendly lad, he was much loved by all his colleagues, including Nelson, and whenever Nelson changed ships, Weatherhead went with him as one of his 'followers'. He was therefore present with Nelson throughout the long campaign in the Mediterranean and served ashore with him in Corsica in 1794, where he nearly died of a combination of malaria and dysentery.

Having fought at Nelson's side at the Battle of Cape St Vincent (14 February 1797) in HMS *Captain*, Weatherhead was promoted lieutenant and moved with his patron into the *Theseus*. He took part in the assault on Santa Cruz de Tenerife (July 1797) where he was in Nelson's boat in the night attack on 24/25 July. Despite the hail of shot and shell, he managed to get ashore onto the beach but was hit in the stomach and was found, close to death, by one of the Spanish defenders, Bernardo Cólogan, who tore up his shirt to make bandages and arranged for him to be returned to his ship in a special cradle. After lingering, apparently without pain, he eventually slipped away on 29 July. 'He was the Darling of the Ship's Company,' wrote his friend and fellow Norfolkman, Midshipman William Hoste, '& universally beloved by the every person who had the pleasure of his Acquaintance.' Chief among these was Nelson. Lacking sons of his own, and increasingly disappointed with his stepson Josiah Nisbet, he often bestowed paternal affection on promising young officers, and it was one of the tragedies of his life that he often lost them. He wrote to Weatherhead's father, '. . . Believe me I have largely partaken in our real cause for grief in the loss of a most excellent young man . . . when I reflect on that fatal night, I cannot but bring sorrow and his fall before my eyes.'

SEE ALSO
Hoste, Tenerife

Websites devoted to Nelson

Nelson's remarkable popularity has even extended to cyberspace. There are a number of sites on the World Wide Web devoted to him and his exploits and they are growing monthly: at the last count (September 2001) there were at least ten devoted exclusively to him and many more with Nelsonian connections.

The most extensive is the Nelson Society site www.nelson-society.org.uk, which currently features over 120 pages. There are essays by eminent Nelson scholars on some of Nelson's key battles, and other aspects of his life, and regular notices of Nelsonian events. Perhaps the most original is the site of The 1805 Club www.admiralnelson.org. This has been prepared as if Nelson himself was writing it and his life and career are told almost exclusively in his own words. It also includes extracts from Nelson's letters to Emma Hamilton, arranged so as to chart the development of their relationship. Finally, it has an excellent 'links' page, which takes the surfer on to all the other main 'Nelsonian' sites.

Wellington, Duke of (Arthur Wellesley) (1769–1852)

Wellington and Nelson never served together and they met only once, for about an hour. But it was Wellington who, in his great campaign in Spain between 1809 and 1814, reaped the harvest of what Nelson had sown at the Battle of Trafalgar (21 October 1805) and he was always keenly aware of how much he owed his success to the support of the Royal Navy.

Wellington served throughout the great war with France: first in the disastrous campaign in Flanders in 1794, then in India where he first won fame, particularly by his victory at the Battle of Assaye during the Second Mahratta War in 1803. Returning home in the autumn of 1805, he was in the waiting room of the offices of the secretary of state for war and the colonies, Lord Castlereagh, on the morning of 13 September. He was joined by Nelson and the two men talked briefly. Unfortunately, we have only Wellington's side of the story, told many years after the event, and he was characteristically disdainful of Nelson's initial conversation, which was 'in really a style so vain and silly as to surprise and almost disgust me.' But then Nelson left the room, apparently to find out the name of the man to whom he was talking, and when he returned, 'all that I thought a charlatan style had vanished . . . in fact he talked like an officer and a statesman.'

Indeed, although he did not appreciate it at the time, the young general had fallen under the spell of Nelson's remarkable charm. Ever afterwards, Wellington remembered him as 'a very superior man' and it is clear that, in the course of a brief half hour's conversation, Nelson managed to pass on to him a clear vision of what could be achieved by the imaginative use of seapower. Later, at the height of his campaign in Spain, in 1813, Wellington told one of Nelson's captains, Sir Thomas Byam Martin, 'If anyone wishes to know the history of this war, I will tell them that it is our maritime superiority gives me the power of maintaining my army while the enemy are unable to do so.'

SEE ALSO
Trafalgar campaign

William IV, King (1765–1837)

The third son of King George III, Prince William Henry, later the Duke of Clarence, was sent to sea in the Royal Navy in 1779. While serving as a midshipman in the battleship HMS *Barfleur* in the West Indies fleet in 1782, he met Nelson, then still a junior captain. The two formed a friendship, which was further cemented when they served together in the West Indies in 1786/7. Prince William, who had by then been given accelerated promotion to the rank of captain, commanded the frigate HMS *Pegasus*, with Nelson as his senior officer. So close did they become that, when Nelson married Frances Herbert on the island of Nevis on 11 March 1787, William attended the wedding and gave the bride away.

By then, however, the two men were already embroiled in a dispute that was to hold up Nelson's career for almost five years, when the Prince had a

Prince William, Duke of Clarence. This engraving shows the prince in about 1782, when he first met Nelson.

disagreement with his first lieutenant William Schomberg, and Nelson failed to defuse the potentially embarrassing incident. He also allowed the Prince to flout naval rules, thus earning the displeasure of the Admiralty and, indeed, of the King himself. So, between 1788 and 1793, Nelson was unable to get any employment, despite repeated requests.

Although promoted to rear admiral in 1790 (when still only twenty-five), William never served at sea again. But he always retained his bluff seaman's

Nelson's wounds. This pen and wash drawing by William Bromley captures the moment when Nelson was struck in the face by gravel thrown up by a French round shot during the siege of the Corsican town of Calvi, 12 July 1794.

manner and kept in touch with many of the officers with whom he had served, chief among them Nelson, with whom he kept up a regular correspondence on naval matters. He later made this correspondence available to Nelson's first official biographers, Clarke and M'Arthur, but it has recently been discovered that they suppressed a significant part of it, containing sensitive or secret material (see transcript on page 268). When Nelson died, William wrote to a friend, 'I do think it possible, but for one of my dearest relations, to have felt what I have, and still do, for poor Nelson.' He attended the funeral service in St Paul's Cathedral and, with his usual informality, left his place in the procession to shake the hand of Nelson's brother-in-law, George Matcham, saying, 'I am come to pay my last duties here, and I hope you and I shall never meet on such a like occasion.'

After a life troubled by political intrigue, family quarrels and doomed love affairs, he eventually became King, following the death of his elder brother, George IV, in 1830. He reigned over a tumultuous period in British political history with great dignity and passed on a stable monarchy to his niece Victoria. Although simple, down-to-earth and occasionally even rather comical, he nonetheless had an underlying decency that made him loved and he rejoiced in the title of 'The Sailor King'.

SEE ALSO
Funeral, Lord Hood, Frances Nelson, New York, Schomberg

LATEST RESEARCH
Tom Pocock, *Sailor King*, Sinclair-Stevenson (London 1991)
Colin White, 'The Nelson Letters Project', *The Mariner's Mirror* 87 (November 2001)

Wounds, Nelson's

In 1802, during the brief period of peace following the Treaty of Amiens, Nelson jotted down a list of his main wounds, 'His Eye in Corsica, His Belly off Cape St Vincent, His arm at Teneriffe, His Head in Egypt,' and then added ruefully, 'Tolerable for one war'. It was indeed a 'tolerable' list, one that no other senior officer could match. And, in fact, it was not even complete.

The first wound Nelson received was relatively

minor, so much so that he barely mentioned it and it is often omitted from accounts of his wounds, including his own. All that is known of it is from two brief references in his letters, from which we learn that he received a 'sharp cut in the back' during the siege of Bastia in Corsica. Even the date is uncertain, although it may have occurred on 12 April 1794 when, as he recorded in his journal, Captain Clerke of the Army was severely wounded, and a Corsican guide killed, by a roundshot fired from the French defences.

The next wound was much more serious. On 12 July 1794, while directing his ship's guns, set up in a shore battery during the siege of Calvi, a French shot struck the battery rampart in front of him driving a shower of earth, sand and pebbles into his face, lacerating it and badly damaging the eye. Characteristically, he made light of the incident in his letters home, and to Lord Hood, his commander-in-chief, and so it has tended to be presented as a relatively minor injury in most biographies. But a recently discovered letter reveals that he had to be carried out of the battery to his tent, which suggests that the actual blow was much more disabling than he admitted. The lacerations healed, leaving no visible sign other than a partially erased eyebrow, but the eye itself never recovered. To the end of his life, he could only distinguish light from dark with it and so it was virtually useless to him. Modern ophthalmological experts have tried to reconstruct exactly what caused the blindness and the most favoured theory would appear to be a severe internal haemorrhage; although a detached retina is also possible. What is certain, however, is that the eye itself remained intact, so that to all external appearances it was undamaged. There was certainly no need for him to wear the mythical eyepatch so beloved of modern film-makers and cartoonists.

Three years later, Nelson was again wounded, this time at sea, and during a major battle. At the height of the Battle of Cape St Vincent (14 February 1797), while in the thick of the action in HMS *Captain*, he

Nelson's wounds. William Bromley's pen and wash drawing of Nelson's wound at Tenerife was based on early accounts, which were inaccurate. In fact, Nelson was still in the boat when his arm was hit and the arm was not shot off, as shown here. However, like all Bromley's illustrations, this is a vivid and realistic impression of the scene.

was struck in the stomach by a large splinter of wood from a shattered rigging block. As at Calvi, he made light of the wound, reporting himself, for the benefit of the official casualty list, as 'bruised but not obliged to leave the deck.' Once again, modern research has revealed that the wound was rather more serious than he suggested. A recently discovered private account of the battle by the commanding officer of the *Captain*, Ralph Miller, has revealed that the blow was so severe that Nelson '…wou'd have fallen had not my arms support'd him.' He added, 'I was shockingly alarmed at the idea of losing him,' which suggests that it appeared to be serious, even fatal, at the time.

Following the battle, Nelson began to encounter problems with the wound and, reconstructing his symptoms, modern medical research suggests that he had suffered a severe abdominal trauma, which could have killed him. As it was, he was left with a weakness, or hernia, which troubled him for the rest of his life. Although normally dormant, it was exacerbated by coughing, when it would form a lump in his side the size of a man's fist, causing him considerable pain.

His next, and most disabling, wound was again the result of a shore operation: this time, an attack in boats on the town of Santa Cruz in Tenerife (24/25 July 1797). Nelson was struck in the upper right arm by a musket ball just as he was preparing to land from his boat, his arm raised to draw his sword. He was taken back to his flagship HMS *Theseus*, where the arm was immediately amputated, without anaesthetic. To begin with, the arm appeared to be healing well but complications set in and, eventually, he was forced to go home to Britain to recover. He was in such pain that he had to take opium every night in order to sleep, and he lost so much weight that he appeared almost emaciated and his normally sandy hair turned white temporarily. Eventually, however, after over four months of suffering, the arm healed almost overnight and he recovered very quickly. Thereafter, it appears to have given him little trouble, apart from occasional 'phantom' pains, usually linked to changes in the weather: indeed the stump soon became one of his trademarks. He gave it a nautical nickname, calling it his 'fin', and would use it humorously to identify himself to strangers. It was also a useful barometer for gauging his mood: his subordinates quickly noticed that, when he was agitated, it would twitch uncontrollably: 'The admiral is working his fin,' they would say, 'do not cross his hawse, I advise you!'

Less than a year after losing his arm, Nelson was again badly wounded, this time in the head, at the Battle of the Nile (1 August 1798), by a piece of flying scrap metal known as 'langridge'. On this occasion, there was no doubt about the seriousness of the wound: indeed he clearly thought it was fatal, collapsing into the arms of the captain of the *Vanguard*, Edward Berry, with the words, 'I am killed. Remember me to my wife.' A flap of skin from his damaged forehead had fallen over his good eye, blinding him with blood, and giving the impression that he was fatally hurt. In fact, although messy and very painful, the wound itself was fairly superficial, but for months afterwards he suffered splitting headaches and nausea.

His final, and fatal, wound at the Battle of Trafalgar (21 October 1805) was well documented at the time by the surgeon of HMS *Victory*, Dr William Beatty, and has been much analysed and discussed by medical experts ever since. Striking Nelson on the left shoulder with a force that threw him onto his knees, the French musket ball smashed two ribs and tore through his left lung, severing a major artery on the way. Then, having fractured his spine, it lodged beneath his right shoulder blade. Nelson felt death enter with it for, when the horrified Hardy bent over his stricken friend, he heard the rueful words, 'Hardy, I believe they have done it at last. My backbone is shot through.' He was taken below to the *Victory*'s cockpit where he took over three hours to die and, for most of that time, he was in agony. In the end, he died from massive internal bleeding, although even if the artery had not been severed, he would almost certainly have died from his spinal injuries. However, in that case, death would have taken even longer to release him from his pain.

SEE ALSO
Beatty, Calvi, Death, Eyepatch, Health, Nile, Tenerife

LATEST RESEARCH
Peter Gray, 'Turning a blind eye', *Trafalgar Chronicle* 10 (2001), The 1805 Club
Ann-Mary Hills, 'His Eye in Corsica', *The Nelson Dispatch* 6 (July 1998), The Nelson Society
———— , 'Nelson's wounds: the evidence of the artists', *The Nelson Dispatch* 7 (April 2000), The Nelson Society
Leslie LeQuesne, 'Nelson and his surgeons', *Journal of the Royal Naval Medical Service* 86 (2000)
Colin White, *1797: Nelson's Year of Destiny*, Sutton and Royal Naval Museum (Stroud & Portsmouth 1998)

The
Appendices

Nelson – *in his own words*

NELSON WAS a prolific, and very vivid, writer. This even applies to his official despatches, which are much less formal than those of his contemporaries. His ordinary letters, especially those addressed to friends and family, have a directness, and an engaging eagerness, that are close to actual speech. So, reading them, we can almost hear Nelson speaking.

The following documents have been chosen for the glimpses they give us of Nelson. Most are taken from his own correspondence and some have been discovered only recently and so are published here for the first time. Nelson's distinctive spelling, punctuation and capitalisation have been retained. The other passages have been included because they include glimpses of him seen through the eyes of his contemporaries, or describe key events in his life.

1. Nelson the wooer

It is often said that Nelson's relationship with his wife was rather cold and formal. In fact, many of his letters to her are full of affection and yearning for her company, as this one, written just six months before their marriage, demonstrates.

Boreas, English Harbour, August 19, 1786

My dearest Fanny,

Having seen in this day's newspaper that a vessel cleared out from St. John's to Nevis a few days ago, I feel vexed not to have had a letter in the office for you: however, if I can help it, I will not be behind-hand again. To write letters to you is the next greatest pleasure I feel to receiving them from you. What I experience when I read such as I am sure are the pure sentiments of your heart, my poor pen cannot express, nor indeed would I give much for any pen or head that could describe feelings of that kind: they are worth but little when that can happen. My heart yearns to you, it is with you, my mind dwells upon nought else but you. Absent from you, I feel no pleasure: it is you, my dearest Fanny, who are everything to me. Without you I care not for this world; for I have found lately nothing in it but vexation and trouble.

These you are well convinced are my present sentiments: God Almighty grant they may never change. Nor do I think they will: indeed there is, as far as human knowledge can judge a moral certainty they cannot: for it must be real affection that brings us together, not interest or compulsion which make so many unhappy.

Monday, seven in the evening; As you begin to know something about sailors, have you not often heard that salt water and absence always wash away love?? Now I am such a heretic as not to believe that faith: for behold every morning since my arrival, I have had six pails of salt water at day-light poured upon my head, and instead of finding what the seamen say to be true, I perceive the contrary effect: and if it goes on so contrary to the prescription, you must see me before my fixed time. At first I bore absence tolerably, but now it is almost insupportable; and by and by I expect it will be quite so. But patience is a virtue, and I must exercise it upon this occasion, whatever it costs my feelings. I am alone in the Commanding Officer's house, while my ship is fitting, and from sun-set until bed time I have not a human creature to speak to: you will feel a little for me I think. I did not use to be over fond of sitting alone. The moment old *Boreas* is habitable in my cabin, I shall fly to it, to avoid mosquitoes and melancholies. Hundreds of the former are now devouring me through all my clothes. You will, however, find I am better: though when you see me I shall be like an Egyptian mummy, for the heat is intolerable. But I walk a mile out at night without fatigue, and all day I am housed. A quart of goat's milk is also taken every day, and I enjoy English sleep, always barring mosquitoes, which all Frank's care with my net cannot keep out at present. What nonsense I am sending you. But I flatter myself the most trivial article concerning me, you feel inter-

264

ested in. I judge from myself; and I would rather have what passes in your mind, than all the news you could tell me, which did not concern you.

May every blessing attend my far better half and may I soon be with you, is the sincere wish of your most affectionate

Horatio Nelson

SOURCE
George Naish, *Nelson's Letters to his Wife*, Navy Records Society (London 1958)

2. The Battle of the Nile, 1/2 August 1798

Nelson wrote even his official despatches in a direct and vivid style, knowing that they would be published. He began this particular despatch himself while the Battle of the Nile was still raging and when he himself was recovering from a severe head wound.

Vanguard, off the Mouth of the Nile, 3 August 1798

My Lord,

Almighty God has blessed his Majesty's Arms in the late Battle, by a great Victory over the Fleet of the Enemy, who I attacked at sunset on the 1st of August, off the Mouth of the Nile.

The Enemy were moored in a strong Line of Battle for defending the entrance of the Bay, (of Shoals,) flanked by numerous Gun-boats, four Frigates, and a Battery of Guns and Mortars on an Island in their Van; but nothing could withstand the Squadron your Lordship did me the honour to place under my command. Their high state of discipline is well known to you, and with the judgment of the Captains, together with their valour, and that of the Officers and Men of every description, it was absolutely irresistible. Could anything from my pen add to the character of the Captains, I would write it with pleasure, but that is impossible.

I have to regret the loss of Captain Westcott of the *Majestic*, who was killed early in the Action; but the Ship was continued to be so well fought by her First Lieutenant, Mr. Cuthbert, that I have given him an order to command her till your Lordship's pleasure is known.

The Ships of the Enemy, all but their two rear Ships, are nearly dismasted: and those two, with two Frigates, I am sorry to say, made their escape; nor was it, I assure you, in my power to prevent them. Captain Hood most handsomely endeavoured to do it, but I had no Ship in a condition to support the *Zealous*, and I was obliged to call her in.

The support and assistance I have received from Captain Berry cannot be sufficiently expressed. I was wounded in the head, and obliged to be carried off the deck; but the service suffered no loss by that event: Captain Berry was fully equal to the important service then going on, and to him I must beg leave to refer you for every information relative to this Victory. He will present you with the Flag of the Second in Command, that of the Commander-in-Chief being burnt in *L'Orient*.

Herewith I transmit you Lists of the Killed and Wounded, and the Lines of Battle of ourselves and the French.

I have the honour to be, my Lord, your Lordship's most obedient Servant,

Horatio Nelson

SOURCE
Nicholas Harris Nicolas, *The Dispatches and Letters of Vice Admiral Lord Nelson*, Henry Colburne (London 1844–1846), Vol III, pp56–57

3. Nelson gives thanks for the victory at the Battle of the Nile

Nelson never claimed all the credit for his victories. As these two memoranda, written immediately after the Battle of the Nile, show, he also acknowledged the assistance he had received from his officers and men – and from God!

TO THE RESPECTIVE CAPTAINS OF THE SQUADRON

Vanguard off the Mouth of the Nile, 2nd day of August, 1798

Almighty God having blessed His Majesty's Arms with Victory, the Admiral intends returning Public Thanksgiving for the same at two o'clock this day; and he recommends every Ship doing the same as soon as convenient.

Horatio Nelson

To the Captains of the Ships of the Squadron

Vanguard, off the Mouth of the Nile, 2nd day of August, 1798

The Admiral most heartily congratulates the Captains, Officers, Seamen, and Marines of the Squadron he has to honour to command, on the event of the late Action; and he desires they will accept his most sincere and cordial Thanks for their very gallant behaviour in this glorious Battle. It must strike forcibly every British Seaman, how superior their conduct is, when in discipline and good order, to the riotous behaviour of lawless Frenchmen.

The Squadron may be assured the Admiral will not fail, with his Dispatches, to represent their truly meritorious conduct in the strongest terms to the Commander-in-Chief,

Horatio Nelson

Source
Nicolas, *op cit*, Vol III, p61

4. Nelson in action

Nelson was a very impulsive, eager man, who exuded energy and retained to the end of his life an engaging boyish enthusiasm. He could also be irritable and short-tempered when things went wrong.

Most contemporary accounts of Nelson are rather too conscious of his status as a hero and so he usually comes over as rather wooden and even aloof. A rare exception is this marvellous account of Nelson – complete with Norfolk accent – directing the chase of Le Généreux, *one of the French battleships that had escaped from the Battle of the Nile. It was written by one of his midshipmen, George Parsons.*

February 18, 1800

'Deck there!! The stranger is evidently a man of war – she is a line of battleship, my lord, and going large on the starboard tack.'

'Ah! An enemy, Mr Staines. I pray God it may be *Le Généreux*. The signal for a general chase Sir Ed'ard [the Nelsonian pronunciation of Edward], make the *Foudroyant* fly!'

Thus spoke the heroic Nelson and every exertion that emulation could inspire was used to crowd the squadron with canvas, the *Northumberland* taking the lead, with the flagship close on her quarter.

'This will not do, Sir Ed'ard; it is certainly *Le Généreux* and to my flagship she can alone surrender. Sir Ed'ard, we must and shall beat the *Northumberland*.'

'I will do my utmost my lord; get the engine to work on the sails – hand butts of water to the stays – pipe the hammocks down and each man place shot in them – slack the stays, knock up the wedges and give the masts play – start off the water, Mr James, and pump the ship. The *Foudroyant* is drawing ahead and at last takes the lead in the chase. The admiral is working his fin (the stump of his right arm), do not cross his hawse I advise you.'

The advice was good, for at this moment, Nelson opened furiously on the quartermaster at the conn, 'I'll knock you off your perch you rascal if you are so inattentive. Sir Ed'ard, send your best quartermaster to the weather wheel.'

'A strange sail ahead of the chase!' called the lookout man.

'Youngster, to the masthead. What! going without your glass and be damned to you? Let me know what she is immediately.'

'A sloop of war or frigate, my lord,' shouted the young signal midshipman.

'Demand her number.'

'The *Success* my lord.'

'Captain Peard. Signal to her to cut off the flying enemy – great odds though – thirty-two small guns to eighty large ones.'

'The *Success* has hove-to athwart-hawse of the *Généreux* and is firing her larboard broadside. The Frenchman has hoisted his tricolour with a rear admiral's flag.'

'Bravo – *Success*, at her again!'

'She has wore round my lord, and firing her starboard broadside. It has winged her, my lord – her flying kites are flying away together. The enemy is close on the *Success* who must receive her tremendous broadside.'

The *Généreux* opens her fire on her little enemy and every person stands aghast, afraid of the consequences. The smoke clears away and there is the *Success*, crippled it is true, but bull-dog like, bearing up after the enemy.

'The signal for the *Success* to discontinue the action and come under my stern,' said Lord Nelson, 'she has done well for her size. Try a shot from the lower deck at her Sir Ed'ard.'

'It goes over her.'

'Beat to quarters and fire coolly and deliberately at her masts and yards.'

The *Généreux* at this moment opened her fire on us; and as a shot passed through the mizzenstaysail, Lord Nelson patting one of the youngsters on the head asked him jocularly how he relished the music; and observing something like alarm depicted on his countenance, consoled him with the information that Charles XII ran away from the first shot he heard, though afterwards he was called 'The Great', and deservedly from his bravery. 'I therefore,' said Lord Nelson, 'hope much from you in future.'

Here the *Northumberland* opened her fire and down came the tricoloured ensign, amidst the thunder of our united cannon.

SOURCE
George Parsons, *Nelsonian Reminiscences*, Gibbings (London 1905; new edition Chatham Publishing, London 1998)

5. Nelson the leader

Nelson was loved by most of those who served with him. This recently discovered letter, written to Captain Sir Narbonne Thompson, son of Admiral Sir Charles Thompson who had served with Nelson at the Battle of Cape St Vincent, demonstrates why. Note the phrase ' the children of departed officers are a natural legacy to the survivors' – Nelson always did his best to assist the careers of the sons of former colleagues. The letter is transcribed exactly as Nelson wrote it.

Victory febry: 22nd: 1804

Dear Sir

It was only this day that I received your letter of Sept: 30th: and I can assure you that if there was the smallest chance of promotion by your coming to the Medn: I should receive you with pleasure but circumstanced as I am the prospect at present would be hopeless unless with a Admiralty order for promotion. However the time may arrive when if you are

not promoted (but which I sincerely hope will not be the case) it may be in my power to be useful to you and you have my full permission to make application to me. For although I had not the honor of being very intimate with your worthy Father yet I had known him several years as an honor to the Service and I feel that the children of departed officers are a natural Legacy to the survivors. With these sentiments you are sure of the sincere good wishes and services of Dear Sir Your faithful Servant

Nelson & Bronte

I remember you most perfectly in the *Prince George* and have often been pleased to hear so good an account of you as a gentleman and an officer

SOURCE
Nelson Museum, Monmouth: E525

6. Nelson the lover

Nelson and Emma Hamilton became lovers in early 1800 and their first child, Horatia, was born in January 1801. Nelson left his wife and set up home with the Hamiltons. But he was often absent at sea and so the lovers kept up an almost daily correspondence. Nelson burned Emma's letters but she kept all of his and so we have an intimate record of the progress of their affair. In this letter, written shortly after the birth of Horatia, Nelson pours out his love and sexual passion for the woman he now regards as 'my own dear wife.'

March 1st, 1801, 9 o'clock

Now my own dear wife for such you are in my eyes and in the face of heaven I can give full scope to my feelings, for I daresay Oliver will faithfully deliver this letter. You know, my dearest Emma, that there is nothing in this world that I would not do for us to live together, and to have our dear little child with us. I firmly believe that this campaign will give us peace, and then we will set off for Bronte. In twelve hours we shall be across the water and freed from all the nonsense of his [*ie* Sir William Hamilton's] friends, or rather pretended ones.

Nothing but an event happening to him could prevent my going, and I am sure you will think so, for unless all matters accord it would bring 100 of tongues and slanderous reports if I separated from her [*ie* Lady Nelson] (which I would do with pleasure the moment we can be united; I want to see her no more), therefore we must manage till we can quit this country or your uncle [Sir William] dies. I love, I never did love any one else. I never had a dear pledge of love till you gave me one, and you, thank my God, never gave one to any body else.

I think before March is out you will either see us back, or so victorious that we shall insure a glorious issue to our toils. Think what my Emma will feel at seeing return safe, perhaps with a little more fame, her own dear loving Nelson. Never if I can help it, will I dine out of my ship, or go on shore, except duty calls me. Let Sir Hyde [Parker] have any glory he can catch – I envy Him not. You, my beloved Emma, and my country, are the two dearest objects of my fond heart – <u>a heart susceptible and true.</u> Only place confidence in me and you never shall be disappointed.

I burn all your dear letters, because it is right for your sake, and I wish you would burn all mine – they can do no good, and will do us both harm if any seizure of them, or the dropping even one of them, would fill the mouths of the world sooner than we intend.

My longing for you, both person and conversation, you may readily imagine. What must be my sensations at the idea of sleeping with you! It setts me on fire, even the thoughts, much more would the reality. I am sure my love & desires are all to you, and if any woman naked were to come to me, even as I am this moment from thinking of you, I hope it might rot off if I would touch her even with my hand. No, my heart, person, and mind is in perfect union of love towards my own dear, beloved Emma the <u>real bosom</u> friend of her, all hers, all Emma's.

I had a letter this day from the Rev. Mr. Holden, who we met on the Continent; he desired his kind compliments to you and Sir William: he sent me the letters of my name, and recommended it as my motto – <u>Honor est a Nilo</u> – HORATIO NELSON. May the Heavens bless you my love, my darling angel, my heaven-given wife, the dearest only true wife of her own till death.

<u>Monday morning.</u> – Oliver is just going on shore; the time will ere long arrive when Nelson will land to fly to his Emma, to be for ever with her. Let that

hope keep us up under our present difficulties. Kiss and bless <u>our</u> dear Horatia – think of that.

SOURCE
Alfred Morrison, *The Hamilton and Nelson papers*, Privately printed (1893/4)

7. Nelson at Copenhagen

Nelson wrote more about Copenhagen than any of his other battles. His official account was a short 700-word despatch to Sir Hyde Parker detailing the main events but he also wrote a number of personal accounts, to various friends, that provide a fascinating contrast to the more formal public version. Among them were three to his friend William, Duke of Clarence (later King William IV). These letters were later omitted from the published editions of Nelson's correspondence, probably because they contain references to Nelson's conversations with the Danish Crown Prince Frederick on 3 April 1801. In 1808, Frederick (who was Clarence's first cousin) became King of Denmark, following the death of his father, Christian VII. Clarence and his advisors may have felt that it was not a tactful moment to publish Nelson's controversial opinions. This transcript was taken from the original manuscript.

St George April 4th 1801

Sir

I believe I may congratulate Your Royal Highness on the recent success of our Incomparable Navy which I trust has not tarnish'd its ancient splendour. It was my good fortune to Command such a very distinguish'd sett of fine fellows, and to have the arrangement of the attack. The loss of services in the stations assigned to them of three sail by their getting on shore prevented our success being so compleat as I intended, but I thank God under those very untoward circumstances for what has been done.

I send Your Royal Highness a list of the Enemy's force as they lay from the Southward to the Crown islands. On the 3rd I had a long conference with His Royal Highness the Prince Royal of Denmark and he was so good as to allow me to state fully my opinion on the present state of Denmark and we considered its unnatural and unprovoked alliance agst us. His assurances always went that his Intentions where [*sic*] perfectly misunderstood that his uncle [George III] had been deceived and that he never would be the

Enemy of England that all his object was to protect his Commerce & to be at peace with all the world however H R Hs requested we would suspend hostilities 'till he could call a Council & endeavour to make some sensible propositions, so we parted and this Evening I expect he will send them to Sir Hyde. I am not very sanguine as to its making a peace for they are now afraid of the Russians.

Our ships are refitting some must go to England & the rest will in 4 days certainly be ready for any Service. I can assure Your R H that since the 24th of March I have not had scarcely any Sleep or rest either of body or mind, I could say much which would be improper to put to paper. I hope to be in England by the middle of May if we are allowed to go on very soon agt Revel I trust it will be a Blockade of Cronstad for the summer when I shall quit, for my Constitution is gone and it is only the Spirit of duty to my Sovereign & Country that enables me to stand up against all I have had to encounter. I do not mean all here part has been in England but why should I trouble you with my grievances. May Every Blessing be pour'd on Your Royal Highness's head and Believe Me as Ever Your Most attached and faithful servant

Nelson & Bronte

His Royal Highness Duke of Clarence

Apl 5th from appearances I believe we must do to War again with Denmark they are this day got to work again on their fortifications

SOURCE
British Library, Add Ms 46356, f37

8. Nelson the public speaker

Nelson was away at sea for so much of his life that there were not many opportunities for him to make public speeches. However, in 1802, during the brief Peace of Amiens, he made a triumphal tour of South Wales and the Midlands with the Hamiltons. He was often called upon to speak at public dinners and appears to have had a 'stock' speech which he gave, with small variations, everywhere. This is a version of it that he used at a dinner in Monmouth.

Gentlemen I beg leave to return you my most respectful thanks for the honour done me in drinking my health and also for the acknowledgement of the important public services you are pleased to say I have rendered the country. It was my good fortune to have under my command some of the most experienced officers in the English Navy, whose professional skill was seconded by the undaunted courage of British sailors: and whatever merit might attach itself to me, I must declare that I had only to show them the enemy and Victory Crowned the Standard!

In my own person I have received an overflowing measure of the Nation's gratitude, far more than I have either merited or expected; because the same success would have crowned the efforts of any British Admiral who had under his command such distinguished officers and such gallant crews.

Gentlemen I shall now speak to you as an Englishman: if war was again to take place I should send every ship, every regular soldier out of the kingdom and leave the nation to be protected entirely by the courage of her sons at home. In all the histories of Kingdoms and States that I have read it was the want of unanimity among themselves that produced their fall and that alone will be able to effect the overthrow of our own. For so long as the people continue to unite Hand and Heart (as we have seen with the late threatened invasion by the French) we have nothing to fear either from their efforts or from those of all the world united in arms against us.

SOURCE
Edward Gill, *Nelson and the Hamiltons on tour*, Sutton (Stroud 1987)

9. Nelson the father

Nelson adored children and one of the sadnesses of his marriage to Fanny Nelson was that they did not have any children of their own. So when Emma Hamilton bore him a daughter, he was delighted and could not for long maintain the fiction that he was her 'godfather'. Here, in his first letter to her, written when she was just two and a half years old, he openly acknowledges his relationship to her.

Victory, off Toulon, October 21st, 1803

My dear child,
Receive this first letter from your most affectionate Father. If live, it will be my pride to see you virtuously brought up; but if it pleases God to call me, I

trust to Himself: in that case, I have left Lady H. your guardian. I therefore charge you, my Child, on the value of a Father's blessing, to be obedient and attentive to all her kind admonitions and instructions.

At this moment I have left you, in a Codicil dated the 6th of September, the sum of four thousand pounds sterling, the interest of which is to be paid to your guardian for your maintenance and education.

I shall only say, my dear Child, may God Almighty bless you and make you an ornament to your sex, which I am sure you will be if you attend to all Lady H.'s kind instructions; and be assured that I am, my dear Horatia, your most affectionate Father,

Nelson and Bronte

SOURCE
Nicolas, *op cit*, Vol V, p260

10. Nelson the administrator

In May 1803, Nelson was appointed commander-in-chief of the Mediterranean, one of the most important posts in the Royal Navy. As well as watching the French and Spanish fleets, and keeping his own fleet well supplied and in fighting trim, he also had to play a pivotal role in the complex diplomacy of the region, keeping in touch with allies and friendly powers and watching over the activities of pirates operating out of ports of the North African coast. During his two years in command – during which time he never set foot on shore – Nelson showed that he was a skilled administrator as well as a fighting admiral.

This letter, written to Sir Evan Nepean, the secretary to the Admiralty, gives a good idea of the many different balls he had to keep in the air at any one time. This transcript was taken from the original manuscript.

Victory Janry: 14th: 1804

Private

My Dear Sir Evan

I am truly sorry to find by your kind note that you have been so much indisposed, but as the spring gets on I hope you will be perfectly well, and keep so, your King, County, (& friends) all in their several stations benefit so much by your ability and kindness that none of the three partys can spare you.

I bow of course with all due defferance [*sic*] to their

Lordships superior wisdom, but cannot alter my opinion, the upper works of the *Gibraltar* being fir & her Bottom Mahogany the upper works are actually seperating from her bottom. The *Kent* is very bad. *Renown* we have just coiled her with <u>three</u> Inch rope she will soon be ruined. *Superb* we have with large Iron bolts and frappings kept her Scarf of the Stem in its place. I can have no wish to part with the very finest ships in the service and the best manned, it could only be from a wish to save them for future service. I shall complain no more, I ought at this time of Service to know what Ships and Men can do.

By desire of Lord Hobart [the Foreign Secretary] I correspond with him on the state of the different powers in this Country, therefore I will [not] trouble you with a repitition, but this I have asserted that if we do not seize Sardinia France will have it. I am now keeping it from Invasion (8000 men are ready to start from Corsica) by my keeping Vessels constantly at Madalena, but the French will soon have it in spite of me.

I have just received the Thanks of Sir Thos: Trigge for my constant care and attention for the comfort of the [Gibraltar] garrison and that they have ample protection for <u>their</u> trade. There are times when as any Sea Officer knows the Navy could not protect a merchant vessel from Row boats, and Tangier and [*illegible*] being except at particular moments the very worst positions for protecting the Trade. Tariffa, Cabrista Point, & Ceuta are the places to watch.

I am always my Dear Sir your most obliged friend

Nelson & Bronte

I hope the French fleet will now soon put to sea

SOURCE
Lloyds Collection, L187

11. Nelson describes to Emma Hamilton his arrival with the fleet off Cádiz

Following a brief spell of leave in England after his epic chase of the French to the West Indies, in the summer of 1805, Nelson was sent back out to Cádiz to command the fleet assembled there to counter the threat posed by the large

Combined Franco-Spanish fleet. He arrived on 28 September and, the following day, his forty-seventh birthday, he gave a dinner party in the Victory *at which he explained his plans for fighting the expected battle. Here, he describes to Emma his arrival and the effect his plan had on his captains. Parts of this famous letter have been published many times before; but this is the first time that the complete letter – including the private passages intended for Emma at the end of the first paragraph – has been published.*

Victory, October 1ˢᵗ, 1805

My dearest Emma,

It is a relief to me, to take up the Pen, and write you a line for I have had, about 4 o'clock this morning, one of my dreadful spasms, which has almost enervated me, it is very odd I was hardly ever better than yesterday. Fremantle stayed with me till eight o'clock, and I slept uncommonly well; but was awoke with this disorder. My opinion of its effect, some one day has never altered, however, it is entirely gone off, and I am only quite weak but I do assure you my Emma that the uncertainty of human life makes the situation of you and dear Horatia dearest to my affectionate heart, you and Horatia fly to my mind and my last breath happen when it will, will be offered up in a prayer for a blessing on you.

The Good people of England will not believe that rest of body and mind is necessary for me. But perhaps this spasm may not come again these six months. I had been writing seven hours yesterday perhaps that had some hand in bringing it upon me.

I got round Cape St Vincent the 26ᵗʰ but it was the 28ᵗʰ before I got off Cadiz and joined Adl Collingwood but it was so late I did not communicate 'till next morning.

I believe my arrival was most welcome, not only to the Commander of the Fleet, but also to every individual in it; and, when I came to explain to them the Nelson touch, it was like an electric shock. Some shed tears all approved, it was new, it was singular, it was simple and, from Admirals downwards, it was repeated, it must succeed, if ever they will allow us to get at them. You are, my Lord surrounded by friends who you inspire with confidence. Some my dear Emma may be Judas's but the majority are certainly much pleased with my commanding them.

The Enemy's fleet is 35 or 36 sail of the Line in Cadiz, the french have given the Dons an old 74 to repair and taken possession of the *Santa Anna* of 112 guns. [Admiral] Louis is going into Gibraltar and Tetuan to get supplies of which the fleet is much in want and Admiral Knight as I am told has almost made us quarrel with the Moors of Barbary however I am sending Mr Ford and money to put us right again. God bless you Amen Amen Amen

SOURCE
British Library, Eg 1614

12. Nelson's plan of attack at Trafalgar

Over dinner on 29 September 1805, Nelson explained his brilliant tactical plan to his captains. He then wrote this famous memorandum, setting out his ideas in detail.

(Secret) *Victory*, off Cadiz, 9ᵗʰ October, 1805

Memorandum.

Thinking it almost impossible to bring a Fleet of forty Sail of the Line into a Line of Battle in variable winds, thick weather, and other circumstances which must occur, without such a loss of time that the opportunity would probably be lost of bringing the Enemy to Battle in such a manner as to make the business decisive, I have therefore made up my mind to keep the Fleet in that position of sailing (with the exception of the First and Second in Command) that the Order of Sailing is to be the Order of Battle, placing the Fleet in two Lines of sixteen Ships each, with an Advanced Squadron of eight of the fastest sailing Two-decked Ships, which will always make, if wanted, a Line of twenty-four Sail, on whichever Line the Commander-in-Chief may direct.

The Second in Command will, after my intentions are made known to him, have the entire direction of his Line to make the attack upon the Enemy, and to follow up the blow until they are captured or destroyed.

If the Enemy's Fleet should be seen to windward in Line of Battle, and that the two Lines and the Advanced Squadron can fetch them, they will probably be so extended that their Van could not succour their Rear.

I should therefore probably make the Second in

Command's signal to lead through, about their twelfth Ship from their Rear, (or wherever he could fetch, if not able to get so far advanced); my Line would lead through about their Centre, and the Advanced Squadron to cut two or three or four Ships a-head of their Centre, so as to ensure getting at their Commander-in-Chief, on whom every effort must be made to capture.

The whole impression of the British Fleet must be to over-power from two or three Ships a-head of their Commander-in-Chief, supposed to be in the Centre, to the Rear of their Fleet. I will suppose twenty Sail of the Enemy's Line to be untouched, it must be some time before they could perform a manoeuvre to bring their force compact to attack any part of the British Fleet engaged, or to succour their own Ships, which indeed would be impossible without mixing with the Ships engaged.

Something must be left to chance; nothing is sure in a Sea Fight beyond all others. Shot will carry away the masts and yards of friends as well as foes; but I look with confidence to a Victory before the Van of the Enemy could succour their Rear, and that the British Fleet would most of them be ready to receive their twenty Sail of the Line, or to pursue them, should they endeavour to make off.

If the Van of the Enemy tacks, the Captured Ships must run to leeward of the British Fleet; if the Enemy wears, the British must place themselves between the Enemy and the Captured, and disabled British Ships; and should the Enemy close, I have no fears as to the result.

The Second in Command will in all possible things direct the movements of his Line, by keeping them as compact as the nature of the circumstances will admit. Captains are to look to their particular Line as their rallying point. But, in case Signals can neither be seen or perfectly understood, no Captain can do very wrong if he places his Ship alongside that of an Enemy.

Of the intended attack from to windward, the Enemy in Line of Battle ready to receive an attack. [For the rough diagram which Nelson inserted here, see Nicolas, Vol VII p91.]

The divisions of the British Fleet will be brought nearly within gun shot of the Enemy's Centre. The signal will most probably then be made for the Lee Line to bear up together, to set all their sails, even steering sails, in order to get as quickly as possible to the Enemy's Line, and to cut through, beginning from the 12 Ship from the Enemy's Rear. Some Ships may not get through their exact place, but they will always be at hand to assist their friends; and if any are thrown round the Rear of the Enemy, they will effectually complete the business of twelve Sail of the Enemy.

Should the Enemy wear together, or bear up and sail large, still the twelve Ships composing, in the first position, the Enemy's Rear, are to be *the* object of attack of the Lee Line, unless otherwise directed from the Commander-in-Chief, which is scarcely to be expected, as the entire management of the Lee Line, after the intentions of the Commander-in-Chief, is signified, is intended to be left to the judgment of the Admiral commanding that Line.

The remainder of the Enemy's Fleet, 34 Sail, are to be left to the management of the Commander-in-Chief, who will endeavour to take care that the movements of the Second in Command are as little interrupted as is possible.

Nelson and Bronte

SOURCE
Nicolas, *op cit*, Vol VII, pp89–92

13. Nelson's last letter to Emma Hamilton

The Combined French and Spanish fleets emerged from Cádiz on 19 October and Nelson gave chase with his fleet until he finally intercepted them on the morning of 21 October. During those busy days, he found time to write this brief letter to Emma. It was left opened and unfinished on his desk. The version reproduced here has been taken directly from Nelson's manuscript. Note that he wrote 'Traf-la-gar' – this suggests he may have pronounced the name of the Cape in the correct Spanish fashion and not in the anglicised way common today.

Victory Octr: 19th: 1805
Noon Cadiz ESE 16 Leagues

My Dearest beloved Emma the dear friend of my bosom the Signal has been made that the Enemy's Combined fleet are coming out of Port. We have very little Wind so that I have no hopes of seeing them before to-morrow. May the God of Battles crown my endeavoùrs with success at all events I will take care that my name shall ever be most dear to you and Horatia both of whom I love as much as my own life, and as my last writing before the battle will be to you so I hope in God that I shall live to finish my letter after the Battle. Mayʹ Heaven bless you prays your Nelson & Bronte.

Octr. 20th in the morning we were close to the mouth of the Streights but the Wind had not come far enough to the Westward to allow the Combined fleets to Weather the shoals off Traflagar [*sic*] but they were counted as far as forty Sail of Ships of War which I suppose to be 34 of the Line and six frigates, a Group of them was seen off the Lighthouse of Cadiz this Morng. but it blows so very fresh & thick weather that I rather believe they will go into the Harbour before Night. May God Almighty give us success over these fellows and enable us to get a Peace.

Endorsed by Emma Hamilton

This letter was found open on <u>His</u> desk & brought to Lady Hamilton by Capn Hardy.

Oh miserable wretched Emma
Oh glorious & happy Nelson

SOURCE
Oliver Warner, *Nelson's Last Diary*, Seeley Service (London 1971), pp73–75

14. Nelson's last prayer

Early in the morning of 21 October, Nelson wrote a prayer in his private pocket book, which summed up his feelings at the climatic moment in his career. Clearly anxious that it should be preserved for posterity, he then made an exact copy of it. His instinct was right: the prayer has long been admired as one of the finest ever penned by a fighting man and it is still read out every Trafalgar Day on the quarter-deck of HMS Victory and in countless other church services all over the world. The version reproduced here has been taken directly from Nelson's manuscript.

Monday Octr 21st 1805 at day Light saw the Enemys Combined fleet from East to E.S.E bore away made the Signal for Order of Sailing, and to prepare for Battle the Enemy with their heads to the Southward, at seven the Enemy wearing in succession.

May the Great God whom I worship Grant to my Country and for the benefit of Europe in General a great and Glorious Victory, and may no misconduct in any one tarnish it, and may humanity after Victory be the predominant feature in the British Fleet. For myself individually I commit my life to Him who made me, and may his blessing light upon my endeavours for serving My Country faithfully, to Him I resign myself and the Just cause which is entrusted to me to Defend. Amen. Amen. Amen.

SOURCE
Oliver Warner, *op cit*, pp58–60

15. Chaplain Alexander Scott describes Nelson's death

The most famous account of Nelson's death was written by the Surgeon of HMS Victory, William Beatty, and has been used in all the biographies of Nelson. But there were two other shorter accounts: one by the ship's purser, William Burke, and this one by the chaplain, Alexander Scott. Scott actually lay alongside Nelson throughout the three hours he took to die, rubbing his chest and giving him lemonade to drink. He wrote this poignant account for one of Nelson's friends, the politician George Rose, who had promised to look after Emma Hamilton if Nelson should die.

[Lord Nelson] lived about three hours after receiving his wound, was perfectly sensible the whole time, but compelled to speak in broken sentences, which pain and suffering prevented him always from connecting. When I first saw him, he was apprehensive he should not live many minutes, and told me so; adding, in a hurried, agitated manner, though with pauses, 'Remember me to Lady Hamilton! Remember me to Horatia! Remember me to all my friends. Doctor, remember me to Mr. Rose: and tell him I have made a will, and left Lady Hamilton and Horatia to my Country.' He repeated his remembrances to Lady Hamilton and Horatia, and told me to mind what he said, several times.

Gradually he became less agitated, and at last calm enough to ask questions about what was going on; this led his mind to Captain Hardy, for whom he sent and inquired with great anxiety, exclaiming aloud, he would not believe he was alive, unless he saw him. He grew agitated at the Captain's not coming, lamented his being unable to go on deck, and do what was to be done, and doubted every assurance given him of the Captain's being safe on the quarter-deck.

At last the Captain came, and he instantly grew more composed, listened to his report about the state of the Fleet, directed him to anchor, and told him he should die, but observed, he should live half an hour longer. 'I shall die, Hardy,' said the Admiral. 'Is your pain great, Sir?' 'Yes, but I shall live half an hour yet – Hardy, kiss me!' The Captain knelt down by his side, and kissed him. Upon the Captain leaving him to return to the deck, Lord Nelson exclaimed very earnestly more than once 'Hardy, if I live I'll bring the Fleet to an anchor; if I live I'll anchor if I live I'll anchor;' and this was earnestly repeated even when the Captain was out of hearing.

After this interview, the Admiral was perfectly tranquil, looking at me in his accustomed manner when alluding to any prior discourse. 'I have not been a great sinner, Doctor,' said he.

SOURCE
Nicolas, *op cit*, Vol VII, p246

16. Nelson's nephew, George Matcham, describes the state funeral

Nelson's body was brought home to England on board HMS Victory, *preserved in a barrel of brandy. After lying in state in the Painted Hall at Greenwich Hospital, the body was transported up the River Thames to London in a splendid river procession. It was then taken to St Paul's Cathedral, where it was finally laid to rest immediately beneath the great dome. Among the mourners was Nelson's fourteen-year-old nephew George Matcham, who recorded the ceremony in his diary.*

Thursday, Jan. 9th

Rose at 6. Put on our full dress, and went to Clarges St. Took up the Boltons. Drove to the Earls, where breakfast was laid out. Saw the two sons of Lord Walpole, gentlemanly looking. Were not received at all by the Earl, not introduced to anybody. Put on there the Cloaks, &.

About half past eight the Mourning Coaches came. Lords Merton and Nelson went in the first, drawn by six horses. My Father, Mr. Bolton, Tom and myself in the second, and Messers Barney, Walpole and Fielding (son to the great Fielding) went in the third as Relations. Went into St. James Park. Found there a vast number of carriages, waited for some time. Saw the Duke of York at the head of his Troops, a handsome man, but shorter then the rest of the Royal Family. He talked a good deal to the Aids de Camp. Saw Mr. Naylar as Herald, I thought his dress very ridiculous, his garment being covered with Armorial Bearings, &c. Saw all the Captains and Admirals much confused, not being able to find their carriage.

From hence we moved by slow degrees and about one arrived at the Horse Guards, where the Procession was joined by the Prince of Wales, and Duke of Clarence. The body was then put into the Car, which represented the stern and bow of the *Victory*. (This description was taken from the *Times*.) The Case modelled at the ends in imitation of the hull of the Victory, its head towards the horses was ornamented with a figure of Fame, the Stern carved and painted in the naval style with the word 'Victory' in yellow raised letters on the lanthorn over the Poop. The Coffin with its head towards the Stern with an English Jack pendant over the Poop, and lowered half Staff. There was a Canopy over the whole supported by Pillars in the form of Palm Trees and partly covered with Black Velvet richly fringed, immediately above which in the front was inscribed in gold the word Nile at one end, on one side the following motto HOSTE DEVICTO REQUIEVIT behind the word TRAFALGAR and on the other side the motto of is arms 'Palmam qui meruit ferat.' The Car was drawn by six led horses.

When the Coffin was brought out of the Admiralty there seemed to be a general Silence, and every one appeared to feel for the Death of so noble and such a good Man. Poor Mr. Scott (with another gentleman) came to our Carriage and requested the Heralds to let him go in the same Coach with us. We were happy to receive him. After he had shaken us all heartily by the hand, he said with Tears in his Eyes 'Ah poor Fellow! I remained with him as long as I could and then they turned me away.'

The procession moved on slowly, the soldiers lining the streets, and the Band playing the Dead

March in Saul. At Temple Bar it was joined by the Mayor and suite, who took their place after the Prince of Wales. As it past the Regiments of the Dukes of York and Sussex, they stood still, and ordered that no salute should be made.

At St. Paul's we got out, and walked in procession up the Passage. It was the most aweful sight I ever saw. All the Bands played. The Colours were all carried by the Sailors and a Canopy was held over the Coffin, supported by Admirals. When we arrived at the Choir, the relations were placed at each side of the coffin on which was the Coronet placed on a Cushion. The service was read by the Bishop of Lincoln, but he did little justice to the occasion as his tone was monotonous and heavy. The Bishop of Chichester read the first lesson.

When the body was conveyed to the Dome for interment, the Prince of Wales passed close by us. He was dressed in the Order of the Garter. Next him was the Duke of York, and he was followed by the Duke of Clarence, who shook my Father by the hand, saying 'I am come to pay my last Duties here, and I hope you and I shall never meet on such a like occasion.' The organ played a Dirge meanwhile, the service went on, the Body was lowered and the Herald declaring the Titles of the Deceased broke the Staves and threw them into the Grave.

There were 5 Dukes, besides the Royal Family. Mr. Fox, Mr Sheridan and Tierney were present. After waiting some time we got to Clarges St. and went to Bromton about 8 with Mr. Scott.

SOURCE
E Eyre Matcham, *The Nelsons of Burnham Thorpe*, John Lane (London 1911)

Nelson's Ships

EVEN THOUGH his life is so well documented, biographies of Nelson are sometimes vague, or even inaccurate, about the ships in which he served and the exact periods during which he served in them. This is scarcely surprising since such information is usually taken from his autobiographical 'Sketch of My Life', and it now appears that some of the dates he gave are wrong.

Recent research into the logs of the ships in which he is known to have served is beginning to piece together a more accurate picture. The list below represents our current state of knowledge but new information is still emerging.

JANUARY–MAY 1771
Raisonnable (64-gun Third Rate battleship), Captain Maurice Suckling
Midshipman

MAY 1771–MAY 1773
Triumph (74-gun Third Rate battleship), Thames Guardship, Captain Maurice Suckling
Captain's servant, then midshipman
From May 1771 to July 1772, Nelson was in fact on board a West Indies merchantman the Mary Ann, *commanded by John Rathbone.*

MAY–OCTOBER 1773
Carcass (8-gun bomb vessel), Captain Skeffington Lutwidge, Polar Expedition
Captain's coxswain

OCTOBER 1773
Triumph (74-gun Third Rate battleship), Captain Maurice Suckling
Midshipman

OCTOBER 1773–MARCH 1776
Seahorse (24-gun Sixth Rate frigate), Captain George Farmer
Able seaman, then midshipman

MARCH–MAY 1776
Dolphin (24-gun Sixth Rate frigate), Captain James Pigot
Midshipman

SEPTEMBER 1776–APRIL 1777
Worcester (64-gun Third Rate battleship), Captain Mark Robinson
Midshipman and acting lieutenant

APRIL–DECEMBER 1777
Lowestoffe (32-gun Fifth Rate frigate), Captain William Locker
Lieutenant

DECEMBER 1777–JULY 1778
Little Lucy
Nelson commanded this schooner, as a 'tender' to the Lowestoffe.

JULY–DECEMBER 1778
Bristol (50-gun Fourth Rate ship), Flagship of Sir Peter Parker
Lieutenant

DECEMBER 1778–JUNE 1779
Badger (16-gun brig-sloop)
Master and commander

JUNE 1779–MARCH 1780
Hinchinbrooke (28-gun Sixth Rate frigate)
Post captain

MARCH–SEPTEMBER 1780
Janus (44-gun Fifth Rate frigate)
Captain
Although nominally in command of the Janus, *Nelson was so ill following the Nicaraguan campaign that he was never able to serve in her.*

SEPTEMBER/OCTOBER 1780
Lion (64-gun Third Rate battleship), Captain Hon William Cornwallis
For passage home only.

In England on half pay, recovering from the diseases he caught during the Nicaraguan campaign

OCTOBER 1781–JULY 1783
Albemarle (28-gun Sixth Rate frigate)
Captain

Peacetime: on half pay in France and England

MARCH 1784–DECEMBER 1787
Boreas (28-gun Sixth Rate frigate)
Captain

Peacetime: on half pay in England

JANUARY 1793–JUNE 1796
Agamemnon (64-gun Third Rate battleship)
Captain, and subsequently Commodore

JUNE–SEPTEMBER 1796
Captain (74-gun Third Rate battleship), Captain Edward Berry
Commodore

SEPTEMBER 1796
Diadem (64-gun Third Rate battleship), Captain George Towry
Commodore

OCTOBER–DECEMBER 1796
Captain (74-gun Third Rate battleship), Captain Ralph Miller
Commodore

DECEMBER 1796–13 FEBRUARY 1797
La Minerve (38-gun Fifth Rate frigate), Captain George Cockburn
Commodore

13/14 FEBRUARY 1797
Captain (74-gun Third Rate battleship), Captain Ralph Miller
Commodore

14 FEBRUARY 1797–MARCH 1797
Irresistible (74-gun Third Rate battleship), Captain George Martin
Commodore

MARCH–MAY 1797
Captain (74-gun Third Rate battleship), Captain Ralph Miller
Commodore, and subsequently rear admiral

MAY–AUGUST 1797
Theseus (74-gun Third Rate battleship), Captain Ralph Miller
Rear admiral

AUGUST/SEPETMBER 1797
Seahorse (38-gun Fifth Rate frigate), Captain Thomas Fremantle
For passage home only

In England on half pay, recovering from the loss of his arm

MARCH 1798–JUNE 1799
Vanguard (74-gun Third Rate battleship), Captain Edward Berry/Captain Thomas Hardy
Rear admiral

JUNE 1799–JULY 1800
Foudroyant (80-gun Third Rate battleship), Captain Thomas Hardy/Captain Edward Berry
Rear admiral

JULY 1800
Alexander (74-gun Third Rate battleship), Captain Alexander Ball
For passage home only

Travelling home through Germany with the Hamiltons

JANUARY/FEBRUARY 1801.
San Josef (112-gun First Rate battleship), Captain Thomas Hardy
Vice admiral

FEBRUARY/MARCH 1801
St George (98-gun Second Rate battleship), Captain
Thomas Hardy
Vice admiral

29 MARCH–2 APRIL 1801
Elephant (74-gun Third Rate battleship), Captain
Thomas Foley
Vice admiral

2 APRIL–JUNE 1801
St George (98-gun Second Rate battleship), Captain
Thomas Hardy
Vice admiral

JUNE 1801
Kite (16-gun brig-sloop), Lieutenant Stephen Digby
For passage home only

On half pay in England

27/29 JULY 1801
Unité (32-gun Fifth Rate frigate)
Vice admiral

AUGUST 1801
Medusa (32-gun Fifth Rate frigate), Captain John
Gore
Vice admiral

SEPTEMBER/OCTOBER 1801
Amazon (38-gun Fifth Rate frigate), Captain Samuel
Sutton

Peace of Amiens – on half pay in England

MAY 1803
Victory (100-gun First Rate battleship), Captain
Thomas Hardy
Vice admiral

MAY–JULY 1803
Amphion (32-gun Fifth Rate frigate), Captain
Thomas Hardy
Vice admiral

JULY 1803–21 OCTOBER 1805
Victory (100-gun First Rate battleship), Captain
Thomas Hardy
Vice admiral

Summary

Ships in which Nelson served, or which he commanded:
Agamemnon (64), *Albemarle* (28), *Amazon* (38),
Amphion (32), *Badger* (16), *Bristol* (50), *Boreas* (28),
Captain (74), *Carcass* (8 bomb), *Diadem* (64), *Elephant*
(74), *Foudroyant* (80), *Hinchinbrooke* (28), *Irresistible*
(74), *Janus* (44), *Little Lucy* (tender), *Lowestoffe* (32),
Medusa (32), *La Minerve* (38), *Raisonnable* (64), *St
George* (98), *San Josef* (112), *Seahorse* (i) (24), *Theseus*
(74), *Triumph* (74), *Unité* (32), *Vanguard* (74), *Victory*
(100), *Worcester* (64).

Ships in which Nelson took passage:
Alexander (74), *Dolphin* (24), *Kite* (16), *Lion* (64),
Seahorse (ii) (38).

Chronology

1758   29 September, Horatio Nelson born at Burnham Thorpe, Norfolk.

1767   26 December, Catherine Nelson, Nelson's mother, dies.

1771   Joins HMS *Raisonnable* as a midshipman. August, sails to the West Indies in a merchant ship.

1773   June to September, joins Arctic expedition. Joins HMS *Seahorse* and sails to East Indies.

1775   Invalided from his ship suffering from malaria. Returns to England. War of American Independence begins.

1777   April, passes examination for lieutenant. Appointed to HMS *Lowestoffe* for service in the West Indies.

1778   September, appointed first lieutenant of HMS *Bristol*. December, appointed commander of HMS *Badger*.

1779   June, promoted to post captain, appointed to command HMS *Hinchinbrooke*.

1780   Takes part in the Nicaraguan expedition (Capture of Fort San Juan). Falls ill and returns home to England. Sits for portrait by John Rigaud.

1781   Appointed to command HMS *Albemarle*.

1782   Joins North American squadron. Visits Quebec and New York.

1783   War of American Independence ends. Returns home. Visits France.

1784   Appointed to command HMS *Boreas*. Sails for West Indies.

1785   May, meets Frances Nisbet.

1786   Appointed ADC to Prince William Henry.

1787   11 March, marries Frances Nisbet at Nevis. Returns to England. Placed on half pay. Lives at Burnham Thorpe with his wife.

1793   Beginning of the French Revolutionary War. 26 January, appointed to command HMS *Agamemnon*. June, sails for the Mediterranean. September, visits Naples. Meets Sir William and Lady Hamilton.

1794   January to August, Corsican campaign. 12 July, right eye injured at Calvi.

1795   14 March, Battle of Gulf of Genoa. HMS *Agamemnon* in action with the *Ça Ira*.

1796   March, appointed commodore. Joins HMS *Captain*.

1797   14 February, BATTLE OF ST VINCENT. Created Knight of Bath. Promoted rear admiral. Hoists flag in HMS *Theseus*. 24 July, failure of attack on Santa Cruz, Tenerife. Loses right arm. Returns home and goes to Bath to recover. Sits for portrait by Lemuel Abbott.

1798   March. Hoists flag in HMS *Vanguard* and joins fleet off Cádiz. April, enters Mediterranean in command of a detached squadron. July, in pursuit of the French Toulon fleet with Napoleon on board. 1 August, destroys the French fleet at Aboukir Bay, BATTLE OF THE NILE, badly wounded in the head. Created Baron Nelson of the Nile. 22 September, arrives at Naples. 23 to 26 December, rescues Neapolitan royal family from advancing French army and takes them to Palermo.

1799   23 January, the French capture Naples. Sits for portrait by Guzzardi. Begins relationship with Emma Hamilton. 8 June, transfers his flag to HMS *Foudroyant*. June, assists in the recapture of Naples. Orders the execution of Commodore Caracciolo. Created Duke of Bronte by King of Naples.

1800   June, recalled home. Returns overland with the Hamiltons. August, in Vienna. Sits for portrait by Füger. Life mask taken for bust by Thaller and Ranson. 6 November, arrives at Great Yarmouth. Sits for portraits by Hoppner and Beechey.

1801   Publication of first biography to appear between its own covers. Separates from his wife. 1 January, promoted to vice admiral.

13 January, hoists flag in HMS *San Josef*.
*c*30 January, Emma Hamilton gives birth to their first daughter, Horatia.
12 March, sails, with Hyde Parker, to the Baltic.
2 April, THE BATTLE OF COPENHAGEN. Flies flag in HMS *Elephant*. Created viscount.
6 May, succeeds Parker as commander-in-chief.
June, returns home.
27 July, appointed to command anti-invasion forces in the Channel.
Hoists flag in HMS *Medusa*.
15 August, failure of attack on Boulogne.
September, buys Merton Place, Surrey.
1 October, armistice signed between Britain and France.
22 October, returns home to Merton.

1802   25 March, Treaty of Amiens (end of the French Revolutionary War)
26 April, Rev Edmund Nelson dies.
July and August, tours South Wales and the Midlands with the Hamiltons.

1803   6 April, Sir William Hamilton dies.
16 May, Napoleonic war begins. Appointed C-in-C Mediterranean.
18 May, hoists flag in HMS *Victory*.
6 July, joins the fleet off Toulon.

1804   Blockades French in Toulon.

1805   April to July, chases French fleet to West Indies and back.
18 August, arrives in England. To Merton on leave.
14 September, rejoins the *Victory* at Portsmouth.
28 September, takes command of the fleet off Cádiz.
21 October, THE BATTLE OF TRAFALGAR. Killed in action.
6 November, news of Trafalgar arrives in England.
First monuments erected (in County Cork, Ireland, and Taynuilt, Scotland).
4 December, the *Victory* arrives at Portsmouth with Nelson's body on board.
5 December, Day of Thanksgiving for Trafalgar.

1806   8 January, funeral procession on the River Thames.
9 January, funeral service in St Paul's Cathedral.

1807   Birmingham monument erected.

1808   Montreal monument erected.

1809   Clarke and M'Arthur's *Life* published

1813   Southey's *Life* published.
Liverpool monument erected.

1814   Launch of first HMS *Nelson*, 120-gun battleship.

1841   Nelson, New Zealand, founded.

1843   Trafalgar Square column and statue completed.

1844   First volume of Nicolas's *Dispatches and Letters* published.

1867   Maclise's 'Death of Nelson' mural in Houses of Parliament completed.
Nelson Monument in Trafalgar Square finally completed by addition of Landseer's lions.

1891   The Navy Exhibition, Chelsea. Many Nelson relics included.

1895   The Navy League founded.

1899   Mahan's *Life* published.

1905   Trafalgar Centenary celebrations

1918   *Nelson* released – first full-length Nelson film.

1922   HMS *Victory* placed in dry dock, launch of the 'Save the *Victory* Fund'.

1925   Launch of seventh HMS *Nelson*, battleship.

1927   Restoration of HMS *Victory* completed.

1937   National Maritime Museum opened. Nelson relics on display.

1939   Victory Museum opened. Nelson relics on display.

1942   *Lady Hamilton* (film) released.

1947   Oman's *Nelson* published.

1951   Statue erected in Portsmouth.

1966   Dublin monument blown up by IRA.

1972   Lambert McCarthy Gallery opened at Royal Naval Museum, to contain Nelson memorabilia collection of Mrs Lily McCarthy CBE.

1994   Monument to Emma Hamilton erected in Calais.

1995   Beginning of 'The Nelson Decade'.

Bibliography

Over a thousand books have been written about Nelson and new titles appear every year. The following are some of the key titles, with particular reference to books that have been consulted in the preparation of this book.

For a full Nelson bibliography see:
Leonard W Cowie, *Lord Nelson 1758–1805: A Bibliography*, Greenwood (Westmouth, CT, 1990)

The main biographies

For a full discussion of the 'Top Twenty' Nelson biographies, and a discussion of their content and history, see: Nash, Michael, 'Building a Nelson Library', in Colin White (ed), *The Nelson Companion*, Royal Naval Museum (Portsmouth, 1995)

Bennet, Geoffrey, *Nelson, the Commander*, Batsford (London 1972)

An excellent modern examination of Nelson as a commander, with some useful insights based on the author's own naval experience.

Clarke, James Stanier & MacArthur, John, *The Life of Admiral Lord Nelson, KB*. T Cadell & W Davies & W Miller, 2 vols (London 1809)

The 'official' biography, to which Earl Nelson, Lady Nelson and a number of Nelson's family, friends and naval colleagues contributed material. Contains some very doubtful stories, especially about Nelson's childhood, many of which have been repeated unquestioningly in subsequent biographies. Also contains many transcripts of Nelson's letters, which modern research has shown were very heavily edited, even censored.

Mahan, Alfred Thayer, *The Life of Nelson, the Embodiment of the Sea Power of Great Britain*, Sampson Low (London 1897)

Still the best biography on Nelson's naval career, and particularly good on aspects which other biographies neglect, notably the Italian campaign of 1795/6 and the Mediterranean campaign of 1803–1805. Less sure-footed on his personal life, with some unattractive Victorian moralising about Emma Hamilton.

Nicolas, Nicholas Harris, *The Dispatches and Letters of Vice-Admiral Lord Viscount Nelson*, Henry Colburn (London 1844–1846)

A superb seven-volume collection of Nelson's despatches and letters, arranged chronologically, and with extensive footnotes so that it reads almost like a biography. Some of the letters – notably those to Fanny Nelson and the Duke of Clarence – were taken from Clarke and M'Arthur's biography, and have therefore been heavily edited. A little thin on Nelson's private life, with little material relating to Emma Hamilton.

Oman, Carola, *Nelson*, Hodder & Stoughton (London 1947)

Still the best study of Nelson the man, distilled from faithful reading of hundreds of his letters. Particularly good on his relationships with women, and the first of Nelson's biographers to judge Emma Hamilton fairly. Less detailed on the battles and no new insights on his ability as a commander.

Pocock, Tom, *Horatio Nelson*, Bodley Head (London 1987)

The best modern all-round biography, offering a first rate introduction to all aspects of Nelson's story, written in a warm and accessible style. Particularly good on descriptions of places where Nelson lived and served, all of which the author has visited himself.

Southey, Robert, *The Life of Nelson*, John Murray (London 1813)

Still regarded as one of the greatest of the Nelson biographies – but more because of its superb style than its content, some of which is now known to be inaccurate. Best read in the 1922 edition, with an introduction by Geoffrey Callender, which corrects most of the mistakes.

Warner, Oliver, *A Portrait of Lord Nelson*, Chatto & Windus (London 1953)

Another excellent all-round introduction to Nelson's life and career. The first to mention Nelson's first mistress, Adelaide Correglia. Includes a useful list of the main portraits.

White, Colin (ed), *The Nelson Companion*, Royal Naval Museum (Portsmouth 1995)

A set of essays by leading Nelson experts on key aspects of 'The Nelson Legend': relics, commemoratives, portraits, biographies, Nelson sites, monuments, letters.

Other titles

Anon, *The Letters of Lord Nelson to Lady Hamilton*, Thomas Lovewell (London 1814)

Beatty, William, *Authentic narrative of the death of Lord Nelson*, T Cadell & W Davies (London 1807)

Beresford, Lord Charles & Wilson, Herbert, *Nelson and his times*, Harmsworth (London 1897)

Bethune, John Drinkwater, *A narrative of the battle of St Vincent with anecdotes of Nelson before and after that battle*, Saunders & Otley (London 1840)

Bradford, Ernle, *Nelson. The essential hero*, Granada (London 1979)

Browne, G Lathom, *Nelson. The public and private life of Horatio, Viscount Nelson*, T Fisher Unwin (London 1891)

Bryant, Arthur, *Nelson*, Collins (Glasgow 1970)

Buckland, Kirstie, *The Miller Papers*, The 1805 Club (Shelton 1999)

Callender, Geoffrey, *The Life of Nelson*, Longmans, Green (London 1912)
_____ (ed), *Southey's Life of Nelson*, J M Dent (London 1922)

Charnock, John, *Biographical memoirs of Lord Viscount Nelson*, H D Symonds & J Hatchard (London 1806)

Clarke, Richard, *The life of Horatio Lord Viscount Nelson*, J & J Cundee (London 1813)

Coleman, Terry, *Nelson: the man and the legend*, Bloomsbury (London 2001)

Corbett, Julian, *The campaign of Trafalgar*, Longmans, Green (London 1910)

Dawson, Warren, *The Nelson Collection at Lloyd's*, Corporation of Lloyd's (London 1932)

Duncan, Archibald, *The life of the late most noble Lord Horatio Nelson*, J Nuttall (Liverpool 1806) & James Cundee (London 1806)

Eyre-Matcham, Mary, *The Nelsons of Burnham Thorpe*, The Bodley Head (London 1911)

Fenwick, Kenneth, *HMS Victory*, Cassell (London 1959)

Fitchett, W H, *Nelson and his captains*, Smith, Elder (London 1904)

Fraser, Flora, *Beloved Emma*, Weidenfeld & Nicolson (London 1986)

Gardiner, Robert (ed), *Fleet Battle and Blockade*, Chatham Publishing (London 1996)
_____ (ed), *Nelson against Napoleon*, Chatham Publishing (London 1997)
_____ (ed), *The Campaign of Trafalgar*, Chatham Publishing (London 1997)
_____ *Warships of the Napoleonic Era*, Chatham Publishing (London 1999)

Goodwin, Peter, *Countdown to Victory*, Manuscript Press (Portsmouth 2001)

Grenfell, Russell, *Nelson the sailor*, Faber & Faber (London 1949)

Guimerà, Agustín, *Nelson and Tenerife*, The 1805 Club (Shelton 1999)

Gutteridge, H C (ed), *Nelson and the Neapolitan Jacobins*, Navy Records Society (London 1903)

Harris, David, *The Nelson Almanack*, Conway (London 1998)

Harrison, James, *The life of the Right Honourable Horatio Lord Viscount Nelson*, C Chapple (London 1806)

Hibbert, Christopher, *Nelson. A personal history*, Viking (London 1994)

Howarth, David, *Trafalgar. The Nelson Touch*, Collins (London 1969)

Howarth, David & Howarth, Stephen, *The Immortal Memory*, J N Dent (London 1998)

Jeaffreson, John, *Lady Hamilton and Lord Nelson*, Hurst and Blackett (London 1888)

Kennedy, Ludovic, *The Band of Brothers*, Oldhams (London 1951)

Kerr, A E F, *The Sailor's Nelson*, Hurst & Blackett (London 1932)

Laughton, John Knox, *Nelson*, Macmillan (London 1895)
_____ *The Nelson memorial. Nelson and his companions in arms*, George Allen (London 1896)

Lavery, Brian, *Nelson's Navy*, Conway (London 1989)
_____ *Nelson and the Nile*, Chatham Publishing (London 1998)
_____ *The Battle of the Nile*, The 1805 Club (Shelton 2000)

Legg, Stuart (ed), *Trafalgar: an eyewitness account of a great battle*, Rupert Hart-Davis (London 1966)

Lloyd, Christopher, *Nelson and Sea Power*, The English Universities Press (London 1973)
_____ *The Nile campaign. Nelson and Napoleon in Egypt*, David & Charles (Newton Abbot 1973)

Lloyd, Frederick, *An accurate and impartial life of the late Lord Viscount Nelson*, J Fowler (Ormskirk 1806)

Mackenzie, Robert, *The Trafalgar Roll*, George Allen (London 1913)

McCarthy, Lily, *Remembering Nelson*, The Royal Naval Museum (Portsmouth 1995)

McGowan, Alan, *HMS Victory: her construction, career and restoration*, Chatham Publishing (Chatham 1999)

Marriott, Leo, *What's left of Nelson*, Dial House (Shepperton 1995)

Minto, Countess of (ed), *Life and Letters of Sir Gilbert Elliot, First Earl of Minto.* (London 1874)

Moorhouse, E Hallam, *Nelson in England. A domestic chronicle*, Chapman & Hall (London 1913)

Morrison, Alfred, *The Hamilton & Nelson papers*, privately published (1893/4)

Morriss, Roger, *Nelson: the life and letters of a hero*, Collins and Brown (London 1996)

Morriss, Roger & Lavery, Brian & Deuchar, Stephen, *Nelson: an illustrated history*, Laurence King & National Maritime Museum (London 1995)

Naish, George P B, *Nelson's letters to his wife*, Navy Records Society (London 1958)

Nash, Michael (int), *The Nelson masks*, Proceedings of the Symposium on the Nelson Masks, Portsmouth, 1992, Marine Books (Hoylake 1993)

Orme, Edward & Blagdon, Francis, *Orme's graphic history of the life, exploits, and death of Horatio Lord Nelson*, Longmans, Hurst, Rees & Orme (London 1806)

Padfield, Peter, *Nelson's war*, Hart-Davis, MacGibbon (London 1976)

Pettigrew, Thomas Joseph, *Memoirs of the life of Vice-Admiral Lord Viscount Nelson*, KB, T & W Boone, 2nd ed, 2 vols (London 1849)

Pocock, Tom, *Nelson and his World*, Thames & Hudson (London 1968)
_____ *The Young Nelson in the Americas*, Collins (London 1980)
_____ *Nelson's Campaign in Corsica*, The 1805 Club (Shelton 1994)
_____ *Nelson's Women*, André Deutsch (London 1999)

Pope, Dudley, *England Expects*, Chatham Publishing (London 1998)
_____ *The Great Gamble*, Chatham Publishing (London 2001)

Pugh, P D Gordon, *Nelson and his surgeons*, E & S Livingstone (Edinburgh 1968)

Rawson, Geoffrey (ed), *Letters from Lord Nelson*, Staples Press (London 1949)
_____ *Nelson's Letters from the Leeward Islands*, The Golden Cockerel Press (1953)

Rodger, Nicholas, *The Wooden World*, Collins (London 1986)

Russell, Jack, *Nelson and the Hamiltons*, Antony Blond (London 1969)

Schom, Alan, *Trafalgar: countdown to battle*, Michael Joseph (London 1990)

Thompson, G, *The life of the Right Honourable Horatio Lord Viscount Nelson, Baron of the Nile*, J S Pratt (London 1841)

Thursfield, James R, *Nelson and other naval studies*, John Murray (London 1909)

Tracy, Nicolas, *Nelson's Battles*, Chatham Publishing (London 1996)

Tunstall, Brian, *Nelson*, Duckworth (London 1933)

Tushingham, Eric & Mansfield, Clifford, *Nelson's Flagship at Copenhagen: HMS Elephant*, The Nelson Society (2001)

Walder, David, *Nelson*, Hamish Hamilton (London 1978)

Walker, Richard, *The Nelson portraits*, Royal Naval Museum (Portsmouth 1998)

Warner, Oliver, *Nelson and the age of fighting sail*, American Heritage (New York 1963)
_____ *Nelson's battles*, Batsford (London 1965)
_____ *Nelson's last diary*, Seeley Service and Co (London 1971)

White, Colin, *The Battle of Cape St Vincent*, The 1805 Club (Shelton 1997)
_____ *1797: Nelson's Year of Destiny*, Royal Naval Museum (Portsmouth 1998)

White, Joshua, *Memoirs of the professional life of the Right Honourable Horatio Lord Viscount Nelson*, James Cundee (London 1806)

Wilkinson, Clennell, *Nelson*, Harrap (London 1931)

Additionally, *The Nelson Dispatch* (Journal of the Nelson Society) and *The Trafalgar Chronicle* (Journal of The 1805 Club) are rich sources of current Nelsonian research.

For details of these societies, and their current secretaries, contact them at their websites:
The 1805 Club: www.admiralnelson.org
The Nelson Society: www.nelson-society.org.uk

Alternatively, details can be obtained from:
Colin White, Director Trafalgar 200, National Maritime Museum, Park Row, Greenwich, LONDON SE10 9NF.

Index

Ship names are in italics. All ships are British Royal Navy unless otherwise indicated. Relationships are to Vice-Admiral Horatio Nelson. Page references in *italics* are to illustrations, page references in **bold** are to major articles on the subject.

Abbreviations:
Adm = Admiral; Capt = Captain;
Cdre = Commodore;
Den = Denmark; Fr = France;
GB = British merchant ship;
Lt = Lieutenant;
Lt-Col = Lieutenant- Colonel;
Lt-Gen = Lieutenant-General;
Neth = Netherlands;
R/A = Rear-Admiral;
Rev = Reverend; Sp = Spain;
US = United States;
V/A = Vice-Admiral

Abbott, Lemuel 47, *50*, **50-1**, *112*, 136-7, *167*, 207-8, 209, 279
Aboukir Bay, battle of *see* Nile, battle of
Active 249
Acton, Sir John 43
Addington, Henry (Lord Sidmouth) 37, **51**, 56, 206, 236, 251
Admiralty and Navy Board 16, **51-2**, *52*, 71, 79, 81, 106, 122-3, 128, 144, 151, 175, **183**, 207, 220, 226-7, 228, 237, 247, 250, 252
Agamemnon 18, 21, **52-4**, *53*, 55-6, 62, 66, 77-8, 81, 89-90, 92, 97, 102, 107-8, 125, 127, 137, 141, 146, 151, 153, 155, 181, 198, 229, 258, 277-9
Agincourt 54
Agincourt Sound **54**, 221
Ajax 68
Albemarle 15-16, **54-5**, 71, 91, 109, 151, 191-2, 225, 251, 277-9
Alexander 278, 59, 252, 277
Alexandria 168, 196
Algeciras, battle of 219
Algiers 90, 154
Allemand, R/A 82
Allen, Tom **55-6**
Allot, Dean 77
Amaranthe 201
Amazon 278
America 65, 71, 91, 95, 148, 150-1, 176, 191, 203, 217, 219, 279
War of 1812 95
War of Independence *15*, 15-16, 56, 59, 75, 90, 96, 105, 109, 115, 117, 125, 134, 139, 152, 154, 159, 163, 167, 176, 192, 199, 203, 233, 251, 254, 256, 279
Amiens, Peace of 39-41, 51, 55, **56**, 68, 92, 98, 106, 118, 123, 127, 139, 152-3, 159, 161, 164, 169-70,

183, 188, 219, 246, 254, 257, 260, 269, 278, 280
Amphion 154, 278
Andrews, Elizabeth 17, **56**
Andrews, George 56
Antigua 17, **57**, 178
Arctic 14, *57*, **57-8**, 169, 279
Arethusa 179
'Armed Neutrality of the North' 32, 36, 99, 105, 233
Asia 95
Atkinson, Thomas **58**
Attwood, Thomas 129
Austen, Capt Francis 169
Austria 18, 25, 44, 82, 131, 156, 182, 190, 241, 246-7, 256

Bacchante 154
Badger 15, 97, 204, 276, 278-9
Bagley, James 150
Bahamas 251
Ball, Capt Sir Alexander **59**, 61, 170, 252, 277
'Band of Brothers' 21, 26, 39, 59, **59-61**, *60*, 65, 68, 96, 122, 124, 139, 146, 152, 161, 169, 179, 193, 222, 234
Barbados 247
Barfleur 46, 97, 151, 192, 220, 259
Barham, Lord 81, **175**, *175*, *241*, 247-8
Bastia 18, **61-2**, 80-1, 88, 107, *127*, 149-50, 152, 176, 223, 261
Bath 23, **63**, 66, 149, 187, 279
Beatty, Sir William **63**, 110, *110*, 111, 114, 149, 162, 185-6, *211*, 262, 273-4
Bedford 133
Beechey, Charles 64
Beechey, Sir William **64**, *64*, 208
Belleisle 154, 203
Bellerophon **64-5**, *65*, 75, 118, 168, *182*
Bellona 235
Berbice 163
Berry, Capt Sir Edward 24, 28, 54, 61, *65*, **65-6**, 130, 148, 235, 252, 262, 265, 277
Berwick 221
Bienfaisant 169
Bille, Cdre Steen 124
Blackwood, Capt Sir Henry 61, **68**, *119*, 245
Blanche 215
Blenheim 251
Bligh, Capt William **68-9**, 102
Bolton, Capt Sir William 55
Bolton, Horatio (cousin) 114
Bolton, Susannah (sister) 81, 121-2, 171, 188-9, 191, 274
Bolton, Thomas (brother-in-law) 16, 122, 188-9, 191, 274
Bolton, Thomas (nephew) 114
Bonaparte, Napoleon *see* Napoleon I
Boreas 15-16, 56-7, **71**, 97, 124, 151, 178, 186, 190-1, 277-9
Bornholme (Den) 124

Boscawen, Adm Edward 158-9, 232
Boulogne 39, **71-3**, *72*, 92, 164, 201, 246, 280
Bounty 68-9
Bowen, Capt Richard 217
Bowen, Richard *73*, **73-4**
Bowyer, R/A George 97
Boydell, Josiah 114
Boyne 163
Braham, John 118
Braithwaite, Capt 96
Brest 42, **74**, 83, 95, 106, 158, 200, 206, 240, 246-7, 256
Briarly, Alexander 235
Bristol 15, 96, 167, 179, 203, 217, 276, 278-9
Britannia 20, 87, 90, 125
Bromley, William 15, 79, *261-2*
Bronte, dukedom of **74**, 114, 191, 225, 279
Brontë, Rev Patrick 225
Brueys d'Aigallers, Adm François de 26, *75*, **75-6**, 167, 196-7
Bruix, Adm 184
Bucentaure (Fr) *76*, 164, 245, 256
Buckingham 203
Buenos Aires 207
Burford 66
Burke, Walter 110-11, 162
Burnham Thorpe 13, 55, **76-7**, 77, 121, 153, 180, 187, 190, 212-13, 279

Ça Ira (Fr) 18, 90, 127, 136, 137, 168, 279
Cádiz 20-1, 24, 26, 42-5, 55, 59, 66, 68, 74, 76, *78*, 79, *79*, 82-3, 97-8, 131, 134, 139, 153-4, 159, 175-6, 184, 199-200, 217, 219, 229-31, 235, 238, 241, 244-5, 247, 256, 270-1, 279-80
Calais 188, 246, 280
Calder, V/A Sir Robert **78-80**, 81-2, 106, 134, 200, 241, 247, 256
'Calder's Action' *see* Cape Finisterre, battle of
Caldwell, Capt Benjamin 53
Calvi 18, *80*, **80-1**, 107, 176, 261, 279
Cambridge 167
Camperdown, battle of 25, 69, 237
Canada 109, 139, 177, 225-6
Canada 106, 219
Canopus 169
Cape Finisterre, battle of 68, **81-2**, 106, 134, 169, 211, 241, 247, 256
Cape of Good Hope 118, 207, 213
Cape Ortegal, battle of 45, **82**, *83*, 245
Cape Spartel, battle of 134
Cape St Vincent, battle of *map 84-5*, *19*, 19-21, 30, 32, 44, 50, 55, 58, 63-6, 74, 78-9, **82-8**, *86*, *89*, 90, 93, 95, 97, 111, 115, 117, 125, 127, 139, 147, 152-4, 159, 176, 179, 198, 216-18, 226, 229-30, 250, 254, 258, 260, 261-2, 279

Capraia 18, 21, **88-9**, 156-7
Captain 20-1, 54, 66, 87-9, *89*, 90, 97, 116, 176, 229, 261-2, 277-9
Caracciolo, Cdre Prince Francesco 30, **90-1**, 125, 185, 279
Carcass 57-8, 169, 276, 278
Carnegie, William, Earl of Northesk **90**
Caroline, Princess of Wales 128, 137
Cartagena 215
Carver, Nathaniel **91**
Casa Bianco, Cdre 197
Castlereagh, Lord 258
Castor 250
Censeur (Fr) 137
Ceres (Sp) 215
Chatham **92-3**, *93*, 206, 232, 252
Chatham, Lord 94
Chesapeake river 95
Cisneros, R/A Don Balthazar de 217
Clarence, HRH Prince William, Duke of (William IV) 13, 16, 21, 25-6, 33-4, 46, 57, 63, 67-8, 71, 105, 115, 149, 151, 161, 186, 192, 219-20, *259*, **259-60**, 268-9, 274-5, 279
Clerke, Capt 261
Clinton, Sir William 33
Cobb, Wheatley 126-7
Cochrane, Adm Sir Alexander 95
Cockburn, Capt Sir George 88, **94-5**, 147, 152, 215, 277
Codrington, Adm Sir Edward **95-6**, 129
Collingwood, V/A Cuthbert Lord 45, 68, 90, **96-8**, *97*, 119, 134, 139, 154, 163, 176-8, 218, 233, 245, 248, 256
Collins, Capt Sir John 221
Cólogan, Bernardo 258
Colossus 179, 218
Comyn, Rev Stephen **99**
Concepcion (Sp) 78
Conqueror 76
Cook, Capt James 69
Cooke, Capt John 64
Copenhagen, battle of *map 100-1*, 11, 33-6, *34-5*, 44, 51, 54-6, 58, 61, 69-70, 92, 99, **99-105**, *103-104*, 124, 127, 133, 135, 148, 201-3, 209, 211-13, 221, 227, 233, 235, 250, 268-9, 280
blind eye signal 69-70, 102, 125, 133, 203, 227
second battle of 152, 163, 252
Córdoba, Teniente General José de 82-3, 217
Corfu 75
Cornwallis, Adm Sir William 42, 81, **105-6**, 108, 152, 220, 247, 277
Cornwallis, Cuba 106, *108*
Correglia, Adelaide 18, **107-8**, 127
Corsica 18-19, 53, 88-9, **107**, 107-8, 115-17, 137, 150, 151-2, 153-6,

176, 178, 254, 258, 260-1, 279
see also Bastia, Calvi
Corunna 152
Cosmo-Kerjulien, Capt 245
Courageux 139
Crescent 218
Cronstadt 159
Crown 220
Cuba 202, 216, 230
Culloden, 20, 86, 147, 220, 250
Culverhouse, Lt John 147, 215
Curieux 247

Dannebrog (Den) 69, 102, 124
Davidson, Thomas *119*
Davison, Alexander 39-40, 44, 50, **109**, 113, 174, 178, 187, 223, 226, 257
de Burgh, Lt-Gen 88
de Koster, Simon *10*, 40, 51, 209
de Vins, General 156
Deal 92
Defiance 133
Denmark 33-6, 54, 69-70, 99-105, 124, 133, 148, 203, 213, 216, 233
see also Copenhagen, battle of
Devis, Arthur *110*, **114**, 120, *120*
Diadem 277-8
Dickens, Charles 177
Digby, Lt Stephen 278
Director 69
Dixon, Capt Charles 251
Dogger Bank, battle of 68-9, 202, 218
Dolphin 276, 278
Dominica 199
Dreadnought 122, 227
Dresden 131
Drinkwater, Capt John **115**, 147
Dubourdieu, Cdre 154
Duckworth, V/A Sir John 162, 169
Duguay Trouin (Fr) 82
Dumanoir de Pelley, Adm 82, 245
Dumas, Jacques 168
Duncan, Adm Adam, Lord 25, 237
Duncan, Major John 116
Dundas, Major-General 62

East India Company 166, 171, 233
East Indies station 14, 106, 122, 152-3, 220, 249-51, 279
Edgar 179, 235
Egypt 26-8, 59, 75-6, 118, 126, 169-70, 196, 256
see also Nile, battle of
Elba 18, 21, 94-5, 115, **116**, 117, 156, 215
Elephant 70, 125, 201, 227, 233-4, 278
Elgin, Lord 153
Elliott, Sir Gilbert 19, 26, 62, 88-9, 107-8, 115-16, **116-17**, 159, 174
Emerald 58
Esterhazy, Prince Nicholas 131, 190
Euryalus 68, 256
Eurydice 154
Excellent 97, 218
Experiment 166

Falconer, William 63
Falmouth 163, 249

Farmer, Capt George **122**, 249, 276
Farrer, Rev Richard 56
Fearney, William 216
Ferdinand I, King of Naples and Sicily 18, 29-30, 42, 50, 55, 74, 90, 111, *112*, 113, 142, 181-2, 183-5, *185*, 201, 214, 240, 252, 279
Ferrol 79, 81, 247
films **122-3**, *123*, 280
Finlayson, Midshipman John 70
Fischer, Cdre Olfert 69, 102-3, *104*, **124**, *124*
Foley, Capt Thomas 27, 61, 70, **124-5**, 152, 179, 197, 278
Foote, Capt Edward 184
Formidable 233
Forsyth, Thomas 40
Fortitude 218
Foudroyant 66, 91, 99, **125-7**, *126*, 131, 142, 148, 159, 170, 184, 201, 214, 252, 266, 277-8
Francis II, Emperor of Austria 131
Franklin (Fr) 196, 219, 235
Frederick, Crown Prince of Denmark 36, 103, 105, 124, 233, 268
Fremantle, Capt Sir Thomas 61, 108, **127**, 137, 170-1, 217, 277
Fremantle, Mrs Betsey 127
Füger, Heinrich 51, 131, 208, 279

Galatea 161
Ganges 127
Ganteaume, Adm 106, 247
Gardner, Cdre Alan 220
Gautier, Col Francisco 216
Gell, R/A John 125
Généreux (Fr) 66, 125, 170, 198, 235, 266-7
Genoa 88-9, 155-6
  Gulf of Genoa, battle of 18, 90, *136*, **137-8**, 155, 279
George III, King of England 16, 24, 26, 51, 57, 128, **130**, 145, 151, 192, 219-20, 259, 259-60, 268
George, Prince of Wales (George IV) 32, 128, 130, 209, 260, 274-5
George V, King of England 255
Germany 31, 40, 113, 126, **131**, 142, 146, 149, 178, 190, 214
Gibraltar 43, 54, 62, 69, 74, 78, 95, 115, 118, *132*, **132-3**, 134, 139, 147, 153-4, 172, 202, 245-7
  Gut of Gibraltar, battle of 152, 161, 219
Gibraltar 270
Gibson, Mrs Mary 188
Gillespie, Dr 172
Glatton 69, 102
Glorious First of June, battle of 64, 68, 97, 220, 250
Gloucester 158
Goliath 27, 125, 152, 197
Gore, Capt John 278
Gorgon 88
Gourly, Lt 88
Grasse, Adm F-J-P de 218
Graves, Adm Samuel 133
Graves, R/A Sir Thomas *133*, **133**
Gravina, Adm Don Frederico **134**, *134*, 245

Great Yarmouth 32, 102, 131, **134-5**, 142, 146, 177, 180, 214, 216, 219, 279
Greece 95-6, 153
Greenwich and Greenwich Hospital 50, 56, 63, 98, 113-14, 128, *135*, **135-7**, 148, 152, 156, 162, 167, 180, 223
Grenada 247
Grenville, Charles 145
Greville, Sir Charles 140-1
Greyhound 153
Guardian 213
Guernsey 71
Guerrier (Fr) 152
Guillaume Tell (Fr) 66, 68, 125-6, 196, 198
Gutiérrez, General Don Antonio 22, **138**, *138*, 231
Guzzardi, Leonardo 209, 279

Hallowell, Capt Benjamin 96, 126, **139**, 152
Hamilton, Catherine Lady 145-6
Hamilton, Emma Lady 11-13, 17, 28, *29*, 30-2, 39-43, 47, 56, 66-8, 74, 92, 96, 108, 111, 113, 115, 117-18, 121-3, *123*, 125-7, 130-1, 134-5, **139-44**, *140-3*, 145-6, 149, 156, 159, 166, 169-74, 178, 180, 182, 184, 186-8, 190-1, 198-9, 201, 206, 209, 212-14, 216, 222, 226, 228-9, 234-5, 238, 240, 244, 250-1, 257, 267-8, 270, 272-3, 277, 279-80
Hamilton, Sir William 17, *29*, 30, 39-41, 56, 92, 96, 118, 125-6, 131, 134-5, 140-1, *141*, 142-3, *145*, **145-6**, 149, 155, 169-71, 173-4, 180, 182, 184, *185*, 187-8, 190, 199, 206, 214, 240, 257, 267-8, 277, 279-80
Hardy, Capt Thomas Masterman 17, 45, 56, 61, 66, 68, 110-11, *119*, **146-8**, *147*, 162, 188, 215, 234, 245, 262, 273-4, 277-8
Harmony (US) 91
Harvey, Capt Eliab 232
Harwich 220
Hawke, Adm Edward 158, 166-7
Haydn, Franz Joseph 190
Heard, Sir Isaac 94, *128*, 129
Herbert, John 186, 191
Hinchinbrooke 15, 97, 105, 192, 276, 278-9
Hobart, Lord 270
Holsteen (Den) 124
Hood, Adm Alexander, first Viscount Hood 17-8, 46, 55, 62, 71, 81, 94, 106, 107, 118, 130, 134, 137, 141, 146, *150*, **150-2**, 154-5, 159, 176, 181, 192, 219-20, 221, 240, 254, 261
Hood, Samuel second Lord Bridport 74, 114
Hood, V/A Sir Samuel, first baronet **152-3**, 231, 265
Hood, Charlotte (niece) 74, 114
Hoppner, John 51, *208*, 209
Horatio 223
Hornby, Capt Phipps 154
Hoste, Capt Sir William 17, 21,

153, **153-4**, 258
Hotham, Adm William 18, 44, 53, 89, 137, 153, **154-5**, 155, *155*, 159, 238, 250
Howe, Adm Lord 64, 68, 95, 134, 154, 202, 204, 254
Hughes, Adm Sir Edward 249
Hughes, Adm Sir Richard 16, 54-5, 57, 71, 179
Hyères, battle of 89, 127, 153, 155, **155**, 168, 238, 250

Implacable 82, 152
  see also Duguay Trouin
Inconstant 116, 127, 137
Intrépide (Fr) 95
Invincible 68
Ireland 18-19, 68, 95, 176, 216, 249
Iris (Fr) 91
Irresistible 90, 277-8
Italy 18-19, 26, 75, 88-9, 107-8, 116, 127, 131, **156-7**, *157*, 182
  see also Leghorn, Naples, Rome

Jamaica 105-6, 108, 203-4
Janus 97, 276, 278
Jervis, Adm Sir John *see* St Vincent, Adm Lord

Keats, Capt Sir Richard 43, 61, *161*, **161-2**, 236-7
Keith, Adm Lord *117*, **117-18**, 126, 131, 153, 169-70, 184, 246
Kempenfelt, Adm Richard 254
Keppel, Adm Augustus 254
King, Capt James 251
King George (GB) 131
Kite 278

La Maddalena Islands 54, 221, 254
La Reunion (Fr) 218
Langara, Adm 78
Lapenotiere, Lt John **163**, 245
Latouche Tréville, Adm Louis de 39, 71-3, 76, 92, **163-4**, *164*, 256
Leander 66, 234-5
Leeward Islands station 17, 57, 106, 178
Leghorn 18, 107-8, *108*, 116, 126-7, 131, 156, 188
Leigh, Vivien *123*, *123*
Lepée, Frank 55
Lewis, Thomas 156
Lion 105-6, 277-8
Lisbon 83, 90, 115
Lissa, battle of 154
Little Lucy 167, 203, 276, 278
Locker, Capt William 15, 20, 50, 55, 63, 96, 108, 136-7, **166-7**, *167*, 180, 203, 276
Logan, Major James 88
London 233
Lord Nelson 223
L'Orient (Fr) 59, 64, 75, 96, 126, 139, **167-8**, *168*, 174, 196-7, 265
Louis, Capt Sir Thomas **169**
Lowe, Sir Hudson 95
Lowestoffe 14-15, *15*, 96, 167, 276, 278-9
Lucas, Capt Jean 233, 245
Lutwidge, Capt Skeffington 58, **169**, 276

Lynx 221
Lyon, Henry 140

Madagascar 251
Maitland, Capt Frederick 65, *182*
Majestic 265
Malmesbury, Lord 134
Malta 26, 54, 59, 118, 125, 142, 168, **170-1,** 172, 193, 250
Malta 139
Maniace, George 74
Maria Carolina, Queen of Naples and Sicily 42, 50, *112*, 113, 141-2, 145, 172, 182, 184, 201, 252, 279
Marsden, William 163
Martin, Capt George 277
Martinique 74, 90
Mary Ann (GB) 14, 211
Mary 235
Matcham, Catherine (sister) 39, 122, **171-2,** 188-9
Matcham, George (brother-in-law) 171-2, 188-9, 260
Matcham, George (nephew) 39, 128-9, 150, 172, 274-5
Matthews, Robert 225-6
Mediator 97
Medusa 92, 278, 280
Meleager 94-5, 147
Merton Place 39, 42-3, 56, 68, 92, 109, 117, 122, *142*, 143-4, 146, 162, 172, *173*, **173-4,** 180, 188, 213, 244, 257, 280
Middleton, Charles *see* Barham, Lord
Mignonne 176
Milford Haven 146
Miller, Capt Ralph 21, 87, 153, **175-6,** 262, 277
Minerva (Naples) 91, 185
Minerve 88, 94-5, 115, 147, 215, 277-8
Minorca 41-2, 184
Minotaur 169
Minto, Lord *see* Elliott, Sir Gilbert
Missiessy, R/A 247
Monarca (Sp) 64
Monmouth 90
Montagu, Adm James 161
Montefiore, Sir Moses 144
Montpelier House 191
Montreal 217
Moore, General Sir John 111, 152
Moreno, Teniente General Joaquin 86-7
Morrison, Alfred 166
Moutray, Capt John 178
Moutray, Mary 17, 57, 97, **178-9,** *179*
Mullan, Matthew 216
Murray, Capt George 172, **179-80**
Mutine 147, 153

Naish, George 166
Naples 18, 28-31, 36, 42-3, 47, 90, 108, 111, 113, 118, 124, 131, 141-2, 145-6, 153, *181*, **181-2,** 199, 209, 214, 226, 240, 252, 279
  Civil War in 11, 30, 90-1, 125, 145-6, 148, 182, **183-5,** 250
  see also Ferdinand I, Maria

Carolina
Napoleon I, Emperor of the French 18, 26, 37, 44, 65, 75, 81, 95, 107-8, 116, 120, 127, 131, 156, 163-4, 168, 170, 176, *182*, **182-3,** 193, 196, 200, *205*, 240, *241*, 246-7, 256, 279
  invasion threat 37-9, 44, 51, 81-2, 91-2, 95, 105-6, 118, 163-4, 169, 173, 175, 200-1, 211, 241, 246-7, 256, 280
  surrender of 118
Nelson, Anne (sister) 56
Nelson, Catherine (mother) 12, 13-14, 51, 76, 121-2, 171, 279
Nelson, Catherine (sister) *see* Matcham, Catherine
Nelson, Charlotte (niece) *see* Hood, Charlotte
Nelson, Rev Edmund (father) 13, 23, 40-1, 63, 76, 121, *121*, 122, 143, 149, 154, 187, 212, 280
Nelson, Frances Lady (wife) 16-18, 23, 31-2, 40, 42, 50, 63, 71, 76-7, 99, *107*, 109, 121-2, 140, 142-4, 148-9, 152, 157, 167, 173, *186*, **186-8,** 191, 198, 204, 213-14, 220, 222, 259, 264-5, 279
Nelson 223, *224*
Nelson, Horatia (daughter) 32, 42, 68, 74, 111, 113, *113*, 125, *142*, 143-4, 170, 172, 174, 180, **188-9,** 189, 191, 201, 206, 216, 222, 228-9, 234, 244, 268-71, 273, 280
Nelson, V/A Horatio *10*, *29*, *38*
  appearance 46-8, *49*, 50-1, **150,** 207-9, 228, 262
  birth and childhood 13-14, 279
  character 11, 13-14, 16, 20-1, 30, 32-3, 37, 39-40, 41-2, 44, 46-8, 51, 67, 71, 79-80, 91, 99, 103, 105, 121, 123, 148, 160, 162, 184-5, 201-2, 222, **228-9,** 231, 250, 258-9
  death of 17, 45, *48*, 63, 66, 68, 91, 98, 106, *110*, **110-11,** 114, 117-18, 122, 130, 136, 148-9, **162,** 171, 204, 206, 212, 221-2, 228, 245, 248, 254, 262, 273-4, 280
    return of body and funeral 46, *46*, 51, 64, 68, 77, 90, **96,** 98, 122, 126, *127-9*, **128-9,** 130, *132*, 133, 137, 139, 152, 160, **185-6,** 200, 204, 246, 254, 256, 260, 274-5, 280
  education 14, **220-1,** 223
  family **113-4, 121-2,** 206
  health 11, 14, 16, 37, 39, 47, 51, 54, 56, 63, 71, 92, 108, 122, 126, 131, 142, **148-9,** 279
  honours 21, 24, *28*, 41, 50, *50*, **74, 93-4,** *94*, 110-11, **111-13,** *112*, 129-30, 191, 226, 228, 279-80
  in House of Lords 40, 51, 56, 219, 224
  joins Navy *12*, 14, 76, 211, 220, 228, 279
  letters 12-13, 16, 18, 20-3, 31-4, 42, 53, 55, 63, *67*, 68, 77, 105, *114*, **115,** 121, 143-4, 149, 159,

161, *165*, **166,** 167, 172-3, 180, 187-9, 192, 198-9, 201, 213, 222, 229, 234-6, 238, 250-1, 257-8, 264-73
  marriage 16-17, 71, 220, 259, 279
  portraits *10*, 40, *50*, 50-1, *57*, 58, *60*, *64*, *79*, *98*, *107*, *110*, *112*, *119*, 120, *120*, 131, 136, 148-9, 162, 167, 187-8, *207-8*, **207-9,** 279
  masks **171,** *171*, 209, 279
  promotions 11, 14-15, 54, 78, 97, 203-4, 227-8, 276-9
  religion 23-4, 43-4, 47, 54, 74, 99, *212*, **212-13,** 229, 265, 273-4
  reputation
    in lifetime 23, *27*, 28, 31, 33, *36*, 40, 43, 45-6, 50, 55, 63-4, 81, 83, 87-8, 115, 117, 127, 131, 198, 257
    posthumous 13, 46-8, *49*, 57, 59, **66-7,** 69-70, 99, 114-15, 118-20, 122-3, *123*, 130, 154, 156, 162, **176-8,** *177*, 178, **180,** 191, 205, *211*, **211-12, 223-4,** 232-3, *248*, 248-9, 254, 258, 280
  signatures **224-5,** *225*
  strategy and tactics 13, 18-23, 26-7, 32-3, 37, 42, 44-5, 53, 71-3, 87, 98, 102, 137-8, 197, 231-2, **235-9,** 244-5, 247-8, 250-1, 256, 271-2
  and women 11-13, 16-18, 30-2, 40, 42, 47, 56, 66-7, 96-8, 108-9, 125-7, 130, 139-45, 186-8, 198, 201, 212, 214, 250, 264-5, 267-8, 272-3
    see also Andrews, Elizabeth; Correglia, Adelaide; Hamilton, Emma; Moutray, Mary; Nelson, Frances; Simpson, Mary
  wounds *19*, *24*, 27-8, 30, 87, 99, 118, 125, 149, 209, 229, **260-2,** *261-2*
    loss of right arm 11, 22-4, 46-7, 54-5, 63, 66, 125, 130, 135-6, 149, 153, 167, 176, 187, 198, 204, 207, 209, 224, 231, 235, 252, 260, 262, 277, 279
    loss of sight of right eye 11, 18, *120*, **120,** 180, 197-8, 223, 260-1, 279
  will 68, 144
Nelson, Horatio (nephew) 113, 191
Nelson, Maurice (brother) 109, 121, 183
Nelson, Susannah (sister) *see* Bolton, Susannah
Nelson, Thomas, second Earl (nephew) 122
Nelson, William, first Earl (brother) 71, 74, 94, 113, 115, 122, 171-2, *190*, **190-1,** 220
Nelson's Column 115, 118, 178
Nepean, Sir Evan 270
Neptune 127, 217
Netherlands 25, 95, 124, 237
Nevis Island 16-17, 186, **191,** 259,

279
New York 55, 151, 191-2, **191-2,** 251, 279
Newbolt, Henry 233
Newcastle, Duke of 105
Nicaragua *see* San Juan
Nicolas, Sir Nicholas Harris *114*, 115, 166, 173, 188, 234
Nile, battle of the *map 194-5*, 11, 25-8, 26, *27*, 33, 44, 58-9, *60*, 61, 64, 66, 72, 75-6, 94, 96, 99, 109, 111, 113, 117-18, 125, 130-1, 139, 141-2, 147-8, 152-3, 159, 167-70, 176, 182-3, 187, 190, **192-8,** *196-7*, 209, 212, 217, 219, 224-6, 233, 235, 237, 246, 250, 252, 256, 262, 265-6, 279
Nile 223
Nisbet, Josiah (first husband of Frances Lady Nelson) 186
Nisbet, Midshipman Josiah (stepson) 17, 22, *107*, 186, 188, **198,** 231, 258
Northumberland 266

Oliver, Francis 144, **199**
Olivier, Laurence 123, *123*
Oneglia 156
Orde, Sir John *199*, **199-200**
Orion 95, 218-19
Orme, Daniel *207*
Ostend 92
Otter 125

Packenham, Capt 68
Palermo 30, 47, 90, 125, 142, 183-4, **201,** 209, 252, 279
Pallas 105
Parker, Capt Edward 17, 39, 73, 92, **201-2**
Parker, Adm Sir Hyde 32-3, 35-6, 70, 102, 105, 125, 127, 133, 135, 159, 201, *202*, **202-3,** 221, 227, 233, 235, 250, 280
Parker, Adm Sir Peter 15, 68, 167, 179, **203-4,** *204*, 217, 276
Parsons, Midshipman George 55, 91, 266-7
Pasco, Capt John 119, 156, **204-5,** *205*, 213, 248
Paston School 14
Paxton, Sir William 178
Pégase (Fr) 159
Pegasus 16, 57, 71, 219, 259
Penelope 68
Penzance 249
Peterel 116
Pettigrew, Thomas 166
Peuple Souverain (Fr) 219, 235
Phipps, Capt the Hon C 57-8, 169
Phoenix 82, 202
Pickle 163, 245
Pigot, Capt James 276
Pitt, William, the Elder 205
Pitt, William, the Younger 43, 51, 57, 159, 175, 177, *205*, **205-6,** 226, 235, 241
Plymouth 96-7, 125, **206**
Pocock, Nicolas *103*
Polson, Colonel 192
Popham, Adm Sir Home Riggs 68, *206*, **207,** 245

Portsmouth 23, 42-3, 55, 58, 63, 65,
    99, 105, 114, 125, 150-1, 154,
    172-3, 176-7, *177*, 180, 188, 204,
    204-5, 206, **209-10**, *210*, 220,
    248, 254-5, 280
Prague 131
Prince 97, 217
Prince George 161, 267
Prince of Wales 80
Principe de Asturias (Sp) 134

Quebec 17, 55, 109, 158, 191,
    225-6, 279
Quebec 122
Queen Charlotte 95, 216
Quiberon Bay, battle of 105, 158,
    166-7

Racehorse 57-8
Radstock, Lord 154
Raisonnable 14, 92, **211**, 220, 228,
    276, 278-9
Ranson, Matthias 171, 279
Rathbone, Lt John 211
Redoutable (Fr) 45, *45*, 222, 228,
    232, 233, 245
Resistance 251
Revolutionnaire (Fr) 64
Rigaud, Francis 50, 167, 189, 208,
    279
Riou, Capt Edward 102, **213**
Ripley, Thomas 51
Robinson, Capt Mark 276
Robust 118
Rochefort 65, 82, 246
Rodney, Adm Sir George 53, 90,
    106, 151, 154, 169, 176, 192, 218,
    233, 237
Rome 29, 146, 153, 169, 183, 250
Romney, George 140, *140*
Rose, George 273
Rose 88
Rosily, Adm 256
Rotterdam (Neth) 117
Roundwood 173, 187, **213-14**
Royal Sovereign 68, 154, 222, 245
Ruffo, Cardinal Fabrizio 184-5,
    214, 250
Russell 218
Russia 32, 36, 96, 99, 105, 152, 159,
    203, 219, 233, 246
Ryves, Capt George 54

Saintes, battle of the 53, 59, 106,
    151-2, 192, 218, 233, 237
Salvador del Mundo (Sp) 218
San Cristobal (Sp) 134
San Domingo, battle of 54, 66, 162,
    169
San José (Sp) 20, 55, 87, 93, 126,
    216, 229
San Josef 32, 58, 99, 148, 206,
    277-8, 280
    see also San José
San Juan 15-16, 54, 63, 106, 108,
    149, **192**, *193*, 277, 279
San Nicolas (Sp) 20, 55, 66, 87, *89*,
    216, 229
Sandy Hook 151, 191-2
Sané, J N 167
Sans Culottes (Fr) 137
Sans Pareil (Fr) 250

Santa Anna (Sp) 245
Santa Cruz de Tenerife 21-5, 28,
    30, 46, 55, 58, 63, 71, 73-4, 127,
    138, 147, 152-3, 176, 198, 209,
    224, *230*, **230-2**, 234-5, 250, 258,
    260, 262, 279
Santa Margarita 82
Santa Sabina (Sp) 95, 147, **215-16**
Santíssima Trinidad (Sp) 74, 87, 90,
    95, 97, 127, 134, **216-17**, *217*,
    218, 245
Sapphire 166
Sardinia 54, 170, 172, 252
Saumarez, Adm James, Lord 61,
    152, 161-2, **217-19**, *218*, 250,
    254
Saunders, Adm Charles 158
Schomberg, Capt Isaac 16, 71, 151,
    219-20, 259
Scott, John 172, 221, **222**
Scott, Rev Alexander 48, 54, 110,
    110, 111, 162, 173, 213, **221-2**,
    273-4, 274
Seahorse (1) 14, 17, 122, 149, 249,
    276
Seahorse (2) 184, 277
Secker, Sergeant 111
Shakespeare, William 59, 220,
    222-3, 238
Shannon 96
Sherman, James 177
Shirley, General Sir Thomas 57
Sicily 30, 74
    see also Palermo
Sidmouth, Lord *see* Addington,
    Henry
Silliman, Benjamin 150
Simpson, Mary 17, 109, 191, **225-6**
Slade, Sir Thomas 64, 71, 252-3
Smith, Adm Sir Sidney 136, 176
Smith, Capt John 90
Solana, Marquis de 78
Southey, Robert 46, 66-7, 245
Spain 15, 19-22, 41-5, 54, 66, 68,
    74, 78-9, 81-*2*, 82-7, 90, 94-5, 97,
    107, 118, 132, 134, 147, 152, 157,
    159, 161, 169, 175-6, 192, 200,
    211, 215-17, 230-2, 244-7, 250,
    254, 256, 258
Spartiate (Fr) 252
Spencer, George, Lord 19-20, 24,
    26, 125, 152, 200, 202, **226-7**,
    257
Spencer, Lady 46, 186-7, 226
Spicer, Lt James 88
Spithead 68, 209
St George 32, 58, 99, 125, 133, 148,
    216, 221, 233, 278
St Helena 95
St Kitts, battle of 106, 151, 218-19
St Vincent, Adm Lord (Sir John
    Jervis) 13, 17, 19-21, 23, 26, 32,
    36-7, 39, 51, 59, 66-7, 73-4, 78,
    82-3, 86-7, 90, 92, 95, 97, 106-7,
    115-16, 118, 139, 147, 152-3, 157,
    158, **158-60**, 163, 176, 182, 188,
    193, 199-202, 215, 217-19, 223,
    226-7, 230, 235, 250-2, 254
Stanlynch Park 191
Stewart, Colonel Sir William 33,
    35, 70, 203, **227**
Strachan, Capt Sir Richard 41, 82,

83
'Strachan's Action' *see* Cape
    Ortegal, battle of
Stuart, Don Jacobo 215
Stuart, Lt-Gen the Hon Charles
    80-1
Success 266-7
Suckling, Capt Maurice (uncle)
    14-15, 58, 122, 148, 151, 166, 183,
    192, 203, 211, 220, **227-8**, 276
Suckling, William (uncle) 56
Suffren, Adm 179
Superb 161-2, 236
Surridge, Mr 122
Surveillante (Fr) 122
Sutton, Capt Samuel 278
Sweden 203, 233
Swiftsure 96, 139
Sykes, John 78, **229**

Tancredi (Naples) 90
Temeraire 232, **232-3**
Tenerife *see* Santa Cruz de
    Tenerife, battle of
Terpsichore 74, 217
Terrible 169
Thaller, Franz 131, 171, 209, 279
Thames 250
Theseus 21, 55, 58, 90, 153, 176, 231,
    258, 262, 277-9
Thesiger, Capt Sir Frederick 103,
    233-4
Thompson, Adm Sir Charles 71,
    125, 267
Thompson, Capt Sir Narbonne
    267
Thompson, Sir Thomas Boulden
    234, **234-5**
Thunder 78
Tigre 139
Tisiphone 218
Tonnant (Fr) 196
Toulon 18, 25, 41-2, 54, 75, 89-90,
    107, 116, 118, 134, 137, 139, 141,
    146, 151, 154, 164, 169-70, 172,
    175-6, 181-2, 184, 200, **239-41**,
    246-7, 252, 254, 279-80
Towry, Capt George 277
Trafalgar, battle of *map 242-3*, 11,
    28, 41, 43-6, *45*, 51, 54-5, 58, 64,
    66, 68, 76, 78, 80-2, 90, 94-6,
    98-9, 105-6, 110-11, 114, 117, 127,
    130, 133-4, 139, 144, 148-51, 154-
    6, 161-4, 171-2, 174-5, 176-7, 178,
    180, 186, 188, 191, 204, 206-7,
    209, 213, 217, 219, 221-2, 227-8,
    232, 235-9, *240-1*, **241-9**, *244*,
    248, 252, 254-6, 258, 262, 280
    'England expects . . .' signal
        118-20, *119*, 183, 204, 207,
        245, 248, 254
Trafalgar 223
Trevenen, Lt James 251
Trinidad 247
Triumph 97, 148, 276, 278
Troubridge, Adm Sir Thomas 17,
    20, 39, 59, 61, 86, 122, 142, 147,
    159, 184, 214, 219, 231, *249*,
    249-51
Troubridge, Midshipman Edward
    251
Turkey 50, 68, 94, 95-6, 113, 169,

176
Turk's Island 55, **251**
Turner, J M W 233

Udney, John 108
Unité 278
Ushant, battle of 53, 74, 122, 169,
    179, 254

Vanguard 27, 29, 59, 66, 99, 125,
    146, 148, 183, 197-8, 201, 219,
    252, 262, 277-9
Vanneau 88
Venerable 152
Vengeur (Fr) 220
Venice 75
Victory 44-5, *45*, 54-5, 58,
    63-4, 68, 71, 76, *86*, 92, 95,
    110-11, 114-15, 118-20, *119*,
    127-9, *132*, 133, 139, 144, 156,
    162, 173, 177-8, 180, 186, 188,
    204, 209-10, 213, 218-19, 221-2,
    232-3, 236-7, 245, 247-9, 251,
    252-5, *253*, *255*, 262, 274, 278,
    280
Vienna 117, 131, 171, 190, 199, 208
Vigo Bay 82, 247
Ville de Paris (Fr) 106, 151, 218
Villeneuve, Adm Pierre de 42-4,
    68, 76; 78-9, 82, 134, 198, 200,
    241, 244-5, 247, **255-6**, *256*
    transatlantic voyage 42-3, 79, 81,
        106, 132, 139, 144, 161, 172,
        175, 200, 228, 241, 246-8,
        256-7, 280
Volage 154

Walcheren 95
Wales 40, 56, **257**, 269, 280
Walpole, Mary 228
Walpole, Sir Robert 121
Ward, Rev Philip (son-in-law) 113,
    189
Warne, Lt-Col Roger 56
Warspite 68
Warwick 117
Watson, Capt John Rowley 176
Weatherhead, John 17, 21, **258**
Wedgewood, Josiah 145
Wellington, Arthur Duke of 46-7,
    64, 95-6, 227, **258-9**
West Indies station 14, 16-17, 42-3,
    54-5, 57, 66, 71, 73, 75-6, 96-7,
    105-6, 108, 124, 132, 139, 151,
    158-9, 162-3, 167, 186-7, 191,
    207, 218-19, 221, 246-8, 252,
    256-7, 259, 279-80
Westcott, Capt 265
Whitehead, Lt John 23
Windsor Castle 176
Winthuysen, R/A Don Francisco
    216
Wolfe, General James 158, 225
Woolnough, Midshipman Joseph
    46
Worcester 14, 209, 276, 278
Wynne, Mr and Mrs Robert 127

Yule, John 156

Zealous 152, 265